Cultivating Creative Collaboration in Student Virtual Teams in Higher Education:

Design and Climate

Jill E. Nemiro
California State Polytechnic University, Pomona, USA

IGI Global
Scientific Publishing
Publishing Tomorrow's Research Today

Vice President of Editorial	Melissa Wagner
Director of Acquisitions	Mikaela Felty
Director of Book Development	Jocelynn Hessler
Production Manager	Mike Brehm
Cover Design	Jose Rosado

Published in the United States of America by
IGI Global Scientific Publishing
701 East Chocolate Avenue
Hershey, PA, 17033, USA
Tel: 717-533-8845
Fax: 717-533-7115
Website: https://www.igi-global.com E-mail: cust@igi-global.com

Library of Congress Cataloging-in-Publication Data

LCCN: 2025006747 (CIP Data Pending)
ISBN13: 979-8-3373-0375-8
Isbn13Softcover: 979-8-3373-0376-5
EISBN13: 979-8-3373-0377-2

British Cataloguing in Publication Data
A Cataloguing in Publication record for this book is available from the British Library.

This book is dedicated to Jerri Louise Nemiro, the first teammate I ever had.

Table of Contents

Detailed Table of Contents

leaders who are equipped to thrive in the evolving digital landscape of modern organizations.

In this chapter the authors discuss how team personality composition (i.e., team narcissism) influences virtual team performance via team processes (i.e., information sharing and team conflict). Evidence was found for the negative impact of team narcissism on information sharing. The relationship between narcissism and team conflict was not supported. Information sharing predicted virtual team performance. Practical implications regarding staffing and virtual team collaboration in higher education are discussed at the end of the chapter.

Maximizing creativity in virtual teams requires the intentional integration of key elements. This chapter guides teams in cultivating a collaborative culture by increasing awareness of how members listen and respond to one another. The instructional strategies presented can be incorporated into course curricula, fostering lifelong habits for effectively participating in or leading teams. Through simulations, the chapter provides opportunities for immediate practice in building a team environment rooted in trust, psychological safety, and open communication. It emphasizes active listening across differences and the development of structured agreements that balance flexibility and creativity. Additionally, it highlights the critical role of a collaborative team mindset in sustaining effective teamwork.

Fostering a creative environment in virtual teams is possible, but it is more difficult than for traditional face-to-face teams. In order to support creativity in virtual teams we need to deliberately create a human-centered team. The most effective way to

Preface

OVERVIEW

Over the last 20 years, creativity has been shown to be a critical element to contemporary organizations, especially as global competition, the need for innovation, and technological advances have intensified. The rise of technological advances has produced an increase in remote work and virtual teams, especially within business settings to deal with global competition and the rise of non-routine work (Nemiro, 2023). Rudimentary or routine work that was once performed by individuals has become automated, and much of the work that remains is knowledge-based and non-routine, which requires creativity and critical thinking (Mohrman et al., 1995; Nemiro, 2007, 2023). Virtual teams have been defined as teams with members in which communication and work tasks are accomplished primarily through technology and are contrasted with traditional teams that accomplish work face-to-face (Nemiro, 2004, 2025).

Prior to the pandemic, having students gain virtual team experience was considered valuable due to the increasing awareness that students may be expected to work remotely at least some of the time in the future (Cleary & Slattery, 2009). Further, research revealed that students working in virtual teams in academic settings reported benefits (such as flexibility) and shared that their experiences were overall positive (Goold, Augar & Farmer, 2006; He et al., 2008). However, the coronavirus pandemic in 2020 generated an even greater increase in the use of remote work and virtual teams not only in business but in higher education as well. As mandatory lockdowns were enforced globally, faculty and students, previously used to teaching and learning face-to-face, were forced to transition to virtual instruction, and to adapt team assignments into virtual team assignments (Cornella-Dorda et al., 2020). This was done quickly with limited opportunities for students to develop the skills for working on virtual teams before having to engage in them to complete course requirements (Charteris et al., 2021; Jensen & Trespalacios, 2022). Not only were there limited training opportunities for students to learn how to work effectively in virtual teams, but limited textbooks tailored to students on virtual teamwork skills as well.

Today, the trend toward remote work and virtual teams is not going away. Many businesses have recognized the benefits of remote work done during the pandemic, and as a result, have continued to find ways to give employees the option of working remotely, moving into what has now been referred to as "a new normal way of working" (Dans, 2020; McKnight, 2021). Over time, there has been a dramatic increase in the amount of time Americans work remotely from home — up from 0.4% in 1965 to 61.5% in May 2020 during the COVID-19 pandemic, to a still high of 28.1% in June 2023 (Barrero, Bloom & Davis, 2023). Now, even after the pandemic, hybrid and remote work and virtual teams continue to be used as forms of work, and some employees actually prefer them. Since this new way of working appears to be here to stay, students need opportunities to practice virtual teamwork skills before embarking on the workplace, and faculty in higher education need to provide them with these types of learning situations.

Thus, it is crucial to teach students how to work effectively in virtual teams to prepare them for their future careers. *Cultivating Creative Collaboration in Student Virtual Teams in Higher Education: Design and Climate* provides university faculty and students, and business professionals with an in-depth understanding of how to design academic courses and business training experiences that can offer students and employees hands-on experiences to develop virtual teamwork skills. This edited book is composed of chapters from renowned academics and professionals from across the globe, who specialize in virtual teamwork and collaboration. The book has two major aims: 1) to nurture students' professional development by enhancing their creativity while working in virtual teams, and 2) to provide faculty with relevant knowledge, expertise, and case examples to assist them in designing and implementing effective virtual team learning experiences in their courses.

Remote and/or hybrid work will continue to be a part of the future workplace, and virtual teams are a key part of how that work gets done. To prepare students to enter the workplace, higher education needs to offer students experiences to learn how to effectively collaborate in virtual teams. Faculty, in creating experiential virtual team assignments within their courses, can assist students in gaining relevant knowledge and skills needed for virtual work, increasing their level of comfort and readiness to engage in virtual teams in the future.

TARGET AUDIENCE

The primary target audience for *Cultivating Creative Collaboration in Student Virtual Teams in Higher Education: Design and Climate* is college-level students and faculty in business, communication studies, computer information systems, education, educational leadership, engineering, general business, international business, instructional design, instructional technology, management and human resources, organizational development and change, organizational psychology, and technology and operations management. In addition, many universities offer professional certificates and/or extension programs to employees across the globe. These programs may use this book in courses offered to working professionals on virtual teamwork. Businesses may also use this book in company training programs on virtual collaboration and teamwork. Even students and business professionals who are not part of virtual teams may find the content of this book transferable to their in-person teams. This book is an excellent resource for educational leaders, educators, instructional designers, technology instructors, human resource (HR) managers, business leaders, professionals, researchers, academicians, and more.

While this book may be used as a stand-alone text for an academic course or professional training experience, it is best used in conjunction with Nemiro's (2026) edited book, *Sustaining Creative Collaboration in Student Virtual Teams in Higher Education: Resources, Norms and Protocols, and Continual Assessment and Learning* (also published by IGI). In addition, Nemiro's (2025) *Creativity in Virtual Teams: Key Components for Success,* Second Edition is a valuable resource as well, as detailed in the next section.

ORGANIZATION OF THE BOOK

The chapters selected for this edited book, *Cultivating Creative Collaboration in Student Virtual Teams in Higher Education,* and the accompanying edited book, *Sustaining Creative Collaboration in Student Virtual Teams in Higher Education* are organized into sections that align with the key components of virtual team creativity as laid out in Nemiro's (2025), *Creativity in Virtual Teams: Key Components for Success,* Second Edition. Those components are Design, Climate, Resources, Norms and Protocols, and Continual Assessment and Learning, and are shown in Figure 1. The five components initially emerged from interviews with professionals from the fields of organizational consulting, education, and engineering (Nemiro, 2004). Taken together, *Cultivating Creative Collaboration in Student Virtual Teams in Higher Education* (this book) and *Sustaining Creative Collaboration in Student Virtual Teams in Higher Education* (accompanying book), extend the application of

Nemiro's five key component model to higher education audiences. *Cultivating Creative Collaboration in Student Virtual Teams in Higher Education* focuses on the key components of Design, and Climate, while *Sustaining Creative Collaboration in Student Virtual Teams in Higher Education* concentrates on the key components of Resources, Norms and Protocols, and Continual Assessment and Learning.

Figure 1. Key Components for Creativity in Virtual Teams

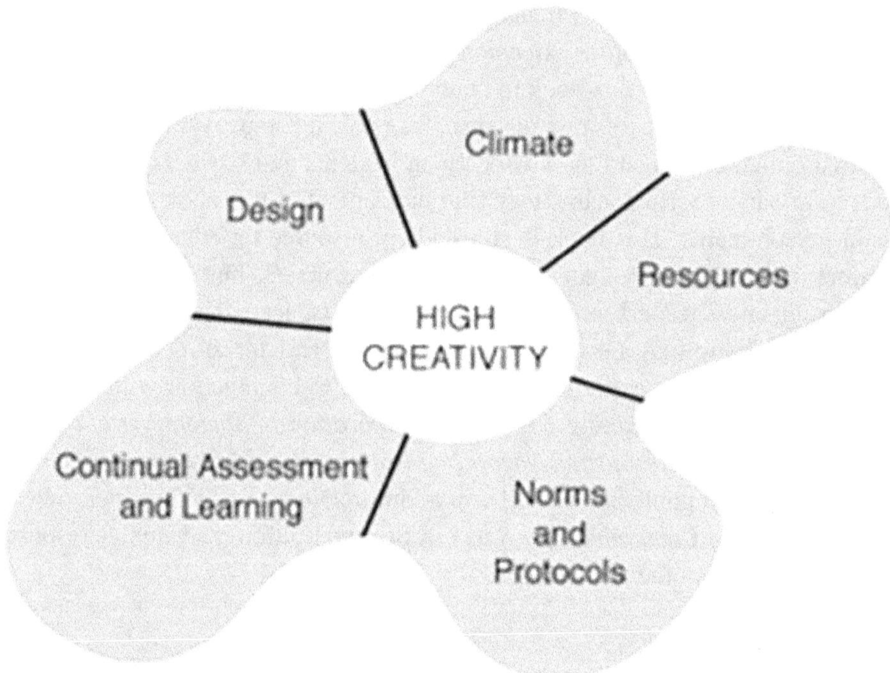

Source: Nemiro, J. E. (2025). Creativity in Virtual Teams: Key Components for Success. Second Edition, Cognella Academic Publishing.

As Figure 1 illustrates, creativity is highest when all five key components are in place – when the *design* is appropriate, the *climate* is supportive of creativity, the *resources* are sufficient, the proper *norms and protocols* are agreed on and adhered to, and the team takes the time for *continual assessment and learning*. Each key component is further described below.

Design

The component of Design includes mapping out an effective creative process and work design approach for a virtual team and choosing an appropriate leadership structure to guide the virtual team toward higher levels of creativity. Applying the Design component to higher education, the first five chapters in this book, *Cultivating Creative Collaboration in Student Virtual Teams in Higher Education*, discuss how to embed teamwork into the design of online courses. Chapters 1 and 2 outline valuable models for integrating teamwork into the design of online courses. Chapter 3 offers strategies and tools to assist in designing creative and high performing student virtual teams. Chapter 4 lays out a case study that illustrates the design of an interactive MBA online course to help students develop leadership skills in virtual environments. Chapter 5 explores an initial part of design – team composition, and the impact personality traits like narcissism can have on virtual team performance.

Climate

The essential component of Climate, the attitudes, feelings, and behaviors that characterize life within a team and organization, details how to build and maintain *a sense of connection* within a virtual team, a necessary element for creativity in virtual teams. Connection involves the elements that need to be in place for a team to develop and maintain identity and a sense of community. Connection involves task connection (made up of dedication/commitment and goal clarity) and interpersonal connection (made up of information sharing, personal bond, and trust). As the creative work is under way, a series of *team member and management conditions* must be in place to stimulate creativity. Those conditions include acceptance of ideas and constructive tension, challenge, collaboration, freedom, management encouragement, and sufficient resources and time to complete the creative work. For creativity in virtual teams, team members and managers also need a variety of *skills and competencies*, including developing self and interpersonal awareness, supportive communication, cross-cultural communication, conflict resolution, problem solving and decision making, stress management, time management and personal productivity, developing and motivating others, positive political skills, knowledge management, data gathering, and information access skills, and career advancement.

Applying the component of Climate to student virtual teams, the last five chapters in this book, *Cultivating Creative Collaboration in Student Virtual Teams in Higher Education*, offer guidance and concrete simulations, exercises, and practices for building a climate that supports creativity in virtual teams. Chapter 6 shares a variety of simulations and structured exercises to help virtual teams build trust, psychological safety, and voice. Chapter 7 reviews how rituals may be used to help virtual teams become human-centered, with team members feeling a sense of connection and belonging. Chapter 8 reveals how the difficulty of a virtual team's initial task can impact key climate variables, such as information sharing and psychological safety, and offers suggestions to strengthen both prior to assigning difficult tasks. Chapter 9 recommends a series of exercises and practices that come from the field of sports that can be adapted for virtual teams to build needed skills and competencies. Lastly, Chapter 10 offers strategies and tools for building relationships within student virtual teams, and for building technological and interpersonal competencies needed by the members of those teams.

Resources

Once a connection between team members is established, team members need sufficient resources to accomplish their creative work. The component of Resources includes the communication tools available to support a virtual team's creative process; the linear and intuitive creativity techniques that foster higher levels of creativity and idea generation; and the variety of software tools that have been developed to enhance the creativity of individuals and teams.

Applying the Resources component to student virtual teams, the initial three chapters in the accompanying book, *Sustaining Creative Collaboration in Student Virtual Teams in Higher Education*, focus primarily on a pressing technological advancement – artificial intelligence (AI) and how virtual teams can use it.

Norms and Protocols

The component of Norms and Protocols outlines the appropriate communication and project and task management norms and protocols that virtual teams need to consider, agree on, and respect and adhere to while working virtually. Communication behavior norms include: a) Availability and acknowledgment norms, where team members agree on when and how they will be available for collaboration and how quickly they will respond to requests; b) Appropriateness of specific communication tools, norms that determine for what purposes or circumstances individual communication tools will be used by the team; c) Protocols or rules of etiquette for the use of each communication tool; d) Rules governing when communication should occur between the entire team, and when it may be appropriate for communication to only occur within certain subgroups; and e) the unique balance the team desires between frequency of structured forms of communication (e.g., scheduled virtual meetings) and unstructured forms of communication (e.g., spontaneous emails, texts).

Project/task management norms include: a) Developing a creative process project lifecycle map, which entails clarifying inputs needed, listing creative tasks to be performed during each stage of the team's creative process, and recording any changes in the life cycle for similar future projects; b) Determining which team tasks can be done routinely and which require creativity, so teams are both creative and efficient; c) Assigning roles and responsibilities to individual team members with respect to the tasks that need to be completed and gaining the entire team's joint agreement on these roles to ensure accountability; d) Timeframes (agreed upon deadlines for when certain actions need to be completed by), and accountability norms that spell out actions to be taken to ensure on-time delivery of task-related output and what will occur if members do not meet up to their responsibilities; e) Protocols for working in a shared workspace and exchanging files back and forth, to ensure that all team members have current project-related information and that the shared workspace is organized; and f) Norms for how the team's work will be reviewed, revised, and finally approved. Agreed-upon norms need to be documented in a formal team charter or agreement, and those charters should be revised as needed when mutual expectations change.

Applying the Norms and Protocols component to student virtual teams, two chapters in the accompanying edited book, *Sustaining Creative Collaboration in Student Virtual Teams in Higher Education*, deal specifically with the development and use of team charters in student virtual teams.

Continual Assessment and Learning

The final component of Continual Assessment and Learning includes ensuring that the virtual team has opportunities for assessment and learning. It is especially important at the close of each creative project for the team to take the time to evaluate and assess what worked and what could be improved. Applying the Continual Assessment and Learning component to student virtual teams, the last four chapters in *Sustaining Creative Collaboration in Student Virtual Teams in Higher Education* discuss how to encourage and build continual learning, assessment, and improvement of the virtual team opportunities offered to students in higher education.

DETAILED DESCRIPTION OF THE CHAPTERS

Each chapter in this book, *Cultivating Creative Collaboration in Student Virtual Teams in Higher Education*, which focuses on the components of Design and Climate, is described in detail in this section. (Chapters in the accompanying book, *Sustaining Creative Collaboration in Student Virtual Teams in Higher Education*, which cover the components of Resources, Norms and Protocols, and Continual Assessment and Learning are discussed in the Preface of that book.)

Design

Chapter 1 - Designing Successful Virtual Team Experiences: A Lifecycle Approach for Instructors. In this chapter, McKenna Sperry, Aliza Aldana, and Thomas O'Neill offer a guide for instructors to assist them in embedding teamwork into the design of an online course. In doing so, a three-phase team lifecycle approach is utilized, including 1) Team Launch, during which student virtual teams develop trust and create norms for collaboration; 2) Task Launch, through which instructor-designed tasks are designed to develop teamwork skills in students; and 3) Performance Cycles and Evaluation, during which students collaborate in their virtual teams to work on tasks and engage in ongoing reflection and feedback to complete their tasks. As each of these three phases is reviewed, the key challenges students may face are detailed, and recommended strategies, practices, and resources for instructors are shared to help them design effective virtual teamwork experiences for students at each phase.

Chapter 2 - Classrooms as Learning Labs for Virtual Collaboration and Learner Agency: Collaborative Learning, Learning Lab, Agency, Threefold Path to High-Performance Virtual Teams. In this chapter, Trina Hoefling views the online classroom as a learning lab to prepare students for their professions and for today's workplace. To assist instructors in designing their online courses as learning labs, Hoefling first describes key principles for adult and online learning, the benefits of redesigning online courses for collaborative groupwork (such as, how to design for accessibility and inclusion, flexibility and group negotiation, swift trust, communication, and the practice of critical thinking in a group), and the challenges that may accompany online courses (for example, variance in learner motivation and readiness for the digital learning environment, technology difficulties, and team members not contributing). Then, Hoefling offers *The Threefold Path to High-Performance Teams*™ as a model that anticipates and addresses the challenges faced by students when working in virtual teams. The model's three paths that instructors can adapt in their classrooms include: a) the first path which develops responsibility, clarity, expectation of agency, and swift trust in student virtual teams; b) the second pathway which supports the culture and climate of supportive learning, and c) the third pathway which leads to successful learning as evidenced by successful assignments, and delivers workforce-ready graduates.

Chapter 3 - Designing Virtual Teamwork for Creativity: Strategies for Higher Education. Andi Asrifan and Syahruddin have written a chapter that serves as a primer on how to design virtual teamwork experiences for creativity in higher education. After reviewing the definition, importance, history, and challenges of virtual teams in higher education, this chapter provides faculty with strategies and tools to assist them in designing student virtual teams that are both creative and high performing. Specific strategies covered include a) strategies for building a creative virtual team through selecting diverse team members, establishing team roles and responsibilities, and fostering a collaborative culture; b) strategies for enhancing creativity in virtual teams, including techniques for brainstorming and ideation, for encouraging risk-taking and experimentation, and for establishing regular feedback loops during the creative process; and c) strategies for assessing and sustaining virtual team performance with the use of metrics for evaluating team effectiveness, and continuous improvement practices. A variety of tools and technologies available for virtual collaboration, and techniques to integrate and ensure the utilization and accessibility of these technologies are also shared. The chapter also shares a series of case studies to illustrate best practices of the proposed strategies and tools.

Chapter 4 - From Distance to Connection: Engaging Leadership Development in Virtual Settings. Lily Blocker offers a case study of the design of an interactive MBA online course to help students develop individual and team leadership skills within virtual environments. Four key course assignments that Blocker has designed, tested, and fine-tuned are described; those assignments include the Media Analysis, Leader Interview Project, Group Dinner, and Team Virtual Case Study. The media analysis builds in students the ability to apply leadership theory to real-world examples and promotes independent critical thinking. The group dinner develops interpersonal connections and communication through informal peer interaction and constructive feedback. The leader interview connects theory and practice by requiring students to interact with professionals, practice their digital communication skills, and reflect on leadership adaptability. The virtual case study serves as the culminating project in the course, requiring real-time virtual collaboration and reflection. Taken together, these four assignments integrate theory, practice, and feedback to build students' necessary leadership skills for virtual work.

Chapter 5 - The "Dark Side" of Personality: Examining Narcissism in Virtual Teams. A key starting point for any virtual team in terms of design is deciding on the composition of the members on the team. Krisztina Szabo and C. Shawn Burke take a unique perspective on virtual team composition by suggesting that those individuals with narcissistic personality tendencies (such as admiration, validation seeking, and a strong need for dominance) may intensify the interpersonal and communication challenges that virtual teams face. The chapter details a research project with undergraduate student teams that examines how narcissism impacts team performance (i.e., team decision-making accuracy) via team processes (i.e., information sharing and relationship conflict). Results indicated that team narcissism was significantly and negatively related to information sharing, and information sharing predicted virtual team performance. Because narcissism was significantly and negatively related to information sharing, Szabo and Burke suggest that composing student virtual teams to have lower levels of narcissism should foster virtual team collaboration. However, as this may not always be doable, Szabo and Burke also provide a valuable set of recommendations for handling narcissistic personality issues in virtual teams to foster information sharing and effective collaboration within higher education settings.

Climate

Chapter 6 - Maximizing Collaborative Creativity: Learning and Practices for Instilling an Intentional Team Culture. This chapter focuses on cultivating team cultures in virtual teams that support creativity, through building trust, psychological safety, and voice. To accomplish this, L. Michelle Bennett shares a series of simulations and structured exercises that allow for practice of both task-oriented and relationship-oriented aspects of teamwork. The simulations and structured exercises described in the chapter can be used to help virtual team members a) build trust and psychological safety with their team, b) learn how people feel heard using a collaborative mindset, c) learn how to empathetically listen to other team members for understanding, and d) balance structure and flexibility to maximize productivity and innovation. These simulations and exercises, when integrated effectively into curriculum along with virtual team project learning, can become integral to virtual team development for students in higher education.

Chapter 7 - Designing a Supportive Climate for Human-Centered Virtual Teams: The Role of Rituals. In this chapter, Tracey Rockett and Stacy Grau highlight how faculty can help students foster creativity in virtual teams, by making their virtual teams more "human-centered". Human-centered virtual teams prioritize the needs, well-being, and experiences of each team member by fostering connection, psychological safety, and an overall sense of belonging. Rockett and Grau propose that rituals serve as the "how" to design the driving forces of team cohesion, team processes, and psychological safety that lead to creativity in human-centered virtual teams. While Rockett and Grau share useful rituals to assist students and faculty in building each of these driving forces in student virtual teams, they also encourage those same virtual teams to create their own rituals. To assist them in doing so, Rockett and Grau offer a set of guidelines for ritual design.

Chapter 8 - Information Sharing and Psychological Safety in Virtual Teams. Joshua Fairchild, Addison LeGrand, Jaelyn Rose Bentzinger, and Katie Pfeiffer explore the impact of initial team task difficulty (challenging versus easy) on the development of several team climate factors predictive of information sharing and team performance, those factors being psychological safety, collective efficacy (team's shared perception that they are able to succeed at a particular task), and team viability (team's capacity for growth required for success in future performance). Fairchild and his co-authors conducted an empirical study involving the use of virtual reality technology, where student virtual teams were given tasks to complete (some extremely simple, some extremely difficult), and were also asked to complete surveys on team cohesion, psychological safety and team viability. Results showed that when the virtual teams experienced difficult tasks, it impaired the development of psychological safety within the team, which in turn hindered team viability and collective efficacy. Fairchild and his colleagues suggest that if virtual teams can develop a sense of cohesion early on, then even if they are faced with tackling a challenging task, psychological safety and information sharing may not be as impacted. To accomplish this, the chapter authors encourage faculty to include course assignments to bolster team cohesion and psychological safety early on, prior to assigning a difficult task; and to encourage students to engage in meaningful engagement with difficult concepts and civil, task-focused disagreement.

Chapter 9 - Teamwork in Action: Harnessing Sports to Boost Creative Collaboration in Virtual Teams. Amitava Pal, Kavita Mathad, and M. Rajkumar uniquely draw parallels between sports teams and virtual teams, proposing that the same fundamental skills are needed in both types of teams for effective collaboration and creativity; those skills include clear communication, defining roles, maintaining strong communication, trust-building, and adaptability. In addition, the chapter illustrates how key practices in sports can be adapted for use in virtual teams to enhance collaboration, communication, and performance, and foster creativity in virtual settings.

Chapter 10 - Creative Collaborative Applications for Virtual Language Learning Experiences. Başak Eda Hancı-Azizoglu, Abdullah Özgel, Şevket Tekin, Eşref Can Yılmaz, and Hüseyin Kafes offer a framework of strategies and tools to assist educators and students in developing virtual teams in language acquisition with a focus on productivity, creativity, and sustained motivation. Strategies are laid out for building and maintaining relationships in virtual teams, building a learning community, fostering collaborative creativity, and for maintaining productivity and engagement in student virtual teams in language acquisition. The chapter also describes a set of required competencies for virtual teamwork, and the strategies to build each of these competencies – Digital-Age Interpersonal and Adaptive Competencies; Technological Adaptability and Tool Integration; Collaboration, Motivation, and Engagement; and Creating an Inclusive and Productive Virtual Learning Environment. While this chapter focuses on student virtual teams in language acquisition, the strategies and tools described can be used by educators in other academic areas in higher education as well.

FINAL THOUGHTS

All one needs to do is look at the diversity of chapter contributors to this book, *Cultivating Creative Collaboration in Student Virtual Teams in Higher Education*, and to the accompanying book, *Sustaining Creative Collaboration in Student Virtual Teams in Higher Education*, to comprehend the complexity of virtual teams and collaboration and the indisputable need for effective practices. Across both books, fifty-four authors from around the world, including Austria, Canada, Finland, India, Indonesia, Morocco, Türkiye, and the United States, make up the list of distinguished academics and professionals specializing in virtual teamwork and collaboration who have contributed to these books. Working with this esteemed list of contributors has been both humbling and inspiring. It has pushed me to design, implement, and assess my own ways of working virtually, and how I teach my students to do the same. I have learned immensely from what the chapter contributors have shared, and I am forever grateful to them for what they have offered me and those of us who want to continue to help students learn how to function effectively in this new way of working virtually. I hope you will find the same as you read the chapters in this book. Enjoy your journey on the way to cultivating creative collaboration in student virtual teams in higher education.

Jill E. Nemiro
California State Polytechnic University, Pomona, USA

REFERENCES

Barrero, J. M., Bloom, N., & Davis, S. J. (2023). The evolution of work from home. Economics Working Paper Report 2311, Stanford University, Hoover Institute, September. https://siepr.stanford.edu/publications/working-paper/evolution-working-home

Charteris, J., Berman, J., & Page, A. (2021). Virtual team professional learning and development for practitioners in education. *Professional Development in Education*, *47*(4), 638–650.

Cleary, Y., & Slattery, D. (2009, August). Virtual teams in higher education: Challenges and rewards for teachers and students [Paper presentation]. *AISHE International Conference.*

Cornella-Dorda, S., Garg, L., Thareja, S., & Vasquez-McCall, B. (2020). Revising agile teams after an abrupt shift to remote. In *The Path to the Next Normal* (pp. 86–93). McKinsey and Company. https://www.mckinsey.com/capabilities/people-and-organizational-performance/our-insights/revisiting-agile-teams-after-an-abrupt-shift-to-remote

Dans, E. (2020, December 30). Could 2021 be the year remote working becomes the new normal? *Forbes*. https://www.forbes.com/sites/enriquedans/2021/12/30/could-2021-be-the-year-remote-working-becomes-the-newnormal/?sh=14726674680b

Goold, A., Augar, N., & Farmer, J. (2006). Learning in virtual teams: Exploring the student experience. *Journal of Information Technology Education*, *5*, 477–490.

He, J., Wang, P., & Li, Z. (2008). Issues and best practices of virtual teamwork in online learning environment. In *Proceedings of The 31st Annual Convention of the Association for Educational Communications and Technology (AECT)* (pp. 92–98). Research and Theory Division of AECT. members.aect.org/pdf/Proceedings/proceedings08/2008/08_11.pdf

Jensen, S., & Trespalacios, J. (2022). Designing virtual teams for K-12 teachers. *The Journal of Applied Instructional Design*, *11*(2). Advance online publication. DOI: 10.51869/112/sjjt

McKnight, A. (2021, June 21). Are you prepared to staff for the new normal? *Quad.com*. https://www.quad.com/resources/are-you-prepared-to-staff-for-the-new-normal/

Mohrman, S. A., Cohen, S. G., & Mohrman, A. M.Jr. (1995). *Designing team-based organizations: New forms for knowledge work*. Jossey-Bass.

Nemiro, J. (2007). The building blocks for creativity in virtual teams. In MacGregor, S., & Torres, T. (Eds.), *Higher creativity for virtual teams: Developing platforms for co-creation* (pp. 98–121). Information Science Reference/IGI Global.

Nemiro, J. E. (2004). *Creativity in virtual teams: Key components for success.* Pfeiffer/Wiley.

Nemiro, J. E. (2023). Chapter 18: Virtual teams. In R. Reiter-Palmon & S. Hunter's (Eds.), *Handbook of Organizational Creativity: Group and Individual Influences,* Second edition (pp. 269-290). Elsevier Publishing.

Nemiro, J. E. (2025). *Creativity in virtual teams: Key components for success* (2nd ed.). Cognella Academic Publishing.

Series AISHE-C. (2009). The National University of Ireland, Maynooth. https://www.researchgate.net/publication/266909262_Virtual_Teams_in_Higher_Education_Challenges_and_Rewards_for_Teachers_and_Students

Acknowledgment

I would like to offer my sincere appreciation to:

- All the contributing authors for their wonderfully creative chapters, for their knowledge and expertise, and for their thoughts on how to better prepare students for the virtual workplace.
- The many peer reviewers whose keen feedback made the chapters shine even more! Most of the chapter authors also served as peer reviewers, and I highly appreciate their taking on this additional task.
- Elizabeth Barrantes, Managing Editor of Book Development at IGI Global Scientific Publishing, whose timely and kind guidance helped me so much to manage this project.
- My psychology colleagues at California State Polytechnic University, Pomona who encouraged me, some of whom served as peer reviewers on chapters in the book as well.
- Professor Penny for her daily reminders that there is more in life than crafting an edited book, like stopping to take her for a walk. And to Miso who made sure I took breaks near the end of editing the book.
- Angel Mikey for smiling down on me while I was trying to stay focused.
- David, whose daily encouragement and love helped me to stay on the path.
- Nancy, who believed in me and offered me comfort and prayers for a successful outcome.
- Sara and Rachel – for being the creative, precious gems in my life.
- You, the reader, for allowing me to share these awesome chapters with you!

Jill E. Nemiro
California State Polytechnic University, Pomona, USA

Section 1
Design

Chapter 1
Designing Successful Virtual Team Experiences:
A Lifecycle Approach for Instructors

McKenna P. Sperry
https://orcid.org/0009-0006-6686-6845
University of Calgary, Canada

Aliza J. Aldana
https://orcid.org/0009-0000-1829-595X
University of Calgary, Canada

Thomas A. O'Neill
https://orcid.org/0000-0002-8336-5763
University of Calgary, Canada

ABSTRACT

Team-based learning is the norm in higher education courses. However, in many online courses, students are expected to navigate teamwork independently with few supports built into the course design. Ultimately, this can lead to ineffective teamwork and negative learning experiences. This chapter presents a comprehensive lifecycle approach to supporting virtual team success, focusing on the design of three essential team development phases: 1) team launch, 2) task launch, and 3) performance cycles and evaluation. Drawing on established theoretical models and empirical research, the authors provide instructors with practical strategies, activities, and tools to help students develop teamwork competencies and support

DOI: 10.4018/979-8-3373-0375-8.ch001

overall team effectiveness in virtual learning environments.

INTRODUCTION

Team-based learning has become an important pedagogical practice in higher education, offering numerous benefits for students. Indeed, team projects can foster the development of teamwork skills, which have become widely recognized as an essential competency in the workplace. For instance, a recent report by the National Association of Colleges and Employers found that over 80% of employers evaluating job candidates seek evidence of teamwork ability (NACE, 2024). Teamwork projects can also enhance student learning, having been positively associated with a variety of beneficial learning outcomes (e.g., Gokhale, 1995; Lohmann et al., 2019; Terenzini et al., 2013). As such, incorporating teamwork into course design can strengthen learning while also providing an opportunity for skill development that will foster success in the job market. However, despite the value of teamwork projects, many student teams are left to "figure it out" on their own and struggle to collaborate effectively. Teams are unlikely to reach their full potential unless structural support is built into the course design. When this support is not provided, students and instructors alike may have negative experiences, perpetuating teamwork as a "dreaded" aspect of coursework. Teamwork challenges may be further exacerbated in online courses, as virtual collaboration can be more difficult to navigate and troubleshoot (e.g., Gilson et al., 2015; Hertel et al., 2005). However, with a thoughtful approach to integrating teamwork into course design, many challenges can be reduced or mitigated.

As such, the purpose of this chapter is to provide a guide for instructors seeking to effectively embed teamwork into online courses. We take a team lifecycle approach and discuss the phases teams progress through, from their initial formation to the completion of their final project. In doing so, we describe the key challenges that teams must navigate throughout their lifecycle, and recommend strategies, practices, and resources for instructors to scaffold teamwork at each phase. We emphasize that teamwork aspects of course design should be ongoing, and urge instructors to avoid what might be an all-too-familiar picture: forming the teams, throwing in a brief "team-building" activity, and sending them off to complete their project, intervening only if problems arise.

Instead of a haphazard approach, imagine the following scenario, in which teamwork development, monitoring, and feedback are embedded into the design of the course from start to finish:

At the start of the semester, engineering students in a first-year design course join breakout rooms on Zoom to meet their project team members for the semester. Assigned to teams with peers they had never met before, many students hesitate to turn on their cameras, and long, awkward pauses fill the breakout rooms. To help students form connections, the instructor introduces a series of icebreakers specifically designed to address some of the challenges inherent in virtual teamwork. Students are encouraged to share a bit about their typical approach to teamwork and how they tend to navigate conflict, which gradually coaxes shy faces onto the screen. Later in the week, the teams establish their own team contracts, discussing how best to communicate, set meeting times, and collaborate using the various digital tools at their disposal. Once rapport is established between team members, the instructor presents an ambitious design challenge: to design and build a fully automated, portable indoor garden by developing individual modules using prototyping kits sent to each team member.

Teams quickly realize that designing an automated indoor garden is no simple task and that there is no "right" solution. They have to be creative in their approach to integrating moisture sensors, LED grow lights, and water pumps, while ensuring their individual modules "fit together" seamlessly. Early meetings involve breaking the challenge down into smaller, interdependent tasks. Some members investigate optimal plant growth conditions, while others experiment with wiring circuits and writing basic control scripts. To prevent teams from letting the work pile up until the final deadline, the instructor requires them to submit progress reports, participate in virtual design reviews, and present their initial prototypes for feedback. Alongside these deliverables, the instructor uses an anonymous evidence-based feedback assessment for students to evaluate each other's contributions in key areas such as commitment and high standards. This assessment allows students to recognize hidden contributions, or, in some cases, acknowledge when a teammate was not fully engaged and subsequently re-establish accountability and action feedback.

The once-disjointed virtual meetings evolve into spirited problem-solving sessions as students begin to find a rhythm with their work and plug away at mid-semester deliverables. Students share their screens to debug code together, troubleshoot sensor failures, and develop their designs. Most implement structured weekly check-ins, while some use shared task boards to keep track of responsibilities. Although miscommunications still happen, such as the occasional message getting buried in a group chat, teams have solid strategies for managing their workflow, in part due to a workshop on effective team communication and decision-making. At this stage, the most successful teams are those who actively monitor both their technical progress and their teamwork processes.

As the end of the semester draws near, teams transition from prototyping individual modules virtually to meeting in person a couple of times to assemble and test the whole system. They simulate various conditions to ensure that the water pump activates only when the soil is dry and that the grow lights adjust based on the plant's needs. In some cases, last-minute failures, like sensor malfunctions, force teams to pivot quickly. Through these challenges, students experience firsthand the iterative nature of engineering design.

The semester culminates in a final report accompanied by a virtual pitch presentation. During the presentation, teams showcase video demonstrations of each module in action, discuss their conceptualization and assembly process, and share simulation results to illustrate the system's performance. The instructor and teaching assistants grade the designs on efficiency, innovation, and feasibility. After students log off from this final meeting, they reflect on their teamwork experience and complete the peer feedback assessment a second time. Instructors adjust final teamwork grades based on assessment results, which ensures that final grades fairly reflect each student's level of engagement and effort.

Naturally, the scenario described above is a gold-standard, desirable outcome which most teams will only strive for. However, integrating structural teamwork support into course design can help teams improve their functioning and move toward achieving high-performance teamwork (e.g., Donia et al., 2018; Mathieu & Rapp, 2009; O'Neill et al., 2017; Rapp & Mathieu, 2007). Through a series of carefully implemented training, development, and feedback opportunities, teams can be supported as they progress from their starting point – no more than a collection of individuals – to becoming a true team, working interdependently to solve problems and adapting as needed to meet new and emerging challenges (Kozlowski et al., 1999).

The authors belong to the Individual and Team Performance (ITP) Lab (wpsites.ucalgary.ca/itp-lab/), led by Dr. Thomas O'Neill, whose members developed the ITP Metrics website (www.ITPmetrics.com), which features a teamwork assessment platform and resources. ITP lab members conduct research on team effectiveness and the impact of teamwork interventions, training, and assessments. Additionally, the lab has been advising instructors on teamwork-specific components of their course design for over a decade and observed student team success as a result of implementing the activities and assessments outlined in this chapter. Moreover, the lab's research on student team functioning and establishing optimal cadences for deploying teamwork assessments has contributed to data-driven insights on how to best support teams in educational settings. Thus, we aim to bring our knowledge and expertise to equip instructors with evidence-based practical tools and actionable advice for integrating teamwork into online course design at each phase of the team's lifespan.

The team lifecycle model presented in this chapter is also grounded in decades of research on team development and team effectiveness (e.g., Hackman, 1987; Mathieu et al., 2008; Salas et al., 2015), including research specific to both virtual teams (e.g., Bell & Kozlowski, 2002; Ortiz De Guinea et al., 2012) and student teams (e.g., Donia et al., 2018; O'Neill et al., 2020). The model is structured into three phases: 1) team launch, 2) task launch, and 3) performance cycles and evaluation. Each phase integrates seminal team development frameworks (e.g., Kozlowski et al., 1999; Marks et al., 2001; Gersick, 1988) and applies them to the virtual student team context. The remainder of this chapter is divided into three main sections to reflect the three phases in the model. We begin by discussing *Phase I: Team Launch,* during which student teams are charged with developing trust and creating norms for how they will work together. Next, we describe *Phase II: Task Launch*, which is characterized by training teamwork skills and instructor-designed tasks that are well-suited to teamwork. Finally, we present *Phase III: Performance Cycles and Evaluation*, during which teams are working together to complete tasks. In this third and final phase, teams participate in ongoing reflection and feedback, and move through several smaller cycles of performance as they work toward completing their final project. Within each section of the chapter, we begin by describing the phase's theoretical grounding, empirical support, and contextualize virtual student teamwork challenges. We then detail practical strategies, applications, and tools that instructors can embed into course design to help teams successfully navigate the phase. Figure 1 summarizes the lifecycle model, its foundations, and recommended applications.

Figure 1. Team Lifecycle Model and Applications

	Phase I	Phase II	Phase III
	Team Launch	Task Launch	Performance Cycles and Evaluation
Description	First interactions after teams are formed. Teams are tasked with building strong relationships and creating norms for how to work together.	Team members are introduced to the project, which is intentionally designed to be well-suited to teamwork. Prior to starting taskwork, students receive training on teamwork skills and effective use of virtual tools.	Teams work on tasks, moving through performance cycles which include phases for task completion and time for goal-setting, strategizing, and reflecting as they progress toward their final goal. Formative and summative feedback for both teamwork and taskwork are provided.
Key Challenges for Student Virtual Teams	• Develop trust within a short timeline. • Develop relationships solely through technology. • Create a shared understanding of how to work together.	• Develop teamwork skills that can be applied throughout the project and beyond. • Learn how to collaborate effectively through technology.	• Differentiate use of media based on the needs of the task and collaboration. • Take time to reflect, debrief, and strategize after one task is completed but before work on the next task begins.
Reccomendations and Key Actions	• Align team formation strategy with the learning objectives of the course. • Implement meaningful icebreakers and team-building activities to help teams establish a foundation of trust.	• Design team tasks (or projects) that require students to stretch their knowledge, skills, and abilities. • Influence teamwork cadences and interactions through external structures (e.g., milestones) and training to help teams maintain consistent interaction and progress.	• Align assessment and evaluation with team performance cycles (i.e., planning, execution, reflection, and adjustment over time). • Design an effective evaluation system: balance taskwork and teamwork, establish appropriate grade weightings, and use reliable assessment tools.
ITP Metrics Resources	• Early-stage assessments for team members to get to know each other: Conflict Management Styles and Personality (debrief materials available). • Team chartering guides and templates.	• Teamwork training to help teams navigate conflict and decision-making: SUIT (instructional materials and activities available).	• Mid- and late-stage assessments to evaluate overall teamwork functioning and individual competencies: Team Health and Peer Feedback (orientation and debrief materials available).

Further Reading

De Jong et al. (2016), Gilson et al. (2015), Ilgen et al. (2005), Klein et al. (2009), Kozlowski et al. (1999), Marks et al. (2001), Maruping and Agarwal (2004), O'Neill et al. (2020), Tuckman (1965).

Note. The team lifecycle model presented in this chapter is composed of three phases: 1) team launch, 2) task launch, and 3) performance cycles and evaluation. For each phase, we provide a description, outline key challenges for student virtual teams, and offer recommendations and resources.

PHASE I: TEAM LAUNCH

The *Team Launch* phase begins with the creation of the team, and encompasses initial interactions between team members. During this early phase, team building and norm creation take center stage. Specifically, team building focuses on building relationships and developing trust between team members, whereas norm creation involves team members getting aligned on how they will interact with each other. Both are essential ingredients for effective teamwork and will eventually serve to support effective taskwork. By the end of the *Team Launch* phase, the team should have a foundation of trust, shared understanding about how to work together, and clarity about the purpose of the team.

Theoretical Foundation

The *Team Launch* phase draws from established models of team development and research findings on team life cycles. Theoretical frameworks on team development often include a stage representing the team's initial establishment. For example, Kozlowski et al. (1999) describe this phase as *team formation*, and Tuckman (1965) labels it *forming*. In both frameworks, the formation phase is associated with team members seeking to understand one another, the purpose of the team, their role on the team, and how they will work together. As such, this phase is heavily grounded in building social relationships and trying to establish a shared understanding of the team's purpose, each individual's interest in it, their backgrounds, and global expectations for performance. For example, Ilgen et al.'s (2005) review of team life cycle literature found team formation as one of three major categories of research conducted on team development, and that the content of this research is largely focused on trust, relationship building, exploring how to work together, and understanding the structure and nature of the team. Ultimately, teams with members that successfully build positive relationships and intentionally plan how they will work together to accomplish goals have better team outcomes (for examples, see Cox & Bobrowski, 2016; De Jong et al., 2016; Johnson et al., 2022; Mathieu & Rapp, 2009; Newman et al., 2017). As such, our *Team Launch* phase's emphasis on both team building and norm creation reflects decades of theoretical development and empirical research on early-phase teamwork.

Key Considerations for Virtual Student Teams

We want to draw attention to three important considerations for virtual student teams in the *Team Launch* phase. First, given that student teams typically have a short lifespan (i.e., the length of the project), there is a limited timeframe to build relationships. In other words, trust does not have time to develop organically as it might in a long-term team, which aligns with Kramer et al.'s (1996) conceptualization of swift trust. The authors explain how teams with a limited tenure expedite the process of building trust by focusing on role-based interactions and using categorical assumptions to reduce uncertainty (e.g., professional credentials). Second, and relatedly, virtual teams have more difficulty establishing and maintaining trust than in-person teams, having fewer natural touchpoints, no face-to-face communication, and being less likely to engage in casual non-task related conversation (e.g., Breuer et al., 2016; Gilson et al., 2015; Jarvenpaa & Leidner, 1999). Yet, trust remains foundational to successful teamwork (De Jong et al., 2016).

Taken together, these first two considerations highlight the importance of incorporating team-building activities early in the semester to support the development of interpersonal relationships in student virtual teams, who are challenged by both timeline *and* proximity constraints. Indeed, scholars have found that team member familiarity plays an important role in virtual team functioning (Maynard et al., 2019) and that team-building activities (including those specifically intended to foster relationship building) are positively associated with team outcomes (for a review, see Klein et al., 2009). The third consideration in the *Team Launch* phase for student virtual teams is that communicating solely via technology (i.e., as virtual teams do) provides fewer non-verbal cues than face-to-face communication, and can easily lead to miscommunication, misunderstanding, and conflict, all of which can impair team functioning (e.g., Gupta et al., 2023; Hertel et al., 2005; Hinds & Mortensen, 2005). To alleviate these potential challenges, teams might develop team norms related to technology use, such as what kinds of technology are best suited for what kinds of messages (e.g., Sperry, Aldana, O'Neill, Mimovic, Gibson, & McLarnon, under review). As such, we now turn our discussion to the practical application of the theoretical foundations of the *Team Launch* phase to course design, which details specific strategies for tackling this phase in student virtual teams.

From Theory to Practice

Instructors set the tone for how students will engage in their teams from the outset. The theory-focused portion of the *Team Launch* phase underscores the importance of team building and norm creation; however, translating that knowledge into the course requires careful consideration and planning. By designing opportunities for students to get to know each other and guiding them to establish and clearly document team norms, instructors can proactively address some of the common challenges associated with virtual teamwork, such as difficulty building trust without face-to-face interaction. In the next section, we offer practical guidance and tools that draw from the research findings and theoretical frameworks discussed above to help instructors effectively form teams.

Team Formation Considerations

There is a lack of evidence on practices for forming teams that align with all course types and environments, which isn't surprising. Given the learning outcomes, content, and delivery methods that vary between courses, there is no "one-size-fits-all" approach. Taking into account Hackman's (1987) work and more recent work by Mathieu et al. (2014), effective team formation begins with aligning the structure of the team to the goals and learning objectives of the course. This may involve using best judgment and then iterating based on feedback from previously taught courses. For example, an instructor teaching a project-based engineering course might initially form teams by grouping students with diverse technical skills and backgrounds to encourage cross-disciplinary collaboration. Of course, functional diversity contributes to conflict (Cronin & Weingart, 2007; Maguire & Keceli, 2024), and therefore, conflict management strategies and training would be beneficial. If, for whatever reason, the task does not require diversity of interests and expertise, the instructor may elect to design less functionally diverse teams. After observing team dynamics and gathering feedback from students (Hastings et al., 2023), the instructor might adjust their approach in future iterations by incorporating a self-selection component, random assignment, or using personality assessments to better match communication styles within teams. In summary, prioritizing the design of the course and group project to support effective teamwork should take precedence over weighing the pros and cons of various team formation strategies, as the success of the team often hinges on clear alignment of objectives.

The ITP Metrics (www.ITPmetrics.com) Team Designer is a tool that can help instructors group students based on complementary knowledge and perspectives. Specifically, the Team Designer allows instructors to create teams that are balanced on both stable and fluid characteristics, such as gender, personality, and background training. Ensuring representation in teams is especially important in programs where there tend to be imbalances in one or more characteristics. For example, based on our observations supporting teamwork in engineering courses, there tend to be a handful of groups that are primarily female-identifying, despite the fact that in most engineering programs, 80% of students identify as male (Engineers Canada, 2021); this may be a deliberate choice by the instructor or the result of students' preferences when choosing team members. However, for team tasks that require diversity in perspectives and skills, the Team Designer can help instructors form more balanced teams. Furthermore, the tool includes a schedule-matching option to maximize available meeting times in students' calendars. To access the Team Designer and deploy it, a prospective user must create an account to access the dashboard. The tool will be visible at the bottom of the dashboard.

Although team formation approaches should vary depending on the course and the type of group project(s) assigned, instructors should strive to be rigorous in their process and communicate to students *why* they chose the formation approach they did. Applying transparency, precision, and thoughtfulness to team formation can support student buy-in by demonstrating that their teams were constructed to optimize learning outcomes and set them up for success (Twigg & Valluri, 2024). Instructors should communicate the rationale behind team assignments and share the criteria used to form teams where appropriate.

Team Building

Effectively launching a virtual team requires early efforts to establish relationships and trust among members. However, building trust in virtual teams is a significant challenge due to the lack of face-to-face interaction (Lechner & Tobias Mortlock, 2022). In traditional, co-located teams, trust often develops naturally through casual interactions, shared experiences, and nonverbal communication, such as body language and tone of voice. Virtual teams, on the other hand, must navigate an environment where these subtle but crucial cues are absent, leaving trust-building to rely heavily on clear communication, consistent behaviour, and mutual accountability (Gilson et al., 2015).

Trust is impossible to cultivate without a foundation of psychological safety. Psychological safety, conceptualized by Edmondson (1999), is defined by the absence of interpersonal threat, which allows team members to behave more openly and take risks (Harvey et al., 2019; Newman et al., 2017). A notable drawback of virtual teamwork is that it can be isolating, as team members tend to interact with each other only when they must. These silos make it difficult for students to develop meaningful relationships with their team members where they feel comfortable taking risks. Promoting psychological safety can have positive consequences for constructive conflict, including knowledge sharing, idea exchange, and feedback-seeking (O'Neill & McLarnon, 2018; O'Neill & Salas, 2018). When team members feel psychologically safe, they are more likely to engage in open and honest communication, share opinions, and tackle conflict effectively. In contrast, a lack of psychological safety can lead to avoidance behaviours, reduced participation, and a decline in team effectiveness, particularly in virtual settings where disengagement may be more common and easier to hide (Lechner & Tobias Mortlock, 2022).

To address these challenges, in the following sections, we provide examples of impactful icebreakers (i.e., early-stage assessments for team members to get to know each other) and introduce chartering as a team-building activity. Together, these tools and activities can help team members better understand each other's working styles from the outset and establish a foundation of trust.

Icebreakers. Icebreakers that encourage team members to share personal experiences, including their teamwork approaches and preferences, can help team members connect, which is especially important for virtual teamwork. The Personality and Conflict Management Style assessments on ITP Metrics offer insights into individual working styles and highlight potential areas of compatibility or tension within the team.

The Conflict Management Styles assessment (O'Neill, Aldana, Espinoza, Sperry, Brykman, & Donia, 2024) evaluates students' tendencies to use five different styles of conflict management derived from the dual concern model, which posits that conflict management is a function of high or low concern for self and high or low concern for others (De Dreu et al., 2001; Rahim & Bonoma, 1979). The accompanying individual report converts raw scores into percentile scores to illustrate students' preferred styles. The report is intended to increase students' awareness of their conflict management preferences and highlight scenarios in which each style would be most effective. The free debriefing activity available through ITP Metrics adds value by encouraging students to reflect on their tendencies, share their experiences with group members, and discuss how their styles might influence team dynamics. Student reactions to this icebreaker have been very positive, with most reporting that it helps them get to know one another more quickly (O'Neill et al., 2024). By encouraging proactive conversations about managing conflict, instructors support team members in understanding each other and navigating disagreements constructively.

The Personality assessment evaluates students across five major dimensions of personality, often referred to as the "Big Five" (i.e., openness, conscientiousness, extraversion, agreeableness, and emotionality; Goldberg et al., 2006). It was originally developed by Johnson (2014) and then was built into ITP Metrics based on research by O'Neill and colleagues (e.g., O'Neill & Allen, 2011). In addition to these factors' consistent relationship to important workplace criteria, they can promote self-insight and help students become better acquainted with their team members. The accompanying report provides students' scores on each Big Five factor and is intended to increase awareness of how their personality traits might influence their interactions and relationships with team members. The debriefing activity prompts students to share insights from their personality profiles, explore how their traits align with or differ from those of their team members, and consider how these differences might influence teamwork. Instructors can use these reflective discussions to encourage students to recognize their unique contributions and appreciate the strengths of their team members. In both of these icebreaker activities, it is important that instructors emphasize that there are no "better" or "worse" conflict management styles or personality characteristics, as it can alleviate students feeling self-conscious about their scores.

Team Chartering. Early in a team's lifecycle, it is common for members to have different expectations about how to work together; however, these divergent expectations can solidify into counterproductive norms (Cox & Bobrowski, 2016). Since team norms emerge whether they are deliberately set or not, misaligned expectations can lead to coordination challenges and conflict. Virtual teams are especially prone to this reality, given the ambiguity of digital environments, where there are fewer opportunities for immediate clarification. A team charter, which documents the team's agreed-upon operating procedures and norms, provides a framework for how to work together. This framework can reduce the risk that members are operating under different expectations, in addition to enhancing team performance (Mathieu & Rapp, 2009). Virtual teams face challenges such as coordinating schedules, asynchronous communication, and maintaining accountability. Chartering can mitigate these challenges by providing clear guidelines on foundational aspects of team functioning early in the team's lifecycle (Sperry et al., under review).

ITP Metrics offers comprehensive materials for instructors who wish to implement chartering into their courses. The *Resources* webpage provides a detailed team charter template designed to guide teams through the process of defining expectations, communication protocols, meeting structures, conflict resolution strategies, stress management plans, and accountability measures. Teams are tasked with collaboratively specifying norms in each of these areas, creating a "living document" that serves to maintain alignment throughout the project while allowing flexibility to be amended as the team evolves. The webpage also equips instructors with a slide deck to outline what chartering is and how to carry it out effectively, as well as practical tips to facilitate inclusive discussion and ensure charters are sufficiently detailed. The key goal at this stage is to activate the students' thinking about what they are expecting from the team experience and their peers, and to communicate those expectations so that discrepancies can be discussed and expectations tempered against reality.

PHASE II: TASK LAUNCH

Once teams have established foundational relationships and norms, they are ready to begin tackling taskwork. Teams must move beyond the relationships they have built and norms they have established to create concrete workflows and actions. The *Task Launch* phase is marked by two central themes, both of which can be embedded within course design by instructors: designing engaging tasks that are well-suited for teamwork and teamwork training. Notably, teamwork *training* differs from team *building* described in the first phase. Team building is focused on establishing relationships, trust, and shared understanding, whereas teamwork training focuses on developing essential skills and abilities for high-performance teamwork (e.g., effective communication, conflict management, etc.). As such, a successful *Task Launch* phase promotes positive and productive teamwork by structuring tasks in a way that encourages and facilitates teamwork and by training students on teamwork skills that students can draw upon as they work with their team.

Theoretical Foundation

The *Task Launch* phase is grounded in theory and research on task design (e.g., Cohen, 1994; Hackman & Oldham, 1975;1976;1980) and training critical skills and abilities for effective teamwork (e.g., Lacerenza et al., 2018; O'Neill et al., 2017; Salas et al., 2008). Regarding task design, some types of tasks are ideal for teamwork, while others are more well-suited for independent work (Hackman, 2002). By definition, teamwork involves working interdependently toward a common goal (e.g., Hackman, 1987; Salas et al., 2015). As such, tasks that involve interdependence are fundamental for team projects. The degree of interdependence can range widely, where higher interdependence (i.e., more reciprocal, simultaneous rather than sequential, and requiring more complex workflows) is more complex and increases the need for strong teamwork skills such as communication and coordination (Kozlowski et al., 1999). Additionally, Hackman and Oldham (1975; 1976; 1980) suggest that to be engaging, tasks should have specific characteristics such as the team feeling the task is important, the task being open-ended such that it might be tackled in various ways, and that it requires a variety of skills to complete. Cohen (1994) similarly suggests that student teams specifically benefit from tasks that require elaborate discussion and interaction with one another, are based around ill-structured problems, and use problems that are "real" (i.e., important and likely to be meaningful to the students). Both models are foundational in guiding task design considerations, and are reflected in our recommendations for developing teamwork tasks in the From Theory to Practice section.

Teamwork training, the second major theme in the *Task Launch* phase, is also essential for success in team projects (e.g., Salas et al., 2008; Shuffler et al., 2018). Effective teamwork requires specific skills and abilities beyond individual technical proficiency, and it has been well-established that the *way* the team works together influences team performance (e.g., LePine et al., 2008). In other words, simply collecting a group of high-performing individuals will not guarantee team effectiveness (Lacerenza et al., 2018): a team of experts does not make an expert team (Reyes & Salas, 2019). The ways in which teams work together, widely referred to as team processes (i.e. team members' interdependent acts that convert inputs into outputs to achieve shared goals; Marks et al., 2001), can be targeted in teamwork training such that members build skills and abilities to effectively enact team processes such as coordination and conflict management. Indeed, research findings support the efficacy of teamwork training, with multiple reviews concluding that it is positively associated with a variety of team outcomes, including improvements in team performance (e.g., Hughes et al., 2016; Salas et al., 2008). As such, evidence suggests that investing time to incorporate teamwork training into course design is likely to be worthwhile and enhance the success of team projects.

Key Considerations for Student Virtual Teams

We want to draw attention to two considerations specific to virtual student teams in the *Task Launch* phase. First, regarding task design, instructors should be strategic in designing tasks that can be completed only through virtual means (i.e., ensuring there is no component that would require students to be in the same geographic location, time zone, or to see one another in person to complete the project). For example, it would likely be challenging to ask virtual teams to complete a material or physical deliverable (unless a great deal of care goes into ensuring that sufficient contributions can be made virtually and scaffolding students on effectively dividing roles). It is also essential that students have access to whatever virtual tools and platforms might be required for the successful completion of the project. For inspiration, we refer the reader to work by Dr. Vas Taras and his initiative, X-Culture (e.g., Taras et al., 2024).

The second consideration relates to teamwork training: although both virtual and face-to-face teams require the same foundational teamwork skills, virtual team members additionally need to have a high degree of competence using technology (Krumm et al., 2016). While most students today *are* likely to be proficient in using technology, they may *not* know how to use it effectively for collaboration. There is a collection of theories which inform our understanding of how teams can best use technology to effectively communicate and complete tasks (e.g., *Media Richness Theory*- Daft & Lengel, 1986; *Media Synchronicity Theory*- Dennis et al., 2008; *Task-Technology Fit Theory*- Goodhue, 1988). Taken together, these theories focus on different features of technological platforms, how well they meet the needs of a given task, the nature of collaboration needed, and how closely they mimic face-to-face interaction, suggesting that the team's ability to successfully perform is impacted by the technology used. For example, Maruping and Agarwal (2004) recommend ways for virtual teams to manage interpersonal processes through technology, identifying what kinds of media are best suited to different circumstances (e.g., when navigating team member emotions, use media that mimics face-to-face interaction, such as a video meeting). The model also generally suggests that teams should use media that is closer to face-to-face interaction for most interpersonal processes early in their lifecycle, but that many of these can be transitioned to less rich media (e.g., email or instant messaging) as the team moves to later stages in its development (note that this is a simplification; for the full model, see Maruping & Agarwal, 2004). As such, teamwork training for virtual teams might include specific content on how to effectively collaborate through technology.

From Theory to Practice

As we have demonstrated, positive teamwork experiences and team success are heavily dependent on how instructors design the task and how they equip students with practical collaboration skills as they work towards deliverables. Teams that are assigned well-designed tasks tend to perform better, remain motivated, and experience greater satisfaction because they engage students and require them to stretch their knowledge, skills, and abilities (Cohen, 1994). Additionally, training on essential teamwork skills, such as communication and conflict management, can benefit students by preparing them to navigate group dynamics effectively (Hollenbeck et al., 2004). As such, in the next section we provide actionable guidance for achieving success in the *Task Launch* phase. Specifically, we outline research-informed criteria for designing "good" team tasks and teamwork training activities to support students in working together.

Designing Motivating and Engaging Team Tasks

Hackman and Oldham's Job Characteristics Model (1975;1976;1980), extended to the team (e.g., Hackman, 2002), offers a useful framework for thinking about what makes a "good" (team) task. When students perceive their project as important and impactful (referred to as *task significance* in the model), they are more likely to stay invested in their team's success. Tasks should also present an all-encompassing, cohesive challenge instead of being trivial or disjointed (referred to as *task identity* in the model). Additionally, the task should require students to draw on a range of skills while having the freedom to approach it in the way they choose to promote creative problem-solving (referred to as *skill variety* and *autonomy,* respectively, in the model). The following sections offer considerations for instructors derived from these guiding principles.

Complexity and "Stretch" Requirements. Complex tasks reduce the risk that a single high-performing student singlehandedly completes the project, and instead motivates all team members to contribute (Campion et al., 1993). By contrast, smaller tasks that can be wrapped up in one or two "all-nighters" undermine collaboration and can result in disengagement. If a task is easily subdivided into siloed portions, where each student works largely in isolation, teams lose the benefits of reciprocal feedback and shared learning. Tasks that are "whole" or "complete" (i.e., those representing an end-to-end service, product, or solution) tend to promote collective brainstorming, iterative testing of ideas, and reflective conversations about what is or isn't working. For example, a large-scale case study can be considered "whole" or "complete" when it requires students to identify a real-world problem, gather relevant data, plan strategic interventions, implement (or simulate) those interventions, and critically evaluate the results.

Open-Ended Problems That Require Creativity. Working on a task where there is no single "right" answer requires teams to think creatively. The open-ended nature of case studies, community-engaged projects, or design prototypes requires students to collaboratively share, consider, and decide on how to move forward. Often, these teamwork processes can be a catalyst for innovative solutions that represent multiple perspectives. Furthermore, students are more inclined to take ownership of and engage deeply with the team's work when they feel there is a strong "real-world" applicability. For example, Bremner et al. (2014) found that students who engaged in a professional communication project where they were given large amounts of freedom increased their motivation and commitment to producing excellent promotional materials. Similarly, Mathieu et al. (2006) found that empowered teams (i.e., teams that experience greater decision-making authority and responsibility) demonstrated enhanced performance outcomes. We encourage instructors to consider how they can connect the project to relevant professional contexts to encourage creativity and commitment. For instance, partnering with external stakeholders (e.g., community organizations or industry professionals) gives students the opportunity to address tangible needs, challenges, and deliverables.

Promoting Peer Learning. Team tasks that demand interaction among team members, interdependence of activities, and reciprocal information exchange and learning promote peer learning in addition to effective teamwork (Cohen, 1994). For instance, if students have different but complementary knowledge (e.g., an engineering capstone course open to students in mechanical, electrical, civil, and other streams), a well-structured project demands the integration of all these perspectives (Maguire & Keceli, 2024). Teams must not only share what they know but also refine their understanding through group discussion and feedback loops, leading to richer, more enduring learning.

Teamwork Cadences

Teamwork ebbs and flows depending on factors internal to team members (e.g., schedules, personal commitments), external factors (e.g., deadlines, resource availability), and project stage (e.g., strategy and planning, action and execution). These rhythms guide how and when teams interact, share updates, and accomplish project goals (Larson et al., 2020; Marks et al., 2001). Although instructors can't directly influence internal factors, they can shape external conditions, such as milestones and feedback intervals, to help teams maintain consistent routines and stay on track. This structure is particularly important in virtual environments, where members can quickly lose momentum or struggle with accountability if interactions are sporadic.

Milestones and Mid-Project Deliverables. Milestones and mid-project deliverables play a pivotal role in helping students avoid procrastination by establishing regular "mini deadlines" rather than one high-stakes submission. Given that teams tend to ramp up their work on a project right before a deadline (e.g., Larson et al., 2020), setting up smaller interim checkpoints can encourage them to consistently plug away at the project instead of rushing through tasks in last-minute sprints. These milestones provide opportunities for teams to share in-progress work and for instructors to gauge teams' collective progress and address any emerging coordination or quality issues. Specifically, they are an optimal point for instructors to provide timely feedback and guide students toward self-correction, ensuring that misunderstandings or uneven workloads are corrected early rather than at the eleventh hour.

Instructors might consider milestones such as rough drafts, interim presentations, or progress reports. Importantly, each milestone should be associated with a tangible output, which can encourage a sense of collective responsibility and urgency. This sequential structure keeps the project at the forefront of students' minds and ensures teams' trajectories remain relatively consistent as they work through milestones.

Planning and Routines. Without a clear structure and process for tackling tasks, even the most innovative project designs fall flat (Lantz et al., 2019). Yet, many students lack experience in organizing workflows, making it difficult for teams to develop effective routines. Regular touchpoints can help to ensure team members are "on the same page" and reduce the likelihood of confusion or duplicated efforts. These routines and touchpoints are especially important for virtual teams, as they tend to struggle with coordinating tasks and aligning efforts. Getting into a routine leads to "entrainment," which creates a self-fulfilling prophecy of good (or bad) team performance habits (Harrison et al., 2003).

We encourage instructors to think about what routine recommendations they can offer students to enable effective teamwork. For instance, instructors might suggest implementing regular team meetings (i.e., weekly or biweekly) to re-align on priorities or, depending on the course, daily "huddles" to discuss the day's objectives. Given the impact of meeting quality on team success, these suggestions can help teams prevent dysfunctional interaction patterns (Kauffeld & Lehmann-Willenbrock, 2012). Furthermore, resources distributed by instructors, such as a team meeting template, may provide students with helpful guidance on how to approach tracking progress and documenting key conversations and decisions.

Establishing effective routines is largely about increasing predictability. Clear roles can also increase predictability by minimizing redundancy and confusion. Having a designated project manager who oversees scheduling meetings, tracks progress, and keeps members updated is beneficial. Meanwhile, other roles (e.g., subject matter experts, editors, presenters) can be assigned according to individual strengths and interests. If coordination issues become apparent as teams start tackling their projects, we recommend that instructors encourage students to re-visit role-related terms in their team charter (if applicable). Teams with vague, broad role-related terms or those who have had little or no conversations about roles are more likely to experience coordination challenges. In these cases, instructors might advise these teams to re-visit, clarify, and flesh out roles so that all team members understand how their contributions support the team's mission.

Training to Strengthen Virtual Teamwork

Effective collaboration in virtual teams extends beyond simply working together online; it requires deliberate strategies to enhance team processes. This section introduces technology training and the SUIT framework as two key approaches for strengthening virtual teamwork.

Technology Training. Virtual teams rely heavily, and often exclusively, on technology to coordinate their work, communicate effectively, and manage their deliverables (Bell & Kozlowski, 2002). Although most students are "digitally fluent" (i.e., they have experience using various digital tools), they might lack an intentional strategy for selecting the right tools for different aspects of teamwork (Maruping & Agarwal, 2004). Furthermore, they may be unaware of how to translate their digital proficiencies into collective practices that support team effectiveness. Technology competence is equally about establishing effective collaboration norms and practices as it is about using the right tools (Sperry et al., under review).

Instructors should ensure students are aware of the technologies available to them and provide guidance on how to use these tools strategically. For example, teams might be advised on when to communicate synchronously (i.e., a virtual meeting) versus asynchronously (i.e., email or instant message). According to *Media Synchronicity Theory*, communication that requires rapid back-and-forth interaction between members, such as brainstorming or complex decision-making, is best suited to synchronous communication, while information that can be understood at face value or requires reflection prior to a response is better suited for asynchronous communication (Dennis et al., 2008).

Introducing students to these concepts and their practical applications through a brief technology training session at the beginning of a project can enhance workflow efficiency. Furthermore, encouraging teams to set expectations for how and when to use platforms can help to reduce confusion down the line. The ITP Metrics' team charter template has a section on communication modalities and practices that can help teams establish clear norms around their use of digital tools. This documentation can provide a helpful basis for instructors to support teams struggling with collaboration due to technology-related issues.

SUIT Training. Beyond using the right tools, effective teamwork demands information-sharing, decision-making, and conflict resolution. The SUIT framework, based on constructive controversy theory and tested on student learning teams, can improve team interactions (O'Neill et al., 2017; O'Neill et al., 2020). Constructive controversy theory assumes that each team member has unique knowledge, skills, and opinions to contribute to a discussion, and that fully exploring these diverse perspectives can lead to innovative solutions and comprehensive decisions (Tjosvold, 2008). SUIT applies the principles that underlie constructive controversy in simplified, easy-to-understand steps that help teams navigate complex discussions. By presenting four key stages—Sharing, Understanding, Integrating, and Team Decision-Making—SUIT ensures that all team members contribute insights, actively listen to one another, and collaboratively refine their ideas before committing to a path forward.

The materials available through ITP Metrics introduce the theory, describe the steps, and present a variety of activities for students to practice (e.g., structured role play, unstructured decision-making exercise, etc.). Delivering this training early in the task launch phase can help teams overcome common pitfalls associated with information sharing, processing, planning, and developing a shared mental model (i.e., a collective understanding).

PHASE III: PERFORMANCE CYCLES AND EVALUATION

In the final phase of the lifecycle model, *Performance Cycles and Evaluation,* teams begin their taskwork. Although "doing" may appear to be the most straightforward phase, there are cycles of performance within the broader project, and key considerations for formative and summative evaluation. The way the team works together as tasks progress tends to be complex, dynamic, and reciprocal in nature, which is why we refer to performance *cycles* rather than suggesting a single linear path toward completing the final project. As such, the final phase of the team lifecycle model has two major themes: performance cycles and team monitoring and evaluation. It culminates in the team completing its final project and completion of its lifecycle.

Theoretical Foundation

The theoretical basis for the *Performance Cycles and Evaluation* phase lies in the wealth of research on how teams work together over time (e.g., Gersick, 1988; Larson et al., 2020; Marks et al., 2001) and how to monitor and evaluate student learning teams (e.g., Donia et al., 2018; McLarnon et al., 2019; O'Neill et al., 2020). In a broad sense, teams tend to increase their capability for teamwork and taskwork over time (Kozlowski & Bell, 2003), and their networks of interdependence become increasingly dense and complex (Kozlowski et al., 1999). This general phase of teamwork, where taskwork is being completed, aligns with Tuckman's (1965) *Performing* stage of team development and Ilgen et al.'s (2005) *Functioning* categorization of literature on team life cycles. At this point, teams should be able to effectively enact teamwork and be capable of adapting and problem solving to complete tasks. However, in addition to the broad and general characterization of teams in this phase, there are more fine-grained considerations related to the smaller performance cycles of the team.

As such, more nuanced, dynamic, and temporally focused models that recognize the complexity of team performance cycles have garnered substantial attention. As teams progress on their large project, completing smaller tasks and assignments that contribute to the final goal, they tend to change the nature, pacing, and engagement in their work (e.g., Larson et al., 2020; Waller et al., 2002). For example, Marks et al. (2001) developed a seminal framework of team performance cycles, which are broadly divided into three overarching phases: transition phase processes (i.e., evaluation and planning-related activities, such as specifying and prioritizing goals), action phase processes (i.e., activities that directly contribute toward goals, such as coordinating interdependent work), and interpersonal processes (i.e., processes that teams use to navigate relationships, such as conflict management). Teams tend to cycle between transition and action phases, where an action phase (i.e., performance on a task) is followed by a brief transition phase (i.e., planning, debriefing, and reflection), and subsequently another action phase. Naturally, these phases are likely to be highly fluid and overlapping, where teams may be working toward multiple goals at any given time (i.e., they may be in an action phase for one goal and a transition phase for another). However, transition phases are an important opportunity for reflection and formative feedback on how the team is performing and a time to make adjustments as needed before starting the next action phase. In addition to cycling through phases of planning and doing, Larson et al. (2020) found that teams tend to increase their extent of engagement in team processes as deadlines approached. Ilgen et al. (2005) similarly address the nature of dynamic and reciprocal relationships by noting in their model that team outputs (e.g., performance on some task) transform back into team inputs on subsequent goals and tasks (in what they coin the input-mediator-output-input, IMOI, model).

Finally, the conclusion of the team, which in a course context is associated with getting a final grade and completing the project, has been coined by Tuckman and Jensen (1977) as the *Adjourning* phase and in Ilgen et al. (2005) literature review as *Finishing*: the end of the team's life cycle. As such, the *Performance Cycles and Evaluation* phase of the team life cycle model culminates with the completion of the final deliverable and disbandment of the team.

Key Considerations for Student Virtual Teams

The main consideration for student virtual teams in the *Performance Cycles and Evaluation* phase ties back to the considerations we outlined in the first two phases as well: virtual teams collaborate via technology, which can be complex to manage effectively (e.g., Gilson et al., 2015; Rapp & Rapp, 2021). As teams progress through action and transition phases, frequent and inclusive communication in alignment with the outlined team norms is imperative. For example, as teams are in transition phases (i.e., goal setting, reflecting on teamwork, and feedback; see From Theory to Practice section for examples), they may choose to opt to communicate via richer media platforms, particularly if conversations are emotionally sensitive (Maruping & Agarwal, 2004). In contrast, whereas tasks are being executed by individuals (depending on how interdependent they are), updates and check-ins via instant message or email may suffice more often. What is important is that teams maintain an awareness and commitment to their norms, willingness to re-visit them as needed, and keep ongoing and inclusive communication practices. The practice of regular and iterative feedback interspersed with phases of teamwork activity seems like a wise practice (e.g., McLarnon et al., 2019; O'Neill et al., 2020). As such, we move to the application section of the *Performance Cycles and Evaluation* phase, discussing how instructors can pace feedback and reflection to the team's performance cycles.

From Theory to Practice

Thoughtfully designed evaluations and feedback can mitigate issues that arise when team members struggle to share critical information, fall behind on their contributions, or have difficulty adapting their strategies to changing circumstances. By providing timely feedback that aligns with performance cycles, instructors can help teams navigate challenges and adjust their approach before reaching key deadlines. In the next section, we offer guidance on embedding evaluation and reflection opportunities into course design to support students in developing teamwork competencies and guide them toward successful project completion.

Connecting Teamwork Cadences to Performance Cycles

Teamwork cadences (discussed in the *Task Launch* phase) can serve as natural points for evaluation. While teamwork cadences are characterized by the pace of work and focus as teams transition between planning and action activities, "performance cycles" refer to the repeated pattern of team activities over time (i.e., planning, execution, reflection, and adjustment; Marks et al., 2001). By aligning evaluations with these intervals, instructors can provide targeted feedback when teams need it most, which can help regulate their motivation and activities (DeShon et al., 2004). Furthermore, tying assessments to performance cycles can help teams and instructors identify issues before they snowball, which is especially crucial for virtual teams since digital environments can reduce the visibility of individual contributions and behind-the-scenes happenings (McLarnon et al., 2019).

Mid-project milestones and deliverables (discussed in the *Task Launch* section) can be coupled with evaluation (e.g., grades for deliverables, teamwork assessments and accompanying debrief activities). Multiple, strategically timed evaluations create opportunities to improve contributions and behaviours incrementally, which impact learning and the quality of final deliverables (Donia et al., 2018). For example, instructors can structure a mid-project milestone to be followed by a mark and feedback for the submission, in addition to peer evaluations, allowing students to reflect on individual contributions and team dynamics while the project is in progress (O'Neill et al., 2019; O'Neill et al., 2020).

Evaluation Considerations

An effective evaluation system provides students with clarity on expectations, ensures accountability, and presents opportunities for growth. The following sections outline best practices for designing well-structured team assessments, including balancing taskwork and teamwork, establishing appropriate grade weightings, and using reliable assessment tools.

Taskwork and Teamwork. To accurately assess students' learning and contributions, evaluations should address both task outcomes (i.e., project quality, deliverables) and teamwork behaviours (i.e., communication, emphasizing high standards; Salas et al., 2015). Whereas taskwork focuses on the final product and how well it meets course objectives, the teamwork component assesses how effectively the team functioned throughout the project. Importantly, taskwork should reflect technical quality and the application of learned skills. Conversely, assessing teamwork can help ensure fair recognition of individual contributions and prevent social loafing, especially when students have an opportunity to course-correct, which we discuss in greater detail in the Formative Versus Summative section. Instructors should use separate rubrics for teamwork and taskwork evaluation. This distinction reinforces that teamwork is not just a means to an end but a core competency.

Weighting. Students have many competing demands, and therefore, they may be tempted to focus the most effort on the areas representing the largest proportions of course grades. If teamwork is weighted too lightly in overall grades, students will likely be less engaged in team activities, ultimately undermining team effectiveness (O'Neill et al., 2020). It also signals that teamwork is not an important feature of the course.

In order to weight the teamwork component of a course appropriately, instructors should consider how much time they expect students to spend on teamwork. We recommend assigning at least 20% of the overall grading distribution to teamwork. Furthermore, instructors can adjust individual teamwork grades based on peer feedback, which can uncover hidden contributions (or lack thereof). If students know their team members' assessments of their teamwork contributions matter, they will likely be more motivated to contribute. For example, an instructor might assign 20% of students' overall grades to teamwork development activities and peer evaluations, which could include completion marks for participating in icebreakers and assessments (e.g., peer feedback and team dynamics), as well as averaging peer ratings for each team member at the end of the project.

Formative Versus Summative. Well-designed evaluation balances formative feedback and assessment (i.e., growth-oriented) with summative assessment and feedback (i.e., grade-oriented). Both are important and should not be conflated (Murphy & Cleveland, 1995). On the one hand, formative assessment is "low stakes", meaning that it carries minimal (or completion-based) grade implications; instead, it encourages students to reflect on their contributions and commit to improving and actioning their team members' feedback before final deliverables are due. Although formative assessment is often focused on taskwork (e.g., a progress report or small mid-project deliverable), formative feedback on teamwork should also be integrated into evaluation. For example, teams might complete a formative assessment at the midpoint of the project that gives them a snapshot of their overall team health, which can help them determine what's working and what's not, guiding refinements to their communication strategies, task coordination, and other teamwork practices (O'Neill et al., 2019). Summative assessment, on the other hand, is "high stakes" because it's used at the end of the project to determine final grades. Effective formative assessment scaffolds performance on summative assessments by making student learning (and areas for improvement) visible early on in the project, giving students an opportunity to pivot and adapt before the summative evaluation. However, to reap the benefits of formative assessment, it is crucial that instructors provide formative feedback well in advance of the deadline for the final project deliverable such that teams have time to adjust and revise their work (i.e., repeated cycles of feedback throughout project progression).

As discussed in the Weighting section, instructors can use peer feedback to assess individual contributions at the project's conclusion. Accountability theory suggests that translating end-of-project peer feedback to student grades (e.g., scaled to 5-10% of their overall grade in the course) reduces social loafing, increases perceptions of fairness, and supports overall team health (O'Neill et al., 2020). However, summative peer feedback should only be used after students have had an opportunity to action formative peer feedback. Specifically, structured team reflection activities following formative assessments allow teams and individual team members to discuss key takeaways and set goals for improvements. Instructors can facilitate these debrief sessions by prompting teams with meaningful, relevant questions, which we will discuss further in the Assessments and Debriefs from ITP Metrics section.

Reliable and Valid Tools. Assessment tools should be evidence-based (i.e., shown to be reliable, valid, accurate, etc.), aligned with the learning objectives of the course, and timed with milestones in the course. Students' teamwork growth over the course of a project will be largely determined by the quality, clarity, and relevance of the feedback they receive. Well-designed assessments not only measure individual and team performance but also provide actionable insights that help students refine their strategies and approach to teamwork. By using valid, reliable tools such as the ITP Metrics Peer Feedback assessment and Team Dynamics assessment, instructors can ensure that students receive structured, research-backed feedback on key teamwork competencies.

To ensure fairness and transparency, instructors should use clear assessment criteria so students understand the expectations for teamwork from the start of the semester (O'Neill et al., 2019). For example, introducing students to the specific teamwork competencies they will be assessed on early in the semester allows them to align their behaviours and contributions accordingly.

Assessments and Debriefs from ITP Metrics

The assessments developed by the ITP lab for the ITP Metrics platform are designed to evaluate and improve teamwork dynamics. These assessments, based on over a decade of research, are widely used in academic and professional settings to evaluate, monitor, and report on a multitude of individual and team metrics. Furthermore, they are correlated with team performance outcomes (O'Neill et al., 2018; O'Neill et al., 2020), making them an appropriate option for instructors looking to integrate off-the-shelf teamwork assessments into their courses. By embedding ITP Metrics assessments into a course, instructors can provide students with data-driven insights on their individual and team contributions, and support teams in recognizing and addressing challenges proactively.

Before deploying any ITP Metrics assessment, instructors should pre-brief (i.e., orient) students to explain the purpose of the assessments, how the results will be used, and which aspects of the assessments are anonymous versus visible to all team members. Transparency is critical from the outset so that students understand why they are being assessed and feel motivated to meaningfully engage with the assessment feedback they receive throughout the course of the semester.

Peer Feedback. The Peer Feedback assessment helps students gain insight into their teamwork effectiveness by evaluating five key teamwork competencies: (1) commitment to the team's work (2) communicating with team members; (3) having a strong foundation of KSAs (Knowledge, Skills, and Abilities); (4) emphasizing high standards; and (5) keeping the team on track. Research conducted on student learning teams indicates the assessment is reliable and valid (O'Neill et al., 2019). Students complete anonymous peer evaluations, where they rate their team members on each of the five competencies. They also complete a self-evaluation to compare their self-perceptions to their team members' observations. The resulting report from the assessment provides students with a visual five-point plot comparing self-ratings to average peer ratings. Furthermore, by aggregating written feedback from team members, the report can help students identify teamwork strengths and areas for improvement.

As we discussed in the Evaluation Considerations section, mid-project peer feedback can help team members course-correct before final deliverables and evaluations. End-of-project peer feedback can be used to adjust grades in order to recognize individual contributions. Considering this recommended process, instructors should encourage students to reflect on their feedback and set personal improvement, which we cover in the Debriefing, Reflecting, and Integrating Feedback section.

Team Health. The Team Health (CARE) assessment evaluates overall team functioning in four key areas: Communication, Adaptability, Relationships, and Education. Students answer a series of questions about how their team functions related to these key areas. These questions are drawn from previously published scales that were chosen for their psychometric properties and, when integrated, are valid and reliable indicators of team functioning (O'Neill et al., 2018; O'Neill et al., 2020). Individual feedback is aggregated to produce team-level quantifiable results. The resulting report highlights where teams excel and where they could benefit from focusing more time and effort and offers customized recommendations for strengthening team processes.

Instructors can implement a mid-project Team Health assessment to help teams understand what's working and what's not as they continue to work through tasks and find their teamwork groove. These insights can set the stage for open, honest discussions about team dynamics and empower teams to set collective goals to enhance teamwork processes.

Debriefing, Reflecting, and Integrating Feedback. Assessment results are most valuable when they lead to meaningful reflection and action. Teams that regularly reflect on their performance and identify areas for growth are more likely to innovate (Schippers et al., 2017). These debriefings can take the form of after-action reviews or the FACTs framework, to name a few examples (Keiser & Arthur, 2021; Rose et al., 2022). However, without structured debriefing, students may struggle to interpret feedback, feel defensive, or miss key opportunities for growth. A meaningful debriefing process ensures that assessment results translate into improved teamwork, communication, and project outcomes (O'Neill et al., 2019).

Instructors can access debriefing slide decks for each of the ITP Metrics assessments through the *Assessments* webpage. Following each assessment, we recommend that instructors dedicate approximately 45 minutes during class time to facilitate a debrief session where students can review their results, discuss takeaways, and commit to actioning feedback. The slide decks include information about creating a safe and constructive debriefing environment, giving and receiving feedback, and setting individual and team goals. After introducing these concepts, instructors can assign teams to breakout rooms where they can analyze their results using the structured prompts provided in the slides.

CONCLUSION

In sum, we have presented a series of actions instructors can take throughout the semester to embed teamwork into course design. We described evidence-based practices and free tools developed from theoretical and empirical research that have demonstrated benefits for student teams. Through the thoughtful integration of teamwork at each phase of the team's lifecycle - *Team Launch, Task Launch,* and *Performance Cycles and Evaluation* - instructors can help student teams reach their full potential, provide them with more positive experiences of group work, and foster the development of essential teamwork skills.

Although this chapter details specific tools, activities, and assessments that are aligned with each lifecycle phase, it is not exhaustive. For example, there are dozens of widely accessible, valid team formation activities; however, given our background, we chose to highlight resources available through ITP Metrics because of the features it contains. Despite virtual teamwork becoming increasingly prevalent in postsecondary courses, it is important for researchers and instructors to recognize that many student teams operate in a hybrid mode, where teams coordinate, execute tasks, and monitor progress both in-person and through digital tools. The lack of consensus and specificity regarding what constitutes hybrid teamwork more broadly is also relevant in education settings. Future research and resources could expand on the considerations and recommendations we present in this chapter, with a specific focus on hybrid student teams. Additionally, course coordinators and curriculum designers could integrate key takeaways from this chapter to scaffold the development of teamwork competencies across multiple courses, ensuring consistency and supporting skill progression. Ultimately, instructors are poised to design, guide, and support students through virtual teamwork experiences, which present significant challenges and opportunities in preparing students for the increasingly virtual workforce.

REFERENCES

Bell, B. S., & Kozlowski, S. W. J. (2002). A typology of virtual teams: Implications for effective leadership. *Group & Organization Management*, *27*(1), 14–49. DOI: 10.1177/1059601102027001003

Bremner, S., Peirson-Smith, A., Jones, R., & Bhatia, V. (2014). Task design and interaction in collaborative writing: The students' story. *Business and Professional Communication Quarterly*, *77*(2), 150–168. DOI: 10.1177/2329490613514598

Breuer, C., Hüffmeier, J., & Hertel, G. (2016). Does trust matter more in virtual teams? A meta-analysis of trust and team effectiveness considering virtuality and documentation as moderators. *The Journal of Applied Psychology*, *101*(8), 1151–1177. DOI: 10.1037/apl0000113 PMID: 27228105

Campion, M. A., Medsker, G. J., & Higgs, A. C. (1993). Relations between work group characteristics and effectiveness: Implications for designing effective work groups. *Personnel Psychology*, *46*(4), 823–847. DOI: 10.1111/j.1744-6570.1993.tb01571.x

Cohen, E. G. (1994). Restructuring the classroom: Conditions for productive small groups. *Review of Educational Research*, *64*(1), 1–35.

Cox, P. L., & Bobrowski, P. E. (2016). The team charter assignment: Improving the effectiveness of classroom teams. *Journal of Behavioral and Applied Management*, *1*(2), 789–805.

Cronin, M. A., & Weingart, L. R. (2007). Representational gaps, information processing, and conflict in functionally diverse teams. *Academy of Management Review*, *32*(3), 761–773. DOI: 10.5465/amr.2007.25275511

De Dreu, C. K. W., Evers, A., Beersma, B., Kluwer, E. S., & Nauta, A. (2001). A theory-based measure of conflict management strategies in the workplace. *Journal of Organizational Behavior*, *22*(6), 645–668. DOI: 10.1002/job.107

De Jong, B. A., Dirks, K. T., & Gillespie, N. (2016). Trust and team performance: A meta-analysis of main effects, moderators, and covariates. *The Journal of Applied Psychology*, *101*(8), 1134–1150. DOI: 10.1037/apl0000110 PMID: 27123697

Dennis, A. R., Fuller, R. M., & Valacich, J. S. (2008). Media, tasks, and communication processes: A theory of media synchronicity. *Management Information Systems Quarterly*, *32*, 575–600.

DeShon, R. P., Kozlowski, S. W. J., Schmidt, A. M., Milner, K. R., & Wiechmann, D. (2004). A multiple-goal, multilevel model of feedback effects on the regulation of individual and team performance. *The Journal of Applied Psychology*, *89*(6), 1035–1056. DOI: 10.1037/0021-9010.89.6.1035 PMID: 15584840

Donia, M. B. L., O'Neill, T. A., & Brutus, S. (2018). The longitudinal effects of peer feedback in the development and transfer of student teamwork skills. *Learning and Individual Differences*, *61*, 87–98. DOI: 10.1016/j.lindif.2017.11.012

Edmondson, A. (1999). Psychological safety and learning behavior in work teams. *Administrative Science Quarterly*, *44*(2), 350–383. DOI: 10.2307/2666999

Engineers Canada. (2021). *Trends in engineering enrolment and degrees awarded in 2016–2020*. https://engineerscanada.ca/reports/enrolment-and-degrees-awarded-report/canadian-engineers-for-tomorrow-2020

Gersick, C. J. G. (1988). Time and transition in work teams: Toward a new model of group development. *Academy of Management Journal*, *31*(1), 9–41. DOI: 10.2307/256496

Gilson, L. L., Maynard, M. T., Jones Young, N. C., Vartiainen, M., & Hakonen, M. (2015). Virtual teams research: 10 years, 10 themes, and 10 opportunities. *Journal of Management*, *41*(5), 1313–1337. DOI: 10.1177/0149206314559946

Gokhale, A. A. (1995). Collaborative learning enhances critical thinking. *Journal of Technology Education*, *7*(1), 22–30.

Goldberg, L. R., Johnson, J. A., Eber, H. W., Hogan, R., Ashton, M. C., Cloninger, C. R., & Gough, H. G. (2006). The international personality item pool and the future of public-domain personality measures. *Journal of Research in Personality*, *40*(1), 84–96. DOI: 10.1016/j.jrp.2005.08.007

Gupta, S., Pathak, G. S., & Biswas, B. (2023). The roles of conflict management and psychological empowerment in virtual teams. *Information Technology & People*, *37*(8), 66–108. DOI: 10.1108/ITP-04-2022-0265

Hackman, J. R. (1987). The design of work teams. In *Handbook of Organizational Behavior* (pp. 315-342).

Hackman, J. R., & Hackman, R. J. (2002). *Leading teams: Setting the stage for great performances*. Harvard Business Press.

Hackman, J. R., & Oldham, G. R. (1975). Development of the job diagnostic survey. *The Journal of Applied Psychology*, *60*(2), 159–170. DOI: 10.1037/h0076546

Hackman, J. R., & Oldham, G. R. (1976). Motivation through the design of work: Test of a theory. *Organizational Behavior and Human Performance*, *16*(2), 250–279. DOI: 10.1016/0030-5073(76)90016-7

Hackman, J. R., & Oldham, G. R. (1980). *Work redesign*. Addison-Wesley.

Harrison, D. A., Mohammed, S., McGrath, J. E., Florey, A. T., & Vanderstoep, S. W. (2003). Time matters in team performance: Effects of member familiarity, entrainment, and task discontinuity on speed and quality. *Personnel Psychology*, *56*(3), 633–669. DOI: 10.1111/j.1744-6570.2003.tb00753.x

Harvey, J.-F., Johnson, K. J., Roloff, K. S., & Edmondson, A. C. (2019). From orientation to behavior: The interplay between learning orientation, open-mindedness, and psychological safety in team learning. *Human Relations*, *72*(11), 1726–1751. DOI: 10.1177/0018726718817812

Hastings, E. M., Ojha, V., Austriaco, B. V., Karahalios, K., & Bailey, B. P. (2023). Composing team compositions: An examination of instructors' current algorithmic team formation practices. *Proceedings of the ACM on Human-Computer Interaction*, *7*(CSCW2), 1–24. https://doi.org/DOI: 10.1145/3610096

Hertel, G., Geister, S., & Konradt, U. (2005). Managing virtual teams: A review of current empirical research. *Human Resource Management Review*, *15*(1), 69–95. DOI: 10.1016/j.hrmr.2005.01.002

Hinds, P. J., & Mortensen, M. (2005). Understanding conflict in geographically distributed teams: The moderating effects of shared identity, shared context, and spontaneous communication. *Organization Science*, *16*(3), 290–307. DOI: 10.1287/orsc.1050.0122

Hollenbeck, J. R., DeRue, D. S., & Guzzo, R. (2004). Bridging the gap between I/O research and HR practice: Improving team composition, team training, and team task design. *Human Resource Management*, *43*(4), 353–366. DOI: 10.1002/hrm.20029

Ilgen, D. R., Hollenbeck, J. R., Johnson, M., & Jundt, D. (2005). Teams in organizations: From input-process-output models to IMOI models. *Annual Review of Psychology*, *56*(1), 517–543. DOI: 10.1146/annurev.psych.56.091103.070250 PMID: 15709945

Jarvenpaa, S. L., & Leidner, D. E. (1999). Communication and trust in global virtual teams. *Organization Science*, *10*(6), 791–815. DOI: 10.1287/orsc.10.6.791

Johnson, J. A. (2014). Measuring thirty facets of the Five Factor Model with a 120-item public domain inventory: Development of the IPIP-NEO-120. *Journal of Research in Personality*, *51*, 78–89. DOI: 10.1016/j.jrp.2014.05.003

Johnson, W. H., Baker, D. S., Dong, L., Taras, V., & Wankel, C. (2022). Do team charters help team-based projects? The effects of team charters on performance and satisfaction in global virtual teams. *Academy of Management Learning & Education*, *21*, 236–260.

Kauffeld, S., & Lehmann-Willenbrock, N. (2012). Meetings matter: Effects of team meetings on team and organizational success. *Small Group Research*, *43*(2), 130–158. DOI: 10.1177/1046496411429599

Klein, C., DiazGranados, D., Salas, E., Le, H., Burke, C. S., Lyons, R., & Goodwin, G. F. (2009). Does team building work? *Small Group Research*, *40*(2), 181–222. DOI: 10.1177/1046496408328821

Kozlowski, S. W., Gully, S. M., Nason, E. R., & Smith, E. M. (1999). Developing adaptive teams: A theory of compilation and performance across levels and time. In Ilgen, D. R., & Pulakos, E. D. (Eds.), *The changing nature of work performance: Implications for staffing, personnel actions, and development* (pp. 240–292). Jossey-Bass.

Kozlowski, S. W. J., & Bell, B. S. (2003). Work groups and teams in organizations. In Borman, W. C., Ilgen, D. R., & Klimoski, R. J. (Eds.), Handbook of psychology: Vol. 12. *Industrial and organizational psychology* (pp. 333–375). John Wiley & Sons, Inc. DOI: 10.1002/0471264385.wei1214

Lacerenza, C. N., Marlow, S. L., Tannenbaum, S. I., & Salas, E. (2018). Team development interventions: Evidence-based approaches for improving teamwork. *The American Psychologist*, *73*(4), 517–531. DOI: 10.1037/amp0000295 PMID: 29792465

Lantz, A., Ulber, D., & Friedrich, P. (2019). Why work in teams, and for what are teams effective? In A. Lantz, D. Ulber, & P. Friedrich, *The Problems with Teamwork, and How to Solve Them* (1st ed., pp. 1–29). Routledge. https://doi.org/DOI: 10.4324/9780429056024-1

Larson, N. L., McLarnon, M. J. W., & O'Neill, T. A. (2020). Challenging the "static" quo: Trajectories of engagement in team processes toward a deadline. *The Journal of Applied Psychology*, *105*(10), 1145–1163. DOI: 10.1037/apl0000479 PMID: 31985237

Lechner, A., & Tobias Mortlock, J. (2022). How to create psychological safety in virtual teams. *Organizational Dynamics*, *51*(2), 100849. DOI: 10.1016/j.orgdyn.2021.100849

Lohmann, G., Pratt, M. A., Benckendorff, P., Strickland, P., Reynolds, P., & Whitelaw, P. A. (2019). Online business simulations: Authentic teamwork, learning outcomes, and satisfaction. *Higher Education, 77*(3), 455–472. DOI: 10.1007/s10734-018-0282-x

Maguire, D., & Keceli, Y. (2024). The impact of formation and diversity on student team conflict. *Active Learning in Higher Education, 25*(3), 409–423. DOI: 10.1177/14697874221144998

Marks, M. A., Mathieu, J. E., & Zaccaro, S. J. (2001). A temporally based framework and taxonomy of team processes. *Academy of Management Review, 26*(3), 356–376. DOI: 10.5465/amr.2001.4845785

Maruping, L. M., & Agarwal, R. (2004). Managing team interpersonal processes through technology: A task-technology fit perspective. *The Journal of Applied Psychology, 89*(6), 975–990. DOI: 10.1037/0021-9010.89.6.975 PMID: 15584836

Mathieu, J., Maynard, M. T., Rapp, T., & Gilson, L. (2008). Team effectiveness 1997-2007: A review of recent advancements and a glimpse into the future. *Journal of Management, 34*(3), 410–476. DOI: 10.1177/0149206308316061

Mathieu, J. E., Gilson, L. L., & Ruddy, T. M. (2006). Empowerment and team effectiveness: An empirical test of an integrated model. *The Journal of Applied Psychology, 91*(1), 97–108. DOI: 10.1037/0021-9010.91.1.97 PMID: 16435941

Mathieu, J. E., & Rapp, T. L. (2009). Laying the foundation for successful team performance trajectories: The roles of team charters and performance strategies. *The Journal of Applied Psychology, 94*(1), 90–103. DOI: 10.1037/a0013257 PMID: 19186898

Mathieu, J. E., Tannenbaum, S. I., Donsbach, J. S., & Alliger, G. M. (2014). A review and integration of team composition models: Moving toward a dynamic and temporal framework. *Journal of Management, 40*(1), 130–160. DOI: 10.1177/0149206313503014

Maynard, M. T., Mathieu, J. E., Gilson, L. L. R., Sanchez, D., & Dean, M. D. (2019). Do I really know you and does it matter? Unpacking the relationship between familiarity and information elaboration in global virtual teams. *Group & Organization Management, 44*(1), 3–37. DOI: 10.1177/1059601118785842

McLarnon, M. J. W., O'Neill, T. A., Taras, V., Law, D., Donia, M. B. L., & Steel, P. (2019). Global virtual team communication, coordination, and performance across three peer feedback interventions. *Canadian Journal of Behavioural Science, 51*, 207–218.

Meyerson, D., Weick, K. E., & Kramer, R. M. (1996). Swift trust and temporary groups. In Kramer, R. M., & Tyler, T. R. (Eds.), *Trust in organizations: Frontiers of theory and research* (pp. 166–195). Sage Publications, Inc., DOI: 10.4135/9781452243610.n9

Murphy, K. R., & Cleveland, J. N. (1995). *Understanding performance appraisal: Social, organizational, and goal-based perspectives*. Sage Publications, Inc.

National Association of Colleges and Employers. (2024, December 9). *What are employers looking for when reviewing college students' resumes?* https://naceweb.org/talent-acquisition/candidate-selection/what-are-employers-looking-for-when-reviewing-college-students-resumes

Newman, A., Donohue, R., & Evan, N. (2017). Psychological safety: A systematic review of the literature. *Human Resource Management Review*, *27*(3), 521–535. DOI: 10.1016/j.hrmr.2017.01.001

O'Neill, T. A., Aldana, A. J., Espinoza, J. A., Sperry, M. P., Brykman, K. M., & Donia, M. B. L. (2024). Conflict management styles assessment and feedback for student self-awareness and team development. *Assessment & Evaluation in Higher Education*, *49*(8), 1091–1104. DOI: 10.1080/02602938.2024.2350682

O'Neill, T. A., & Allen, N. J. (2011). Personality and the prediction of team performance. *European Journal of Personality*, *25*(1), 31–42. DOI: 10.1002/per.769

O'Neill, T. A., Boyce, M. A., & McLarnon, M. J. W. (2020). Team health is improved when peer evaluation scores affect grades on team projects. *Frontiers in Education*, *5*, 1–10. DOI: 10.3389/feduc.2020.00049

O'Neill, T. A., Deacon, A., Gibbard, K., Larson, N., Hoffart, G., Smith, J., & Donia, B. L. M. (2018). Team dynamics feedback for post-secondary student learning teams. *Assessment & Evaluation in Higher Education*, *43*(4), 571–585. DOI: 10.1080/02602938.2017.1380161

O'Neill, T. A., Hancock, S., McLarnon, M. J. W., & Holland, T. (2020). When the "SUIT" fits: Constructive controversy training in face-to-face and virtual teams. *Negotiation and Conflict Management Research*, *13*(1), 44–59. DOI: 10.1111/ncmr.12154

O'Neill, T. A., Hoffart, G. C., McLarnon, M. M., Woodley, H. J., Eggermont, M., Rosehart, W., & Brennan, R. (2017). Constructive controversy and reflexivity training promotes effective conflict profiles and team functioning in student learning teams. *Academy of Management Learning & Education*, *16*(2), 257–276. DOI: 10.5465/amle.2015.0183

O'Neill, T. A., Larson, N., Smith, J., Donia, M., Deng, C., Rosehart, W., & Brennan, R. (2019). Introducing a scalable peer feedback system for learning teams. *Assessment & Evaluation in Higher Education*, *44*(6), 848–862. DOI: 10.1080/02602938.2018.1526256

O'Neill, T. A., Pezer, L., Solis, L., Larson, N., Maynard, N., Dolphin, G. R., Brennan, R. W., & Li, S. (2020). Team dynamics feedback for post-secondary student learning teams: Introducing the "Bare CARE" assessment and report. *Assessment & Evaluation in Higher Education*, *45*(8), 1121–1135. DOI: 10.1080/02602938.2020.1727412

Ortiz De Guinea, A., Webster, J., & Staples, D. S. (2012). A meta-analysis of the consequences of virtualness on team functioning. *Information & Management*, *49*(6), 301–308. DOI: 10.1016/j.im.2012.08.003

Rahim, A., & Bonoma, T. V. (1979). Managing organizational conflict: A model for diagnosis and intervention. *Psychological Reports*, *44*(3, Suppl.), 1323–1344. DOI: 10.2466/pr0.1979.44.3c.1323

Rapp, T. L., & Mathieu, J. E. (2007). Evaluating an individually self-administered generic teamwork skills training program across time and levels. *Small Group Research*, *38*(4), 532–555. DOI: 10.1177/1046496407300479

Rapp, T. L., & Rapp, A. A. (2021). Managing virtual sales teams: Challenges and evidence-based recommendations. *Organizational Dynamics*, *50*(1), 100821. DOI: 10.1016/j.orgdyn.2020.100821

Reyes, D. L., & Salas, E. (2019). What makes a team of experts an expert team? In Subotnik, R. F., Olszewski-Kubilius, P., & Worrell, F. C. (Eds.), *The psychology of high performance: Developing human potential into domain-specific talent* (pp. 141–159). American Psychological Association., DOI: 10.1037/0000120-007

Salas, E., DiazGranados, D., Klein, C., Burke, C. S., Stagl, K. C., Goodwin, G. F., & Halpin, S. M. (2008). Does team training improve team performance? A meta-analysis. *Human Factors*, *50*(6), 903–933. DOI: 10.1518/001872008X375009 PMID: 19292013

Salas, E., Shuffler, M. L., Thayer, A. L., Bedwell, W. L., & Lazzara, E. H. (2015). Understanding and improving teamwork in organizations: A scientifically based practical guide. *Human Resource Management*, *54*(4), 599–622. DOI: 10.1002/hrm.21628

Schippers, M. C., West, M. A., & Edmondson, A. C. (2017). Team reflexivity and innovation. In Salas, E., Rico, R., & Passmore, J. (Eds.), *The Wiley Blackwell Handbook of the Psychology of Team Working and Collaborative Processes* (1st ed., pp. 459–478). Wiley. DOI: 10.1002/9781118909997.ch20

Shuffler, M. L., Diazgranados, D., Maynard, M. T., & Salas, E. (2018). Developing, sustaining, and maximizing team effectiveness: An integrative, dynamic perspective of team development interventions. *The Academy of Management Annals*, *12*(2), 688–724. DOI: 10.5465/annals.2016.0045 PMID: 30931078

Sperry, M.P., Aldana, A.J., O'Neill, T.A., Mimovic, A., Gibson, C.B., & McLarnon, M.J.W. (Under Review). Hybrid and remote team chartering: Creating clarity in an increasingly virtual world.

Taras, V., McLarnon, M., Steel, P., & O'Neil, T. (2024). Reducing freeloading in Global Virtual Teams: A quasi-experimental approach. *Journal of World Business*, *59*(5), 101566. DOI: 10.1016/j.jwb.2024.101566

Terenzini, P. T., Cabrera, A. F., Colbeck, C. L., Parente, J. M., & Bjorklund, S. A. (2001). Collaborative learning vs. lecture/discussion: Students' reported learning gains. *Journal of Engineering Education*, *90*(1), 123–130. DOI: 10.1002/j.2168-9830.2001.tb00579.x

Tjosvold, D. (2008). Constructive controversy for management education: Developing committed, open-minded researchers. *Academy of Management Learning & Education*, *7*(1), 73–85. DOI: 10.5465/amle.2008.31413864

Tuckman, B. W. (1965). Developmental sequence in small groups. *Psychological Bulletin*, *63*(6), 384–399. DOI: 10.1037/h0022100 PMID: 14314073

Tuckman, B. W., & Jensen, M. A. C. (1977). Stages of small-group development re-visited. *Group & Organization Studies*, *2*(4), 419–427. DOI: 10.1177/105960117700200404

Twigg, A., & Valluri, N. (2024). Improving student team formation in design classrooms using a novel approach. In Zaphiris, P., & Ioannou, A. (Eds.), *Learning and Collaboration Technologies* (Vol. 14723, pp. 256–271). Springer Nature Switzerland., DOI: 10.1007/978-3-031-61685-3_19

Waller, M. J., Zellmer-Bruhn, M. E., & Giambatista, R. C. (2002). Watching the clock: Group pacing behavior under dynamic deadlines. *Academy of Management Journal*, *45*(5), 1046–1055. DOI: 10.5465/3069329

APPENDIX: ITP METRICS TOOLS AND RESOURCES

Team Designer: an instructor tool for forming student teams that are balanced on both stable and fluid characteristics, such as gender, personality, and background training.

Conflict Management Styles assessment: evaluates individuals' tendencies to use five different styles of conflict management derived from the dual concern model (https://www.itpmetrics.com/assessment.info).

Personality assessment: evaluates individuals across the five major dimensions of personality, commonly referred to as the "Big Five" (https://www.itpmetrics.com/assessment.info).

Team Charter template and materials: guides teams through the process of "chartering", which includes defining expectations, communication protocols, meeting structures, conflict resolution strategies, stress management plans, and accountability measures (https://www.itpmetrics.com/team.resources).

SUIT training: introduces four key steps—Sharing, Understanding, Integrating, and Team Decision-Making—to help teams navigate difficult conversations respectfully and effectively (https://www.itpmetrics.com/team.resources).

Peer Feedback assessment: provides anonymized evaluations of individuals' teamwork competencies across five key domains derived from the literature on high-performing teams (https://www.itpmetrics.com/assessment.info).

Team Health assessment: evaluates overall team functioning in four key areas: Communication, Adaptability, Relationships, and Education (https://www.itpmetrics.com/assessment.info).

Chapter 2
Classrooms as Learning Labs for Virtual Collaboration and Learner Agency:
Collaborative Learning, Learning Lab, Agency, Threefold Path to High-Performance Virtual Teams

Trina L. Hoefling
https://orcid.org/0009-0007-6887-1274
University of Southern California, USA

ABSTRACT

Instructors can adapt curriculum so that learners have the competencies needed for a fulfilling career working well with others, together or apart. A curriculum can easily embed teamwork, coach learners into good study habits, and teach them how to write, present, follow instructions, and think critically. Today's instructors guide learners to creatively imagine and innovate beyond perceived limitations, including distance and time barriers of online learning and remote work. Groups can be learning labs where learners work together, hold each other accountable, and deliver group assignments. Today's workforce must collaborate and work well with others. This chapter provides a framework for designing and managing online courses for creative collaboration. Instructors will share responsibility for a successful learning experience by engaging learners in decisions and creating future team leaders. The framework lays out three pathways that develop a workforce that is competent, innovative, connected, engaged, flexible, and virtual.

DOI: 10.4018/979-8-3373-0375-8.ch002

INTRODUCTION

Your classroom – online or blended – is a ripe pathway for learners to practice collaboration on online and hybrid temporary teams, with students learning together as well as individually. Once a course is designed for creative collaboration, your job gets easier while still being able to impart knowledge to learners, facilitate their skill development, and prepare them for today's workplace.

How you facilitate your course and assign group projects can develop core virtual teaming competencies. The digital classroom is also a "place" for learners to grow a personal network of lifelong professional colleagues who have learned by working together with shared responsibility for outcomes. "Estimates show between seventy and eighty percent of all jobs are never posted. That 'hidden job market' can be difficult to tap into without having a powerful network," according to Forbes Council member Jeffrey Ton (Ton, 2020). Networking isn't just about jobs, though. Today's professionals can't know everything and must learn quickly. In the fast-changing workplace, it's common to need to get reliable advice from people we trust and rely on for their subject matter expertise and, sometimes, discretion or ability to explain things clearly. Google search or AI summary doesn't replace solid knowledge or advice from a trusted colleague. Your classroom is a learning lab for everyone to grow their professional networks that can serve them, if maintained, for a lifetime.

When learners realize they have some responsibility for the learning experience, they focus on more than just the grade, thereby developing a broader understanding of agency that includes considering their classmates. To help you accomplish collaboration, this chapter describes design and facilitation principles that support engaged learners and prepare them to be members of and lead high-performance collaborative, virtual teams that can adapt, innovate, and continuously perform. Everything shared in this chapter applies in both blended and fully online courses, though for simplicity, I will proceed referring only to online learning in fully remote or blended environments.

This chapter provides a pathway to:

1. Redesign activities and assignments to require coordinated student effort using a simple hybrid team model, the Threefold Path to High-Performance Virtual Teams™.
2. Teach communication and peer learning strategies in virtual and hybrid environments while continuing to teach course content.
3. Establish clear expectations for online interactions and shared responsibility for learning from peers and the instructor.

4. Incorporate regular check-ins and feedback loops to monitor progress and address issues on teams, modeling skilled professional hybrid work accountability practices.
5. Foster a supportive and inclusive learning culture where learners feel psychologically safe to try new things.

Online learning is ubiquitous, synchronous, and asynchronous; it is the ideal environment to embed solid remote team member competencies. For blended courses, the online learning environment provides a learning lab for the remote aspects of most jobs today. Digital technology brings an opportunity to rethink your classroom course design to leverage the Learning Management System (LMS), rethinking assignments for collaborative learning.

Learners use online platforms and tools to connect to the course, the instructor, and each other to complete the course and assignments. The learning platform and collaborative tools allow student teams to interact and work on shared assignments in ways that replicate hybrid and remote work teams. The online learning environment prepares learners to establish a virtual presence, becoming value-added contributors to high-performance learning teams. They develop the written and oral communication and critical thinking skills needed to negotiate, collaborate, and cooperate. These are among non-negotiable competencies for digital literacy in the workplace (Hoefling, 2017).

Collaborative learning happens through asynchronous discussion boards, group chats, project teams with shared folders and co-created documents, video conferencing with and without the instructor, polls, and other collaborative tools usually contained within the learning management system. By leveraging easily navigated tools, instructors can easily introduce the intentional use of adult learning principles that support collaborative online learning.

ADULT LEARNING PRINCIPLES AND ONLINE LEARNING

Blended and online learning easily aligns with solid adult learning methodology. For example, people learn best with spaced learning and by applying concepts experientially. Research proves that adults embed learning more deeply when they learn collaboratively and in similar environments to where they will deploy the skills learned, often a virtual team (Morris, 2019) (Hoefling, 2017). The online classroom is a rich environment to apply adult learning principles while also developing remote teaming skills. The ubiquitous nature of online learning gives learners time for iterative, spaced, meaningful, double-loop learning. Learners can consume and digest knowledge through regularly scheduled learning packets on demand, supported by instructor-led class discussions and presentations. They receive feedback through instructor evaluation but also from classmates, especially when working in groups or with peer advisors. This practice prepares students to lead regular meetings where people gather to help each other or peer review work, get feedback on a certain project, or just brainstorm ideas. The practice creates a safe place that reflects the company culture, beginning in your classroom.

Online learners develop teaming skills through various graded and not-graded group work opportunities, which helps them learn to:

- Communicate through multiple platforms and forums.
- Craft working agreements across time and space.
- Foster team support using boundaries and habits that foster team support.
- Accountability behaviors and strategies for managing mutual responsibilities.
- Embed intentional feedback loops that ease remote collaboration.

Online learning fits with how adults really learn (Boser, 2017). Adults learn most effectively when certain conditions are met. These classroom conditions are initiated through developing instructor classroom practices that can be applied regardless of the area of professional study. Review the following principles and innovate simple practices in your classroom. Whether in a blended format, fully online, or in a traditional learning environment, design courses that help everyone learn their discipline *and* develop teamplay. Simple adaptations such as these continuously foster best practices for lifelong learning leaders. Teach learners to follow a simple model, explained in the next section, that replicates the workplace, the Threefold Path to High-Performance Learning™. When developing courses, consider the following design practices: agency and self-management, bite-sized learning, effective use of synchronous learning, and connect page to practice. How well are you already preparing learners to exercise these practices? Where can you improve?

Agency and Self-Management

Begin by encouraging learners to develop study habits with rhythms and flows that prioritize their learning as an integrated aspect of their lives. Flexible, online learning accommodates personal calendars and lifestyles and has been a driver toward more online learning. At the same time, many learners need help learning how to manage all their responsibilities, including course group work, without the structure of a traditional classroom. Since many learners will be (or are) remote or hybrid workers, they need the same discipline at work. Use the classroom to help them cultivate good prioritization and work habits.

As the instructor, expect, for example, that all work will be completed on time unless discussed with you first. You may negotiate deadlines for individual learners due to circumstances; however, planning and communication are needed. Suggest group members prioritize course activity that impacts others before self-managed assignments, and coach learners into good virtual work habits if needed.

In general, many adults don't feel comfortable as learners. They feel vulnerable and don't want to look stupid. This hesitancy increases when working or learning online (Hoefling, 2017). Some learners struggle to grasp course material and must ask their questions or ask for help but do not ask or may not know how to get assistance, especially online. Some hesitate to reach out if an online instructor doesn't make it clear how. Instructors should assume not every question is asked and encourage learners to speak up for themselves in multiple ways. The use of quick polls, quizzes, or word clouds to capture student learning provides a quick assessment of the readiness to move on to new material. You and the class can quickly see group learning progress, often opening discussions and questions that learners might not have asked without the assessment prompt. Welcome the questions, even when it means backing up or slowing down. This practice sets a condition for student agency.

Another simple way to coach learners into sharing the responsibility for a climate of shared responsibility is to set virtual office hours and encourage all learners to avail themselves of the benefit. Be willing to stay informally after synchronous sessions, holding open-ended virtual after-hours where learners lead the agenda. Your interest in how they are doing can provide agency for learners, encouraging them to speak up for themselves when they know you are interested in them. Your care opens the space for them to give you feedback, too. Ask them about your pacing and the course flow. Thank learners when they offer a comment or question.

Consider simple changes in how you end learning modules to encourage student agency. For example, do not close a lecturette with "Any questions?" Instead, expect questions. One suggestion is to use the following script, "Before we move on, let us break into five-minute triads to share your most important learnings. Ask your team for help with any questions you may have and bring back any remaining questions. Minimally, be ready to share one top team takeaway with the large class. Any questions before breaking out?"

Bite-Size Learning

Make It Stick: The Science of Successful Learning (Peter C. Brown, 2014) summarizes adult learning research by saying that more complex learning comes from self-testing and bite-sized, progressive learning over time. The book's summary of adult learning suggests providing learners with regular challenges that get more difficult. This enables them to practice applying skills in slightly new situations each time. Introducing incrementally harder challenges helps grow competence and embeds memory more than other approaches. Teaching a concept in one session and then moving on to a new topic slows learning retention. Online learning is ideal for bite-sized learning objectives with time for reflection and integration of material, leading to higher retention of class material.

Bite-sized learning is commonly called "micro-learning," (Brew, 2025) learning in the moment just enough to move forward. This is frequently applied in the workplace with digital tutorials or bots, as well as single-objective learning modules. Micro-learning can focus on a singular objective learned over a single activity or in support of a larger macro-design. This is a particularly effective strategy when presenting complex topics in the classroom. Concepts can be presented in chaptered or segmented chunks or videos such as YouTube or Instagram clips. Include a small activity with all topics, minimally a guided discussion or a short breakout activity. Chunking the concepts followed by activity helps learners process material.

When the instructor takes the time to set up the micro-learning clearly, the learners know

- what they are learning and how it reflects a learning goal,
- why the activity has value,
- how the micro-learning module connects to previous and future learning,
- how to incorporate course material into assignments.

Provide guidance that frames the micro-learning goal. For example, before watching a video clip, pose a focusing question or instruct viewers what to notice. This helps learners actively focus and engage with the material and the group activity rather than being passive. They are primed to consider information that prepares them for the group assignment.

Use Synchronous Course Time Wisely

Most lectures and "downloaded information" should be asynchronous. Do bite-sized lecturettes in synchronous sessions. Take no more than ten minutes to explain a concept. When learners "download" information asynchronously, they can do so when they are at their mental best and digest slowly, if need be. It also means that synchronous live sessions are more interactive. Long videos and reading preparation should be assigned to be completed asynchronously. If you want to provide a longer lecture, consider prerecording it. Expand on the lecture by setting up online searches that send small teams to look for answers to specific questions or examples of lecture points made, for example. By doing so, learners develop digital competency and applying the lesson plan concretely. Because they do this in teams, they are learning cooperation. Social media and search engines are great instructor aids, so use them.

Connect Page to Practice

In *Learn Better (2017)*, Ulrich Boser urges learners to engage with the material *and each other* to retain course material. Peer learning increases the depth of learning and retention. "You want to learn the systems, or the analogies, of the relationships between things in a certain field, and how they interact with each other. Then ultimately you gain that knowledge so that you can shift your own thinking, so when you see a new problem you're better able to solve it...Doing things that are a little bit more difficult, require you to make connections, is a better way to learn" (Boser, 2017). In other words, how learners engage with course material *and* each other is important. Help the learners see the connection of the information from the material through experience with fellow learners.

Connect peer learners using the course content to open the conversation and learners' eyes, helping them connect all the pieces into an integral, holistic understanding of course objectives. A coaching client and business owner, Lidiane Mocko, states that "Based on my experience with the online MBA program at the university, sharing professional experiences and learning from the experiences of my classmates was key to my learner experience" (L. Mocko, personal communication, January 25, 2025). Encourage learners to share their lived experiences and resources. Have learners post their work for classmates, record podcasts, collaborate on a Wiki, and present in class or discussions. Help learners to build, extend, and maintain their professional networks of connections that bring them value inside and outside of the course.

Peer Learning

Every course serves as an opportunity for learners to work together on multiple temporary team assignments. *Have learners think and discuss together.* They speak up and learn better together if they are learning in a climate where they feel welcomed as human beings. It is the instructor's job to welcome learners and show them the way to connect with each other, especially online. As an example, asynchronously before a course starts, I introduce myself to the class. I not only share the syllabus, but also tips to thrive, how to navigate the platform, and other instructions for the course. I post a welcome video, introducing myself as a professional experienced in the course focus. In an interactive discussion thread, I introduce myself by answering the same set of questions I ask learners to answer. Essentially, I break the ice with them and help them bridge the digital divide with each other. When learners introduce themselves with a set of suggested questions to answer, beginning with their personal Why, it sets the expectation of participation and sharing information. Why did they enroll in the program? What is their career history and future goals? What time zone are they in? This helps me connect the course material to student readiness, and they begin to connect with each other. It begins to expand emotional bandwidth as a temporary team and learning cohort with you as the learning leader. If you make the effort, respond to each student's introduction, welcoming them. They appreciate it.

Group Discussions, Activities, and Graded Team Assignments

Learners learn as much from each other as they do the instructor (Uday S Bhowal, UT Collaborative Education, Cockrell School of Engineering, UT Austin, 2022). Everyone's participation plays a key role in peer learning. Requiring and enforcing student participation in asynchronous discussions will augment or deepen those participation opportunities occurring during live sessions. This requirement deepens student agency and provides peer-to-peer bite-sized learning. They also hear explanations and examples from more than the instructor, often helpful for integrating complex material.

Asynchronous session discussions can challenge assumptions and broaden thinking when you also participate. Invite other perspectives, broaden perspectives shared with a contrary experience, and facilitate thinking critically together. Have learners analyze what is accurate or wrong with a scenario, ideally from a learner's experience, as it applies to a learning objective. This can be accomplished throughout the course in various ways but must use breakout activities. In smaller groups, everyone is involved in co-learning. Ask groups to discuss and answer higher-level questions such as "What is really going on here?" What might be the reason for ___? What evidence points to that?" "What can you conclude from these data?" "How did you come to that conclusion?" or "What are the pros and cons?". Consider having each group focus on a different question so that each group report adds to the breakout group's learning. Reports also provide practice in presenting to an audience, another core communication skill for today's workforce.

Another simple method for group discussion is to have each student take a stand on a key issue by requiring them to vote at the start of a topic, then conduct an activity where group members defend or change their positions, finally coming to a group conclusion. Provide the learners the opportunity to discuss links between course concepts and their experience or current events with each other (e.g., volunteer activities, internships, study abroad, work experiences). Throughout the course, look for ways to facilitate learners talking with each other in both large discussions and small learning teams, in synchronous sessions, and beyond.

Scheduled Posted Summaries and Takeaways

Reflection is a key element of adult learning (Imel, 1992). Have the learners reflect on what they have just learned independently, through group discussion, a group activity, or by teaching one another. In asynchronous discussions or live session chat at the end of a section, learners can post their takeaways that link broader course objectives or previous discussions to a given learning objective for that session. For example, before signing off, have students post in chat, "What was the significance of what we did today to the overarching course objectives?" Invite them to ask questions of you after they have had time to reflect on the lessons learned in an asynchronous discussion thread (E.J. Dallimore, 2016).

Learners improve their understanding when they must verbalize – ask and answer questions. Learning is enhanced when both instructors and learners reciprocally inquire, listen, and respond. Resilience and honest communication develop as co-learners give and receive feedback. This practice applies to learning course content as well as how to work with others in group settings. As shared in a personal conversation with colleague and retired graduate school online program director Dr. Patricia Greer, "No one gets through school without a little help from their friends" (P. Greer, personal communication, January 22, 2024).

BENEFITS OF REDESIGNING COURSES FOR COLLABORATIVE GROUPWORK

Other benefits of redesigning courses to engage learners collaboratively through group work in blended and online learning environments include responsibility for accessibility and inclusion, flexibility and group negotiation, swift trust in diverse teams, communication, and the practice of critical thinking in a group. Classroom practice with these skills improves all online interactions, immediately crossing over into workforce readiness. Once learners are exposed to structured online learning and virtual teamwork, they bring a better structure to their remote/group work experiences.

Accessibility and Inclusion

Online learning allows learners from diverse geographical locations and diverse backgrounds to participate in group work. Assignments should be structured to include required divergent positions, encouraging learners to advocate for their assigned "position" balanced with a commitment to inquiry. This forces diversity of thought with an eye to a better understanding of assignments, creative approaches, and co-developed outcomes. Positional debates and analysis deepen learner engagement with content and each other to complete assignments.

Flexibility Through Negotiated Team Responsibilities

Learners can contribute to group projects based on personal strengths, lived experiences, and professional goals, sometimes at their own pace and schedule. Group discussions and negotiations clarify roles and responsibilities while learners get to know one another, essential to all successful work teams and a skill to be developed.

Diverse Perspectives and Swift Trust

Increase learner skills in active listening, cooperation, and collaborative team habits by expecting a wide range of diverse views. Consider using quick personality profiles – validated or simple popular assessment tools to assemble diverse groups. Learners benefit from working with different group compositions and accepting various team roles. Assignments can be structured to provide practice in team behaviors essential on temporary or fast-forming teams, establishing swift trust (Mills & Wren, 2019), and helping develop relationships quickly. This practice will prepare learners to do so professionally, as teams, teammates, and team assignments often evolve and change.

Improved Communication Skills

Career (and team) success depends on expressing ideas clearly and effectively in a digital environment. In decades of asking graduate learners what their primary workplace challenge is, I hear the same response repeatedly – poor communication. It is a broad answer, but also quite simply true. Professionals must continuously communicate in organizations where communication is always imperfect. Look for opportunities to give learners practice. Course group projects and discussions provide invaluable experience in communicating with fellow learners across time and space. Provide practice communicating in many ways – written and on screen, with you and each other, using media and through tools. Stress the learning goal of good communication as learners and emerging leaders, and model good communication. Following is a sample communication checklist for learning teams to address.

- Ensure clarity.
- Establish roles and responsibilities early in assignments.
- Develop project/assignment plans and team agreements.
- Negotiate any needed group adaptations.
- Anticipate and plan for logistical, relational, and performance conflicts. (Learners may need help with this. Consider recommending a conflict management model, building it into the course design or tutorials.)
- Think together asynchronously and synchronously.
- Assess progress and ensure team commitments are met.
- Support teammates during challenges and interferences that happen occasionally.
- Hold each other accountable with respect and kindness.
- Produce high-quality group work.

Enhanced Critical Thinking

Learners gain more insight and deepen their thinking when coursework is structured to encourage information-sharing and wrestling with course material by engaging with peers. Ask students for their professional experiences related to the topics explored in class. Have them consider where a concept could be applied in their current workplace or share a reflection. This articulation engages critical thinking. Instructional design needs to facilitate learners' transferring learning to remembered experience. This wrestling with concepts is not natural in a passive online learning environment. Activate their thinking in graded and ungraded activities. Cascade assignments to build learning over time with aspects of group work built in throughout the class. Structure peer review discussions of upcoming individual assignments, increasing the likelihood of a submitted assignment that hits the mark.

These are the primary benefits of embedding collaborative group work into courses, though the shift to a more collaborative online classroom brings predictable challenges. Plan for the most common ones.

CHALLENGES IN THE ONLINE CLASSROOM

Anticipate predictable challenges when designing a learner-centric, collaborative curriculum. Knowing what is likely to happen helps the course instructor plan for challenges, folding them into the learning experience. These challenges include variance in learner motivation and readiness for the digital learning environment, technology difficulties, team members not contributing, underground conflict common on remote teams, and us, the instructors.

Digital Literacy Varies

Just as learners vary in their levels of knowledge and experience about the course learning objectives, so do they vary in their tool competence. If the Learning Management System (LMS) does not have built-in tutorials, consider launching each class with a roadmap for learning, including how to navigate the various aspects of the learning platform. If teaching initial courses in a program, orient learners to the learning platform.

This can be done asynchronously with documents, video tutorials, and announcements. Provide instruction for how to navigate the LMS, assignments, and where to go for help. A virtual office where you respond to questions of other course issues that should be handled quickly. Schedule online office hours to meet privately. Offer optional practice sessions for learners who want to learn how to do online research or navigate the learning management platform, especially if the school does not have platform or program orientation programs. Create a scavenger hunt to learn how to find and use platform and videoconferencing tools. Use gamification tools and activities wherever possible without losing the human touch that you bring as the learning leader.

When with students synchronously in live sessions, plan large group activities that use videoconference tools, such as chat, whiteboards, polls, and annotation tools. Have students use annotation tools to write directly onto a visual. For example, have students place themselves on a spectrum of choice, such as a Likert scale. Show them how to annotate their name or respond anonymously. Conduct live polls to check learner confidence and check in on class progress or assess opinions about course topics. Quick group processes like this take little time and can be on topic or just for fun. They help everyone get to know one another quickly, sometimes anonymously, and provide information about everyone. Multi-task during live sessions by using chat and inviting learners to comment or ask questions there. There are myriad other options to expand digital literacy in a low-risk environment. Tool usage increases comfort using various tools, further preparing them for a digital workplace. The group will also "teach" each other how to assess online sources as they do the activity, sharing critical thinking practices.

A new area to explore embedding digital literacy in your course design is how to think critically about source material that is not verified or AI-generated. Because of the rise of disinformation and AI research that isn't verified, consider a group learning activity where learners validate online sources. AI can be a powerful learning aid, and it is constantly changing, stretching everyone's digital literacy.

Learner Motivation May Need Prodding

Some learners take courses to advance their careers, less driven by a deep need to learn. The motivating force is a future goal, sometimes making it harder to prioritize school. Navigating work, home, and school commitments can be even more complicated when courses require teamwork. Occasionally, learners ask to complete group assignments alone, even though it means more work. Whether it is a lack of motivation, time, or another reason, you must have a plan for such requests.

Group assignments take time to organize, plan, and coordinate, so it is your job to understand their reasons for resisting group work and to convince learners to participate. Ease the way into group work by helping learners get to know each other before group assignments begin. Ease the social barrier of getting to know people through a video screen. Set standards for group work throughout the course, both graded and ungraded assignments, by teaching a simple model for temporary teams to work together quickly. Recommend scheduling and project management tools like Doodle, Trello, Asana, or Slack.

The Threefold Path to High-Performance Teams™ shared in this chapter is a model that anticipates and addresses challenges when teaming virtually. It is easily adapted for the online learning classroom so that reticent group learners quickly learn that teamwork can be efficient and add greatly to individual learning when they have a model to follow. Occasionally, a learner fails a team, but most reticent lone learners thank me later for requiring group work as they continue to apply high-performance virtual team practices in their careers.

Technical and Connectivity Difficulties

Backup plans and workarounds are part of remote work. Technical challenges can derail a group's process. Issues with internet connectivity can leave a group wondering where someone is if no text group backup is in place, for example. Remind learners that telephone conferences can replace virtual conferences when the internet goes down. Your school likely has a protocol for technical issues. Ensure everyone knows how to get help. Encourage text chains, the use of Slack (or another platform), or the learning platform for team communication. Include tutorials for Google Drive and other collaborative tools that are available to them.

Free-Riding Behavior Is A Risk

Learners often do not contribute equally to group projects. Some learners repeatedly take an "easy role" for them, which doesn't stretch their skills. Required or encouraged role-switching develops well-rounded team skills for everyone. For example, some people naturally volunteer to lead small groups, while others seldom want to speak up. Good writers may take the role of integrating assignments into one team voice while others do the research. Early in the class, encourage deploying to strength as they learn to work in groups. As the course progresses, however, encourage or require learners to take on stretch roles while in the psychologically safe environment of their team.

Many want assurances that they will get good grades when taking a role where they are less confident, so have a plan for that. If you want learners to stretch their competencies, find ways to evaluate learning and progress that don't negatively result in a lower formal grade. Keep graded group assignments to no more than 40 percent of learners' grades. This releases undue pressure on grade-conscious achievers to cover for poor teammate inputs. By balancing individual and group grades, learners maintain agency over their overall grade while realizing their agency must also include learning to work well with others.

Construct larger group assignments to have individual components *and* team deliverables. This will ensure that all members contribute to their learning, even if some learners do the minimum. Structure rotating roles and embed feedback mechanisms to assess how the learning groups work together to accomplish assignments. Create communication pathways to you, the professor. Embed peer evaluations. Make it clear that fellow learners have a say in learner performance. Consider peer grades for team performance and make it part of the grading rubric. This increases the pressure for recalcitrant group learners to consider their classmates as a critical component of their academic (and career) success.

Lack of Face-To-Face Interaction Breeds Underground Conflict

Especially if a learning group has a member who is not communicating or delivering on commitments, this can lead to reduced engagement if trust is broken. Learners often hesitate to confront poor team behavior or "rat out" a team member to the professor. They may perceive it to be easier to work around the teammate who doesn't follow through, resenting the extra work placed on everyone else. Instead of leaving teams feeling stranded but without swooping in to mediate, provide a template or micro-learning module managing team conflict and caring confrontation. The first team assignment should include their co-created team agreements regarding communication and how to address team member issues if they happen.

Encourage learners to determine when they should involve a greater authority, such as the professor. They are creating a social contract with each other. You can provide templates for groups to discuss how they will work together and discuss progress. It is worthwhile to remind learners of team formation stages, including storming. This decompresses tension when it naturally occurs. Basically, help them understand what to expect. This is valuable in their professional lives as well.

The last barrier to embedding virtual collaboration into online coursework is the hurdle this chapter will help you overcome.

You, the Instructor

The best of us are lifelong learners. Lifelong learning includes getting better at how we lead learning. At the same time, we know what works for us as instructors. We have developed our teaching habits over time. Despite evidence and good intentions, most of us do not change readily. Before trying something new, most of us want teaching methods that work right the first time. Who wants to fail in front of learners who think you are the expert, or to fail them in their learning goal? It is easy to rely on old habits. Let this book and chapter nudge your desire to become better leaders of collaborative learning.

Start by relying less on the information you share. Instead, get learners doing it. As Maryellen Weimer, PhD and higher education strategist, reminds us, "We know that when there is less talking and more doing, learning increases. And if we are reasonable about that conclusion and not absolutist in ruling out either, most faculty will acknowledge that they should be talking less and have learners doing more" (Maryellen Weimer, 2017).

Assess your learner-centric teaching behaviors. When was the last time you checked your talk-to-listen ratio in your classes? This is easy to do with AI tools like AI Companion or Fireflies. You can have AI monitor your live sessions to get this type of ratio information. There is no absolute ratio, but if you are doing more than sixty percent of the talking in synchronous live sessions, consider reducing that by a third or more.

Another long-term advantage of having learners do more is that there is an opportunity to stay viable as an instructor by learning from the class. We can learn from the new generations. Seek their perspectives on trends in workplaces.

It is reasonable to rely on comfortable teaching practices. Innovative online learning methodologies are not always proven and may yield meek results for the effort. Why put in the effort for a plausible but not guaranteed outcome? We are teachers, after all, and we know our content and what teaching habits have worked for us in the past. Understandably, it is safer to ensure that basic learning happens, though it is not the best choice.

The challenges for online learning have been identified, with strategies to address each. Now the focus turns to the changed role of the instructor or professor- whichever you choose.

OUR ROLE AS INSTRUCTORS HAS BROADENED

The existence of this book points to our broadening responsibilities as educators. We no longer take the podium – virtual or physical – and impart knowledge. If we are an engaging subject matter expert known for being an "edu-trainer", it's easy to stick with what has always worked because learners are mostly satisfied. Engaged learning today is, however, much more than following a well-delivered lecture with Q&A. Online learning is more than a click-through self-paced course with a quiz to test learners' ability to listen and regurgitate content. Our classrooms should be learning labs preparing learners for their professions and today's workplace.

Internships and capstones are traditional learning labs, but learners need more hands-on learning in the classroom. Simple changes can convert your classes into mini-learning labs that better prepare learners for the virtual workplace. Traditional methodologies continue to have their place, but they are not enough. Adult learning methodologies, especially when online, must include learner-centric, Socratic, and experiential approaches. Socratic and experiential learning methodologies involve asking probing questions to stimulate critical thinking and learning through hands-on experiences, followed by reflection. This approach allows learners to actively construct knowledge by engaging with real-world situations. It takes some effort initially in course design, but it does work (LP Stonehouse, L Frick, & T. Codd, various).

This approach requires instructors to be facilitators of learning with learner involvement. To prepare a workforce for continuous innovation, we must educate continuous learners. We must also have a willingness to learn and innovate ourselves. Assuming you are familiar with the course material and have intentionally integrated it into your approach to the new activity, give yourself time to master the activity's instruction and facilitation. Competence comes with practice. The class will appreciate your openness as you "practice" shifting to being a more learner-centric facilitator of learning. They appreciate your willingness to learn as you teach, permitting learners to adapt and try, aka be "imperfect" as they learn.

This is an invitation to share responsibility for learning with learners and developing their agency. It also models the speed of learning and willingness to innovate that today's workplace requires. We get to model innovation and iterative learning, improving as we learn. Learners get to see innovation and continuous improvement in action, sharing responsibility for helping you get even better.

The classroom leader plays a vital role in establishing the classroom tone. Learners can quickly agree upon, if not share, a vision for successful learning. They help define the values that guide their collaborative efforts through clear class agreements. Setting this expectation of shared responsibility encourages learners to help create a psychologically safe environment where everyone can apply new knowledge.

Our self-talk can be strong and persuasive against trying, however. We have limited time and so much important content to cover. We are the experts for a reason, and learners want to hear our stories. It is easy to convince ourselves that we should not rob learners of our expertise. Most learners readily agree, meaning they can sit back, listen, take notes, and get a grade. It's the easy way out.

I invite you as a leader of learning to trust the learning process. Know that your wisdom comes through in ways that do not have to be imparted in lectures. Share your knowledge in other ways. Have learners write their case studies. This allows them to reflect on their professional experiences in a way that paves the way for deeper learning experiences.

Listen carefully during group reports to reinforce good work and state any components not brought up or that may need expert clarification or expansion. Leverage your expertise to deepen the conversation. Embed learning with callouts of key concepts. Yet another way to ensure you cover all concepts fully is to bulk up module summaries, notes that reflect your expertise and the learning objectives. Instructor notes are a gift of knowledge that lives beyond the short time spent in a classroom together. Learners have executive summaries from you, the expert and subject matter expert, for future reference.

Before transitioning to facilitating a collaborative classroom and navigating the challenges that come with it, let's consider the competencies required to be a valued member of high-performance teams in school and at work.

HIGH-PERFORMANCE TEAM COMPETENCIES

Today's professionals must be responsible team players, able to collaborate virtually and maintain interpersonal relationships with coworkers they may only know through a screen. They must excel at accomplishing tasks together and independently. Today's instructors are facilitators who teach learners how to work virtually alone and with others. Facilitating learning involves developing student competencies that extend beyond course-focused learning outcomes and individual assignment objectives. Business leaders want to hire graduates who are ready for virtual, collaborative, and innovative work. Classroom group work is essential to prepare students for this. Adaptability and innovation are core competencies as the workplace rapidly evolves due to changing job requirements and rapid advances in technology and AI, for example. Few professionals have the luxury of learning how to do something once. Most of us must continue to learn throughout our careers as business models, tools, team members, and leaders change.

Additionally, hybrid and remote professionals need relational skills that bridge the digital divide. New teams and joining team members must quickly learn to work well together. They must develop swift trust in fast-formed teams. Extending swift trust means initially assuming that workmates are competent and have integrity (Meyerson, Wick, & Kramer, 1996). Their behaviors will reflect the values of the organization. In other words, they are reliable teammates. Good faith is extended and continues unless evidence emerges to the contrary. The newly formed virtual team (or newly joined team member) needs initial clarity, information, and negotiations about the work the team came together to do. Team members need to understand everyone's roles, contributions, responsibilities, and limits. This kind of "rules of the road" makes swift trust possible and necessary to develop into a team. Ideally, swift trust leads to real trust. Team communication and agreements help teams to perform faster and to do so with less conflict.

Your classroom is a safe place to get good at offering swift trust. Give learners practice. Help them move from swift trust to deeper trust, from formation to performance. Even if every graded assignment is an individual assignment, set up peer learning partners to discuss, review, and advise one another on significant milestones for assignments. This develops a habit of cooperation if not collaboration. While a certain amount of assumed (swift) trust is extended quickly in today's workplaces (and learning environments), *deep trust grows over time* – especially in a fully remote group that meets but does not take steps to get to know each other. Help learners learn to develop relationships as they learn together in your classroom. Peer learning is beneficial as a high-impact adult learning practice, and it prepares learners for a thriving virtual or hybrid career where the foundation of high-performance teams is mutual trust.

The way to a solid foundation of trust is belonging and connection to various components of successful teamwork. Your classroom is a learning lab for learners to connect actively with all components; you are the connective tissue. Connect them to:

- The educational program and course learning objectives, which translated to work, prepare learners to connect with the organization's mission, vision, values, customers, and the job.
- Their role as learners, which translated to work, connects them to their strategic contributions and responsibilities.
- Your expectations and agreed-upon class agreements and team accountability practices.

- You and each other – their professional network, connecting human to human and expanding emotional bandwidth.

Learners today are leaders, formal and informal, as they develop relationships with classmates working on project assignments, managing themselves and each other, and learning how to work in a team. Significantly, by getting to know each other and how to work better together, they also expand their professional networks for the long term.

Many competent, ready professionals struggle to promote themselves or their careers when working in a hybrid, distributed, or remote work environment. People communicate about work as needed, but many teams miss synergistic opportunities that support career growth and workplace well-being. Individuals lose out on career advancement opportunities by neglecting to develop team collaboration skills and virtual communication habits. People remember stellar teammates *and* those who didn't add value. Either way, team behaviors build a reputation that lasts. Engaged online learning invites learners to show up virtually, develop connected relationships, and lead team performance.

Limited visibility limits influence and is also a career risk in today's hybrid and remote workplaces. Your classroom is a safe place to practice assertive collaboration with low stakes in ways that develop lifelong career friendships. To advance their careers faster, provide learners with low-risk opportunities to practice informal leadership and build influence. Help learners embrace relationships with diverse classmates, plan for and develop relationships online, expand personal exposure professionally, and become influential across time, space, platforms, and time zones. Help them speak up, step up, and take various roles in class. You are helping learners find ways to expand professional exposure and develop a good reputation. Your classroom is the best learning lab to become competent, ethical, and reliable virtual team members.

Professors are still subject matter experts and continue to be conveyors of content, but a primary focus is on how we foster professional team collaboration in learning. Weave the way you share content with processes that connect learners. Adapt lesson plans by seeking ways to develop relationship competencies that lead to successful hybrid team play and leadership. Instructional adaptation of curriculum embeds teamwork and other skills as well. We are coaching learners to develop good study habits. We teach them how to write, present, follow instructions, and make a case by thinking analytically and critically. Also very importantly, we teach learners how to creatively imagine and innovate beyond perceived limitations, including the distance and time barriers that come with remote work.

Altogether, these competencies enable learners to develop various ways to work together, support each other, hold each other accountable, and deliver high-caliber team assignments. Self and peer management skills develop over time when learning, helping all learners become future remote team leaders, regardless of their formal titles. When redesigned, team learning becomes a foundational component. The simplest way to begin is to follow the Threefold Path to transform learning from individually focused learning to group-based learning, as shown in Figure 1. By doing so, you and your learners will shift to a mindset of people sharing a learning journey across space and over time.

The Threefold Path of High-Performance Learning™ Leads to High-Performance Virtual Team Competencies

Figure 1. The Threefold Path to High-Performance Virtual Teams

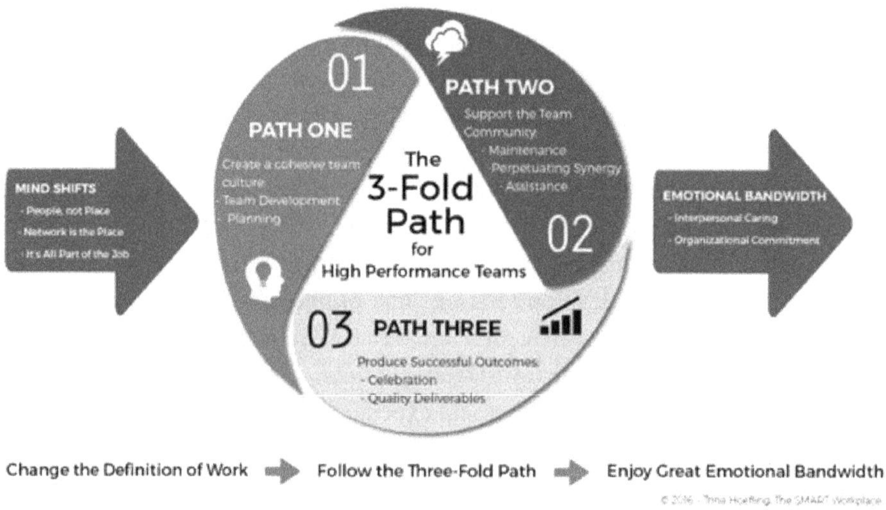

I have been facilitating, teaching, training, and leading virtual teams since the mid-1990s when I co-founded an early adopter company, Telecommuting Success, Inc. Out of that early work, I wrote a seminal book on hybrid teams in 2000, *Working Virtually: Managing People for Successful Virtual Teams and Organizations*, and a 2nd edition in 2017, *Working Virtually: Transforming the Mobile Workplace*

(Hoefling, 2017). The Threefold Path for High-Performance Teams™ is a remote team model that emerged from this work, as illustrated in Figure 1.

This model aligns and overlays nicely with engaged online learning, preparing learners for a hybrid workplace. The pathways are identical and are used to fast-track group assignments that provide a foundation of collaborative practices that learners will use.

Easily adapted for professors to deploy in their classrooms, learner- and group-centric classroom management creates conditions that allow learners to navigate their learning with agency. The Threefold Path prepares learners to work well with others in virtual settings, emphasizing both interpersonal relationships and task-oriented collaboration. The first pathway prepares all learners to be contributors who share responsibility for the classroom experience and later, learning teams. Establish course rhythms, flows, expectations, and standards. The second pathway supports the culture and climate of supportive learning, and the third pathway leads to successful learning as evidenced by well-done assignments.

THE FIRST PATH DEVELOPS CLARITY, EXPECTATION OF AGENCY, & SWIFT TRUST

The more clarity you provide learners about how your classroom will work, the sooner they can relax into learning the content and getting to know classmates rather than learning to understand how you evaluate and grade. The simplest way to model the First Path to High-Performance Teams is to be clear, set expectations, and confirm understandings and commitments. You are their learner leader. Simple behaviors open student agency. Develop your own rhythms and flows that better integrate the synchronous and asynchronous aspects of the course into a clear holistic learning journey to which you and learners are contributing.

The professor models clarity for all, easing the pathway to swift trust by showing learners how to engage and complete coursework. For those new to the learning platform, consider demonstrations and other tutorials. Set the tone by sharing a few class agreements. Assign or suggest a template for team assignment agreements. Best practice tips and templates can prompt effective team habits regarding roles, responsibilities, and how they communicate with and treat each other through assignment progressions. With such guidance, learners establish group norms and agreements for learning teams and can plan how to complete tasks, manage interpersonal issues, and organize themselves into temporary teams.

Learners can quickly agree upon, if not actively work toward, a course vision for successful learning. Allow them to co-determine the values for how to learn together with clear class agreements. Creating this class culture, led by you, invites learners to be agents for their own and group learning. Most will accept an active, shared responsibility for creating a psychologically safe climate where everyone can apply learning. *This is the first path of the Threefold Path to High-Performance Learning™ and, later, high-performance teamwork.*

Simple Ways to Adapt Curriculum for Student Expectations, Clarity, and Agency

- Expect misunderstandings. Online learning requires a lot of writing, as does the mobile workplace. Writing is a flat medium that invites misunderstanding and confusion. Expect learners (and you) to misunderstand discussion posts and written instructions.
- Be a role model and proactively ask questions about discussion posts that are not clear. Learners begin to take more care in their postings to reduce the likelihood they are misunderstood, becoming better writers.
- To avoid answering the same question multiple times, keep a virtual office and post FAQs. Direct learners to the virtual office to ask course questions. (I like to use a discussion thread that is always open called "Our 24-7 Virtual Office.") Anyone can answer a posted question. In my experience, learners often answer each other's questions instead of waiting for me, evidence that they are engaged and supporting one another.
- Launch the course digitally with a welcome video and learning platform tutorials, or share tips to thrive. Ask learners to complete prework or a self-assessment, and most importantly, have learners introduce themselves in a discussion thread or on LinkedIn. Encourage short video introductions. However done, learners introduce themselves in a way that helps them get to know each other and build swift trust as a temporary learning team. Require them to state their professional goals and how the course will help them reach their goals. Ask them to share their experiences and strengths. Encourage them to complete their online profiles and portfolios if they have not already. Grade both participation *and* quality of contribution. Lead by example by introducing yourself and welcoming each student. However, learners are led to meet one another and break the ice interpersonally.
- Communicate up front what is being asked of them for both graded and ungraded assignments, as well as asynchronous and synchronous activities. Include an introduction that includes why it is worthwhile to do each activity. Set any context and reference helpful material. State how the activity is related to learning objectives and upcoming assignments and provide the approximate time range expected to complete the activity. If reporting back, describe what groups should be prepared to share.

- Differentiate between required and recommended reading and videos. Augment required material with digital clips, movies, and experiential exercises that will enhance student understanding of the lesson. Bring reading into live sessions and asynchronous discussions, increasing the probability that the material will be read.
- Determine and communicate clearly how learning will be measured. For example, you may have a multiple-choice or fill-in-the-blank quiz at the end of a module, followed by a page with the right answers. This enables learners to score their own results. Decide if this is a recommended self-assessment or a graded one. If graded, do learners have one attempt, or can they repeat the quiz? Develop rubrics for both individual and group components of all graded team assignments. When teams complete assignments, include a peer review component in the evaluation.
- Prepare discussion questions ahead of time so that students can prepare. Preview what you will cover in the next module. After a lecture or when completing a module, ask a series of questions to bring closure to a subject and to introduce reflective thinking before the next module. Consider breakout group discussions or intergroup quiz challenges to test comprehension.
- Anticipate problems that may occur during the performance of selected assignments. Explain how the learners can remedy these. Tips may either be included within the individual micro module or as general principles for course conduct.

Learning starts with clear understanding and continuous verification of student comprehension, along with shared responsibility for the learning environment. This establishes the foundation for high-performance online learning and, later, for successful virtual teams. The learning progresses along the second path of support.

THE SECOND PATH EXPECTS AND RECEIVES SUPPORT

Today's learners must frequently adapt to a rapidly changing workplace. It is important to view the classroom as a temporary team that develops its own culture, enhances student commitment to learning, and prepares them to be part of work teams, whether fully remote or hybrid. Research in adult learning and decades of experience have shown that learners learn best when they engage as a cohort. Peer learning is crucial for helping learners apply concepts in practice and is vital for teamwork. This includes shared responsibility but also the give-and-take of asking for and offering help to one another.

While some learners may seek out learning partners independently, most will not. They need to be shown how to actively advocate for themselves and support each other as a cohort. Instructors must incorporate peer learning opportunities into the classroom experience. The second pathway involves supporting the learners on their learning journey and teaching them how to support each other. It develops learners' shared responsibility for their own *and each other's* learning.

Open the conversation and your learners' eyes, then care enough to stay involved and ensure relevance to the learning objectives. You are a facilitator of the learning experience as much as you are a content expert. Bridge the virtual distance with team assignments and opportunities to provide peer support. Invite them to answer each other's questions, clarifying and correcting answers as needed. Team assignment groups learn to cooperate because their grades are interdependent. Today's work world requires most professionals to be able to collaborate virtually, so it is part of the instructor's job to get learners ready to succeed, often in virtual teams. Team learning teaches collaboration and team self-management.

Set up team assignments and peer learning to match the workplace, comprised of loosely connected people whose grade (or job performance) is partly based on supporting each other. In other words, no one completes the learning objectives without working with others and being evaluated as a team. If a graded group project doesn't fit the course design, you can still design for group learning. Have learners teach each other through peer reviews and group presentations, with the class providing feedback to presentation groups. This also lightens your grading load and teaches another critical competency: giving and receiving constructive feedback. By working together, they develop virtual team competencies, something often missing in online learning when peer interaction is not required.

Our main job is to be the *human* connection, the instructor who cares enough to facilitate deeper learning and good student choices. Learners struggle to connect online. The digital screen presents a barrier to interpersonal outreach. Care enough about your learners to expand emotional bandwidth. Connect with learners as whole humans, authentically. Learners are open to learning when the instructor is open. People learn better when they feel psychologically safe. Learners welcome knowing their instructor is an interested and real person. Consider showing your real office instead of a virtual background. Let the cat stay on your lap and invite new mothers to hold their sleeping babies. If a current event is relevant to the topic, rip a discussion straight from the headlines, connecting the textbook to real life. Facilitate icebreakers related to holidays and special events. Connect, connect, connect!

Prepare for disconnected, distracted learners, though. For learners who arrive unprepared, model team support while managing expectations to come ready to learn. Reinforce your preferences regarding course preparedness, holding the standard, of course. When teamwork is part of the course, however, it is critical to be ready to accommodate the occasional unprepared team member in ways that won't hold everyone back. Have a hip-pocket activity if learners show up without prework. Provide a generic case study they can use as a substitute. If possible, invite learners to complete prework during the 1st break. Do not slow down learning to accommodate the unprepared. This happens in work teams and reflects real life. Some people arrive just in time, unprepared, while others have done the work and are ready to keep to an agenda.

If you have designed your course for interdependence among learners with shared grades on team assignments, communicate how teams must address those who fail to perform timely or to quality standards. This is a team learning opportunity with consideration to clarifying expectations. Deploy your plan. You are modeling how to support team success and individual occasional slips while keeping the course on schedule and learning on track.

When learners discuss course material through asynchronous discussions and in live sessions, expect learners to speak up clearly and often. Encourage everyone to expand and deepen the conversation, redirecting student questions to classmates for response. Ask questions, share examples that add to or challenge a perspective, and invite others to do the same. Discussion is organic, so share your personality a bit more freely than you might when writing an academic paper. Appreciate your class as learners and valuable contributors to the topic. Welcome humor. Acknowledge powerfully written discussion posts publicly. Encourage participation while adding your content as part of the natural conversation.

By leading with connection and support and by structuring group learning as an embedded design decision, learners will begin to follow the second path of support with each other as well. Help learners develop a sense of responsibility for their peers' well-being. Group work in class leads them to successful careers that are, in reality, at least partially based on how well they help their classmates succeed, not just themselves. Be overt about how peer support grows a lifelong professional network. This also increases psychological safety in learning teams when you are not present. Teams are more likely to resolve mistakes, disagreements, disappointments, poor communication, and conflicts when working with people they know and respect. Group assignments are rich fodder to expand emotional bandwidth by getting to know one another as they learn something new together. Peer support is essential for learners to relax and learn, especially if a grade is involved – a built-in shared responsibility for mutual success. *This is the second path on the threefold path to high-performance learning*™.

Simple Ways to Adapt Your Curriculum for a Supportive Classroom Using the Second Path

- Use platform tools to connect learners. For example, set up a shared folder for learners to upload assignments for peer review, whether voluntary or guided by you.
- Peer learning increases learning transfer, both in the giving and receiving of feedback. Assign or recommend learning partners or teams that stay together throughout a course or extended module, even when they do not work on the same assignment team. If the course is longer, it may be beneficial to rotate partners halfway through.
- Provide peer interviews or self-assessments that "introduce" learners to each other. If pressed for time, assign Prework.
- Encourage learners to connect on LinkedIn and get active with student chapters of professional associations.
- Set up fun team games to gather information or investigate an issue. For example, have teams compete against each other on a digital scavenger hunt with report-outs.
- Ask learners to record a podcast *for their classmates* instead of writing an essay *for you*. Save time grading while increasing learning through peer feedback. This also provides some valuable speaking experience.
- Do not let learners talk you out of group work. It is part of learning and a necessary component.

A Supportive Classroom is an Inclusive Classroom, another aspect of the second path.

Inclusion does not occur naturally in online learning or virtual team environments—especially at first. Online learning and virtual teams cross time zones, distance, cultural, and other differences. Real-world digital teams can lead to isolation, disengagement, and career derailment (Modi, 2021). Business research confirms that team leaders must intentionally cultivate relationships among team members (Jonathan H. Westover, 2024). Online learning teams boost socialization by getting learners connected for a purpose. This builds social capital and prepares learners to bridge digital divides throughout their careers. Lead bonding activities that launch an assignment team, helping bridge the digital divide and letting relationships develop as learners get to know each other. Remind learners that part of the team assignment is to communicate with, support, and learn to depend on each other.

Inclusion in an online or hybrid learning or work environment means bridging physical and emotional distance; in other words, inclusive online classrooms address distance bias. People often struggle to connect across the digital divide, developing a shyness when meeting only online, yet today's workforce must reach out to individuals they may not know well. Course design and instructor facilitation can help bridge this virtual distance and set a tone for learners to establish swift trust and develop confidence and experience in developing relationships with other learners.

Facilitate a classroom culture that functions as a temporary team. Include ongoing icebreakers and learning-focused breakout activities, especially early in a program or course when learners need help getting to know one another. Balance relational connection questions with course content application. For example, in the first live session, instructors can break learners into icebreaker groups and have them report back a summary of course-focused questions along with one more: "What is one thing everyone in this group has in common besides this course?" Consider other simple practices that support inclusivity in the classroom.

- Provide opportunities for learners to engage in multiple ways. For example, a student who is uncomfortable speaking in large Zoom sessions could lead a small group activity.
- Diversity of lived experience, opinion, and approach should be an expected part of the process for team assignments. Build exploration of diverse thoughts into assignment instructions. Guide and instruct learners on how to manage healthy conflicts and misunderstandings.
- Offer opportunities for learners to:
    - o Develop or influence classroom norms and take responsibility for upholding them.
    - o Celebrate the temporary team upon completion of the course or cohort. Recognize peers through nominations and acknowledgments for contributing to one another's learning. Celebrate group accomplishments together.
    - o Build excitement for future endeavors and solidify professional friendships and connections.
- Design projects that require diverse skills and contributions from each team member, with clear deadlines and deliverables for each phase.
- Make learners the teachers. Each student or team researches a specific part of a topic and then shares their knowledge with the group.

Select one or two of the provided suggestions and incorporate these practices into your course. Watch supportive friendships develop as learning happens. This leads us to the third and last path of delivering high-quality assignment results.

THE THIRD PATH OF SUCCESSFUL LEARNING DELIVERS HIGH MARKS

By executing well on the first and second pathways, student teams submit better assignments, and they do so with more confidence and pride. They deliver high-quality results. The third path delivers workforce-ready graduates. Learners share the responsibility for their learning by engaging actively along the pathways of clarity and support, leading to results. *Delivering quality individual and team assignments is the 3rd path in the Threefold Path to High-Performance Learning*™.

Instructors are the learning leaders on all three paths, but the third path carries more responsibility to create learning environments where learners do well individually and as learning team members. It is human to want to know how we are doing before moving forward. Online learners need frequent, informative, and timely feedback to bridge virtual distance. People do better when they know how they are doing. Provide frequent feedback. It is foundational for learners to be able to focus on learning. You do not want learners attempting to figure out how they are doing in the professor's eyes. While that is a useful political skill, it takes the learner's focus off the objectives.

Especially when giving written feedback, read before submitting. Have AI check your tone and content for clarity. The written word is a flat medium and is easily misunderstood. My initial assignment feedback can "read" as harsher than I intended, or my comment may miss context. I model respect for feedback by reading my words through a student's eyes. I often ask AI to rewrite my feedback to be clear and kind. This saves time in the long run with fewer student follow-up questions.

It also shows an expectation of high-caliber work. Today's workforce must be made up of continuous learners. Evaluate student performance with a philosophy of continuous improvement and high standards. Seek opportunities for giving – and receiving – feedback and develop learners' habits of doing the same. Point out strengths, great insights, and learner blind spots. Respect their effort enough to review their work and give authentic feedback. For example, start with one positive comment followed by constructive feedback. End with one or two specific ideas for learners to work on next time. If a group assignment has individual components, provide group feedback publicly and individual comments privately.

Learners will take more accountability when they have feedback to inform them. Human beings want to know that they are okay. Grade timely, at a minimum, but also embed feedback loops throughout the course. Promote continuous improvement through positive and constructive feedback, and with enough time to allow for course corrections. For example, determine *and communicate* how the learners' grasp of the material in each module will be measured. You may want to have an auto-graded multiple-choice or fill-in-the-blank quiz at the end of each section. Learners can see their results and how to improve. These can be one-time assessments, or you might allow repeat assessments; they can be graded or not. The point is to provide frequent and fast feedback in multiple ways so learners can move forward confidently and with self-determination.

A neglected component of high-performance teams and team learning is acknowledgment and celebration (Hoefling, 2017). The Third Path to High Performance involves acknowledging and celebrating the work done. Share stellar assignment segments with the class. This provides exemplars and can be a source of pride. Acknowledge the individual or team's work publicly. Host peer-voted awards as the course ends, honoring learners who exemplify course values. For example, have learners nominate and acknowledge those who contributed the most to live session breakout sessions, provided the best small group leadership, best asynchronous discussion contributions, and so on. As a learning team and individuals, take a moment to appreciate each other and celebrate success.

Simple Ways to Adapt Your Curriculum for High-Quality Assignments and Grades

There are many ways to adapt course design that lead to high-quality assignment submissions. Motivate learners to want to earn high grades.

- Provide feedback in multiple ways. Give learning teams time to debrief.
- Monitor team interactions discreetly through digital means. Utilize AI, tools, and the platform to track learner engagement and provide timely support.
- Identify patterns and trends to streamline the sharing of responsibilities with learners.
- Invite case study examples from student experiences. This takes a concept from lecture to applied practice.
- Incorporate active, outcomes-based, hands-on activities that are collaborative and student-led. For example, have groups analyze an applied case study and discuss recommendations or innovations asynchronously *and* during in-person course time.

- Set milestones for more complex assignments as they digest, analyze, consider, advise, and complete sections of an assignment. Robust learning happens individually and in groups through applied research, discussion, collaborative analysis and evaluation, and recommendations or decisions.
- Compel diverse considerations that synthesize multiple perspectives on a focused learning topic into an articulated summary of understanding and perspective.
- Have learners evaluate each other's team contributions and provide peer feedback on assignments.
- To share responsibility for learning, balance individual and group activities to embed a mindset of being evaluated both individually and as a group.
- Attend to asynchronous aspects of the classroom as well as live sessions.
- Find chances for learners to develop a shared sense of pride. Invite learners to share a recent success in chat or as an icebreaker, providing opportunities to "humble brag".
- Assign learners to validate information and become Wikipedia editors and curators.
- Schedule knowledge parties or live quiz competitions.
- Ask hypothetical situations for the learners to analyze, reflect and record their impressions to defend or adapt based on input from others.
- Balance evaluation methods with shared grades, peer evaluations, individual grades, and self-evaluations.

Basically, find ways to formally and informally get learners to think beyond the regurgitation of established knowledge. Learners become advisory teams that give one another advice and feedback. Help them bring their best intelligence and genuine desire to support one another's learning. Encourage classes to seek feedback and input from their classmates. Regularly embed course reflections that are not graded and may be anonymous. Respond quickly as the evaluator. Respect that online learning is a learning lab for both students and professors.

Follow the Threefold Path principles as you rethink and redesign your courses. With the right course and assignment structure, learners will navigate the Threefold Path to High-Performance Learning™ of clarity, support, and performance. Additionally, you are providing a learning lab for leadership and continuous learning.

ONLINE LEARNING LAB FOR LEADERSHIP AND LIFELONG LEARNING

According to a recent McKinsey Institute study, high-quality leadership is the critical variable in the success of hybrid teams (Aaron De Smet, 2021). Leaders must develop trust and connection with distributed teams. Your students are virtual learners *and* leaders in the classroom. Prepare them to be virtual team members and leaders with team learning that cuts through appearances, pushing learners to produce and perform because others depend on them. Team-based, learner-centric course design forces student agency. Everyone leads, speaks up, and advocates for an approach or a position in ways that develop team leadership skills and self-agency. Leadership opportunities give learners practice in being visible and develop a 'lasting' reputation, harder to do when learning alone or on a disconnected team. Invite opportunities to be strong individual contributors within a learning team.

Leaders must give and receive feedback. Model double-loop learning in structuring a course. Depending on the course, your style, and the nature of the learning outcomes or program, make decisions that balance student agency with instructor classroom management controls and feedback opportunities. Regardless of how much responsibility is shared with the learners, communicate to learners clearly what you and they can expect.

Self-agency shows learners how to engage with you individually and as a team representative. Clarify and communicate how you, as the instructor and temporary learning leader, prefer to be approached for various issues, from assignment clarity to team conflict intervention. Incorporate peer breakout groups and team assignment opportunities every time the class meets synchronously. Group work should be non-negotiable, and rotating roles, including leadership roles, are highly recommended.

There are other less visible ways to embed double-loop learning feedback and increase student ownership of learning outcomes along the Third Path to High-Performance Learning™, such as:

- Teach learners how to give and receive constructive feedback as part of a breakout group activity assignment.
- Provide both asynchronous and synchronous leadership practice opportunities, assigning people to the role if practical.
- Model for learners how to lead virtual meetings and present online. Invite them to practice. For example, have teams lead 5-minute "teaching lecturettes."

CONCLUSION

Today's instructors must rise to the challenge. We are developing a workforce that is digitally literate, professionally competent, respectful, effective, connected, adaptive, flexible, continuously learning, and virtual. Andria Zafirakou, Global Teacher of the Year for 2018, discusses how business executives want education to produce a more compassionate, communicative, and innovative workforce moving forward. She emphasizes the human experience as truly valuable to organizations in the future (Zomorodi, 2020). Today's learner seeks collaboration and connection competence, recognizing that they are not always good at it. Many need to be taught how to work well with others. You are a facilitator of the learning experience as much as you are a content expert. Lead the learning journey and connect your learners. Our main responsibility is to be the human connection, that person who cares enough to assist today's professionals to develop the competencies needed to enjoy a fulfilling career, adapting and learning along the way *with others*.

REFERENCES

Aaron De Smet, B. D. (2021, July 9). It's Time for Leaders to Get Real About Hybrid. *The McKinsey Quarterly*.

Boser, U. (2017). *Learn Better: Mastering the Skills for Success in Life, Business, and School, or How to Become an Expert in Just about Anything*. Rodale Publishing.

Brew, M. (2025). *Microlearning: A Beginner's Guide*. Retrieved from EduMe: https://www.edume.com/blog/what-is-microlearning

Dallimore, E.J., J. H. (2016). Creating a Community of Learning Through Classroom Discussion: Student Perceptions of the Relationships Among Participation Learning, Comfort and Preparation. *Journal on Excellence in College Teaching*, *27*(3), 137–171.

Hoefling, T. (2017). *Working Virtually: Transforming the Mobile Workplace* (2nd ed.). Stylus Publishing.

Imel, S. (1992). *Reflective Practice in Adult Education. ERIC Digest #122*. Retrieved from ERIC Clearinghouse on Adult, Career, and Vocational Education: https://eric.ed.gov/?id=ED346319

Jonathan, H., & Westover, P. F. (2024, November 26). *Cultivating Community and Connection: A New Playbook for the Hybrid Workforce*. Retrieved from Forbes Coaches Council: https://www.forbes.com/councils/forbescoachescouncil/2024/11/26/cultivating-community-and-connection-a-new-playbook-for-the-hybrid-workforce/

Maryellen Weimer, P. (2017, June 28). *The Teaching Professor Blog Faculty Focus: Higher Ed Teaching Strategies*. Retrieved from Faculty Focus Magna Publications: https://www.facultyfocus.com/articles/philosophy-of-teaching/contradictions-think-teaching/?_hsenc=p2ANqtz-8urWzmYpvkRVyNY3i9fSYhmbEw8DtMXy_ImaAyTIHLJi8zWShbE90ZK2269Jys-wcnus45aExy3fo8EZaXRb1-XP93TQ&_hsmi=53632571

Meyerson, D., Weick, K. E., & Kramer, R. M. (1996). Swift trust and temporary groups. In Kramer, R. M., & Tyler, T. R. (Eds.), *Trust in organizations: Frontiers of theory and research* (pp. 166–195). Sage Publications, Inc. DOI: 10.4135/9781452243610.n9

Mills, W. (2019, April 3). *Faculty Focus*. Retrieved from Faculty Focus: https://www.facultyfocus.com/articles/online-education/what-is-swift-trust-and-why-do-i-want-it-in-my-classes/

Morris, T. H. (2019, January 24). *Experiential Learning - A Systematic Review and Revision of Kolb's Theory.* Retrieved from Taylor & Francis Peer Reviewed Journals and Articles - Interactive Learning Environments: https://www.tandfonline.com/doi/abs/10.1080/10494820.2019.1570279

Peter, C., & Brown, H. L. (2014). *Make It Stick: The Science of Successful Learning.* Belknap Press, Harvard University Press.

Stonehouse, L. P. P. A., Frick, R. A., & T. Codd, S. W. (n.d.). *Scholar.* Retrieved from Scholar.Google: Here is a link to multiple scholarly articles about the Socratic, experiential approach. https://scholar.google.com/scholar?q=socratic+and+experiential+learning+theory&hl=en&as_sdt=0&as_vis=1&oi=scholart

Ton, J. (2020, October 15). *Networking: It's Not What You Think.* Retrieved from Forbes Tech Council: https://www.forbes.com/councils/forbestechcouncil/2020/10/15/networking-its-not-what-you-think/

Uday, S. (2022). *Potential of Collaborative Online Learning: A Guide for University Students.* Retrieved from University of Texas Collaborative Online: https://sites.utexas.edu/collaborated/potential-of-collaborative-online-learning/

Zomorodi, M. (2020, September 30). How the Best Teacher Teaches Creativity. *Notes to Self podcast.* https://podcasts.apple.com/us/podcast/note-to-self/id561470997?i=1000451828638

Chapter 3
Designing Virtual Teamwork for Creativity:
Strategies for Higher Education

Andi Asrifan
https://orcid.org/0000-0002-9934-6129
Universitas Negeri Makassar, Indonesia

Syahruddin
Universitas Negeri Makassar, Indonesia

ABSTRACT

This chapter examines the dynamics of virtual teamwork in higher education, emphasizing tactics that foster innovation and collaboration among students. With the growing prevalence of online learning, the necessity for efficient virtual collaboration tools and methodologies is critical. The chapter delineates essential techniques, encompassing the selection of varied team members, the formation of explicit roles, and the promotion of an inclusive culture that fosters open communication. It underscores the need of employing digital tools that enhance brainstorming and project management, so enabling students to participate actively in their learning experiences. The chapter also discusses potential hurdles, including communication impediments and cultural differences, and provides strategies to surmount these limitations. Through the use of these tactics, instructors can cultivate a supportive environment that promotes innovation and equips students for the collaborative requirements of the contemporary workforce.

DOI: 10.4018/979-8-3373-0375-8.ch003

UNDERSTANDING VIRTUAL TEAMWORK

Definition and Importance

Virtual teamwork denotes the collaborative endeavors of individuals who are physically separated and employ digital tools and platforms for communication, information sharing, and collective pursuit of common objectives (Garro-Abarca et al., 2021; Kiely et al., 2022). In higher education, virtual collaboration has gained significance due to the proliferation of online learning environments, globalization, and the demand for adaptable instructional frameworks. The importance of virtual teaming beyond simple collaboration is vital in cultivating creativity among both students and educators.

In conventional educational environments, collaboration typically transpires in person, facilitating impromptu dialogues and prompt feedback. As higher education institutions adjust to the digital context, the dynamics of collaboration have transformed. Virtual collaboration presents distinct chances for innovation by uniting diverse ideas from students across several regions, cultures, and backgrounds (Dincă et al., 2021). This diversity can foster fresh ideas and solutions that may not arise in a homogeneous group.

Furthermore, virtual collaboration promotes the utilization of diverse digital technologies that enhance ideation, project management, and communication. Video conferencing, collaborative documents, and project management software facilitate real-time collaboration across teams, irrespective of their physical locations. This accessibility may enhance involvement, as students who feel intimidated in a conventional classroom may find it simpler to engage in a virtual setting.

The significance of virtual collaboration in higher education is emphasized by the competencies it develops in students. As the workforce increasingly necessitates collaboration through digital platforms, students participating in virtual teamwork are more adequately equipped for future employment (Bennett & McWhorter, 2021). They cultivate crucial competencies such as digital communication, distant cooperation, and adaptability—skills that are vital in the contemporary employment market.

Moreover, virtual collaboration can augment creativity by offering a forum for brainstorming and idea generation that is less restricted by conventional conventions. Students are permitted to express their opinions openly, employ multimedia resources, and participate in asynchronous discussions that facilitate reflection and comprehensive analysis (Lin & Sun, 2024). This flexibility cultivates an environment that promotes creative thinking and allows students to assume responsibility for their learning.

The significance of virtual teams in higher education has been influenced by significant historical and technological developments. In the early 2000s, the emergence of online learning systems such as Moodle and Blackboard facilitated asynchronous learning and established the groundwork for digital collaboration. The emergence of cloud-based applications like Google Docs and Microsoft Teams further expedited real-time, location-independent collaboration. The COVID-19 pandemic acted as a significant motivator, prompting institutions worldwide to implement entirely remote learning environments and standardizing virtual cooperation. In conjunction with these technological advancements, there has been a notable evolution in organizational and pedagogical paradigms—from conventional campus-based instruction to adaptable, hybrid, and virtual educational models. This transition signifies a growing focus on global competency, necessitating students cultivate cross-cultural communication and collaboration abilities to succeed in a linked world. Consequently, virtual collaboration has emerged as an essential element of higher education strategy in the 21st century.

The Evolution of Teamwork in Education

Over the decades, education has changed from face-to-face interactions to virtual partnerships (Singh et al., 2022). Technology, changing educational paradigms, and the requirement for customizable learning environments have driven this growth.

Student collaboration traditionally happened in physical classrooms during group projects, discussions, and cooperative learning (Reyes et al., 2024). This paradigm emphasized face-to-face communication and shared experiences to build connections. Traditional cooperation develops interpersonal skills and camaraderie, but geographical and time constraints can hinder group collaboration.

Technology changed education collaboration (Barron et al., 2022). After computers and the internet arrived in the late 20th century, schools began studying digital communication. Email became the principal form of student collaboration, although it still relied on textual communication. Technology improved collaborative tools, making teamwork more dynamic and engaging.

Online learning platforms enhanced virtual collaboration in the early 21st century. Moodle and Blackboard allow students to communicate, submit homework, and chat online (Maslov et al., 2021). This transition was vital to education, allowing students to collaborate more freely and accommodate varied learning styles and schedules.

COVID-19 accelerated the transition of education collaboration, forcing institutions worldwide to adapt to remote learning (Babbar & Gupta, 2022; Stracke et al., 2022). Zoom and Microsoft Teams became popular, enabling real-time, global communication. This transition highlighted the importance of digital expertise and how virtual cooperation can boost creativity and innovation. Students from different countries and cultures can now collaborate, bringing new perspectives.

Higher education now relies on virtual cooperation, combining traditional methods with modern technology. Online collaborations have transformed student learning and teamwork, creating a more inclusive and flexible educational environment (Singh et al., 2022). To stimulate innovation and prepare students for success in an increasingly interconnected society, we must understand virtual collaboration mechanics.

Challenges of Virtual Teamwork

Although virtual teaming offers various benefits, it also poses certain problems that may impede collaboration and innovation in higher education (Donelan & Kear, 2024). Comprehending these problems is crucial for both instructors and students as they maneuver through the intricacies of a digital landscape.

A primary issue of virtual teamwork is communication limitations. In conventional in-person interactions, non-verbal signals, including body language, eye contact, and vocal tone, are essential for message transmission and rapport establishment (Eklund & Isotalus, 2024). In virtual contexts, these indications are frequently reduced or completely lacking, resulting in misunderstandings and misinterpretations. Written communication, common in virtual collaboration, may lack the subtleties of verbal discourse, hindering team members' ability to completely comprehend one another's objectives. This may lead to irritation, diminished collaboration, and a decrease in team morale.

Moreover, dependence on technology for communication may provide distinct issues. Technical difficulties, like inadequate internet connectivity, software malfunctions, or lack of proficiency with digital technologies, can impede meetings and obstruct productivity. When team members face these challenges, it may result in project timetable delays and a feeling of detachment among participants. It is essential for all team members to be adept in utilizing the requisite tools, however this may necessitate supplementary time and resources for training and support (Chan, 2023).

Time zone disparities provide a substantial obstacle in virtual collaboration, especially within higher education environments that draw an international student population (Singh et al., 2022). Organizing meetings and collaborative sessions can be difficult when team members are located in different time zones. This may result in schedule difficulties, necessitating certain members to attend meetings at inconvenient times, leading to weariness and diminished involvement. Moreover, asynchronous communication can induce delays in feedback and decision-making, thus hindering the creative process and impeding project advancement.

Cultural disparities contribute to the difficulties of virtual collaboration. Team members from varied origins may exhibit differing communication styles, work ethics, and problem-solving techniques. This diversity can foster creativity, but it may also result in conflict if not managed properly. Cultural misunderstandings can generate stress within the team, necessitating the cultivation of cultural awareness and sensitivity among members (Grosskopf & Barmeyer, 2021; Tuohy & Wallace, 2024).

Alongside technological and cross-cultural hurdles, elements related to the home environment pose significant obstacles to virtual teaming. A multitude of students and instructors engage in virtual meetings from communal or multifunctional environments, where disruptions from family members, children, or roommates frequently occur and prove disruptive. The lack of a specialized or ergonomically designed workspace might result in physical discomfort and diminished productivity. Ambient noise, restricted privacy, and insufficient lighting significantly diminish the quality of virtual connection. Furthermore, variations in home circumstances generate inequities; certain students may lack dependable internet access or the requisite gear to engage fully in collaborative activities. These factors lead to disengagement, particularly during prolonged video sessions, resulting in what is sometimes referred to as "Zoom fatigue." Persistent multitasking and cognitive fatigue in these environments reduce attention spans and hinder substantial engagement. Overcoming these obstacles necessitates flexible approaches and compassionate leadership to promote inclusive and efficient virtual collaboration.

Chapter Purpose

The purpose of this chapter is to provide faculty in higher education with information and strategies on how to overcome the challenges just reviewed and to design virtual teams that are both creative and high performing. To do so, the following design areas will be discussed:

1) Strategies for building a creative virtual team through selecting diverse team members, establishing team roles and responsibilities, and fostering a collaborative culture;
2) The variety of tools and technologies available for virtual collaboration, and techniques to integrate and ensure utilization and accessibility of these technologies;
3) Strategies for enhancing creativity in virtual teams, including techniques for brainstorming and ideation, for encouraging risk-taking and experimentation; and for establishing regular feedback loops during the creative process;
4) Strategies for assessing and sustaining virtual team performance with the use of metrics for evaluating team effectiveness, and continuous improvement practices; and

5) Case studies that illustrate best practices of the above design principles.

BUILDING A CREATIVE VIRTUAL TEAM

Selecting Team Members

The success of a virtual team is fundamentally dependent on the meticulous selection of its members (Gifford, 2022). In higher education, where creativity and invention are essential, collecting a varied collection of individuals can greatly augment the team's collaborative capacity. The selection process must emphasize diverse characteristics that enhance creativity, encourage inclusion, and guarantee effective collaboration. Diversity in talents and expertise is a fundamental criterion for selecting team members.

A team consisting of individuals with diverse academic backgrounds, professional experiences, and skill sets can tackle problems from various perspectives and produce a broader range of ideas (Mogavi et al., 2024). Incorporating individuals from disciplines such as design, engineering, business, and the arts can yield unique solutions that integrate diverse views. This interdisciplinary approach enhances the creative process and fosters mutual learning among team members, thereby expanding their individual skill sets.

The diversity of opinion and perspective is equally significant. Team members with diverse cultural, geographical, and social backgrounds offer distinct perspectives that might contest traditional thinking. This diversity can foster innovative dialogues and inspire unconventional solutions. Educators should pick team members who exhibit critical and creative thinking skills, along with open-mindedness and a readiness to investigate novel ideas (Marshall et al., 2021).

Alongside talents and viewpoints, interpersonal attributes are essential to team dynamics. Choosing individuals with robust communication abilities, emotional intelligence, and a cooperative disposition may cultivate a constructive team atmosphere. Effective communication is essential in virtual environments because misunderstandings can readily occur (Alam & Mohanty, 2022). Team members who can express their ideas clearly and engage in active listening enhance team cohesion and productivity. Moreover, people possessing elevated emotional intelligence may adeptly manage disagreements and cultivate robust relationships, which are crucial for sustaining team morale and motivation.

Another significant element is flexibility. In a virtual setting, team members must exhibit adaptability and receptiveness to change, as projects can develop swiftly and necessitate rapid strategic adjustments (Ismail et al., 2023; Kerzner et al., 2022).

Choosing individuals capable of excelling in dynamic environments and adopting new technology will augment the team's overall resilience and creativity.

Ultimately, it is essential to evaluate team chemistry during the selection process. Diversity is crucial, but team members must also collaborate effectively and establish rapport. Implementing team-building activities or preliminary meetings help assess interpersonal dynamics and confirm that chosen individuals can collaborate efficiently (Elforgani et al., 2024).

Establishing Team Roles and Responsibilities

In the context of virtual collaboration, especially in higher education, well-defined roles and duties are crucial for promoting accountability and optimizing the skills of each team member (Stewart et al., 2023; Herriott & McNulty, 2022). Clearly defined responsibilities enable teams to function more effectively, resulting in improved collaboration and innovation.

One of the principal advantages of delineating distinct responsibilities is the enhancement of accountability (Luo et al., 2024). When team members comprehend their distinct roles, they are more inclined to assume ownership of their tasks and contribute significantly to the group's objectives. This accountability enhances individual performance and fortifies the whole team dynamic, since members depend on one another to meet their obligations. Accountability becomes increasingly vital in a virtual environment where direct oversight is frequently restricted (Wu, 2022). Well-defined roles reduce the likelihood of tasks being overlooked, guaranteeing that all elements of a project are attended to.

Furthermore, clearly delineated responsibilities allow teams to utilize each member's distinct talents and abilities. In a heterogeneous team, members contribute varied expertise and viewpoints. By allocating responsibilities that correspond with these strengths, teams can maximize their creative potential (Brown et al., 2023). A person with expertise in graphic design may assume the position of visual communicator, whereas another with robust analytical skills may concentrate on data analysis. This intentional distribution of duties enables team members to operate in their areas of expertise, resulting in superior outputs and inventive solutions.

Defining responsibilities also enhances successful communication within the team (Kim et al., 2022; Smuck et al., 2021). When members understand each other's roles, they can coordinate their activities more effectively and prevent redundancy. This clarity facilitates communication, enabling team members to direct their inquiries and feedback to the relevant personnel. In a virtual setting where communication may be disjointed, this clarity is essential for preserving coherence and guaranteeing uniform understanding among all participants.

Moreover, well-defined positions can improve motivation and morale. When team members comprehend how their contributions integrate into the broader project framework, they are more inclined to feel appreciated and included. This sense of purpose is particularly crucial in virtual environments, where isolation and detachment can occur. Acknowledging and rewarding individual contributions cultivates a positive team culture and motivates individuals to dedicate their utmost efforts to the collaborative process (Javed, 2024).

Fostering a Collaborative Culture

Establishing a collaborative culture is essential for the success of virtual teams in higher education, particularly when the objective is to foster creativity and invention (Khamis et al., 2021). An inclusive atmosphere that fosters free communication and the exchange of ideas enhances team morale and results in more varied and profound viewpoints. To do this, instructors and team leaders may employ many tactics.

Primarily, it is imperative to establish explicit communication guidelines. Teams must establish consensus on preferred communication channels—whether video conferences, instant messaging, or collaborative documents—and delineate expectations for responding. Consistent check-ins and updates enhance participation and guarantee that all perspectives are acknowledged. Fostering a culture in which team members are at ease expressing their opinions and criticism enables the establishment of an environment characterized by trust and transparency (Zolfaghari & Madjdi, 2022). This is especially crucial in virtual environments, where participants may experience isolation or disconnection.

Another efficacious technique is to promote active engagement from all team members. This can be accomplished by conducting organized brainstorming sessions that invite all participants to share ideas without criticism. Methods like round-robin sharing or anonymous idea submissions can facilitate the expression of opinions by quieter members. By appreciating each member's contributions, teams promote a sense of belonging and mutual respect, essential for nurturing creativity (Burt et al., 2022).

Alongside scheduled events, enabling informal opportunities for interaction can further augment collaboration. Virtual team-building activities, including icebreakers and social events, can dismantle barriers and enhance relationships among team members (Schrammel, 2024). Informal encounters can enhance comfort and familiarity, facilitating the sharing of ideas and productive collaboration during formal sessions.

Furthermore, acknowledging and commemorating achievements is essential for cultivating a collaborative culture. Emphasizing personal accomplishments and collective achievements enhances morale and underscores the significance of each member's contribution to the creative process. Educators may establish a method for recognizing contributions, such as commendations during meetings or acknowledgment in team emails, to foster a positive feedback loop that promotes continuous engagement (Menon & Suresh, 2021).

Ultimately, fostering a growth mentality among the team can markedly improve collaboration. Motivating individuals to perceive problems as opportunities for growth and enhancement cultivates resilience and inventiveness. When team members see a secure environment for experimentation, risk-taking, and learning from failures, they are more inclined to propose audacious ideas and participate in innovative problem-solving.

In summary, cultivating a collaborative culture within virtual teams is crucial for optimizing creativity and innovation in higher education. By instituting explicit communication standards, fostering active engagement, facilitating informal contact opportunities, acknowledging contributions, and endorsing a growth attitude, educators can nurture an inclusive environment that encourages open dialogue and the exchange of ideas. These tactics will augment the efficacy of virtual collaboration and elevate the educational experience for all participants.

TOOLS AND TECHNOLOGIES FOR VIRTUAL COLLABORATION

Overview of Collaboration Tools

In the domain of virtual collaboration, especially in higher education, the choice and proficient utilization of digital technologies are essential for improving communication, organization, and creativity. Numerous platforms exist, each tailored to enhance certain facets of collaboration. Comprehending these tools can enable educators and students to select the most appropriate solutions for their collaborative projects (Haleem et al., 2022; Ruiz-Rojas et al., 2024).

Zoom is one of the most prevalent tools for virtual communication. This video conferencing software facilitates real-time meetings, webinars, and debates, permitting face-to-face connection despite geographical dispersion of participants. Zoom's functionalities enhance collaborative and brainstorming endeavors, including breakout rooms, screen sharing, and recording options. The capacity to observe and listen to team members cultivates a sense of connection, which is vital for establishing rapport and promoting open communication (Itzchakov et al., 2023).

Slack is a widely utilized platform that improves communication among team members. This messaging platform facilitates individual and group discussions, permitting users to establish channels for particular subjects or initiatives. Slack facilitates file sharing, integrates with many programs, and allows for tagging team members, so enhancing the organization and accessibility of talks. Its asynchronous feature enables team members to communicate at their discretion, supporting varying schedules and time zones. Slack enhances collaborative efficiency by minimizing email clutter and optimizing communication (Müller, 2023).

Trello is an efficient project management application that employs a visual board system to monitor tasks and progress (Peña et al., 2021). Team members can establish boards for various projects, incorporate cards for particular tasks, and designate roles. Trello's intuitive interface facilitates effortless changes and alterations, simplifying the oversight of deadlines and workflows. This transparency promotes accountability, enabling team members to identify task responsibilities and monitor the project's overall progress.

Microsoft Teams is a multifaceted platform that integrates chat, video conferencing, and file collaboration into a single interface (Deželak et al., 2023). It connects effortlessly with Microsoft Office products, enabling teams to collaborate on documents, spreadsheets, and presentations in real time. This comprehensive solution streamlines cooperation by offering a centralized platform for communication and project management, facilitating connectivity and organization among team members.

Finally, Google Workspace (formerly G Suite) provides a collection of tools such as Google Docs, Sheets, and Slides, which enable collaborative document editing and sharing (Edirisinghe et al., 2024). These cloud-based programs let numerous users collaborate on the same document concurrently, offering real-time feedback and revisions. The simplicity of sharing and commenting facilitates cooperation, enabling team members to directly add their ideas and suggestions within the page.

Integrating Technology into Teamwork

Integrating technology into virtual teamwork is crucial for improving communication and project management in higher education. By implementing best practices, instructors and students can utilize digital tools to foster a more efficient and collaborative environment (Mhlongo et al., 2023; Alenezi, 2023). Here are some techniques to enhance the utilization of technology in virtual collaboration.

Initially, formulating a definitive communication strategy is essential. This plan must delineate desired communication channels, update frequency, and protocols for various interaction kinds. Synchronous meetings are optimal for brainstorming sessions, whereas asynchronous methods like Slack are suitable for continuous discussions and rapid updates. Establishing protocols for communication among team members may prevent misunderstandings and guarantee that all individuals stay informed and involved (Saxena & McDonagh, 2022).

Another optimal technique is to employ project management tools to systematize duties and monitor progress. Platforms like Trello or Asana enable teams to establish boards or lists that delineate specific tasks, dates, and responsibilities. By visually delineating the project, team members may readily identify the tasks to be accomplished and the individuals accountable for each assignment (Bomström et al. 2023). Consistently updating these tools enhances accountability and offers a transparent perspective of the project's status, assisting teams in maintaining focus and adhering to deadlines.

Alongside project management, the use of collaborative document technologies is essential for improving teamwork. Google Workspace facilitates simultaneous editing and commentary on documents, spreadsheets, and presentations. Promoting the utilization of these tools facilitates effortless cooperation, enabling all team members to concurrently share their thoughts and feedback (Zamiri & Esmaeili, 2024). This approach not only enhances the editing process but also cultivates a sense of shared ownership of the final result.

Moreover, cultivating an inclusive environment via technology is vital for augmenting creativity. Employing video conferencing platforms such as Zoom for routine check-ins and team meetings fosters a sense of connectedness among members, despite physical separation (Lal et al., 2023). Integrating icebreakers or casual discussions at the commencement of meetings helps foster rapport and promote open communication. Facilitating the chance for all team members to articulate and exchange their views fosters a culture of inclusivity and collaboration.

Ultimately, offering training and resources for team members on the chosen technology is essential for effective integration. Educators ought to provide instruction on the efficient utilization of available tools, addressing any technical difficulties (Chrimes et al., 2022). This support empowers team members to use technology confidently and boosts overall productivity.

In summary, the incorporation of technology into virtual collaboration necessitates meticulous preparation and implementation. By implementing explicit communication rules, employing project management technologies, promoting collaboration via shared documents, cultivating inclusive meeting spaces, and offering requisite training, teams can improve their communication and project management proficiency. Adhering to these best practices can enhance the efficacy and creativity of virtual teamwork in higher education, facilitating student success in collaborative environments.

Ensuring Accessibility and Usability

In the realm of virtual collaboration in higher education, guaranteeing the accessibility and usability of digital technologies is essential. A varied team typically consists of people possessing differing degrees of technical expertise and distinct accessibility requirements (Li, 2022). To foster an inclusive atmosphere that enables successful participation from all individuals, educators and team leaders must implement solutions that address these variances.

Primarily, it is crucial to perform an initial evaluation of team members' technological competencies. This can be accomplished via surveys or informal chats to assess familiarity with the selected tools. Comprehending the proficiency levels of team members enables leaders to customize training sessions that meet certain requirements (Day et al., 2021). If certain users lack expertise with video conferencing services, specific courses can be offered to familiarize them with capabilities like screen sharing, breakout rooms, and chat tools.

Offering extensive training resources is an essential technique (Zhang & Chen, 2024; Benhelal et al., 2021). These resources may encompass video lessons, user manuals, and frequently asked questions that address the fundamental features of the utilized tools. Establishing a centralized repository for these resources guarantees that team members may readily access information as required. Moreover, providing live training sessions or workshops can enhance experiential learning, enabling participants to pose inquiries and obtain prompt feedback. This method not only bolsters user confidence but also cultivates a sense of community as team members engage in collective learning.

Integrating user-friendly tools is essential for improving usability. Choosing platforms that emphasize intuitive design and clear navigation can markedly lessen the learning curve for team members. Applications like Google Workspace and Trello are recognized for their intuitive interfaces, rendering them accessible to users with diverse technological proficiencies. When implementing new technologies, it is essential to assess their usability and confirm their compatibility with the team's collective competencies.

Furthermore, addressing various accessibility requirements is essential for establishing an inclusive virtual environment (Radanliev et al., 2024). This entails accommodating people with disabilities who may necessitate particular tools or features. Ensuring that video conferencing systems have closed captioning can aid individuals with hearing difficulties. Furthermore, offering alternative formats for shared papers, including audio versions or screen-reader-compatible files, can improve accessibility for all team members.

Fostering a culture of support and collaboration is vital (Siltaloppi & Ballardini, 2023). Team leaders should underscore the need of assisting one another in navigating the tools and exchanging strategies for efficient utilization. Implementing a mentorship structure, wherein seasoned individuals support those facing challenges, can cultivate a collaborative ethos and enhance camaraderie within the team.

STRATEGIES FOR ENHANCING CREATIVITY IN VIRTUAL TEAMS

Techniques for Brainstorming and Ideation

Improving creativity in virtual teams necessitates the application of efficient brainstorming and ideation methods that foster new thought and promote collaboration (Baruah & Green, 2023). In a virtual setting, where direct interactions are restricted, employing structured approaches can enhance the exchange of ideas and guarantee that all team members participate in the creative process. This chapter examines various strategies, such as mind mapping and virtual brainstorming sessions, that can enhance creativity in higher education environments.

Mind Mapping is an effective technique that visualizes ideas and concepts, enabling team members to examine relationships and connections among various thoughts (Ligita et al., 2022). A mind mapping session begins with the identification of a major theme or problem, after which participants are invited to add associated thoughts, which are subsequently structured in a branching structure. This graphic depiction assists teams in perceiving the overarching context and recognizing possible avenues for investigation. Platforms such as MindMeister or Miro provide online mind mapping, permitting team members to interact in real-time while contributing their input. Mind mapping dissects intricate concepts into digestible elements, promoting a profound comprehension of the subject and stimulating innovative thought.

Virtual brainstorming sessions represent an efficacious approach for idea generation within a collaborative setting (Wieland et al., 2022). These meetings can be organized in several formats, including open brainstorming, where participants exchange ideas without critique, or more structured methods, such as round-robin brainstorming, where each team member sequentially presents their thoughts. Team leaders can cultivate an engaging atmosphere by instituting ground rules that foster respect and open-mindedness, so ensuring the acceptance of all views. Participants can engage in real-time discussions, share screens, and utilize collaborative tools like digital whiteboards on Zoom or Microsoft Teams to capture ideas visually. This collaborative structure promotes spontaneity and may result in unforeseen connections and ideas.

Moreover, utilizing brainwriting might be very advantageous in virtual environments. In brainwriting, team members independently document their ideas for a designated duration prior to presenting them to the group (Mengue-Topio et al., 2024). This method enables participants to formulate ideas without the stress of prompt verbal articulation, which can be advantageous for those who may be reluctant to contribute in bigger assemblies. After gathering the initial concepts, the team can deliberate and expand upon them, resulting in more sophisticated and inventive solutions.

Ultimately, integrating inventive ideas and challenges can enhance brainstorming. Team leaders may provide team members with targeted prompts, such as "What if we had no budgetary limitations?" or "How would we tackle this issue if we belonged to an entirely other industry?" These cues stimulate team members to consider innovative approaches and investigate nontraditional solutions (Donate et al., 2022).

Encouraging Risk-Taking and Experimentation

To cultivate creativity in virtual teams, it is imperative to create an environment that promotes risk-taking and experimentation (Khan & Ullah, 2025; Neukam & Bollinger, 2022). When team members feel secure in expressing unique ideas without the apprehension of criticism, innovation thrives. This chapter examines ways for cultivating an environment that fosters creativity and enables individuals to pursue innovative solutions.

A fundamental aspect of promoting risk-taking is the creation of a psychologically safe atmosphere (Kyambade et al., 2024). Team leaders must convey that all ideas are appreciated, irrespective of their unorthodox nature. This can be accomplished by clearly asserting the team's dedication to open conversation and prioritizing constructive comments above criticism. By exemplifying vulnerability, such as disclosing unconventional ideas or acknowledging past missteps, leaders can establish a culture of openness. This approach indicates to team members that taking chances is permissible and that errors are integral to the creative process.

Alongside fostering psychological safety, the execution of planned brainstorming sessions might enhance the exchange of innovative ideas (Mukerjee & Metiu, 2022). Methods like "Yes, and..." can be especially efficacious. This approach promotes collaboration among team members by fostering the enhancement of one another's ideas instead of rejecting them. For instance, if a participant suggests an extravagant idea, others may reply with, "Yes, and we may additionally..." This strategy promotes collaboration and stimulates participants to think broadly, evolving basic ideas into more refined concepts.

Additionally, allocating specific time for testing can promote risk-taking. Team leaders may designate particular sessions for the exploration of innovative concepts or the experimentation of unusual methodologies, free from the constraints of quick results. These experimental sessions might be regarded as opportunities for learning rather than assessments of performance. Permitting team members to investigate and refine their concepts enables teams to uncover unique solutions that may not have arisen in a conventional environment (Magistretti et al., 2023).

Another technique involves acknowledging minor achievements and creative endeavors, irrespective of the results. Acknowledging and praising team members for their propensity to take risks underscores the significance of experimentation (Handy, 2006). This can be accomplished through public commendations during meetings, recognition in team communications, or informal celebrations of innovative contributions. By emphasizing these contributions, teams foster a culture that prioritizes innovation and promotes continuous experimentation.

Ultimately, giving resources and assistance for experimentation is essential. This may encompass access to resources, new technology training, or seasoned team members' mentorship. When individuals possess the requisite resources to investigate their concepts, they are more inclined to undertake risks and participate in innovative problem-solving (Stolz et al., 2022).

Implementing Feedback Loops

The establishment of feedback loops is essential for augmenting creativity and boosting team dynamics in virtual teams within higher education (Zamiri & Esmaeili, 2024). Regular feedback sessions enhance ideas and cultivate a culture of ongoing improvement and collaboration. Implementing systematic methods for delivering and receiving feedback enables teams to improve their creative processes and fortify interpersonal ties.

Regular feedback meetings primarily assist team members by facilitating reflection on their own work and the contributions of others (Mitchell, 2023). These meetings establish a systematic setting in which individuals may articulate their ideas, obtain constructive feedback, and deliberate on potential enhancements. This iterative method enables teams to use each other's talents, resulting in more sophisticated and imaginative solutions. A project team can arrange bi-weekly feedback sessions to evaluate progress, address difficulties, and generate new ideas. This routine check-in not only maintains project alignment but also fosters continuous collaboration.

Furthermore, feedback loops foster a growth mentality among team members. Individuals are taught to perceive constructive feedback as a beneficial learning opportunity rather than as condemnation. This change in viewpoint cultivates resilience and adaptability, which are vital for innovative problem-solving. Normalizing the feedback process enables teams to foster an environment that embraces experimentation and perceives mistakes as essential steps toward success (Devdas, 2024; Gotian, 2022; Swargiary, 2024).

In virtual environments, the characteristics of feedback can be modified to align with the medium. The use of digital collaboration tools, such as Google Docs or project management platforms, enables team members to offer real-time comments and ideas on shared papers (Wu, 2022). This asynchronous feedback system guarantees that all perspectives are acknowledged, irrespective of time zones or varying schedules. Moreover, including anonymous feedback mechanisms can promote more forthright responses, enabling team members to articulate their opinions without apprehension of criticism.

An additional significant element of feedback loops is the function of active listening. In feedback sessions, team members must engage in active listening to comprehensively grasp the viewpoints and recommendations of their colleagues. This entails posing clarifying inquiries and encapsulating essential aspects to exhibit understanding. By cultivating a culture of respectful communication, teams can improve trust and transparency, which are essential for efficient collaboration (Mercader et al., 2021).

It is imperative to address feedback given during sessions. Teams must delineate explicit action items derived from talks, guaranteeing that recommendations are executed and assessed in future sessions (Goodyear et al., 2021). This accountability underscores the significance of the feedback mechanism and illustrates that contributions are esteemed and regarded with seriousness.

In summary, the implementation of feedback loops is essential for enhancing concepts and optimizing team dynamics within virtual teams. Regular feedback sessions, the promotion of a growth attitude, the use of digital tools for feedback, active listening, and diligent follow-up on suggestions can increase creative processes and cultivate a collaborative environment within teams. This method not only results in improved outcomes but also enhances the whole educational experience for all participants in higher education.

ASSESSING AND SUSTAINING TEAM PERFORMANCE

Metrics for Evaluating Team Effectiveness

Evaluating the success of virtual teams in higher education is crucial for comprehending their efficacy and pinpointing areas for enhancement. The assessment procedure must include diverse measures that indicate both the quality of collaboration and the creativity of the team's products (Tanno et al., 2024). By developing explicit assessment criteria, educators may ensure that teams maintain focus on their objectives and consistently improve their performance.

A key criterion for assessing team effectiveness is the output of creativity. The originality, feasibility, and impact of the ideas produced throughout the collaborative process might serve as metrics for measurement. Educators can evaluate creativity by analyzing the variety of ideas offered, the degree of ingenuity demonstrated in the solutions, and the extent to which these ideas fulfill the project's objectives (Suherman & Vidákovich, 2022). For example, teams might be required to present their concepts to a panel or submit their work for peer assessment, allowing for external appraisal of their creative outputs.

A crucial element is the caliber of collaboration among team members. This can be evaluated using different metrics, including communication efficacy, engagement levels, and interpersonal relationships. Surveys and feedback forms can be employed to collect insights from team members on their experiences with communication, trust, and support within the group. Metrics such the frequency of contributions from each member, the number of collaborative talks conducted, and the engagement levels during meetings can yield significant data regarding the overall quality of collaboration (Hopko et al., 2022).

Furthermore, the attainment of project objectives functions as a critical performance indicator. Teams must define explicit objectives at the commencement of their projects, and their capacity to achieve these goals within the specified timeframe is a crucial measure of effectiveness. Assessing the team's compliance with deadlines, completion of assigned tasks, and quality of outputs in relation to the project's objectives can yield an extensive evaluation of their performance (Taherdoost, 2024).

Moreover, team member satisfaction is a crucial statistic that indicates the general well-being of the team dynamic. Regularly administering surveys or feedback sessions can assess team members' impressions of their experiences, including engagement levels, contentment with the collaborative process, and sense of belonging within the group (Walton et al., 2022). Elevated satisfaction levels frequently connect with enhanced performance and creativity, as individuals who perceive themselves as valued and supported are more inclined to contribute productively.

Finally, the evaluation process must include adaptability and responsiveness to input. Teams that exhibit a readiness to assimilate feedback and modify their strategies are more inclined to maintain elevated levels of creativity and collaboration. Assessing how teams integrate feedback into their processes and their capacity to adapt when confronted with obstacles might yield insights into their overall efficacy (Podgórska, 2022).

Continuous Improvement Practices

In the evolving realm of virtual collaboration in higher education, ongoing enhancement strategies are essential for fostering innovation and maintaining consistent team performance. By using tactics for continuous assessment and modification, teams can enhance their processes, promote innovation, and successfully address obstacles (Eisman et al., 2022). This chapter delineates various essential methodologies for executing continuous improvement inside virtual teams.

A fundamental strategy for continual improvement is the implementation of regular reflection sessions. These workshops allow team members to evaluate effective practices and identify areas for enhancement in their collaborative processes. Conducted at critical stages of a project, these reflections promote candid discussions regarding team dynamics, communication efficacy, and creative outcomes. Establishing a secure environment for candid feedback enables teams to pinpoint certain areas for enhancement and formulate concrete improvement strategies (Banerjee et al., 2021).

An additional beneficial practice is the implementation of agile methodologies, which prioritize adaptability and incremental advancement (Daraojimba et al., 2024). Teams may implement frameworks like Scrum or Kanban, which encourage frequent evaluations and flexibility. In a Scrum framework, teams operate in brief sprints, facilitating regular evaluation of objectives and methods. This iterative method allows teams to swiftly adapt to feedback and evolving conditions, promoting a culture of ongoing learning and innovation.

Integrating feedback loops is crucial for ongoing enhancement. As previously noted, regular feedback meetings enable team members to assess their performance and implement required improvements. Fostering a culture in which feedback is not merely accepted but actively pursued can result in substantial improvements in creativity (Zamiri & Esmaeili, 2024). Teams must have explicit methods for delivering feedback, whether anonymous surveys or organized criticism sessions, to guarantee that all perspectives are acknowledged and appreciated.

Furthermore, teams ought to focus on professional development and training opportunities. Organizations can boost team contributions by investing in the development of its people, equipping them with new skills and information. Workshops focused on creative thinking, collaboration tools, or conflict resolution can equip team members with innovative perspectives and methodologies for application in their work (Amankwah-Amoah et al., 2024; Patricio et al., 2022). Ongoing education enhances personal skills and simultaneously augments the collective creativity of the team.

Ultimately, teams ought to adopt a culture of experimentation. Motivating members to explore novel methodologies, instruments, and strategies may result in unforeseen advancements in creativity. Teams can designate time for experimentation, enabling members to investigate creative concepts without the burden of immediate outcomes. Commemorating both achievements and setbacks as educational opportunities underscores the significance of experimentation in the creative process (Oo et al., 2024; Jancovich & Stevenson, 2021).

CASE STUDIES AND BEST PRACTICES

Analyzing real-world instances of effective virtual teams in higher education offers significant insights for promoting creativity and improving collaborative endeavors (Donelan & Kear, 2024). These case studies exemplify best practices that can be emulated by other teams seeking to enhance their virtual collaboration experiences.

A prominent instance is the Global Virtual Teams (GVT) Project at the University of Southern California (USC) (Yates et al., 2022). This initiative included students from various geographical backgrounds in collaborative projects addressing global concerns including climate change and public health. The GVT initiative employed digital platforms such as Zoom and Slack to enhance communication and collaboration across several time zones. A crucial insight gained from this endeavor was the significance of implementing explicit communication channels from the outset. By establishing expectations for response and employing a combination of synchronous and asynchronous communication, the teams sustained engagement and productivity, ultimately resulting in new solutions that incorporated multiple viewpoints (Heilporn et al., 2021).

The University of Massachusetts Amherst has successfully implemented the Virtual Exchange Program. This program linked UMass students with counterparts in international institutions to collaborate on collaborative projects. The event highlighted the utilization of collaborative platforms such as Google Workspace for document sharing and project management. A key insight from this experience was the importance of systematic feedback mechanisms. Regular virtual meetings were convened to evaluate progress, exchange ideas, and offer constructive comments (Karl et al., 2022). This iterative procedure enhanced the projects and fortified team dynamics, as students felt more interconnected and engaged in one another's efforts.

The Creative Collaboration Lab at the University of Toronto exemplifies the promotion of creativity among virtual teams. This program convened students from diverse fields to participate in online design thinking workshops. The laboratory employed mind mapping and brainstorming methodologies, encouraging participants to express unorthodox ideas openly. A key best practice identified in this laboratory was the prioritization of establishing a psychologically safe atmosphere (Sjöblom et al., 2022; Auernhammer & Roth, 2021). By fostering a culture of respect and transparency, team members felt empowered to take risks and pursue new ideas without fear of criticism.

The Interdisciplinary Virtual Team Initiative at Stanford University concentrated on collaborative research endeavors with faculty and students from several departments. This effort emphasized the importance of professional development and training. Workshops on efficient virtual collaboration and innovative problem-solving were conducted, offering participants the requisite skills for meaningful engagement in virtual cooperation (Zamiri & Esmaeili, 2024). The program illustrated that investing in the development of team members not only improves individual skills but also amplifies the team's collective creativity.

CONCLUSION

The chapter emphasized the essential function of virtual collaboration in promoting creativity in higher education. As institutions transition to more digital learning environments, the capacity to formulate effective virtual collaboration strategies is essential. The focus on diversity in team makeup is crucial, as it unites diverse ideas that can foster innovative solutions. Nonetheless, obstacles including communication hurdles, time zone differences, and technical difficulties must be resolved to optimize the efficacy of these cooperation.

Defined duties and responsibilities are crucial for accountability and efficient collaboration, guaranteeing that all members comprehend their contributions. The chapter recommends tactics such as brainstorming, risk-taking, and continual feedback loops to foster a culture of innovation and promote creativity. The incorporation of digital collaboration tools enhances these initiatives by facilitating communication and organizing among team members.

Furthermore, ongoing assessment via metrics and feedback is essential for maintaining team performance and promoting a culture of enhancement. Educational institutions can adopt best practices that improve cooperative learning experiences by analyzing successful case studies. The chapter contends that by emphasizing accessibility, usability, and sufficient training for digital tools, virtual teams can enhance their efficacy and equip students for the challenges of their future employment. In conclusion, the effective execution of virtual teaming tactics is essential for fostering creativity and collaboration in the contemporary educational environment.

REFERENCES

Alam, A., & Mohanty, A. (2022, December). Facial analytics or virtual avatars: Competencies and design considerations for student-teacher interaction in AI-powered online education for effective classroom engagement. In *International Conference on Communication, Networks and Computing* (pp. 252-265). Springer Nature Switzerland. DOI: 10.1007/978-3-031-43145-6_21

Alenezi, M. (2023). Digital learning and digital institution in higher education. *Education Sciences*. Advance online publication. DOI: 10.3390/educsci13010088

Amankwah-Amoah, J., Abdalla, S., Mogaji, E., Elbanna, A., & Dwivedi, Y. K. (2024). The impending disruption of creative industries by generative AI: Opportunities, challenges, and research agenda. *International Journal of Information Management, 102759*. Advance online publication. DOI: 10.1016/j.ijinfomgt.2024.102759

Auernhammer, J., & Roth, B. (2021). The origin and evolution of Stanford University's design thinking: From product design to design thinking in innovation management. *Journal of Product Innovation Management, 38*(6), 623–644. DOI: 10.1111/jpim.12594

Babbar, M., & Gupta, T. (2022). Response of educational institutions to COVID-19 pandemic: An inter-country comparison. *Policy Futures in Education*. Advance online publication. DOI: 10.1177/14782103211021937 PMID: 40478015

Banerjee, A., Taylor, D., Stranz, A., & Wahl, A. (2021). Facilitated reflection meetings as a relational approach to problem-solving within long-term care facilities. *Journal of Aging Studies*. Advance online publication. DOI: 10.1016/j.jaging.2021.100965 PMID: 34794710

Barron, T., Friend, M., Dieker, L., & Kohnke, S. (2022). Co-teaching in uncertain times: Using technology to improve student learning and manage today's complex educational landscape. *Journal of Special Education Technology, 37*(3), 439–446. DOI: 10.1177/01626434211033579

Baruah, J., & Green, K. (2023). Innovation in virtual teams: The critical role of anonymity across divergent and convergent thinking processes. *The Journal of Creative Behavior*. Advance online publication. DOI: 10.1002/jocb.603

Benhelal, E., Shamsaei, E., & Rashid, M. I. (2021). Challenges against CO2 abatement strategies in cement industry: *A review. Journal of Environmental Sciences (China)*. Advance online publication. DOI: 10.1016/j.jes.2020.11.020 PMID: 33985750

Bennett, E. E., & McWhorter, R. R. (2021). Virtual HRD's role in crisis and the post Covid-19 professional lifeworld: Accelerating skills for digital transformation. *Advances in Developing Human Resources, 23*(1), 5–25. DOI: 10.1177/1523422320973288

Bomström, H., Kelanti, M., Annanperä, E., Liukkunen, K., Kilamo, T., Sievi-Korte, O., & Systä, K. (2023). Information needs and presentation in agile software development. *Information and Software Technology, 162*, 107265. DOI: 10.1016/j.infsof.2023.107265

Brown, S. A., Sparapani, R., Osinski, K., Zhang, J., Blessing, J., Cheng, F., & Olson, J. (2023). Team principles for successful interdisciplinary research teams. *American Heart Journal Plus : Cardiology Research and Practice, 32*, 100306. DOI: 10.1016/j.ahjo.2023.100306 PMID: 38510201

Burt, B. A., Stone, B.Jr, Perkins, T., Polk, A., Ramirez, C., & Rosado, J. (2022). Team culture of community: Cultural practices for scientific team cohesion and productivity. *Small Group Research, 53*(6), 855–890. DOI: 10.1177/10464964221097699

Chan, C. K. Y. (2023). A comprehensive AI policy education framework for university teaching and learning. *International Journal of Educational Technology in Higher Education, 20*(1), 38. DOI: 10.1186/s41239-023-00408-3

Chrimes, N., Higgs, A., Hagberg, C. A., Baker, P. A., Cooper, R. M., Greif, R., & Cook, T. M. (2022). Preventing unrecognised oesophageal intubation: A consensus guideline from the Project for Universal Management of Airways and international airway societies. *Anaesthesia, 77*(12), 1395–1415. DOI: 10.1111/anae.15817 PMID: 35977431

Daraojimba, E. C., Nwasike, C. N., Adegbite, A. O., Ezeigweneme, C. A., & Gidiagba, J. O. (2024). Comprehensive review of agile methodologies in project management. *Computer Science & IT Research Journal, 5*(1), 190–218. DOI: 10.51594/csitrj.v5i.717

Day, D. V., Riggio, R. E., Tan, S. J., & Conger, J. A. (2021). Advancing the science of 21st-century leadership development: Theory, research, and practice. *The Leadership Quarterly*. Advance online publication. DOI: 10.1016/j.leaqua.2021.101557

Devdas, D. (2024). *The human equation: Penta factor*. Notion Press.

Deželak, Z., Zabukovšek, S. S., & Bobek, S. (2023). Changes of Collaboration Platforms' Use Perceived by Users Because of COVID: A Research Study of Changes in User Experience of Microsoft Teams Platform. In Birdie, A. K., & Joshi, R. (Eds.), *Reshaping the business world post-COVID-19: Management strategies for sustainable behavior change* (pp. 93–125). Apple Academic Press. DOI: 10.1201/9781003372424

Dincă, M., Lu trea, A., Oni iu, A., Cra ovan, M., & Berge, T. (2021). The effects of disciplinary composition on virtual learning group process dynamics: Students' perspectives. *Sustainability*. Advance online publication. DOI: 10.3390/su13158493

Donate, M. J., González-Mohíno, M., Appio, F. P., & Bernhard, F. (2022). Dealing with knowledge hiding to improve innovation capabilities in the hotel industry: The unconventional role of knowledge-oriented leadership. *Journal of Business Research*, *144*, 572–586. DOI: 10.1016/j.jbusres.2022.02.001

Donelan, H., & Kear, K. (2024). Online group projects in higher education: Persistent challenges and implications for practice. *Journal of Computing in Higher Education*. Advance online publication. DOI: 10.1007/s12528-023-09360-7 PMID: 37359044

Edirisinghe, G. S., Trindade, M. A., & Luo, L. (2024). Game changer: Cloud-based classroom interactions powered by Google Sheets. *Decision Sciences Journal of Innovative Education*, *22*(3), 197–211. DOI: 10.1111/dsji.12316

Eisman, A. B., Kim, B., Salloum, R. G., Shuman, C. J., & Glasgow, R. E. (2022). Advancing rapid adaptation for urgent public health crises: Using implementation science to facilitate effective and efficient responses. *Frontiers in Public Health*, *10*, 959567. DOI: 10.3389/fpubh.2022.959567 PMID: 36091566

Eklund, M., & Isotalus, P. (2024). Having it both ways: Learning communication skills in face-to-face and online environments. *Frontiers in Education*. Advance online publication. DOI: 10.3389/feduc.2024.1270164

Elforgani, M. S. A., Alabsi, A. A. N., & Alwarafi, A. (2024). Strategic Approaches to Design Teams for Construction Quality Management and Green Building Performance. *Buildings (Basel, Switzerland)*. Advance online publication. DOI: 10.3390/buildings14072020

Garro-Abarca, V., Palos-Sanchez, P., & Aguayo-Camacho, M. (2021). Virtual teams in times of pandemic: Factors that influence performance. *Frontiers in Psychology*, *12*, 624637. DOI: 10.3389/fpsyg.2021.624637 PMID: 33679543

Gifford, J. (2022). Remote working: Unprecedented increase and a developing research agenda. *Human Resource Development International*. Advance online publication. DOI: 10.1080/13678868.2022.2049108

Goodyear, P., Carvalho, L., & Yeoman, P. (2021). Activity-Centred Analysis and Design (ACAD): Core purposes, distinctive qualities and current developments. *Educational Technology Research and Development*, *69*, 445–464. DOI: 10.1007/s11423-020-09926-7 PMID: 33456288

Gotian, R. (2022). *The success factor: Developing the mindset and skillset for peak business performance.* Kogan Page.

Grosskopf, S., & Barmeyer, C. (2021). Learning from multi-paradigmatic sensitivity in cross-cultural management? Empirical and theoretical considerations. *International Journal of Cross Cultural Management, 21*(2), 181–202. DOI: 10.1177/14705958211019437

Haleem, A., Javaid, M., Qadri, M. A., & Suman, R. (2022). Understanding the role of digital technologies in education: A review. *Sustainable Operations and Computers, 3*, 275–285. DOI: 10.1016/j.susoc.2022.05.004

Handy, C. (2006). Managing the dream. Learning organizations. In J. Renesch & S. Chawla (Eds.), *Learning organizations: Developing cultures for tomorrow's workplace.* Productivity Print. DOI: 10.4324/9781003578840

Heilporn, G., Lakhal, S., & Bélisle, M. (2021). An examination of teachers' strategies to foster student engagement in blended learning in higher education. *International Journal of Educational Technology in Higher Education, 18*(1), 25. DOI: 10.1186/s41239-021-00260-3 PMID: 34805484

Herriott, H. L., & McNulty, M. A. (2022). Virtual learning impacts communication and teamwork. *The Clinical Teacher.* Advance online publication. DOI: 10.1111/tct.13514 PMID: 35851567

Hopko, S., Wang, J., & Mehta, R. (2022). Human factors considerations and metrics in shared space human-robot collaboration: A systematic review. *Frontiers in Robotics and AI.* Advance online publication. DOI: 10.3389/frobt.2022.799522 PMID: 35187093

Ismail, A., Hidajat, T., Dora, Y. M., Prasatia, F. E., & Pranadani, A. (2023). *Leading the digital transformation: Evidence from Indonesia.* Independently published.

Itzchakov, G., Weinstein, N., Vinokur, E., & Yomtovian, A. (2023). Communicating for workplace connection: A longitudinal study of the outcomes of listening training on teachers' autonomy, psychological safety, and relational climate. *Psychology in the Schools, 60*(4), 1279–1298. DOI: 10.1002/pits.22835

Jancovich, L., & Stevenson, D. (2021). Failure seems to be the hardest word to say. *International Journal of Cultural Policy.* Advance online publication. DOI: 10.1080/10286632.2021.1879798

Javed, H. (2024). Creating a positive workplace culture: diversity, equity, and inclusion initiatives. *Innovative Human Resource Management for SMEs.* DOI: 10.4018/979-8-3693-0972-8.ch020

Karl, K. A., Peluchette, J. V., & Aghakhani, N. (2022). Virtual work meetings during the COVID-19 pandemic: The good, bad, and ugly. *Small Group Research*. Advance online publication. DOI: 10.1177/10464964211015286 PMID: 38603094

Kerzner, H., Zeitoun, A., & Vargas, R. V. (2022). *Project management next generation: The pillars for organizational excellence*. Wiley.

Khamis, T., Naseem, A., Khamis, A., & Petrucka, P. (2021). The COVID-19 pandemic: A catalyst for creativity and collaboration for online learning and work-based higher education systems and processes. *Journal of Work-Applied Management, 13*(2), 184–196. DOI: 10.1108/JWAM-01-2021-0010

Khan, M. T., & Ullah, S. (2025). Balancing innovation: The role of paradoxical leadership and ambidexterity in fostering team creativity. *International Journal of Innovation Science*. Advance online publication. DOI: 10.1108/IJIS-07-2024-0206

Kiely, G., Butler, T., & Finnegan, P. (2022). Global virtual teams coordination mechanisms: Building theory from research in software development. *Behaviour & Information Technology*. Advance online publication. DOI: 10.1080/0144929X.2021.1909141

Kim, J., Lee, H., & Cho, Y. H. (2022). Learning design to support student-AI collaboration: Perspectives of leading teachers for AI in education. *Education and Information Technologies*. Advance online publication. DOI: 10.1007/s10639-021-10831-6

Kyambade, M., Namuddu, R., Mugambwa, J., & Namatovu, A. (2024). I can't express myself at work: Encouraging socially responsible leadership and psychological safety in higher education setting. *Cogent Education, 11*(1), 2373560. DOI: 10.1080/2331186X.2024.2373560

Lal, B., Dwivedi, Y. K., & Haag, M. (2023). Working from home during Covid-19: Doing and managing technology-enabled social interaction with colleagues at a distance. *Information Systems Frontiers*. Advance online publication. DOI: 10.1007/s10796-021-10182-0 PMID: 34483713

Li, L. (2022). Reskilling and upskilling the future-ready workforce for industry 4.0 and beyond. *Information Systems Frontiers*. Advance online publication. DOI: 10.1007/s10796-022-10308-y PMID: 35855776

Ligita, T., Nurjannah, I., Wicking, K., Harvey, N., & Francis, K. (2022). From textual to visual: The use of concept mapping as an analytical tool in a grounded theory study. *Qualitative Research, 22*(1), 126–142. DOI: 10.1177/1468794120965362

Lin, X., & Sun, Q. (2024). Discussion activities in asynchronous online learning: Motivating adult learners' interactions. *The Journal of Continuing Higher Education*. Advance online publication. DOI: 10.1080/07377363.2022.2119803

Luo, W., He, H., Liu, J., Berson, I. R., Berson, M. J., Zhou, Y., & Li, H. (2024). Aladdin's Genie or Pandora's Box for early childhood education? Experts chat on the roles, challenges, and developments of ChatGPT. *Early Education and Development, 35*(1), 96–113. DOI: 10.1080/10409289.2023.2214181

Magistretti, S., Sanasi, S., Dell'Era, C., & Ghezzi, A. (2023). Entrepreneurship as design: A design process for the emergence and development of entrepreneurial opportunities. *Creativity and Innovation Management, 32*(1), 5–21. DOI: 10.1111/caim.12529

Marshall, T., Keville, S., Cain, A., & Adler, J. R. (2021). On being open-minded, wholehearted, and responsible: A review and synthesis exploring factors enabling practitioner development in reflective practice. *Reflective Practice*. Advance online publication. DOI: 10.1080/14623943.2021.1976131

Maslov, I., Nikou, S., & Hansen, P. (2021). Exploring user experience of learning management system. *The International Journal of Information and Learning Technology, 38*(4), 344–363. DOI: 10.1108/IJILT-03-2021-0046

Mengue-Topio, H., Guedira, Y., Lepreux, S., & Kolski, C. (2024). Ideation, Focus Groups, and Brainstorming. In Stephanidis, C., & Salvendy, G. (Eds.), *User experience methods and tools in human-computer interaction* (pp. 34–70). CRC Press. DOI: 10.1201/9781003495161

Menon, S., & Suresh, M. (2021). Enablers of workforce agility in engineering educational institutions. *Journal of Applied Research in Higher Education, 13*(2), 504–539. DOI: 10.1108/JARHE-12-2019-0304

Mercader, V., Galván-Vela, E., Ravina-Ripoll, R., & Popescu, C. R. G. (2021). A focus on ethical value under the vision of leadership, teamwork, effective communication and productivity. *Journal of Risk and Financial Management, 14*(11), 522. DOI: 10.3390/jrfm14110522

Mhlongo, S., Mbatha, K., Ramatsetse, B., & Dlamini, R. (2023). Challenges, opportunities, and prospects of adopting and using smart digital technologies in learning environments: An iterative review. *Heliyon*. Advance online publication. DOI: 10.1016/j.heliyon.2023.e16348 PMID: 37274691

Mitchell, A. (2023). Collaboration technology affordances from virtual collaboration in the time of COVID-19 and post-pandemic strategies. *Information Technology & People*. Advance online publication. DOI: 10.1108/ITP-01-2021-0003

Mogavi, R. H., Deng, C., Kim, J. J., Zhou, P., Kwon, Y. D., Metwally, A. H. S., & Hui, P. (2024). ChatGPT in education: A blessing or a curse? A qualitative study exploring early adopters' utilization and perceptions. *Computers in Human Behavior: Artificial Humans, 2*(1), 100027. DOI: 10.1016/j.chbah.2023.100027

Mukerjee, J., & Metiu, A. (2022). Play and psychological safety: An ethnography of innovative work. *Journal of Product Innovation Management, 39*(3), 394–418. DOI: 10.1111/jpim.12598

Müller, S. (2023). How Slack Facilitates Communication and Collaboration in Seminars and Project-Based Courses. *Journal of Educational Technology Systems*. Advance online publication. DOI: 10.1177/00472395231151910

Neukam, M., & Bollinger, S. (2022). Encouraging creative teams to integrate a sustainable approach to technology. *Journal of Business Research*. Advance online publication. DOI: 10.1016/j.jbusres.2022.05.083

Oo, T. Z., Kadyirov, T., Kadyjrova, L., & Józsa, K. (2024). Design-based learning in higher education: Its effects on students' motivation, creativity and design skills. *Thinking Skills and Creativity*. Advance online publication. DOI: 10.1016/j.tsc.2024.101621

Patricio, R., Moreira, A. C., & Zurlo, F. (2022). Gamification in innovation teams. *International Journal of Innovation Studies*. https://doi.org/DOI: 10.1016/j.ijis.2022.05.003

Peña, J., Bravo, A., del-Río-Ortega, A., Resinas, M., & Ruiz-Cortés, A. (2021, June). Design patterns for board-based collaborative work management tools. In *International Conference on Advanced Information Systems Engineering* (pp. 177-192). Springer International Publishing. DOI: 10.1007/978-3-030-79382-1_11

Podgórska, M. (2022). Challenges and perspectives in innovative projects focused on sustainable industry 4.0—A case study on polish project teams. *Sustainability*. Advance online publication. DOI: 10.3390/su14095334

Radanliev, P., De Roure, D., Novitzky, P., & Sluganovic, I. (2024). Accessibility and inclusiveness of new information and communication technologies for disabled users and content creators in the Metaverse. *Disability and Rehabilitation. Assistive Technology, 19*(5), 1849–1863. DOI: 10.1080/17483107.2023.2241882 PMID: 37585705

Reyes, R. L., Isleta, K. P., Regala, J. D., & Bialba, D. M. R. (2024). Enhancing experiential science learning with virtual labs: A narrative account of merits, challenges, and implementation strategies. *Journal of Computer Assisted Learning, 40*(6), 3167–3186. DOI: 10.1111/jcal.13061

Ruiz-Rojas, L. I., Salvador-Ullauri, L., & Acosta-Vargas, P. (2024). Collaborative working and critical thinking: Adoption of generative artificial intelligence tools in higher education. *Sustainability.* Advance online publication. DOI: 10.3390/su16135367

Saxena, D., & McDonagh, J. (2022). Communication breakdowns during business process change projects–Insights from a sociotechnical case study. *International Journal of Project Management.* Advance online publication. DOI: 10.1016/j.ijproman.2021.11.011

Schrammel, M. (2024). Virtual Social Labs–Requirements and Challenges for Effective Team Collaboration. *Journal of Responsible Technology.* sciencedirect.comDOI: 10.1016/j.jrt.2024.100095

Siltaloppi, J., & Ballardini, R. M. (2023). Promoting systemic collaboration for sustainable innovation through intellectual property rights. *Journal of Co-operative Organization and Management, 11*(1), 100200. DOI: 10.1016/j.jcom.2023.100200

Singh, J., Evans, E., Reed, A., Karch, L., Qualey, K., Singh, L., & Wiersma, H. (2022). Online, hybrid, and face-to-face learning through the eyes of faculty, students, administrators, and instructional designers: Lessons learned and directions for the post-vaccine and post-pandemic/COVID-19 world. *Journal of Educational Technology Systems, 50*(3), 301–326. DOI: 10.1177/00472395211063754

Sjöblom, K., Juutinen, S., & Mäkikangas, A. (2022). The importance of self-leadership strategies and psychological safety for well-being in the context of enforced remote work. *Challenges.* Advance online publication. DOI: 10.3390/challe13010014

Smuck, M., Odonkor, C. A., Wilt, J. K., Schmidt, N., & Swiernik, M. A. (2021). The emerging clinical role of wearables: Factors for successful implementation in healthcare. *NPJ Digital Medicine, 4*(1), 1–8. DOI: 10.1038/s41746-021-00418-3 PMID: 33692479

Stewart, V. R., Snyder, D. G., & Kou, C. Y. (2023). We hold ourselves accountable: A relational view of team accountability. *Journal of Business Ethics.* Advance online publication. DOI: 10.1007/s10551-021-04969-z PMID: 34812211

Stolz, R. C., Blackmon, A. T., Engerman, K., Tonge, L., & McKayle, C. A. (2022). Poised for creativity: Benefits of exposing undergraduate students to creative problem-solving to moderate change in creative self-efficacy and academic achievement. *Journal of Creativity, 32*(2), 100024. DOI: 10.1016/j.yjoc.2022.100024

Stracke, C. M., Burgos, D., Santos-Hermosa, G., Bozkurt, A., Sharma, R. C., Swiatek Cassafieres, C., & Truong, V. (2022). Responding to the initial challenge of the COVID-19 pandemic: Analysis of international responses and impact in school and higher education. *Sustainability, 14*(3), 1876. DOI: 10.3390/su14031876

Suherman, S., & Vidákovich, T. (2022). Assessment of mathematical creative thinking: A systematic review. *Thinking Skills and Creativity*. Advance online publication. DOI: 10.1016/j.tsc.2022.101019

Swargiary, K. (2024). *Redefining reality: My vision for an education rooted in real-world experiences*. Scholar Press.

Taherdoost, H. (2024). Team Building in R&D Projects. In *Innovation through research and development: Strategies for success* (pp. 153–178). Springer Nature Switzerland. DOI: 10.1007/978-3-031-52565-0_8

Tanno, R., Barrett, D. G., Sellergren, A., Ghaisas, S., Dathathri, S., See, A., & Ktena, I. (2024). Collaboration between clinicians and vision–language models in radiology report generation. *Nature Medicine*, 1–10. DOI: 10.1038/s41591-024-03302-1 PMID: 39511432

Tuohy, D., & Wallace, E. (2024). Ensuring effective intercultural communication in the emergency department. *Emergency Nurse*. Advance online publication. DOI: 10.7748/en.2022.e2122 PMID: 35266350

Walton, H., Vindrola-Padros, C., Crellin, N. E., Sidhu, M. S., Herlitz, L., Litchfield, I., & Fulop, N. J. (2022). Patients' experiences of, and engagement with, remote home monitoring services for COVID-19 patients: A rapid mixed-methods study. *Health Expectations, 25*(5), 2386–2404. DOI: 10.1111/hex.13548 PMID: 35796686

Wieland, B., de Wit, J., & de Rooij, A. (2022). Electronic brainstorming with a chatbot partner: A good idea due to increased productivity and idea diversity. *Frontiers in Artificial Intelligence*. Advance online publication. DOI: 10.3389/frai.2022.880673 PMID: 36213166

Wu, T. (2022). Digital project management: Rapid changes define new working environments. *The Journal of Business Strategy*. Advance online publication. DOI: 10.1108/JBS-03-2021-0047

Yates, A., Pedersen Zari, M., Bloomfield, S., Burgess, A., Walker, C., Waghorn, K., & Palmer, F. (2022). A transformative architectural pedagogy and tool for a time of converging crises. *Urban Science (Basel, Switzerland)*, *7*(1), 1. DOI: 10.3390/urbansci7010001

Zamiri, M., & Esmaeili, A. (2024). Strategies, methods, and supports for developing skills within learning communities: A systematic review of the literature. *Administrative Sciences*. Advance online publication. DOI: 10.3390/admsci14090231

Zhang, J., & Chen, Z. (2024). Exploring human resource management digital transformation in the digital age. *Journal of the Knowledge Economy*. Advance online publication. DOI: 10.1007/s13132-023-01214-y PMID: 40479358

Zolfaghari, B., & Madjdi, F. (2022). Building trusting multicultural organizations: Rethinking the influence of culture on interpersonal trust development in the workplace. *Journal of International Management*. Advance online publication. DOI: 10.1016/j.intman.2022.100944

Chapter 4
From Distance to Connection:
Engaging Leadership Development in Virtual Settings

Lily Blocker
https://orcid.org/0000-0003-4354-1897
Stony Brook University, USA

ABSTRACT

This chapter explores the practical and pedagogical strategies for engaging students in virtual teams within management education to prepare future leaders for an increasingly digital and distributed workplace. Drawing on empirical research and original assignments developed from over 15 years of teaching and 5 years of serving as the director of online and in-person MBA programs, the chapter provides instructors with evidence-based, hands-on learning assignments. Assignments are designed around three core learning outcomes: leading effectively, analyzing critically, and acting strategically. The chapter describes specific exercises, including a Media Analysis, Leader Interview Project, Group Dinner, and a Virtual Case Study to illustrate how students can build relationships, share knowledge, and practice leadership in virtual contexts. By embedding real-world relevance and engagement strategies into course design, educators can support the development of impactful leaders who are equipped to thrive in the evolving digital landscape of modern organizations.

DOI: 10.4018/979-8-3373-0375-8.ch004

INTRODUCTION

Designing a modern online course, particularly one focused on virtual teams and leadership, requires an intentional, interactive framework that integrates theoretical learning with hands-on practice and real-world application. This combination is essential for developing and refining the core leadership and collaboration skills students need to succeed in virtual environments. Research consistently underscores that engagement in virtual teams is not something that can be passively assumed; it requires deliberate and sustained efforts, especially when managing the various stages of the virtual team (Purvanova et al., 2021).

To promote sustained engagement, course designs must consider the challenges inherent in virtual teams, such as communication barriers, differing time zones, and varying levels of participation across team members. A well-structured virtual course should not only provide content and assignments but also continuously involve students through regular interaction and feedback loops. Interactive components, such as synchronous and asynchronous discussions, peer feedback, and reflective journaling, provide multiple opportunities for students to engage meaningfully with the course material, their peers, and the practical application of leadership concepts. This constant engagement ensures that students are not just passively absorbing information but are actively involved in a process of learning and development that extends beyond the theoretical to the practical. Engagement in virtual team settings is a dynamic process that must be carefully cultivated from the beginning to the end of the team and projects lifecycle (Panteli, Yalabik, & Rapti, 2019).

To keep students engaged throughout the phases of the course, instructors must employ strategies that facilitate active participation and prevent disengagement. This includes clear and frequent communication, offering flexibility in how students contribute to group work (for example, providing options for synchronous or asynchronous participation), and ensuring that all students feel their voices are heard. Additionally, research shows that the effectiveness of engagement is heavily influenced by the leadership behaviors exhibited within the virtual team. Leaders must be trained to recognize signs of disengagement and employ techniques to bring team members back into the fold, whether through setting clear expectations, fostering trust, or using inclusive decision-making processes (Purvanova et al., 2021). The role of the online instructor becomes that of a virtual team leader, providing ongoing encouragement and guidance to maintain high levels of participation, motivation, and accountability.

Like many online courses, my online MBA Leadership course was developed around the time of the COVID-19 pandemic and has since undergone a great deal of thoughtful revision. The rapid shift to digital learning in the wake of the COVID-19 pandemic highlighted the stark differences between Emergency Remote Teaching

(ERT) and intentionally designed online education. As Hodges and Fowler (2020) emphasize, ERT is a temporary and reactive response, focused on immediate usability rather than long-term effectiveness. Instructors were often required to transition face-to-face content into an online format with little preparation, limited support, and significant resource constraints. The primary concern was maintaining instructional continuity, not creating a high-quality online learning experience. While ERT helped avoid large-scale educational disruption, it also surfaced the limitations of ad hoc digital instruction. Students and faculty alike reported feelings of disconnection, fatigue, and uncertainty. Courses originally designed for in-person engagement often translated poorly to online platforms, revealing the need for a fundamental shift in how virtual education is conceptualized and delivered.

In contrast, effective online teaching must be proactive rather than reactive—rooted in pedagogical intention, thoughtful design, and best practices in virtual learning. Well-developed online courses align learning objectives, assessments, and activities with accessible and inclusive technologies. They are curated thoughtfully to promote active learning, build community, and facilitate regular, substantive interaction with instructors. At institutions like Stony Brook University, we now leverage the publicly available SUNY OSCQR Quality Review rubric to ensure online courses meet high standards of design and delivery.

This transition—from ERT to intentionally designed digital learning—demands time, collaboration, and institutional support. It also requires a reimagining of what virtual learning can offer, not as a substitute for in-person instruction but as a robust, flexible modality in its own right. Faculty development programs, instructional design partnerships, and iterative feedback loops are essential for sustaining this evolution.

Teaching Leadership Online

Effective leadership education must be more than informative—it must be transformational. In online learning environments, where students often balance complex professional, academic, and personal commitments, the design and delivery of instructional content play a crucial role in either enabling or impeding leadership development. For leadership competencies to take root, course materials must be purposefully curated, clearly structured, and explicitly connected to the practical enactment of leadership behaviors and mindsets.

Furthermore, the design of assignments and activities throughout the course should support different stages of the virtual team lifecycle. For example, early stages of team collaboration may focus on building relationships and understanding individual strengths, while later stages may involve deeper, more complex problem-solving and decision-making activities. Assignments that encourage reflection at each stage allow students to engage in self-assessment, analyze their contributions, and adjust as needed. This process encourages critical thinking and continuous improvement, reinforcing the concept that engagement in virtual teams is an evolving process rather than a static event.

In the online MBA course I teach, core assignments such as the Media Analysis, Leader Interview Project, and Group Dinner, and Team Virtual Case Study align with these principles of engagement by requiring students to engage at different levels—individually, with peers, and within virtual team settings. These assignments also allow students to take ownership of their learning, offering opportunities for personal reflection and collaboration. By leveraging a variety of learning modes, from peer feedback and group reflection to real-time case study analysis, the course creates a dynamic and inclusive environment that supports ongoing engagement and skill development throughout the course. In this way, students are better prepared to work effectively in real-world virtual teams, where engagement is critical to success and leadership effectiveness.

Simunich et al. (2024) underscore the importance of framing instructional content not as material to be passively consumed, but as tools to be actively used and applied (p. 87). This distinction is particularly critical in leadership education, where the objective extends beyond comprehension to application in complex, real-world contexts. When resources are presented as optional readings, fragmented videos, or loosely related articles, students—especially those in asynchronous courses—are left to discern what is essential. As Simunich and colleagues warn, "when 'need to know' instructional materials are not clear, students triage and make their own decisions on what to read and what to skip. The danger in this is they might inadvertently skip something that is foundational or crucial" (p. 90).

In the context of leadership development, such ambiguity carries heightened risks. Skipping a foundational reading on psychological safety, for example, may leave students underprepared to lead inclusive teams. Ignoring a reflection prompt on ethical dilemmas may forfeit an opportunity to articulate one's leadership values. Instructional design, therefore, becomes a pedagogical imperative. The curation of course content must not only reduce cognitive overload but also foster the kind of integrative learning that enables students to connect theory to lived leadership practice.

In this chapter, leadership content is designed to function as a bridge between theory and action. Materials are not simply explanatory—they are preparatory. Each resource is selected to support specific competencies and is embedded within an assessment pathway that gives students immediate opportunities to apply their learning. Whether preparing for a leader interview, a team-based case study, or a group dinner, students engage with materials that model the concepts and skills they are expected to demonstrate.

This approach is rooted in a commitment to clarity, equity, and relevance. Content is concise, directly tied to weekly themes, and presented through a variety of formats—including readings, short videos, and reflection prompts—to meet diverse learning preferences. Voices across gender, race, geography, industry, and leadership styles are intentionally included, allowing students to encounter leadership in forms that resonate with their identities and challenge their assumptions. Materials are structured to invite both individual reflection and collaborative inquiry, providing space for critical thinking, feedback, and growth. In the asynchronous MBA leadership course described in this chapter, each week's content includes a limited set of core materials: a short concept video, two to three key readings, and a "prepare-to-apply" activity aligned with a major assignment. For example, prior to the Group Dinner where they practice active listening skills, students read about relational leadership and informal influence, helping them plan how to build trust and cohesion in a virtual team setting.

This instructional design affirms Simunich et al.'s (2024) argument that online education must require students to *do* something with content. Leadership is not memorized—it is practiced. To that end, content is tightly integrated with assignment prompts, performance expectations, and opportunities for feedback. Guides, rubrics, annotated examples, and short "just-in-time" videos scaffold student success. Curated case studies, both real and fictional, offer students opportunities to test leadership theories against dynamic and often ambiguous contexts. Instructor commentary and personalized videos provide additional framing, helping students link abstract principles to concrete professional realities.

Rather than aiming to "cover" as much content as possible, the course design prioritizes depth over breadth. The goal is not to inundate students with information, but to uncover leadership through focused, experiential engagement. This requires deliberate decisions about what to include—and what to omit. Those decisions are grounded in a clear understanding of course competencies and a philosophy of learning that values intentionality, relevance, and application.

This curatorial approach also aligns with broader trends in management education, which increasingly recognize leadership development as nonlinear, iterative, and context-sensitive. Leadership grows through exploration, missteps, reflection, and adaptation. Instructional content must therefore be layered and responsive, offering foundational concepts early and building complexity as students gain confidence and fluency. Open Educational Resources (OER), such as those available through OER Commons, Merlot, or SUNY OER, offer additional flexibility and accessibility, supporting inclusive learning by reducing costs and allowing instructors to tailor materials to the evolving needs of their students. To maintain instructional quality without overwhelming learners, tools like the Wake Forest Workload Estimator can also help ensure that the total time and cognitive load remains manageable. In leadership—as in leadership education—prioritization is a key competency. Educators must model this through thoughtful content selection and pacing.

In sum, curating content for leadership education in online MBA programs requires more than subject-matter expertise. It demands a pedagogical mindset grounded in application, clarity, and developmental growth. By integrating course materials with reflective practice and real-world performance, instructors can prepare students not only to understand leadership—but to enact it meaningfully in the increasingly virtual, complex, and fast-changing environments they will lead.

Applied to instructors, fostering engagement in virtual environments requires a thoughtful, systematic approach that builds over time, aligning with the course's overall learning goals. Rather than viewing each assignment as an isolated task, instructors must consider the course holistically, integrating various elements in ways that support both the individual and collective learning experience. This perspective allows educators to identify key competencies that students need to develop and then design assignments that intentionally target those competencies, scaffolding learning and engagement as students progress through the course.

A well-designed online course takes into account the different phases of the learning process, beginning with creating a foundation for engagement, progressing through deepening interactions, and culminating in opportunities for reflection and application. Early in the course, instructors can focus on setting clear expectations, building rapport, and helping students understand the course structure. These foundational steps are crucial for establishing trust and psychological safety, both of which are necessary for effective engagement (Edmondson, 1999).

Importantly, the structure of assignments should also support the development of soft skills, which are vital for virtual teamwork. These include communication skills, adaptability, conflict resolution, and empathy. Instructors can explicitly design assignments that require students to practice these skills, such as giving and receiving feedback during group projects, providing opportunities for reflection on team interactions, or incorporating peer reviews. By embedding these competencies within assignments, instructors help students gain not only theoretical knowledge but also the practical experience necessary to lead and collaborate effectively in virtual settings.

Instructors also play a pivotal role in sustaining engagement by providing timely, constructive feedback throughout the course. Formative feedback, which focuses on development rather than grades, helps students refine their skills and build confidence in their abilities. For example, feedback on a group dinner activity or media analysis can guide students in understanding how their interactions influence team dynamics and leadership effectiveness. This process of continuous feedback, combined with reflective assignments, helps students internalize lessons and apply them to future collaborative experiences.

Moreover, instructors should remain flexible and responsive to the unique needs of their students, who may come from diverse backgrounds and have different learning preferences and schedules. This adaptability is especially crucial in virtual environments, where students may be balancing multiple commitments or facing challenges in terms of access to technology. Providing a variety of participation options—such as synchronous and asynchronous activities—ensures that all students can engage meaningfully, regardless of their individual circumstances. In this way, instructors create a more inclusive and accessible learning environment that allows students to thrive and actively contribute to the learning community.

Is Your Leadership Course Teaching What You Think It's Teaching?

The digital transition in higher education has brought to light a significant challenge: a widespread disconnect between institutional missions and the actual curriculum, particularly in the domain of leadership development. In *Leadership Reckoning* (Kolditz, Gill, Brown, & Collins, 2021), the authors observe that while leadership is frequently emphasized in university mission statements, strategic plans, and promotional materials, it is rarely accompanied by a coherent, intentional, and measurable approach to its development. This gap is especially concerning in online programs, which are often perceived as less effective in fostering soft skills like leadership. According to Kolditz and colleagues, institutional approaches to leadership development tend to be fragmented and inconsistent, with leadership opportunities scattered across co-curricular activities, workshops, and student clubs, rather than being embedded within a structured curriculum. Without a defined leadership curriculum, clearly articulated competencies, and rigorous methods of assessment, leadership education becomes performative rather than transformative. Consequently, students may graduate from even prestigious institutions without ever receiving direct instruction, feedback, or assessment of their leadership style, ethical decision-making, or interpersonal effectiveness.

The authors also highlight a pervasive absence of evidence-based practices in leadership development programs. While many institutions offer leadership development opportunities, few evaluate their effectiveness or align them with research-backed models from adult development, behavioral science, or organizational psychology. Instead, instructors often rely on anecdotal methods, outdated exercises, or abstract theory, all of which lack the scaffolding necessary for students to internalize and apply leadership skills meaningfully. This failure is not merely a matter of oversight—it reflects a deeper reluctance to treat leadership as a teachable, assessable discipline akin to fields such as finance or operations management. In an era where employers increasingly prioritize emotional intelligence, collaboration, and inclusive leadership, the failure to address this gap in formal education has tangible and far-reaching consequences.

Despite these challenges, online education offers a unique opportunity to bridge this leadership gap—provided that it is designed intentionally. Contrary to outdated assumptions, online platforms possess the flexibility, accessibility, and interactivity necessary to teach, model, and assess leadership development effectively. Virtual environments provide students with the opportunity to engage in leadership practice asynchronously, across geographic, industry, and cultural boundaries—thereby reflecting the distributed and hybrid team dynamics they will encounter in professional settings.

LEARNING OBJECTIVES FOR MY LEADERSHIP COURSE

By creating a curriculum that is intentional, structured, and aligned with the needs of both students and employers, educators can ensure that leadership education remains relevant and effective in preparing future leaders for the challenges of an increasingly digital world. The assignments for this course were designed with three learning objectives. First, students would learn effective leadership skills by being able to correctly identify and apply evidence-based best practices in leadership. The second learning objective was the ability to analyze well. Specifically, students would analyze events for problem solving and interpret information using concepts from class and think critically about why they are occurring. Finally, as future leaders themselves, they would need to be able to act on the information they were learning. The third learning objective was for them to be able to deliver valuable recommendations and feedback, which would improve others' performance through appropriate analysis and carefully communicated strategies. The assignments also included the higher order goals of the MBA program, including formulating ethical policies, formulating a compelling audience in writing and oral communication, and working effectively to collaborate as a team. In short, students would be expected to act as effective leaders and team members after completing the class.

In this chapter, I will present several examples of assignments that I have developed and tested in my online MBA Leadership classes at a large, public university over the past five years. In addition to teaching the online MBA class, I am also the director of both our online and in-person MBA programs, and have taught Leadership for over 15 years. These classes typically enroll 60 students, most of whom are located within driving distance of the university but opt for fully asynchronous learning for various reasons, such as work schedules, commuting, or a preference for more flexible, autonomous learning. It is important to recognize that many of these students prefer virtual communication methods, even when in-person or hybrid formats are available. This highlights a key aspect of the virtual team dynamics often present in modern higher education (Hincapie & Hill, 2024). Having the majority of the students locally allows us to invite them for occasional in-person optional events or activities that support the community feel of the program.

Throughout the course, I frame leadership as a practice rather than a position, emphasizing that leadership is not defined by a title or personality trait, but by behaviors and decisions. This approach encourages students to reflect on and analyze their own leadership experiences, regardless of whether they hold formal authority. By exploring both personal and observed leadership practices, the course underscores that leadership is accessible to all individuals in various contexts. Additionally, the course integrates feedback loops and reflective exercises to help students build emotional intelligence and resilience—crucial traits for effective leadership. Notably, the assignments described below serve as vehicles for fostering this emotional growth, encouraging students to engage with each other in meaningful, reflective ways that cultivate their leadership potential. In the next sections, I highlight four key assignments in the course, which are part of a larger assessment strategy that includes many smaller writing and reflection assignments throughout the course. These four assignments include a media analysis, leader interview paper, group dinner, and team case study. I assign the media analysis three times early on in the class, and usually have the group dinner just after the add/drop date early in the semester as well. The other two assignments, the leader interview and case study, are towards the end of the semester as culminating projects but I introduce the leader interview paper assignment right away to give students the most time to schedule their interview with a leader. I describe each of these assignments in more detail in the following sections.

MEDIA ANALYSIS ASSIGNMENTS

The Media Analysis Assignments serve as foundational exercises that scaffold students' ability to think critically and communicate effectively about leadership and team dynamics in real-world contexts. Completed three times throughout the semester, these short assignments mirror the structure and analytical expectations of the culminating Leader Interview Project, providing students with repeated, lower-stakes opportunities to build and refine the core competencies of observation, analysis, and giving recommendations that are also mirrored in the more high stakes leader interview project at the end of the semester.

For each media analysis, students select a recent public example—published within the month—featuring a specific leader in action. Acceptable media formats include news articles, podcasts, YouTube videos, TV or movie clips, and blogs, among others. Importantly, students must focus on an individual leader rather than an organization, as the assignment emphasizes behavioral and theoretical analysis over descriptive summary.

Each media analysis submission follows a consistent structure that encourages precision and rigor in student writing. Students begin with a brief summary of the selected leadership situation, limited to no more than five sentences. This exercise develops their ability to distill complex material into a clear and concise narrative, a key competency in business communication. The core of the assignment centers on analysis: students are required to examine the selected leadership example using at least two distinct theoretical concepts introduced in class or through the course readings. These concepts must be explicitly identified and applied with specificity to demonstrate a deep understanding of their definitions, mechanisms, and implications. Beyond interpretation, students are asked to formulate a behavioral recommendation that addresses a key leadership challenge or opportunity highlighted in their analysis. This recommendation must be grounded in course theory, encouraging students to not only critique but also propose constructive solutions rooted in evidence-based practices. Finally, students must meet formatting requirements that reflect professional communication standards. This includes adhering to a two-page, double-spaced limit, using APA-style in-text citations, and providing a functional hyperlink to the media source. These formal elements reinforce attention to detail and academic integrity, while also simulating the kind of polished deliverables expected in professional environments.

By engaging with current, dynamic examples, students strengthen their analytical thinking, written communication, and theoretical application skills. The brevity of the assignment encourages conciseness and precision—traits critical in business writing—while repeated iterations allow students to incorporate feedback and improve over time.

Just as important, the Media Analysis Assignments help students test academic concepts against the unpredictability and complexity of real leadership scenarios. Whether analyzing Elon Musk's public communications, Whitney Wolfe Herd's leadership narrative in a podcast, or fictional depictions of team motivation in films, students must determine how well leadership theories map onto actual practice. In doing so, they learn to identify not only congruence but also gaps, tensions, and contradictions between leadership ideals and lived behavior.

The Media Analysis Assignments are especially valuable for students in virtual team settings because they enhance the ability to observe, analyze, and respond to leadership behaviors remotely. In virtual teams, where face-to-face interactions are limited, understanding leadership dynamics through media examples allows students to develop key skills for managing relationships and influence in a digital environment. By analyzing how leaders navigate challenges such as communication barriers, team engagement, and decision-making across distances, students gain insights into the complexities of leading virtual teams. These assignments teach students to apply leadership theories in contexts that mirror the distributed, asynchronous, and often fragmented nature of virtual team interactions. Additionally, by engaging with diverse media forms—such as podcasts, news articles, or video interviews—students build the versatility required to analyze leadership across various virtual communication platforms, preparing them to lead or support virtual teams in their professional careers. Allowing them to choose the industry or topic of the media also creates greater inclusion for whatever the students' interests in leadership are.

This iterative practice also prepares students to approach the more demanding Leader Interview Project with greater confidence, depth, and analytical fluency. The structure of the media assignments—summary, analysis, and recommendation—intentionally mirrors that of the final paper, allowing students to internalize a consistent analytical framework over time. This scaffolded repetition is especially important in leadership education, where students must move beyond memorizing definitions to recognizing patterns, diagnosing behaviors, and articulating grounded insights. By engaging repeatedly in structured analysis of leadership as portrayed in real-world or media-based contexts, students develop not only familiarity with key theoretical models but also the ability to apply those models with increasing precision and sophistication. Much of leadership is reading "between the lines" of what motivates others' behaviors.

This low-stakes, high-frequency format also supports *deliberate practice*, a critical condition for skill development in complex domains such as leadership. Students are not expected to master analysis in their first attempt; instead, they are encouraged to experiment with different approaches, receive formative feedback, and recalibrate their thinking across the three assignments. This feedback loop helps refine their ability to interpret behavior through theoretical lenses, improve the clarity and professionalism of their writing, and articulate recommendations that are both actionable and grounded in course content. As a result, students build confidence not only in their understanding of leadership theory but also in their ability to communicate insights persuasively to a business audience.

Moreover, this iterative process supports several of the core competencies emphasized in the course. Each media analysis reinforces students' capacity to extract meaning from complex leadership situations, translate abstract theory into accessible language, and make informed, critical judgments about leader effectiveness. These are the same skills required for the Leader Interview Project, but exercised here in a controlled, manageable format that reduces performance anxiety and increases engagement.

By the time students arrive at the Leader Interview Project, they have already developed their ability to do leadership analysis: they know how to frame a situation concisely, identify the relevant theoretical frameworks, and offer recommendations rooted in both evidence and empathy. What changes in the final project is the complexity of the task—not the structure itself. Students must now apply these same competencies in a live, interactive setting, requiring deeper synthesis, greater interpretive nuance, and real-time interpersonal skills. In this way, the Media Analysis Assignments serve as both rehearsal and runway: preparing students to meet the demands of the final paper with clarity and confidence.

LEADER INTERVIEW PROJECT

Leadership education is most transformative when students are immersed in experiences that bridge theoretical frameworks with real-world practice. In this paper, students identify a practicing leader, conduct a behavioral interview, and analyze the leader's strategies and challenges using conceptual tools introduced throughout the course. In doing so, students engage in a multi-layered process of inquiry, reflection, and strategic feedback that deepens their understanding of leadership as both a relational and organizational practice.

The assignment builds directly upon the Media Analysis Assignments, which serve as preliminary training in leadership observation and theoretical analysis. Having already completed three media analyses—each involving real-time application of class concepts to public examples—students approach the interview project with a well-developed ability to identify relevant leadership behaviors, apply course concepts with accuracy, and synthesize findings into a clear argument. The Leader Interview Project thus represents both a culmination of these earlier exercises and an extension into a more complex and interactive context.

Students are encouraged to select a leader in a field of personal or professional interest—preferably someone outside of their immediate circle. The leader should hold a position of influence with at least two direct reports or followers. While students are not penalized for interviewing someone they already know, they are urged to use this assignment as an opportunity to build new professional relationships. Past students have successfully leveraged the assignment to gain introductions through mutual contacts or through cold outreach on platforms like LinkedIn. Many report that the interview opened doors to internships, mentorships, and even job offers. These outcomes underscore the developmental value of the assignment, which extends well beyond the paper itself.

The project develops applied analytical thinking, strategic communication, and professional relationship-building. By initiating contact with experienced professionals and structuring a one-on-one interview, students cultivate real-world interpersonal competencies. These skills, previously rehearsed through media analysis in written form, are now practiced in live interaction—initiating dialogue, managing professional tone, and asking targeted, follow-up questions. These experiences are foundational not only for effective leadership, but also for consulting, organizational diagnostics, and stakeholder engagement.

Engaging in direct conversation with a leader requires students to exercise a unique combination of interpersonal, analytical, and strategic thinking skills. Interviewing someone in a position of power or influence builds students' confidence and communication precision, challenging them to listen actively, ask follow-up questions in real time, and maintain a focused yet conversational tone. This process simulates real-world scenarios such as informational interviews, stakeholder meetings, and client consultations, thereby preparing students for high-stakes professional interactions.

Students also strengthen their sense-making abilities, learning how to interpret not only what is said, but also what is implied or omitted. Leaders often express their practices through storytelling, metaphor, or strategic language. Students must parse these narratives for patterns, underlying values, and leadership habits, which requires a combination of emotional intelligence and critical thinking. These skills, initially developed through media analysis, become deeper and more nuanced when exercised in real-time conversation.

A central challenge—and benefit—of the assignment lies in the act of synthesis. Students must integrate firsthand accounts with scholarly literature, making connections between lived experience and theoretical frameworks. Students are tasked not only with summarizing the leader's behavior, but also with interpreting it through the lens of leadership science. For example, they may ask: What does this leader's approach reveal about how power operates in their organization? How do their decisions reflect (or contradict) best practices for motivating teams? Where do their actions align with the course readings, and where do they diverge?

The act of writing this synthesis sharpens students' capacity for structured thinking and strategic communication. They must construct a compelling argument, supported by evidence from both the interview and course texts. Rather than presenting a glowing summary, the goal is to offer a critical, nuanced, and evidence-based interpretation of leadership behavior.

The interview project asks students to test theory versus reality. While the media assignments expose students to curated or dramatized leadership behaviors, the interview paper introduces messier, more ambiguous contexts. The classroom offers conceptual clarity: models are linear, outcomes are measurable, and leadership behaviors are often presented in idealized form. But organizations are messy, and leaders face conflicting priorities, systemic constraints, and human fallibility. This assignment invites students to confront that complexity. For example, a leader may espouse a commitment to inclusivity but operate within a company culture that does not reward dissent. A leader may value transparency yet struggle with how much to share during organizational crises. By examining such tensions, students gain a richer understanding of what leadership actually entails: navigating ambiguity, making tradeoffs, and exercising judgment under pressure.

The final portion of the paper requires students to generate evidence-based recommendations for the leader. This component builds students' ability to provide constructive and actionable feedback—a key competency in leadership and consulting. The recommendations must be tailored to the leader's context and reflect both a respect for their experience and a command of course content. In formulating these suggestions, students practice balancing critique with empathy, and rigor with relevance. Importantly, the students write the recommendations after some reflection and do not actually provide the recommendations to the leader they interviewed as part of the assignment. Both the leader and the student are reminded that the paper is confidential, and the students are allowed to use pseudonyms for the leader and organization if they wish.

In an online leadership course, this project provides students with the opportunity to engage directly with leaders who are navigating the complexities of leading in digital or hybrid environments. In virtual teams, leadership often requires unique approaches to communication, trust-building, and decision-making that differ from traditional, co-located settings. The interview project allows students to gain firsthand insight into these challenges by speaking with leaders who may be actively managing teams remotely or across different time zones. This direct interaction with leaders equips students with a deeper understanding of how leadership theories play out in virtual contexts and offers a real-world perspective on the skills and strategies that are effective in remote environments.

Additionally, the option of interviewing leaders remotely mirrors the types of interactions students are likely to experience in their own professional roles within virtual or distributed teams. It helps students build critical virtual communication competencies such as active listening, questioning, and managing professional tone through digital mediums. These skills are indispensable in virtual team settings, where non-verbal cues are limited, and effective communication requires heightened attention to clarity, empathy, and precision.

Moreover, the Leader Interview Project empowers students to explore how leaders in virtual settings manage issues such as fostering engagement without face-to-face interaction, maintaining team cohesion across distances, and cultivating a strong organizational culture in a decentralized work environment. By examining these real-world scenarios, students not only deepen their theoretical knowledge but also learn how to adapt leadership strategies to the unique challenges of virtual teams. This project equips them with practical insights and strategies that they can apply in their own future virtual leadership roles, enhancing their preparedness to lead and collaborate in the increasingly digital, remote-focused professional landscape.

Taken together, the Media Analysis Assignments and the Leader Interview Project constitute a developmental arc within the course. Beginning with brief, structured opportunities to analyze leadership in the public sphere, and culminating in an extended engagement with a real-life leader, students build the analytical, interpersonal, and critical thinking skills necessary to thrive in complex professional environments. By testing theory against lived experience, learning to ask better questions, and translating observation into insight, students move from practice to mastery. They begin to see themselves not only as students of leadership, but as reflective practitioners capable of discerning patterns, articulating strategies, and offering meaningful, grounded feedback.

LEADERSHIP DEVELOPMENT DINNER

Early in the semester students are randomly assigned in groups for the Leadership Development Dinner, an experience that introduces students to the foundational practices of trust-building, authentic dialogue, and narrative-based leadership. I created this assignment to address a persistent challenge in both online and face-to-face leadership development programs: how to create meaningful connection in environments that often default to transactional or surface-level interaction. By positioning conversation as both a leadership skill and a pedagogical method, this exercise invites students into a shared developmental space where storytelling, vulnerability, and presence are encouraged.

The Leadership Development Dinner is particularly important in the context of virtual or hybrid MBA programs, where relationship-building can be hindered by physical distance and asynchronous communication. Research on virtual team dynamics underscores that trust is not only central to collaboration and performance but also more difficult to cultivate when team members lack opportunities for spontaneous, informal connection (Mutha & Srivastava, 2021). Students are randomly assigned into small groups and asked to coordinate a shared conversation, ideally over a meal or virtual meeting, and then write a reflection paper. Students are asked to bring their whole selves—professional histories, personal values, struggles, and aspirations—into a psychologically safe space created by the explicitly established shared norms of respect, confidentiality, and empathy.

The conversation is guided by a set of questions that are designed to elicit introspection and disclosure. These questions were inspired by Aron et al. (1997), whose research demonstrated that having pairs of people ask each other more and more vulnerable questions could rapidly deepen their bonds. Much like those classic experiments, this dinner exercise encourages students to engage in "big talk"—conversations marked not by resume-style achievements but by reflections on leadership challenges, tensions, and long-term goals. Questions such as "What have you rebelled against in your career?" or "What would you like people to say about you when you retire?" are not just prompts for discussion but invitations into peer empathy.

Each participant, whether moderating or responding, practices critical skills that are central to effective leadership: active listening, perspective-taking, emotional regulation, and story-telling. As students talk together, they are asked to reflect not only on the events themselves, but on what those events mean for their identity as leaders. In doing so, they engage in the kind of reflective processing that adult learning theory identifies as essential for transformative development. This approach is aligned with Kolditz et al.'s (2021) call for a more rigorous, practice-oriented model of leadership education—one in which students are not passive consumers of theory but active participants in their own leadership formation.

Student group facilitators are selected based on alphabetical order (whose first name is first in the alphabet) and tasked with ensuring that all voices are heard and that the group remains focused on the goal of depth over breadth. Students are encouraged to take their time with each question, to ask one another follow-up questions such as "How do you know that?" or "Can you give an example?", and to resist the urge to jump ahead or shift topics too quickly. This structure reinforces the importance of presence and attentiveness, which are especially critical in virtual leadership contexts where cues like body language and tone may be muted or distorted. As Raghuram et al. (2019) note, the quality of attentional presence in virtual settings is strongly correlated with team engagement and cohesion. Thus, the dinner also functions as a rehearsal space for practicing virtual leadership skills in real time.

Students often report that the dinner experience fundamentally changes their approach to the rest of the course. Many describe a comfort and connection in group projects that follow, and some maintain relationships with their dinner groups throughout the semester or even across the entire program. Several students have told me that speaking about their professional struggles helps to reframe those experiences in a more constructive light. The act of naming one's challenges—particularly in front of empathetic peers—can recontextualize setbacks as sources of insight and resilience, thus reinforcing a growth-oriented leadership mindset (Han & Stieha, 2020; Owens & Hekman, 2012; Rogers, Christian, Jennings, & Lanaj, 2023).

The assignment culminates in a two-page reflection paper in which students synthesize what they learned during the dinner, drawing on both peer contributions and their own self-reflections. Students are asked not to use their peers' names, but to refer to others with neutral phrases such as "one of my group members," reinforcing the importance of confidentiality and mutual respect. The paper should integrate specific comments and insights that resonated with the student, and include a third page containing a group photo or screenshot of the meeting.

For students who are unable to attend due to extenuating circumstances, a written alternative is available. In this version, students write a four-page reflection addressing each of the questions. While this format lacks the interpersonal dynamics of the group experience, it preserves the assignment's core goals of self-reflection, narrative formation, and leadership identity development and is a backup option if the group is unable to meet. However, in a class of 60 typically only a few people end up taking the written alternative option as the groups usually do want to meet each other. Ultimately, this assignment builds trust, fosters inclusion, and helps students lead with authenticity in a world where these qualities are urgently needed.

VIRTUAL TEAM CASE STUDY

Finally, the Virtual Team Case Study assignment is designed to help students practice the unique communication barriers in virtual team projects. This assignment simulates real-world conditions by requiring teams to collaborate remotely to solve a leadership challenge presented in a business case. Teams are given limited time—just 40 minutes—to analyze the case and develop a solution. This time pressure mirrors the reality many virtual teams face, where decision-making must often be swift, and collaboration must occur efficiently despite the absence of immediate physical cues. The structure of this assignment encourages students to communicate clearly and effectively under time constraints, a vital skill in virtual leadership. Additionally, it challenges students to engage in rapid problem-solving, making decisive contributions even when the group lacks the luxury of lengthy in-person discussions. Finally, this assignment also takes advantage of archive capability, the ability to record electronically and track the team process as it occurs (Nemiro, 2002). Specifically, I ask teams to make recordings of their synchronous team session so they can refer back to specific behaviors when giving team members feedback.

Before the group meeting, each student is required to complete an individual analysis of the case. This step serves as an essential component of the learning process, teaching students the value of coming prepared to a group meeting with limited time. Preparation and individual accountability are essential in virtual teams, where remote participants do not rely on informal, spontaneous interactions that often occur in physical settings. It also encourages students to reflect on the case independently and develop their own insights before engaging with the group.

Another critical feature of the leaderless format is that it allows students to experience and experiment with various leadership roles within the group. In virtual teams, leadership is not always exercised by one person in a traditional hierarchical manner. Instead, effective virtual leadership often involves emergent leadership, where leadership responsibilities are distributed based on the needs of the team at any given moment (Hoch & Dulebohn, 2017; Charlier, Stewart, Greco, & Reeves, 2016). Some students may take on more of a facilitator role, guiding the discussion and ensuring that all voices are heard, while others may assume a strategic role, driving the analysis and solution development. This flexibility in leadership styles reflects the fluidity required in virtual teams, where traditional leadership roles can be less defined and more dynamic (Purvanova et al., 2021). This assignment encourages students to adapt their leadership behaviors to meet the needs of the team, making them better prepared for future leadership roles in virtual environments.

In addition, the innovation component of the assignment challenges students to think creatively within the context of the case. Students are asked to propose a novel solution or improvement for the organization within the case, testing their ability to apply critical thinking and innovation to real-world business challenges. This section of the assignment encourages students to push beyond conventional solutions and come up with new, viable strategies that could lead to more efficient and effective team or organizational outcomes.

Finally, the assignment includes a debriefing session immediately following the case group meeting. During the debrief, students reflect on their team dynamics, individual contributions, and the effectiveness of their communication using provided questions. This reflection process allows students to engage in self-assessment and peer feedback, which helps them improve their future teamwork and leadership capabilities. The ability to offer and receive constructive feedback in a virtual setting is crucial, as it enhances empathy, emotional intelligence, and the ability to provide actionable advice—all essential skills for leading virtual teams. Research supports this, noting that trust is essential for collaboration in virtual teams, but knowledge sharing is a more direct driver of team effectiveness (Alsharo et al., 2017; Blay et al., 2023). Through this retrospective reflection, students learn how to navigate the nuances of virtual communication and adjust their approach to enhance team performance.

Reflecting on team performance after the completion of the assignment also helps bridge the gap between virtual communication and in-person feedback processes. In a virtual environment, nonverbal cues—such as body language, tone of voice, or immediate facial expressions—are often missing, making real-time feedback more challenging and less intuitive (Lurey & Raisinghani, 2001). By conducting a team debrief, students can engage in a structured review that compensates for these communication gaps, allowing for a clearer understanding of how individual contributions fit into the collective efforts (Handke, Klonek, O'Neill, & Kerschreiter, 2022).

Research on after-event reviews (AERs) supports the idea that reflection improves team learning, enhances problem-solving skills, and strengthens future collaboration (Ellis & Davidi, 2005; Ellis, Mendel, & Nir, 2006). This is especially pertinent in virtual settings, where team members may have less immediate feedback from their peers. AERs facilitate a meta-cognitive process, enabling students to critically analyze their individual and team behaviors, the dynamics of their virtual collaboration, and areas for improvement. These reflective exercises help mitigate the risk of miscommunication, disengagement, or misunderstanding that can arise in virtual teams due to the absence of face-to-face interaction. Additionally, the group reflection exercise in virtual teams fosters psychological safety, a critical element for effective collaboration. In a virtual environment, trust-building takes longer and is more challenging than in traditional, co-located teams (Malhotra, Majchrzak, & Rosen, 2007; Raghuram, Hill, Gibbs, & Maruping, 2019; Shockley, Allen, Dodd, & Waiwood, 2021). A structured debrief provides a safe space for students to openly discuss their experiences, mistakes, and successes without fear of judgment. Psychological safety has been shown to enhance team learning by allowing members to share candid feedback and explore differences of opinion without the threat of conflict (Edmondson, 1999). This kind of safe, open communication is vital in virtual teams where the physical distance can create a sense of isolation, hindering authentic dialogue.

The debrief also provides an opportunity to reflect on the level of dependability and motivation within the team. Research suggests that virtual teams often struggle with issues of accountability due to the lack of daily face-to-face interaction (Alsharo et al., 2017). Reflecting on these aspects during the debrief allows students to evaluate how well they followed through on their commitments and whether they engaged actively in the problem-solving process. Moreover, virtual teams require flexibility and adaptability in leadership roles, and the reflection portion allows students to assess how leadership emerged organically during the collaboration. Reflecting on who naturally took charge and how leadership roles shifted based on task needs helps students understand that leadership in virtual teams is dynamic and responsive (Purvanova et al., 2021). By analyzing their leadership behaviors and the leadership actions of others, students are better prepared to manage leadership transitions in future virtual team settings.

By engaging in a retrospective analysis, students evaluate what worked well in their collaborative process and what did not. This review helps identify root causes of challenges such as delays in decision-making or unclear task assignments, and helps students recognize how they can improve their virtual collaboration strategies moving forward. The process fosters analytical skills as students critically assess their interactions and draw connections between their team dynamics and the leadership principles learned throughout the course. Through the debrief, students also learn to recognize the importance of adapting their leadership styles in response to the team's evolving needs. This reinforces the class's emphasis on adaptive leadership, a key competency in both virtual and real-world team settings, where challenges may arise unexpectedly and require flexible, situational leadership responses.

The reflection exercise also helps to strengthen feedback delivery skills, which are essential for virtual leaders. In remote teams, providing clear, constructive, and actionable feedback requires a higher degree of emotional intelligence and communication precision. Virtual team members cannot rely on the immediate cues of body language or tone that come with in-person communication. The debriefing process gives students the chance to practice delivering feedback in a thoughtful, tactful manner, ensuring that it is both empathetic and constructive (Marlow, Lacerenza, & Salas, 2017). This is essential for maintaining trust and motivation in virtual teams, where miscommunications or poorly delivered feedback can easily escalate into conflict.

The four core assignments in my online course—media analysis, group dinner, leader interview, and team virtual case study—are designed to foster individual and collective leadership development within virtual environments. The media analysis builds foundational skills in applying leadership theory to real-world examples, promoting independent critical thinking. The group dinner emphasizes relationship-building and communication through informal peer interaction and constructive feedback. The leader interview bridges theory and practice by helping students engage with professionals, refine digital communication, and reflect on leadership adaptability. Finally, the virtual case study serves as a capstone, requiring real-time collaboration and reflection, mirroring real-world virtual team dynamics. Together, these assignments integrate theory, practice, and feedback to cultivate essential leadership skills for virtual settings.

INCLUSIVITY, FLEXIBILITY, AND PRACTICE

In designing virtual team assignments, it is crucial to take into account the diversity of student backgrounds, schedules, and communication preferences. The assignments in the course should be thoughtfully structured to accommodate these varying needs while still achieving the course's overarching learning outcomes. By offering students different ways to contribute based on their individual strengths, interests, and availability, the assignments not only foster inclusivity but also ensure that every student can engage meaningfully in the learning process.

For example, the Group Dinner assignment offers both synchronous and asynchronous options, ensuring that students from different time zones or those with varying personal schedules can still participate. The primary goal of this assignment—building relationships and trust—remains intact regardless of whether students are engaging in real-time discussions or contributing asynchronously. The flexibility in format acknowledges the challenge of coordinating group activities in a virtual environment, where logistical constraints are often a barrier to collaboration. This flexibility encourages students to engage in ways that align with their strengths and availability, thus fostering an inclusive learning environment. The ability to collaborate effectively with peers, regardless of their backgrounds or time constraints, mirrors the adaptive leadership skills necessary in virtual workplaces, where teams are often geographically dispersed.

The structure of the assignments in this course also provides ample opportunities for practice, which is essential to skill development. In virtual settings, where face-to-face interactions are limited, students need varied avenues to apply leadership competencies actively. Throughout the course, students are prompted to engage with the material via discussion posts, scenario-based reflections, and peer reviews—each of which provides them with a chance to practice the skills and knowledge they are acquiring. For instance, in the Team Virtual Case Study, students must navigate a complex leadership challenge, working collaboratively with teammates to analyze the case, propose solutions, and reflect on their group dynamics. This assignment, with its combination of synchronous and asynchronous components, allows students to refine both their analytical skills and their ability to work within teams. The debriefing and feedback processes help solidify the learning by encouraging students to reflect on what went well and what could be improved, which is critical in developing leadership skills that will be useful in real-world virtual settings.

Moreover, the course assignments encourage students to explore leadership challenges that resonate personally with their identities, industries, or professional aspirations. By allowing students to connect course content to their own experiences, the assignments become more than just academic exercises; they become opportunities for students to explore their own leadership styles, values, and goals. For example, in the Leader Interview Project, students engage directly with a leader from their chosen field, allowing them to gain insights into leadership practices specific to their area of interest. This personal connection to course material makes the learning process more inclusive and relevant, as students are encouraged to draw from their own professional journeys and challenges. By addressing leadership challenges that are specific to their industries or aspirations, students gain a deeper, more nuanced understanding of leadership that aligns with their career goals and professional identities.

Furthermore, faculty play a pivotal role in creating an inclusive learning environment that honors the diverse perspectives students bring to virtual collaboration. In a virtual classroom, where students may be interacting with peers from different cultural, professional, and geographical backgrounds, it is essential that the course encourages open dialogue and values varied viewpoints. The assignments, by nature, promote this inclusivity by encouraging students to collaborate with peers in ways that leverage their unique perspectives and skills. Faculty facilitate this process by providing flexible pathways for students to meet the learning objectives, recognizing that the diverse backgrounds of students require varied approaches to collaboration and leadership development. By supporting flexible contributions and encouraging self-reflection, faculty ensure that students can engage with the material in a way that feels personally relevant and inclusive, ultimately leading to more meaningful and impactful learning experiences.

In this way, the assignments in an effective online leadership course do not just teach students about leadership in theory; they create real opportunities for students to practice leadership in ways that are flexible, inclusive, and personally relevant. Whether it is through the diverse participation options in the Group Dinner, the real-world application in the Team Virtual Case Study, or the individual insights gained through the Leader Interview Project, each assignment is carefully designed to support the development of leadership skills in a virtual environment. These assignments also foster greater student engagement by encouraging active participation and self-reflection, and by providing meaningful opportunities for practice that align with students' professional interests and aspirations. Ultimately, the course fosters an environment where students not only learn about leadership but also develop the practical skills needed to lead in a virtual world—skills that are adaptable, inclusive, and informed by their personal and professional experiences.

CONCLUSION

Evaluating and assessing students' virtual collaboration skills requires a nuanced approach that goes beyond simply assigning group projects. It involves designing assignments that not only measure students' ability to work together but also foster the development of key competencies such as trust-building, knowledge sharing, leadership, and effective communication. Thoughtfully structured virtual team assignments—such as the Media Analysis, Leader Interview Project, Group Dinner, and Team Virtual Case Study—serve as platforms for students to demonstrate and refine these skills. By embedding opportunities for peer feedback and self-reflection, educators create a low-stakes environment where students can evaluate their own contributions and assess how their behaviors influence team dynamics. This feedback loop is crucial for fostering continuous growth, as it mirrors the iterative nature of professional collaboration and performance reviews.

As virtual work becomes increasingly prevalent, management education has a responsibility to equip students with the tools and insights they need to lead and collaborate effectively in digital environments. Through carefully designed assignments, educators can assess not only students' academic knowledge but also their ability to engage with diverse teams, navigate challenges, and contribute to collective success. By embedding engagement strategies throughout the course design, instructors can bridge the gap between virtual distance and real-world connection, creating a student experience that is both immersive and transformative. Ultimately, by emphasizing the development of virtual collaboration skills and fostering an environment of continuous feedback and self-reflection, educators prepare students to thrive in the evolving landscape of virtual leadership and teamwork.

REFERENCES

Alsharo, M., Gregg, D., & Ramirez, R. (2017). Virtual team effectiveness: The role of knowledge sharing and trust. *Information & Management*, *54*, 479–490. DOI: 10.1016/j.im.2016.10.005

Aron, A., Melinat, E., Aron, E. N., Vallone, R. D., & Bator, R. J. (1997). The experimental generation of interpersonal closeness: A procedure and some preliminary findings. *Personality and Social Psychology Bulletin*, *23*(4), 363–377. DOI: 10.1177/0146167297234003

Blay, T., Froese, F. J., Taras, V., & Gunkel, M. (2023). Convergence of collaborative behavior in virtual teams: The role of external crises and implications for performance. *The Journal of Applied Psychology*, *109*(4), 469–489. DOI: 10.1037/apl0001133 PMID: 37917493

Charlier, S. D., Stewart, G. L., Greco, L. M., & Reeves, C. J. (2016). Emergent leadership in virtual teams: A multilevel investigation of individual communication and team dispersion antecedents. *The Leadership Quarterly*, *27*(5), 745–764. DOI: 10.1016/j.leaqua.2016.05.002

Edmondson, A. (1999). Psychological safety and learning behavior in work teams. *Administrative Science Quarterly*, *44*(2), 350–383. DOI: 10.2307/2666999

Ellis, S., & Davidi, I. (2005). After-event reviews: Drawing lessons from successful and failed experience. *The Journal of Applied Psychology*, *90*(5), 857–871. DOI: 10.1037/0021-9010.90.5.857 PMID: 16162059

Ellis, S., Mendel, R., & Nir, M. (2006). Learning from successful and failed experience: The moderating role of kind of after-event review. *The Journal of Applied Psychology*, *91*(3), 669–680. DOI: 10.1037/0021-9010.91.3.669 PMID: 16737362

Han, S. J., & Stieha, V. (2020). Growth mindset for human resource development: A scoping review of the literature with recommended interventions. *Human Resource Development Review*, *19*(3), 309–331. DOI: 10.1177/1534484320939739

Handke, L., Klonek, F., O'Neill, T. A., & Kerschreiter, R. (2022). Unpacking the role of feedback in virtual team effectiveness. *Small Group Research*, *53*(1), 41–87. DOI: 10.1177/10464964211057116

Hincapie, M. X., & Hill, N. S. (2024). The Impact of Team Virtuality on the Performance of On-Campus Student Teams. *Academy of Management Learning & Education*, *23*(1), 158–175. DOI: 10.5465/amle.2022.0397

Hoch, J. E., & Dulebohn, J. H. (2017). Team personality composition, emergent leadership and shared leadership in virtual teams: A theoretical framework. *Human Resource Management Review, 27*(4), 678–693. DOI: 10.1016/j.hrmr.2016.12.012

Hodges, C. B., & Fowler, D. J. (2020). The covid-19 crisis and faculty members in higher education: From emergency remote teaching to better teaching through reflection. *International Journal of Multidisciplinary Perspectives in Higher Education, 5*(1), 118–122.

Kolditz, T. A., Gill, L., Brown, R. P., & Collins, J. (2021). *Leadership reckoning: Can higher education develop the leaders we need?* Monocle Press.

Lurey, J., & Raisinghani, M. (2001). An empirical study of best practices in virtual teams. *Information & Management, 38*, 523–544. DOI: 10.1016/S0378-7206(01)00074-X

Marlow, S. L., Lacerenza, C. N., & Salas, E. (2017). Communication in virtual teams: A conceptual framework and research agenda. *Human Resource Management Review, 27*(4), 575–589. DOI: 10.1016/j.hrmr.2016.12.005

Mutha, P., & Srivastava, M. (2021). Decoding leadership to leverage employee engagement in virtual teams. *The International Journal of Organizational Analysis*. Advance online publication. DOI: 10.1108/ijoa-07-2021-2856

Nemiro, J. E. (2002). The creative process in virtual teams. *Creativity Research Journal, 14*(1), 69–83. DOI: 10.1207/S15326934CRJ1401_6

Owens, B. P., & Hekman, D. R. (2012). Modeling how to grow: An inductive examination of humble leader behaviors, contingencies, and outcomes. *Academy of Management Journal, 55*(4), 787–818. DOI: 10.5465/amj.2010.0441

Panteli, N., Yalabik, Z., & Rapti, A. (2019). Fostering work engagement in geographically-dispersed and asynchronous virtual teams. *Information Technology & People, 32*, 2–17. DOI: 10.1108/ITP-04-2017-0133

Purvanova, R. K., Charlier, S. D., Reeves, C. J., & Greco, L. M. (2021). Who emerges into virtual team leadership roles? The role of achievement and ascription antecedents for leadership emergence across the virtuality spectrum. *Journal of Business and Psychology, 36*(4), 713–733. DOI: 10.1007/s10869-020-09698-0

Raghuram, S., Hill, N. S., Gibbs, J. L., & Maruping, L. M. (2019). Virtual work: Bridging research clusters. *The Academy of Management Annals, 13*(1), 308–341. DOI: 10.5465/annals.2017.0020

Rogers, B. A., Christian, J. S., Jennings, R. E., & Lanaj, K. (2023). The growth mindset at work: Will employees help others to develop themselves? *Academy of Management Discoveries*, *9*(1), 67–92. DOI: 10.5465/amd.2021.0144

Shockley, K. M., Allen, T. D., Dodd, H., & Waiwood, A. M. (2021). Remote worker communication during COVID-19: The role of quantity, quality, and supervisor expectation-setting. *The Journal of Applied Psychology*, *106*(10), 1466–1482. DOI: 10.1037/apl0000970 PMID: 34855422

Simunich, B., Gregg, A., & Ralston-Berg, P. (2024). *High-Impact Design for Online Courses: Blueprinting Quality Digital Learning in Eight Practical Steps*. Taylor & Francis.

Chapter 5
The "Dark Side" of Personality: Examining Narcissism in Virtual Teams

Krisztina Szabo
https://orcid.org/0009-0006-5715-6489
University of Central Florida, USA

C. Shawn Burke
University of Central Florida, USA

ABSTRACT

In this chapter the authors discuss how team personality composition (i.e., team narcissism) influences virtual team performance via team processes (i.e., information sharing and team conflict). Evidence was found for the negative impact of team narcissism on information sharing. The relationship between narcissism and team conflict was not supported. Information sharing predicted virtual team performance. Practical implications regarding staffing and virtual team collaboration in higher education are discussed at the end of the chapter.

INTRODUCTION

Due to technological advancements and recent global events (e.g., COVID-19), there has been an increasing reliance on virtual teams in both educational and professional contexts (Frost & Duan, 2020; Kolm et al., 2022). Virtual teams, defined as a group of dispersed individuals primarily collaborating through digital communication tools (Bell & Kozlowski, 2002), present unique opportunities and

DOI: 10.4018/979-8-3373-0375-8.ch005

challenges for teamwork. While working in a virtual team offers great flexibility and unprecedented access to talent, these teams often face challenges stemming from team compositional factors (Scott & Wildman, 2015). Highlighting the importance of team composition in the virtual context, Ferrazzi (2014, p. 120; from Dulebohn & Hoch, 2017) stated: "Team composition should be your starting point. You won't get anywhere without hiring (or developing) people suited to virtual teamwork." Team compositional research focuses on how configurations of team member attributes (e.g., age, gender, sex, personality, collective orientation; Bell, 2007; Bell et al., 2011) influence team processes and outcomes. Among the team member attributes investigated, personality traits have been historically considered to be particularly relevant (LePine et al., 2011).

When it comes to the examination of team member personality composition in virtual teams, the majority of the literature has relied on the prominent Big Five typology (Hoch & Dulebohn, 2017). Even though the Big Five personality traits provide valuable insights into team dynamics, there has been a call that research should go beyond the examination of these traits (Roberts & Woodman, 2017). One trait that seems to be particularly relevant in the context of virtual teams is narcissism. The importance of examining narcissism within the context of virtual teams stems from the idea that narcissistic tendencies (e.g., admiration, validation seeking, strong need for dominance, Back, 2018) may amplify the challenges associated with interpersonal interaction in virtual teams. For example, the strong need for dominance and admiration seeking may amplify the already existing challenges with communication and information sharing. Additionally, the strong need for dominance may make it more difficult to develop cohesion and psychological safety within virtual teams due to others not having the ability to speak up. This strong need for dominance and validation seeking may also impact the development of cohesion in virtual teams due to the constant attention seeking serving to create faultlines (i.e., hypothetical dividing lines based on one or more attributes; Lau & Murninghan, 1998) within the team as other team members become frustrated by the inability to have a voice. Despite its potential relevance, narcissism in the context of virtual teams has received little attention in the literature. Therefore, the purpose of the current research is to provide a broader understanding of how narcissism impacts team performance (i.e., team decision-making accuracy) via team processes (i.e., information sharing and relationship conflict) and in doing so provide guidance for team composition and collaboration in the context of virtual teams.

THEORETICAL BACKGROUND

Personality and Team Performance in Virtual Teams

Team composition refers to the configuration of team member characteristics that influences team processes and outcomes (Bell et al., 2018). Historically, compositional variables have been described as either surface-level (i.e., reflecting readily observable characteristics such as age, ethnicity; Jackson & Ruderman, 1995) or deep-level (i.e., involving underlying differences such as values and attitudes; Harrison et al., 1998). Personality is a deep-level compositional variable that reflects relatively stable patterns of behaviors, attitudes, and feelings (Hogan, 1996). At the team level, personality composition refers to the team-level index of personality traits within the team reflecting the strength and/or heterogeneity of a given trait within a team (Prewett et al., 2018).

In both traditional and virtual team literatures, the Five-Factor Model of Personality or the Big Five (i.e., conscientiousness, agreeableness, emotional stability/neuroticism, extraversion, openness to experience; e.g., Goldberg 1990; McCrae & Costa, 1987) has been widely discussed in the context of team performance. In the context of co-located teams, meta-analyses (Barrick & Mount, 1991; Bell, 2007; Peeters et al., 2006) indicated that personality composition at the team level was positively related to team performance (e.g., conscientiousness, $\rho = .11$; agreeableness, $\rho = .12$; extraversion, $\rho = .09$; emotional stability, $\rho = .04$; openness to experience, $\rho = .05$; from Bell, 2007). However, researchers suggested that optimal team composition may differ in virtual teams compared to face-to-face teams (Turel & Zhang, 2010). The impact of personality on virtual team functioning and performance depends on contextual factors, such as the use of communication technologies, that are often absent from face-to-face settings. These communication technologies often provide fewer social cues and decreased social stimulation as compared to communication within face-to-face teams. For instance, while team mean extraversion has been indicated to be beneficial in traditional team settings (Bell, 2007), Dennis and colleagues (2022) found that it had a large negative effect on virtual team performance when teams engaged in text-based computer-mediated communication as extraverts were no longer able to excel in spoken conversations (Dennis et al., 2022).

In the virtual context, the Big Five personality variables have been examined in the context of knowledge sharing behaviors (Hao et al., 2019), leadership emergence (Cogliser et al., 2012; Wilson et al., 2021), cohesion (Sánchez et al., 2018), trust (Flavian et al., 2022; Furumo et al., 2009; Murmu & Neelam, 2022), collaboration (Murmu & Neelam, 2022), communication technology anxiety (Jacques et al., 2009), and performance and effectiveness (Balthazard et al., 2004; Dennis et al., 2022; Turel & Zhang, 2010; Wang & Hsu, 2012). Although the Big Five personality variables provide a valuable starting point for understanding how team personality composition may influence team functioning and outcomes, it is important to examine how other variables may play out in a virtual team setting as virtual teams operate under different conditions (e.g., reliance on digital collaboration tools, reduced social cues, asynchronous communication, etc.) compared to face-to-face teams. More specifically, researchers and organizations should aim to further explore personality traits (e.g., the Dark Triad personality traits; Paulhus & Williams, 2002) that may potentially impede team functioning and provide recommendations for improving collaborative work in the virtual context.

While research on the "bright" side of personality (e.g., team conscientiousness) provides valuable insights into selecting and developing high-performing teams, research on the "dark" side is equally important, as these traits can be disruptive to team dynamics. Virtual teams, where interpersonal interactions are constrained by reduced face-to-face communication, are particularly susceptible to the manipulative, exploitative, and self-serving behaviors linked to Dark Triad traits (Paulhus & Williams, 2002). In the following paragraphs, a member of the Dark Triad, narcissism, and its relevance to virtual teams is discussed.

Narcissism

Narcissism is one of oldest constructs in psychology (Brown et al., 2009). Raskin and Terry (1988, p. 896) defined subclinical narcissism as "self-admiration that is characterized by tendencies toward grandiose ideas, fantasied talents, exhibitionism, and defensiveness in response to criticism; interpersonal relationships are characterized by feelings of entitlement, exploitativeness, and a lack of empathy" and described it on seven dimensions (i.e., entitlement, authority, superiority, exploitativeness, self-sufficiency, vanity, and exhibitionism).

Narcissistic personality traits are characterized by grandiosity, entitlement, and a sense of superiority (Paulhus & Williams, 2002). As a component of the Dark Triad (Paulhus & Williams, 2002), narcissism is also marked by a fundamental lack of empathy (Wai & Tiliopoulos, 2012). Individuals with narcissistic tendencies often exhibit inflated self-importance, dominance, arrogance, self-centeredness, and overconfidence (Paulhus & Williams, 2002). They also tend to possess socially malevolent characteristics, such as aggressiveness, exploitation, emotional detachment, and deceitfulness (Paulhus & Williams, 2002). Additionally, past research has shown that narcissists frequently manipulate others in personal relationships, viewing them as tools for their own success (Campbell et al., 2002). Additionally, in terms of the Big Five personality variables, studies suggest that narcissistic individuals tend to be more extroverted but less agreeable than others (Douglas et al., 2012).

Based on above-mentioned characteristics of narcissistic individuals, perhaps it is no surprise that narcissism has been linked to several undesirable outcomes such as aggression (Du et al., 2022), counterproductive work behaviors (Grijalva & Newman, 2015), and decreased quality of interpersonal relationships (Khodabakhs & Besharat, 2011). In the context of teams, the vast majority of research on narcissism has focused on examining narcissism at the individual level (i.e., leader narcissism) in connection to individual-level processes (e.g., leader emergence; Brunell et al., 2008; Hartel et al., 2023; Nevicka et al., 2011) and team-level outcomes such as creativity (Zhou et al., 2019) and performance (Schmid et al., 2021). Although the impact of individual-level narcissism has received increased attention in recent years (Grijalva et al., 2015), there is little known about how narcissism manifests at the team level and how it may impact team processes and outcomes. In the context of the face-to-face literature on teams, researchers suggested that team-level narcissism impacts coordination (Grijalva et al., 2020), conflict (Bush-Evans, 2020; Lynch et al., 2022), cohesion (Bush-Evans, 2020), team-level task performance and organizational citizenship behaviors (Felty et al., 2015).

While there is an increasing prevalence of narcissism in the modern work environment, the impact of narcissistic tendencies in virtual teams is yet to be explored (Wehrung, 2017). As Cogliser et al. (2012) highlighted, personality traits can influence virtual team members' perception. Since narcissism is characterized by a high level of grandiosity and exhibitionism (Raskin & Terry, 1988), it is likely that narcissistic individuals will engage in self-disclosure behaviors that ultimately impact social perceptions and interpersonal interactions, making this construct particularly relevant to study in the virtual team context. While individuals can engage in self-disclosure for a wide variety of reasons, narcissists may have ulterior motives to do so (e.g., as a form of self-promotion to position themselves above other team members), which ultimately impacts team dynamics.

Beyond the individual level, the emergence of narcissism at the collective level (i.e., team narcissism) can also shape team functioning and consequent outcomes. For instance, in virtual settings, where visibility and recognition may be more challenging to establish compared to face-to-face teams, higher levels of team narcissism could impact team dynamics via heightened competition for status and recognition. As such, team discussions may be dominated by team members seeking recognition for contributions and interpersonal conflict may arise due to competition for attention and credit. Additionally, narcissism at the team level may manifest through an exaggerated sense of team confidence and importance, hindering feedback processes and the collaboration essential for successful team performance. In the next paragraphs, the manner in which narcissism influences virtual team performance through key team processes (i.e., team conflict and information sharing) is delineated.

Hypothesis Development

To represent the association between team composition (i.e., team-level narcissism) and team performance via team processes, we draw from the input-process-output (IPO; McGrath, 1964) and input-mediator-output-input (IMOI; Ilgen et al., 2005) frameworks. The IPO and IMOI frameworks have been traditionally applied in the context of face-to-face teams, but recently these models have been also examined in the context of virtual teams (Dulebohn & Hoch, 2017). The basic premise of both models is that team input factors (e.g., team composition) impact mediators (i.e., team processes and emergent states) which then influence team outcomes (e.g., team performance). Our model depicts that team personality composition (i.e., team-level narcissism) influences virtual team performance via team conflict (i.e., relationship conflict) and information sharing. The model is presented in *Figure 1* below.

Figure 1. Proposed Model

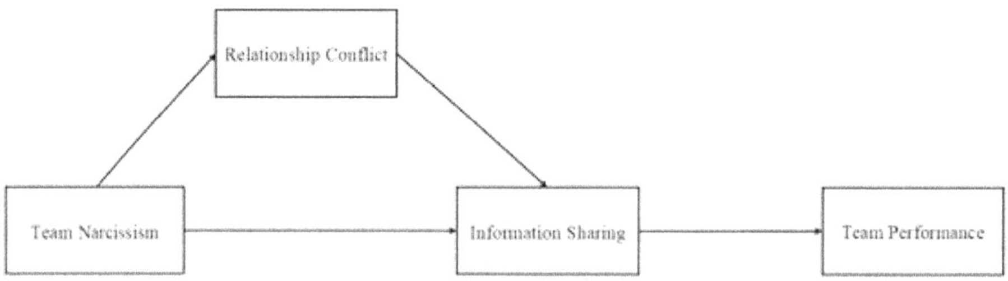

Team Narcissism and Information Sharing

Information sharing refers to the communication related to task details, activities, progress, and the reasoning for making task relevant decisions (Moye & Langfred, 2004). Jehn and Shah (1997, p. 777) defined information sharing as "making statements to other group members about the task." Drawing from the information processing theory, "individuals, as adaptive organisms, adapt attitudes, behavior, and beliefs to their social context and to the reality of their own past and present behavior and situation" (Salancik & Pfeffer, 1978, p. 226). Based on the theory, individuals engage in certain behaviors based on the social cues from the environment. In virtual teams, team members' behaviors are shaped by digital cues and interactions within their online environment. In a virtual setting, narcissistic team members are likely to engage in self-centered behaviors, such as dominating virtual discussions or prioritizing opportunities for personal recognition. These behaviors can signal negative social cues (e.g., exclusivity, competitiveness) to other team members creating an environment that impedes open information elaboration and exchange. Additionally, narcissistic teams may prioritize maintaining a dominant image over fostering transparent communication across team members, leading to selective information sharing. Rather than distributing knowledge equitably, such teams may withhold valuable insights to maintain a competitive edge even within the team itself. Furthermore, collective narcissism can result in overconfidence, as team members collectively reinforce inflated perceptions of their abilities. This overestimation may lead to the dismissal of alternative solutions and perspectives, reducing the depth of task-relevant discussions. This leads to the first hypothesis:

Hypothesis 1: Team narcissism will be negatively related to information sharing.

The Mediating Role of Relationship Conflict

When numerous individuals engage in self-centered behaviors within a team, it is likely that conflict will emerge. DeChurch et al. (2013) described conflict processes as "members' interactions aimed at working through task and interpersonal disagreements" (p. 560). There has been a limited amount of research on narcissism and team conflict at the team level. In a recent study, Lynch and colleagues (2022) found that team mean scores of narcissistic rivalry were associated with increased competitive conflict processes. In another recent study, Boulter et al. (2022) examined different aggregations of team-level narcissism (i.e., average and maximum) as antecedents of within-team conflict profiles which varied in patterns of task, relationship, and process conflict. The results indicated that teams with higher levels of narcissism in terms of mean and maximum scores were likely to occupy dysfunctional conflict profiles (i.e., profiles high in all conflict types).

Based on the agency model of narcissism (Campbell et al., 2006), it is expected that relationship conflict will be present in teams with higher levels of narcissism due to elevated agency (e.g., dominance) and lower communion (e.g., warmth). Relationship conflict refers to "an awareness of interpersonal incompatibilities, includes affective components such as feeling tension and friction" (Jehn & Mannix, 2001, p. 238). With higher collective narcissism at the team level, it is likely that teams will experience disagreements and personal frictions due to members holding grandiose views of themselves (Paulhus & Williams, 2002) and overestimating their cognitive ability and value of contributions (Campbell et al., 2004; Paulhus et al., 2003; Robins & Beer, 2001).

Previous research suggested that intragroup conflict can impact key team processes such as information sharing. For example, Jehn and colleagues (2013) argued that relationship conflict has negative consequences to team functioning due to coalition formation within teams. As a result of coalition formation, team members may be more prone to discussing issues with their private support networks within the team instead of engaging in information sharing with the entire team (Kolb & Bartunek, 1992). This can be particularly problematic in the virtual context, where face-to-face interactions are limited and team members have access to a wide variety of collaboration tools that enable private conversations (e.g., use of private chat). Furthermore, relationship conflict may also lead to intrateam competition that can potentially hinder information sharing. From an information processing perspective, Carnevale and Probst (1998) suggested that conflict leads to higher cognitive load and information processing is impeded as conflict intensifies. In their literature review, Simons and Peterson (2000) noted that relationship conflict limits information sharing and information processing in teams as it shifts the focus from task-related problems to focusing on each other. Therefore, the second hypothesis proposes that team-level narcissism influences information sharing via relationship conflict:

> Hypothesis 2: Relationship conflict will partially mediate the relationship between team narcissism and information sharing.

Information Sharing and Team Performance

Team performance refers to the extent to which the team successfully completed their job (Hackman et al., 1976). As Jehn and colleagues (1999) highlighted, knowledge is likely to be a function of team members' expertise, experience, education, values, goals, history, and demographic characteristics. However, for the team to take advantage of this knowledge, team members must be willing to share it (Griffith & Neale, 2001). The nature of virtual teams allows for diverse membership regardless of physical location, creating an opportunity to access a broad and varied pool of knowledge. Consequently, virtual teams often consist of members with specialized expertise, leading to mutual dependence as each member possesses unique knowledge that others may lack. In this case, sharing unique, expertise-related information is vital to creating a collective understanding of task-relevant information within the team.

Furthermore, in virtual teams, where nonverbal cues are limited, the digital exchange of relevant information plays a crucial role in ensuring that decisions are based on all available knowledge. Without in-person interactions, virtual team members must rely almost entirely on digital platforms—such as video and audio calls, chat, and document sharing—to convey and interpret information. In this context, accurate and timely information sharing provides the foundation for accurate decision making and team performance. This leads to the last hypothesis:

Hypothesis 3: Information sharing will be positively related to team performance (i.e., team decision-making accuracy).

METHODOLOGY

Participants

Participants were undergraduate students from a large Southeastern university and individuals from Prolific's data collection website. The final sample included 62 teams (186 participants) who completed at least 2 rounds of the management simulation game, Tinsel Town. Out of the 186 participants, 73 (39.2%) identified as male, and 111 (59.7%) identified as female and 2 participants (1.1%) preferred not to answer. Participants' age ranged from 18 to 71 ($M = 23.67$, $SD = 9.84$). As far as racial and ethnic background, 54.3% of the participants identified as White/ Caucasian, 13.4% as Black/African American, 26.3% as Hispanic, 10.8% as Asian, 3.2% as Middle Eastern, 0.5% as Pacific Islander, 0.5% as American Indian, and 1.1% as Other (*Note:* participants were allowed to select more than one option). Participants' leadership experience in terms of the number of leadership roles that they were currently holding at the time of the study, or they held within the past 6 months ranged from 0 to 4 ($M = 1.01$, $SD = 1.03$). None of the participants had previous experience participating in Tinsel Town. In terms of college classification, the university sample included 77 (52.4%) freshmen, 29 (19.7%) sophomore, 30 (20.4%) junior, and 11 (7.5%) senior students. The sample demographics along with the breakdown of the SONA and Prolific samples are presented in *Table 1*.

Table 1. Sample Descriptive Statistics

Sample Statistics	**Full Sample**		**SONA Sample**		**Prolific Sample**		
	n=186	**%**	**n=147**	**%**	**n=39**	**%**	χ^2
Gender							13.10***
Male	73	39.20%	52	35.40%	21	53.80%	
Female	111	59.70%	95	64.60%	16	41.00%	
Prefer Not to Answer	2	1.10%	0	0%	2	5.10%	
Race/Ethnic Background							
White/Caucasian	101	54.30%	71	48.30%	30	76.90%	
Black/African American	25	13.40%	19	12.90%	6	15.40%	
Hispanic or Latino	49	26.30%	49	33.30%	0	0.00%	

continued on following page

Table 1. Continued

Sample Statistics	Full Sample		SONA Sample		Prolific Sample		
	n=186	%	n=147	%	n=39	%	χ^2
Asian or Asian American	20	10.80%	17	11.60%	3	7.70%	
Middle Eastern	6	3.20%	6	4.10%	0	0.00%	
Pacific Islander	1	0.50%	1	0.70%	0	0.00%	
American Indian	1	0.50%	0	0%	1	2.60%	
Other	2	1.10%	2	1.40%			
Education							
Freshmen			77	52.40%			
Sophomore			29	19.70%			
Junior			30	20.40%			
Senior			11	7.50%			
	M	*SD*	*M*	*SD*	*M*	*SD*	t(184)
Age	23.67	9.84	19.84	4.18	38.08	11.60	-15.69***
Leadership Experience	1.00	1.02	1.06	1.08	0.77	0.71	1.60*

Note. * $p < .05$, *** $p < .001$

Task

Tinsel Town is a business simulation involving distributed expertise (Devine et al., 2004). It is often used to understand organizational decision-making teams and to foster team development in organizational settings. In the simulation, groups of three individuals act as a management team of a fictional movie studio. For the purpose of the study, an assigned leader was chosen based on having the most leadership experience. Within the team, each team member had distinct roles. These roles were: 1) Vice President, Marketing, 2) Vice President, Research, and 3) Vice President, Development. Throughout the simulation game, the main goal of the team was to maximize a movie studio's profit over three years (three decision periods) by deciding which screenplays to produce based on a limited budget. There was common information provided to all team members (e.g., team goals); however, there was also unique information related to each specific role.

Measures

Demographic Information. Demographic information was measured through a short questionnaire. Participants were asked to indicate their gender, age, ethnicity, educational background, leadership experience, and experience with the simulation game (i.e., Tinsel Town).

Narcissism. Narcissism was measured by Raskin and Terry's (1988) Narcissistic Personality Inventory (NPI). The NPI is a 40-item forced-choice instrument that was used to measure participants' level of non-clinical narcissism. The scores on the NPI range between 0 and 40 where choices are scored positively; the higher the score, the more narcissistic the individual is. In the current sample, the NPI had high internal consistency ($\omega = .85$.) and has demonstrated construct validity when being compared to other instruments measuring narcissism in the past (Jakobwitz & Egan, 2006). Example items include: 1) A. I have a natural talent for influencing people. B. I am not good at influencing people, and 2) A. Modesty doesn't become me. B. I am essentially a modest person.

Historically, there have been different approaches (i.e., trait-oriented and task-oriented) for aggregating personality variables at the team level (Prewett et al., 2009). The trait-oriented approach suggests that staffing should be guided by primarily examining the person-team fit and considers personality traits as either supplementary or complimentary (Prewett et al., 2009). Based on the trait approach, narcissism can be considered as a supplementary fit, emphasizing trait homogeneity for optimal performance. Since we hypothesize narcissism to be a potentially harmful trait in the virtual team context, homogeneity for best performance should occur at the lower end of the scale. Consequently, lower homogeneity on the trait in terms of team scores should benefit the team.

The task-oriented approach represents another line of aggregation methods frequently employed in the literature (e.g., Turel & Zhang, 2010). The task-oriented approach suggests that the task's nature drives the aggregation of the variables at the team level. The most common approaches to specifying operationalization based on the nature of the task have been through using Steiner's (1972) and Thompson's (1967) taxonomies (e.g., LePine et al., 1997). As Mathieu et al. (2014) highlighted, task/workflow interdependence is a critical contextual variable to consider in compositional research. Based on Thompson's taxonomy, Tinsel Town primarily requires pooled interdependence teamwork at the beginning of the simulation (i.e., team members assigned to distinct departments within the simulation with unique information to insert into formulas for each role). However, when team members start sharing their unique information (i.e., results of the calculations) as part of a team discussion, teamwork becomes reciprocal in nature. We operationalize narcissism at the team level using the average score of team members as the additive nature of taskwork serves as the foundation of the simulation and then provide supplementary analyses using team minimum and maximum scores.

Team Conflict. Team conflict was measured using a revised version of Jehn's (1995) Intragroup Conflict Scale (ICS) which consists of two dimensions: task and relationship conflict. The ICS has been widely used by researchers in the past; however, the number of items included in the ICS remains inconsistent across studies. For the purposes of the study, Pearson and colleagues' (2002) refined 6-item scale was used. Items were measured on a 5-point Likert-scale. Example items include: "How much anger was there among the members of the group?" and "How many disagreements over different ideas were there?". Items were captured on a 5-point Likert-type scale ranging from 1 = *none at all* to 5 = *a great deal*. The reliability for the relationship and task conflict subscales across the three rounds were .85 and .86.

Information Sharing. Information sharing was measured by Hoegl and Gemeunden's (2001) Teamwork Quality Scale. The original scale included 10 items. Three items were excluded from the measure due to lack of relevance to the task/experiment: "The team members communicated often in spontaneous meetings, phone conversations, etc.," "The team members communicated mostly directly and personally with each other," and "There were mediators through whom much communication was conducted." Items were captured on a 5-point Likert-type scale ranging from 1 = *strongly disagree* to 5 = *strongly agree*. The reliability of the 7-item revised scale was $\alpha = 0.73$.

Team Performance. Team performance was indicated by the teams' final performance percentage achieved in Tinsel Town, an objective measure. Team performance for each round was calculated via the following formula: team's total profit/maximum profit for given the round*100. The maximum total profit for each of the rounds was provided as part of the simulation's resources. The team's final performance score was calculated by averaging the percentages of the three rounds.

Control Variables

Age. Previous research has indicated that age could be an important variable impacting decision-making as it influences one's tendency to seek out information, diagnose information value, and integrate information to make accurate decision-making choices (Taylor, 1975). Age was included as a control variable due to the differences between the mean of the SONA and Prolific samples, as well as the relatively large standard deviation within the whole sample. Participants' age was aggregated at the team level by the mean.

Data collection platform. The sample of the study included participants from the university's data collection platform, SONA, and Prolific. Since Prolific represents a broader sample (i.e., individuals across the United States versus individuals from a

Southeastern university), data collection platform was included as a control variable to ensure that potential differences between the SONA and Prolific samples have been accounted for. Teams gathered from the SONA platform were coded as 1 and teams gathered from Prolific's platform were coded as 2.

Leader's leadership experience. Leadership experience has been linked to the development of several abilities and skills (e.g., strategic thinking, innovative problem solving, dealing with conflict, motivating people, coping skills, self-confidence; McCall et al., 1988) that could potentially impact team processes and outcomes. Therefore, the team leaders' leadership experience was included in the current study as a control variable. The leader's leadership experience was measured based on the number of leadership roles that they were currently holding at the time of the study and the number of leadership roles that they had in the previous 6 months.

Leader's gender. Although past research in the context of gender and leadership has been inconsistent, there is some evidence supporting the notion of gender differences in leadership (Jonsen et al., 2010). Gibson (1995) suggested that male leadership styles are associated with more agentic qualities (e.g., being ambitious, goal oriented), while female leadership styles tend to be more communal, and people oriented. Agentic qualities have been found to be negatively associated with transformational behaviors, while communal qualities have been associated with transformational behaviors (Poddar & Kirshnan, 2004). Based on these findings, it is expected that the leader's gender may impact team functioning (e.g., information sharing, team conflict). Therefore, the team leaders' gender was included as a control variable in the study and each team was coded based on their leader's gender. Leader's gender was coded as 1 = male and 2 = female.

Procedure

Participants signed up for the study through the university's SONA system and Prolific. The study's time commitment was approximately 2.5 hours. Participants from the university's system received SONA credit, while participants from Prolific received monetary compensation for their participation. Upon signing up for the study, participants were provided with a Zoom link. First, the participants were given a link to the informed consent and completed a demographic measure, leadership, and personality assessment. Upon the completion of the measures, participants were assigned to one of the three roles (marketing, development, research) in the simulation. The leadership role (marketing) was assigned to the person with the most leadership experience. The other two roles were randomly assigned. After the roles were assigned, participants received training on Tinsel Town and their individual role. Each participant was provided with their own binder containing all the necessary information to complete the simulation. At the end of the training, participants could ask any task-related questions to ensure that everyone had a proper understanding of the simulation game.

Once the training was completed, participants engaged in three rounds of Tinsel Town where they were required to work collectively to maximize a functional movie studio's profit over three consecutive years. Participants had 5 minutes at the beginning of each round to silently review their individual information sent through the private chat via Zoom by the experimenter. After the 5-minute review period, participants had 15 minutes to discuss the movies for the given round. At the end of each round, the following questionnaires were completed: individual recommendation sheet, final recommendation sheet (leader), and measures of teamwork. After completing the measures, participants were given feedback regarding their performance in the given round. The team profit was calculated by the researcher based on the guidelines and documentation in Tinsel Town.

Analyses

The proposed hypotheses were tested via path analyses with the lavaan package (version 0.6-19) in R (version 4.4.2).

RESULTS

Descriptive Statistics

The descriptive statistics, variable intercorrelations and reliabilities are presented in *Table 2*. Team minimum narcissism was significantly related to team mean narcissism ($r = .81, p < .001$), team maximum narcissism ($r = .46, p < .001$), and information sharing ($r = -.28, p < .05$). Task conflict was significantly and positively related to relationship conflict ($r = .54, p < .01$). Information sharing was significantly and positively related to team performance ($r = .27, p < .05$). The correlations between the variables along with the means and standard deviations are presented in *Table 2*.

Next, the relationship between the control variables and team performance was examined. Team mean age ($b = -4.29(2.43)$, $\beta = -.22$, $t(60) = -1.76$, $p = .083$), data collection platform ($t(60)=1.070$, $p = .289$), leader's gender ($t(60) = .576$, $p = .567$), and leader's leadership experience ($b = 4.04(19.58)$, $\beta = .03$, $t(60) = .21$, $p = .837$) were not significantly related to team performance. Therefore, the control variables were not included in the path analyses.

Table 2. Team-level Descriptive Statistics, Correlations, and Cronbach's α

Variable	*M*	*SD*	**1**	**2**	**3**	**4**	**5**	**6**	**7**
1. Team Min. Narc.	7.68	4.15	(0.85)						
2. Team Mean Narc.	13.26	4.24	0.81***	(0.85)					
3. Team Max. Narc.	19.13	5.66	0.46***	0.85***	(0.85)				
4. Task Conflict	1.63	0.39	-0.08	-0.04	0.03	(0.86)			
5. Rel. Conflict	1.14	0.24	0.02	-0.04	-0.04	0.54***	(0.85)		
6. Inf. Sharing	4.47	0.31	-0.28*	-0.36**	-0.28*	-0.22*	-0.23*	(0.71)	
7. Team Performance	69.18	10.63	-0.05	-0.08	-0.01	-0.05	-0.17	0.27*	-

*p < .05, **p < .01, ***p < .001.

Hypothesis Testing

Team Mean Narcissism

The proposed model indicated an excellent fit to the data, *CFI* = 1.00, *RMSEA* = .00, *SRMR* = .03. Hypothesis 1 stated that team minimum narcissism would be negatively related to information sharing. The results of the path analysis indicated that team mean narcissism was significantly and negatively related to information sharing (b = -.03 (.01), β = -.37, $p < .001$) supporting Hypothesis 1.

The second hypothesis proposed that relationship conflict would partially mediate the relationship between team-level narcissism (minimum) and information sharing. Team mean narcissism was unrelated to relationship conflict, b = -.00 (.01), β = -.04, p = .76. Relationship conflict significantly and negatively predicted information sharing, b = -.03 (.01), β = -.37, $p < .001$. The indirect effect was estimated via bootstrapping (1,000 iterations). The indirect effect between team minimum narcissism and information sharing was not significant, 95% CI [-.01; .005]. Therefore, Hypothesis 2 was not supported.

Hypothesis 3 stated that information sharing would be positively related to team performance. Information sharing was significantly and positively related to team performance, b = 9.347 (4.24), β = .27, $p < .05$. Thus, Hypothesis 3 was supported.

Although not hypothesized, a significant negative indirect effect was found between team mean narcissism and team performance when examining the indirect effects via bootstrapping 95% CI [-.53; -0.03]. The results of the path analysis are presented in *Table 3* below.

Table 3. Model 1: Team-level Path Analysis Examining Team Average Narcissism

Direct Effects	**b**	**p**	**SE**	**95% CIlower**	**95% CIupper**	R^2
Predicting Relationship Conflict						0.00
Team Average Narcissism	-0.00	0.90	0.01	-0.02	0.01	
Predicting Information Sharing						0.19
Team Average Narcissism	-0.03*	<.05	0.01	-0.04	-0.00	
Relationship Conflict	-0.31*	<.05	0.15	-0.61	-0.02	
Predicting Team Performance						0.07
Information Sharing	9.35*	<.05	4.24	1.03	17.67	
Indirect Effects	b	p	SE†	$B_{95\% \text{ CIlower}}$	$B_{95\% \text{ CIupper}}$	
Team Narcissism → Relationship conflict → Information Sharing	-0.00	0.77	0.00	-0.004	0.005	
Team Narcissism → Information Sharing → Team Performance	-0.26*	<.05	0.13	-0.529	-0.033	

Note. †Standard errors of indirect effects are estimated via percentile bootstrapping (1,000 iterations).
*p < .05, **p < .01, ***p < .001.

Supplemental Analyses

Aggregation Method

Team Minimum Narcissism

Next, we examined the proposed relationships with other aggregation methods (i.e., team minimum and maximum narcissism). The model including team minimum narcissism provided an excellent fit to the data, *CFI* = 1.00, *RMSEA* = .00, *SRMR* = .03. Team minimum narcissism was significantly and negatively related to information sharing (b = - .02 (.01), β = -.27, p < .05). Team minimum narcissism was unrelated to relationship conflict (b = .00 (.01), β = .02, p = .90) and it was marginally significantly related to information sharing, b = - .29 (.16), β = -.22, p = .06. The indirect effect estimated via bootstrapping between team minimum narcissism and information sharing was not significant, 95% CI [-.013; .004]. Similarly to the previous model, information sharing was significantly and positively related to team decision accuracy (b = 9.34 (4.24), β = .27, p < .05). The results of this model are presented in *Table 4* below.

Table 4. Model 3: Team-level Path Analysis Examining Team Minimum Narcissism

Direct Effects	**b**	**p**	**SE**	**95% CIlower**	**95% CIupper**	**R^2**
Predicting Relationship Conflict						0.00
Team Minimum Narcissism	0.00	0.90	0.01	-0.01	0.02	
Predicting Information Sharing						0.13
Team Minimum Narcissism	-0.02*	<.05	0.01	-0.04	-0.00	
Relationship Conflict	-0.29	0.06	0.16	-0.60	0.02	
Predicting Team Performance						0.07
Information Sharing	9.35*	<.05	4.24	1.03	17.67	
Indirect Effects	b	p	SE†	$B_{95\% CIlower}$	$B_{95\% CIupper}$	
Team Narcissism → Relationship conflict → Information Sharing	-0.00	0.95	0.00	-0.013	0.004	
Team Narcissism → Information Sharing → Team Performance	-0.19	0.12	0.12	-0.481	0.004	

Note. †Standard errors of indirect effects are estimated via percentile bootstrapping (1,000 iterations).
*p < .05, **p < .01, ***p < .001.

Team Maximum Narcissism

We also examined the proposed model using the team maximum score for aggregation at the team level. Model 4 provided an excellent fit to the data, CFI = 1.00, $RMSEA$ = .00, $SRMR$ = .04. Team maximum narcissism was significantly and negatively related to information sharing (b = -.02 (.01), β = -.29, p < .05). Similarly to the previous models, team maximum narcissism was unrelated to relationship conflict, b = -.00 (.01), β = -.04, p = .77. Relationship conflict was significantly and negatively related to information sharing, b = -.31 (.16), β = -.24, p < .05. The indirect effect between team maximum narcissism and information sharing via relationship conflict was not significant, 95% CI [-.004; .006]. Information sharing predicted team performance (b = 9.34 (4.24), β = .27, p < .05). The results are presented in *Table 5* below.

Table 5. Model 3: Team-level Path Analysis Examining Team Maximum Narcissism

Direct Effects	**b**	**p**	**SE**	**95% CIlower**	**95% CIupper**	**R^2**
Predicting Relationship Conflict						0.00
Team Maximum Narcissism	-0.00	0.90	0.01	-0.01	0.01	
Predicting Information Sharing						0.13
Team Maximum Narcissism	-0.02*	<.05	0.01	-0.03	-0.003	
Relationship Conflict	-0.31*	<.05	0.16	-0.62	-0.004	
Predicting Team Performance						0.07
Information Sharing	9.35*	<.05	4.24	1.03	17.67	

continued on following page

Table 5. Continued

Direct Effects	b	p	SE	95% CIlower	95% CIupper	R^2
Indirect Effects	b	p	SE†	$B_{95\% CIlower}$	$B_{95\% CIupper}$	
Team Narcissism → Relationship conflict → Information Sharing	-0.00	0.82	0.00	-0.004	0.006	
Team Narcissism → Information Sharing → Team Performance	-0.15	0.06	0.12	-0.320	-0.013	

Note. †Standard errors of indirect effects are estimated via percentile bootstrapping (1,000 iterations). *p < .05, **p < .01, ***p < .001.

Task Conflict

Additionally, the proposed model was examined by including task conflict instead of relationship conflict in the model. While relationship conflict is related to interpersonal differences, task conflict tends to revolve around disagreements with regards to the allocation of resources, and procedures and decisions related to task work (De Dreu & Weingart, 2003). As task conflict has been described as a potentially beneficial type of conflict (e.g., Jehn, 1995), the main interest of this supplementary analysis was to examine whether incorporating task conflict in the model would lead to different results. Overall, the analyses yielded similar results compared to the original model.

Models 6 (*CFI* = 1.00, *RMSEA* = .00, *SRMR* = .01), 7 and 8 (*CFI* = 1.00, *RMSEA* = .00, *SRMR* = .02) indicated excellent fit to the data. Team minimum (b = -.00 (.01), β = -.08, p = .56), average (b = -.00 (.01), β = -*.04*, p = .78), and maximum narcissism (b = .00 (.01), β = *.03*, p = .82) were unrelated to task conflict. The indirect relationship between team narcissism and task conflict was not supported in any of the models. Task conflict was significantly and negatively related to information sharing in Models 6 (b = -.19 (.10), β = -.24, $p < .05$) and 7 (b = -.18 (.10), β = -.23, $p < .05$). Information sharing was predicted team performance in all three models, b = 9.35 (4.24), β = *.27*, $p < .05$. The results are presented in *Tables 6-8* below.

Table 6. Model 4: Team-level Path Analysis Examining Team Minimum Narcissism and Task Conflict

Direct Effects	b	p	SE	95% CIlower	95% CIupper	R^2
Predicting Task Conflict						0.01
Team Minimum Narcissism	-0.00	0.56	0.01	-0.031	0.017	
Predicting Information Sharing						0.13
Team Minimum Narcissism	-0.02*	<.05	0.01	-0.040	-0.005	
Task Conflict	-0.19*	<.05	0.10	-0.379	-0.002	
Predicting Team Performance						0.07

continued on following page

Table 6. Continued

Direct Effects	b	p	SE	95% CIlower	95% CIupper	R^2
Information Sharing	9.35*	<.05	4.24	1.028	17.665	
Indirect Effects	b	p	SE†	$B_{95\% CIlower}$	$B_{95\% CIupper}$	
Team Narcissism → Task Conflict → Information Sharing	-0.00	0.62	0.00	-0.004	0.008	
Team Narcissism → Information Sharing → Team Performance	-0.21	0.13	0.14	-0.504	0.001	

Note. †Standard errors of indirect effects are estimated via percentile bootstrapping (1,000 iterations).
*p < .05, **p < .01, ***p < .001.

Table 7. Model 5: Team-level Path Analysis Examining Team Average Narcissism and Task Conflict

Direct Effects	b	p	SE	95% CIlower	95% CIupper	R^2
Predicting Task Conflict						0.00
Team Average Narcissism	-0.00	0.78	0.01	-0.012	0.009	
Predicting Information Sharing						0.13
Team Average Narcissism	-0.03*	<.05	0.01	-0.029	-0.003	
Task Conflict	-0.18*	<.05	0.16	-0.616	-0.004	
Predicting Team Performance						0.07
Information Sharing	9.35*	<.05	4.24	1.028	17.665	
Indirect Effects	b	p	SE†	$B_{95\% CIlower}$	$B_{95\% CIupper}$	
Team Narcissism → Task Conflict → Information Sharing	-0.00	0.82	0.00	-0.005	0.007	
Team Narcissism → Information Sharing → Team Performance	-0.25	0.06	0.14	-0.553	-0.031	

Note. †Standard errors of indirect effects are estimated via percentile bootstrapping (1,000 iterations).
*p < .05, **p < .01, ***p < .001.

Table 8. Model 6: Team-level Path Analysis Examining Team Maximum Narcissism and Task Conflict

Direct Effects	b	p	SE	95% CIlower	95% CIupper	R^2
Predicting Task Conflict						0.00
Team Maximum Narcissism	0.00	0.82	0.01	-0.015	0.019	
Predicting Information Sharing						0.12
Team Maximum Narcissism	-0.02*	<.05	0.01	-0.028	-0.002	
Task Conflict	-0.17	0.08	0.10	-0.356	0.023	
Predicting Team Performance						0.07
Information Sharing	9.35*	<.05	4.24	1.028	17.665	
Indirect Effects	b	p	SE†	$B_{95\% CIlower}$	$B_{95\% CIupper}$	

continued on following page

Table 8. Continued

Direct Effects	b	p	SE	95% CIlower	95% CIupper	R^2
Team Narcissism → Task Conflict → Information Sharing	-0.00	0.83	0.00	-0.004	0.003	
Team Narcissism → Information Sharing → Team Performance	-0.14	0.07	0.08	-0.308	-0.007	

Note. †Standard errors of indirect effects are estimated via percentile bootstrapping (1,000 iterations). *p < .05, **p < .01, ***p < .001.

DISCUSSION

Summary of Findings

The current study examined the influence of team-level narcissism on team performance via team processes (i.e., information sharing, team conflict). The results of the study indicated that team narcissism (i.e., average, minimum, maximum) was significantly and negatively related to information sharing. Information sharing predicted virtual team performance.

However, we did not find support for the relationship between team-level narcissism (i.e., average, minimum, maximum) and team conflict (i.e., relationship and task). Prior research in the context of face-to-to face teams (e.g., Boulter et al., 2022, Lynch et al., 2022) suggests that team narcissism could contribute to the development of conflict in teams. A potential explanation for the current findings could be related to the study's timeframe. For instance, Lynch et al. (2022) examined the relationship between narcissism and team conflict processes in the context of a longitudinal research over the course of 8 months. In a similar vein, Boulter et al. (2022) examined the association between narcissism and within-team profiles of intragroup conflict in the context of sport teams arguing that they were representative of naturalistic and fully developed teams. Considering the nature of personality, it is plausible that team narcissism could have had a stronger impact on conflict over time. As Paulhus (1998) highlighted, others may initially have favorable impressions of narcissists (Paulhus, 1998). However, over time, these initial positive impressions may turn negative as their true characteristics emerge (Foster & Twenge, 2010). It is also possible that more time was needed for conflict to develop considering the low mean values for both relationship and task conflict and the short timeframe of the study. The other potential explanation is related to the nature of the virtual environment teams operate in. Virtual environments may provide fewer opportunities for immediate emotional reactions and interpersonal clashes compared to in-person environments. In the virtual context where communication is mediated via collaboration tools, emotional reactions may be less apparent and team members may have more time to process and regulate responses potentially mitigating conflict within the team.

Moreover, the results of the supplementary analyses indicated that task conflict was negatively related to information sharing within virtual teams. These findings add to prior conversations regarding whether task conflict could be beneficial for teams though fostering engagement in deep and deliberate task-relevant information processing (see De Dreu & Weingart, 2003). In the context of virtual teams, several factors (e.g., degree of virtuality, use of technology mediated communication, etc.) may act as barriers for task conflict to be beneficial. Additionally, trust and psychological safety might play a key role in whether task conflict leads to beneficial outcomes. In virtual teams, building trust and psychological safety can be more challenging compared to face-to-face teams due to limited social cues and interpersonal interactions. Consequently, without a solid foundation for these emergent states, task conflict may be perceived as more threatening, reducing the likelihood that disagreements can be leveraged productively within the team.

Theoretical Contributions

The present research has theoretical contributions in two areas. First, most research on narcissism in the context of teams has been conducted at the individual level with a focus on narcissistic leadership (e.g., Xiao et al., 2018). Therefore, there is little known about narcissism as a team-level compositional variable. To cover this gap, the current study aimed to provide a broader understanding of how narcissism manifests at the team-level and influence key team processes and outcomes in the virtual context.

The second contribution is related to the conceptualization and aggregation of narcissism at the team level. As Bell (2007) highlighted, it is important to choose appropriate operationalization of team compositional variables. In the current study, narcissism was operationalized in three different ways (i.e., minimum, maximum, average) due to both task-based and trait-based operationalizations receiving mixed support in the literature. We found that all three (i.e., mean, minimum, average) operationalizations of narcissism at the team level yielded similar patterns of relationships. This implies that whether the team's level of narcissism was determined by its most narcissistic member (i.e., team maximum), least narcissistic member (i.e., team minimum), or the average narcissism across the team, its effects on other variables remained consistent. In the current study, we focused on the operationalization of a single team compositional variable, but we encourage future research to further explore how the combination of personality attributes influence team functioning based on more recently developed approaches (e.g., team member attribute alignment approach; Emich et al., 2022).

Practical Implications

The current study has implications related to team composition and collaboration within virtual teams. The results indicated that team-level narcissism was significantly and negatively related to information sharing suggesting that considering team members' personality is a crucial factor that influences team functioning. One potential way to enhance team functioning is to measure team members' personality and compose teams based on the scores. Based on our findings, composing teams to have lower levels of narcissism (i.e., in terms of minimum, average, and maximum scores) should foster virtual team collaboration. While this can be a viable option in some settings, we realize that virtual courses in many universities may involve many students and therefore, the administration of personality measures and the composition of teams might be time and resource consuming. Therefore, we provide a set of practical recommendations related to handling personality issues in virtual teams and ways to foster information sharing and high-quality collaboration within higher education settings:

(1) *Engage in regular, transparent communication and establish clear communication protocols.* The findings of the current study indicated that higher levels of narcissism in teams hinder task-relevant information sharing. To ensure information flow among virtual team members, we suggest using structured agendas for virtual meetings to minimize off-topic discussions and maintain focus on the task. Also, we encourage teams to use university-provided collaborative tools (e.g., Slack, Zoom, Microsoft Teams) to ensure centralized communication and transparency of information flow.
(2) *Establish clear expectations and boundaries to promote role clarity from the beginning of the project.* Explicitly define roles, responsibilities, and acceptable behaviors in team charters or agreements to prevent undesirable behaviors from escalating. By establishing clear, pre-defined roles, teams can prevent narcissistic individuals from overstepping roles and dominating tasks. Teams can use tools such as Google Docs or Notion to document team member responsibilities and keep track of them.
(3) *Establish and enforce team norms.* Teams can create a code of conduct in which they establish ground rules for virtual collaboration with a specific focus on identifying acceptable behaviors and the consequences for violating them. Based on the established norms, team members can address disruptive behaviors and prevent them from escalating into larger issues.
(4) *Leverage narcissistic team members' strengths while keeping team goals in mind.* Although the current paper explored the potential harmful side of narcissism in teams, narcissistic individuals can have several strengths that can be leveraged in

a virtual team setting. As past research highlighted, narcissists are extroverted, motivated to improve their self-image, and tend to showcase confidence (Paulhus & Williams, 2002; Wallace & Baumeister, 2002). Consequently, assigning tasks to them that allow their abilities to shine (e.g., leading presentations, managing public-facing parts of the project) may motivate them to contribute to team tasks. Also, framing tasks highlighting how individual contributions impact team success may appeal to their desire for recognition.

(5) *Promote inclusive participation in projects.* Due to individuals having different personalities in virtual teams, members may voice their opinions to varying degrees. There is substantial literature on narcissism being related to leadership emergence with the initial positive perception of narcissistic leadership rapidly waning over time (Ong et al., 2016). To balance power dynamics in virtual student teams, members can rotate leadership roles for different tasks or meetings to allow equal participation, giving a chance to lead and contribute to the collective success of the team. Additionally, anonymous online polls for decision-making are encouraged so that all team members can voice their concerns and opinions equally.

(6) *Create a system for accountability.* Student teams can implement regular team check-ins to discuss their progress relevant to project milestones, assess and adjust workload when necessary, and keep track of whether everyone is completing their assigned tasks. This also gives an opportunity to teams to identify potential performance gap and discuss how to move forward.

(7) *Celebrate team milestones and goal achievement.* Acknowledging team progress and celebrating achievements can help to shift team members' focus from their individual goals to team goals, as well as create pride in the team's efforts. For example, after completing a major project milestone, teams can hold a virtual celebration in the form of a short Zoom meeting or a celebratory post in the group chat to recognize their collective success.

Limitations and Future Directions

There are several limitations of the current study. The study did not include control variables related to the use of technology (i.e., technological self-efficacy and experience with information and communication technology). Future research should incorporate technological self-efficacy and experience with ICT as control variables when conducting studies in a virtual environment.

Another potential limitation of the study is related to the study's timeframe. In a recent study, Grijalva et al. (2020) examined the impact of narcissism on team functioning in the context of a longitudinal study and found that narcissism's influence on team functioning was strengthened over time. In the current research study, individuals participated in a two-and-a-half-hour simulation game. Consequently, the timeframe of the study may have posed potential limitations regarding the strength of the relationship between narcissism, team processes, and performance. Therefore, it is recommended that future research should examine the impact of narcissism on team performance in the context of a longitudinal research study.

Third, the present study investigated the proposed hypotheses using ad hoc teams from online platforms (i.e., university's SONA system, Prolific) who had no prior experience working together. Therefore, future research should examine the proposed relationships in the context of real-world virtual teams.

Fourth, in the current study, we captured narcissism (i.e., grandiose narcissism) via the Narcissistic Personality Inventory (NPI; Rakin & Terry, 1988). However, other types of narcissism (e.g., vulnerable narcissism) are also worth exploring in the context of future research. Vulnerable narcissism is characterized by fragile self-confidence, preoccupation with grandiose fantasies, and the oscillation between feelings of superiority and inferiority. Whereas grandiose narcissism has been linked to high self-esteem and independent self-construal, vulnerable narcissism has been associated with low self-esteem, interdependent self-construal, and higher attachment anxiety (Rohmann et al., 2012). Given the differences between the two, it is likely that vulnerable narcissism would impact virtual team dynamics differently compared to grandiose narcissism. More specifically, we recommend exploring the connections between vulnerable narcissism and team emergent states (e.g., psychological safety, trust) as well as team processes (e.g., interpersonal processes) for future research.

Lastly, we encourage future research to explore other "dark" personality traits that potentially influence team functioning in virtual teams. In addition to the Dark Triad, other personality traits such as spitefulness and greed (*see* Marcus & Zeigler-Hill, 2015) could influence interpersonal dynamics in virtual teams. Moreover, we also recommend examining how the combination of two or more personality traits (e.g., narcissism and Big Five variables, narcissism and other dark personality traits) impacts teams. To do this, we recommend utilizing recent team compositional approaches (i.e., attribute alignment approach; Emich et al., 2022, Emich et al., 2024) in addition to the traditional team compositional approaches.

CONCLUSION

Examining narcissism at the team level is a relatively new trend in the literature. The current study aimed to provide a broader understanding of how team-level narcissism may impact team performance via team processes (i.e., information sharing and conflict) in the virtual setting. Evidence was found for the negative impact of team-level narcissism on information sharing; however, the results indicated that team-level narcissism was unrelated to both relationship and task conflict. Additionally, we found evidence for information sharing predicting virtual team performance. Considering the increasing use of virtual teams in both educational and organizational settings, team composition is a much needed and quickly evolving area of research that has the potential to enhance team functioning and outcomes.

REFERENCES

Back, M. D. (2018). The narcissistic admiration and rivalry concept. In Hermann, A. D., Brunell, A., & Foster, J. D. (Eds.), *Handbook of trait narcissism: Key advances, research methods, and controversies* (pp. 57–67). Springer. DOI: 10.1007/978-3-319-92171-6_6

Balthazard, P., Potter, R. E., & Warren, J. (2004). Expertise, extraversion and group interaction styles as performance indicators in virtual teams: How do perceptions of IT's performance get formed? *The Data Base for Advances in Information Systems, 35*(1), 41–64. DOI: 10.1145/968464.968469

Barrick, M. R., & Mount, M. K. (1991). The Big Five personality dimensions and job performance: A meta-analysis. *Personnel Psychology, 44*(1), 1–26. DOI: 10.1111/j.1744-6570.1991.tb00688.x

Bell, B. S., & Kozlowski, S. W. (2002). A typology of virtual teams: Implications for effective leadership. *Group & Organization Management, 27*(1), 14–49. DOI: 10.1177/1059601102027001003

Bell, S. T. (2007). Deep-level composition variables as predictors of team performance: A meta-analysis. *The Journal of Applied Psychology, 92*(3), 595–615. DOI: 10.1037/0021-9010.92.3.595 PMID: 17484544

Bell, S. T., Brown, S. G., Colaneri, A., & Outland, N. (2018). Team composition and the ABCs of teamwork. *The American Psychologist, 73*(4), 349–362. DOI: 10.1037/amp0000305 PMID: 29792453

Borg, M. E., Butterfield, K. M., Wood, E., Zhang, H. H., & Pinto, S. (2021). Investigating the impacts of personality on the use and perceptions of online collaborative platforms in higher education. *SN Social Sciences, 1*(40), 1–22. DOI: 10.1007/s43545-020-00053-x PMID: 34693305

Boulter, M. W., Roberts, R., & Hardy, J. (2022). Upsetting the apple cart: Within-team profiles of intragroup conflict and their associations with narcissism. *Psychology of Sport and Exercise, 63*, 102291. DOI: 10.1016/j.psychsport.2022.102291

Brown, R. P., Budzek, K., & Tamborski, M. (2009). On the meaning and measure of narcissism. *Personality and Social Psychology Bulletin, 35*(7), 951–964. DOI: 10.1177/0146167209335461 PMID: 19487486

Bush-Evans, R. (2020). *There's no I in team but there is a me: The influence of narcissism on team processes and organisational outcomes* (Doctoral dissertation, University of Southampton).

Campbell, W. K., Brunell, A. B., & Finkel, E. J. (2006). Narcissism, Interpersonal Self-Regulation, and Romantic Relationships: An Agency Model Approach. In Vohs, K. D., & Finkel, E. J. (Eds.), *Self and relationships: Connecting intrapersonal and interpersonal processes* (pp. 57–83). The Guilford Press.

Campbell, W. K., Goodie, A. S., & Foster, J. D. (2004). Narcissism, confidence, and risk attitude. *Journal of Behavioral Decision Making*, *17*(4), 297–312. DOI: 10.1002/bdm.475

Campbell, W. K., Rudich, E. A., & Sedikides, C. (2002). Narcissism, self-esteem, and the positivity of self-views: Two portraits of self-love. *Personality and Social Psychology Bulletin*, *28*(3), 358–368. DOI: 10.1177/0146167202286007

Carnevale, P. J., & Probst, T. M. (1998). Social values and social conflict in creative problem solving and categorization. *Journal of Personality and Social Psychology*, *74*(5), 1300–1309. DOI: 10.1037/0022-3514.74.5.1300 PMID: 9866189

Cogliser, C. C., Gardner, W. L., Gavin, M. B., & Broberg, J. C. (2012). Big five personality factors and leader emergence in virtual teams: Relationships with team trustworthiness, member performance contributions, and team performance. *Group & Organization Management*, *37*(6), 752–784. DOI: 10.1177/1059601112464266

De Dreu, C. K., & Weingart, L. R. (2003). Task versus relationship conflict, team performance, and team member satisfaction: A meta-analysis. *The Journal of Applied Psychology*, *88*(4), 741–749. DOI: 10.1037/0021-9010.88.4.741 PMID: 12940412

DeChurch, L. A., Mesmer-Magnus, J. R., & Doty, D. (2013). Moving beyond relationship and task conflict: Toward a process-state perspective. *The Journal of Applied Psychology*, *98*(4), 559–578. DOI: 10.1037/a0032896 PMID: 23731027

Dennis, A. S., Barlow, J. B., & Dennis, A. R. (2022). The power of introverts: Personality and intelligence in virtual teams. *Journal of Management Information Systems*, *39*(1), 102–129. DOI: 10.1080/07421222.2021.2023408

Devine, D. J., Habig, J. K., Martin, K. E., Bott, J. P., & Grayson, A. L. (2004). Tinsel Town: A top management simulation involving distributed expertise. *Simulation & Gaming*, *35*(1), 94–134. DOI: 10.1177/10468781032581

Douglas, H., Bore, M., & Munro, D. (2012). Distinguishing the dark triad: Evidence from the five-factor model and the Hogan development survey. *Psychology (Irvine, Calif.)*, *3*(3), 237–242. DOI: 10.4236/psych.2012.33033

Du, T. V., Miller, J. D., & Lynam, D. R. (2022). The relation between narcissism and aggression: A meta-analysis. *Journal of Personality*, *90*(4), 574–594. DOI: 10.1111/jopy.12684 PMID: 34689345

Dulebohn, J. H., & Hoch, J. E. (2017). Virtual teams in organizations. *Human Resource Management Review*, *27*(4), 569–574. DOI: 10.1016/j.hrmr.2016.12.004

Emich, K. J., Lu, L., Ferguson, A., Peterson, R. S., & McCourt, M. (2022). Team composition revisited: A team member attribute alignment approach. *Organizational Research Methods*, *25*(4), 642–672. DOI: 10.1177/10944281211042388

Emich, K. J., McCourt, M., Lu, L., Ferguson, A., & Peterson, R. (2024). Team composition revisited: Expanding the team member attribute alignment approach to consider patterns of more than two attributes. *Organizational Research Methods*, *27*(2), 329–348. DOI: 10.1177/10944281231166656

Felty, R., Whitaker, B. G., Bergman, S. M., & Bergman, J. Z. (2015). The longitudinal influence of narcissism in the team context. *International Journal of Organization Theory and Behavior*, *18*(2), 147–176. DOI: 10.1108/IJOTB-18-02-2015-B001

Flavián, C., Guinaliu, M., & Jordan, P. (2022). Virtual teams are here to stay: How personality traits, virtuality and leader gender impact trust in the leader and team commitment. *European Research on Management and Business Economics*, *28*(2), 100193. DOI: 10.1016/j.iedeen.2021.100193

Foster, J. D., & Twenge, J. M. (2010). Narcissism and relationships: From light to dark. In *The dark side of close relationships II* (pp. 401-428). Routledge/Taylor & Francis Group.

Frost, M., & Duan, S. X. (2020). Rethinking the role of technology in virtual teams in light of COVID-19. *Charles Sturt University Research Output*, 1–7. https://researchoutput.csu.edu.au/en/publications/rethinking-the-role-of-technology-in-virtual-teams-in-light-of-co

Furumo, K., de Pillis, E., & Green, D. (2009). Personality influences trust differently in virtual and face-to-face teams. *International Journal of Human Resources Development and Management*, *9*(1), 36–58. DOI: 10.1504/IJHRDM.2009.021554

Goldberg, L. R. (2013). An alternative "description of personality": The Big-Five factor structure. In *Personality and Personality Disorders* (pp. 34–47). Routledge. DOI: 10.1037/0022-3514.59.6.1216

Griffith, T. L., & Neale, M. A. (2001). Information processing in traditional, hybrid, and virtual teams: From nascent knowledge to transactive memory. *Research in Organizational Behavior*, *23*, 379–421. DOI: 10.1016/S0191-3085(01)23009-3

Grijalva, E., & Newman, D. A. (2015). Narcissism and counterproductive work behavior (CWB): Meta-analysis and consideration of collectivist culture, Big Five personality, and narcissism's facet structure. *Applied Psychology*, *64*(1), 93–126. DOI: 10.1111/apps.12025

Hackman, J. R., Brousseau, K. R., & Weiss, J. A. (1976). The interaction of task design and group performance strategies in determining group effectiveness. *Organizational Behavior and Human Performance*, *16*(2), 350–365. DOI: 10.1016/0030-5073(76)90021-0

Hao, Q., Yang, W., & Shi, Y. (2019). Characterizing the relationship between conscientiousness and knowledge sharing behavior in virtual teams: An interactionist approach. *Computers in Human Behavior*, *91*, 42–51. DOI: 10.1016/j.chb.2018.09.035

Harrison, D. A., Price, K. H., & Bell, M. P. (1998). Beyond relational demography: Time and the effects of surface-and deep-level diversity on work group cohesion. *Academy of Management Journal*, *41*(1), 96–107. DOI: 10.2307/256901

Hoch, J. E., & Dulebohn, J. H. (2017). Team personality composition, emergent leadership and shared leadership in virtual teams: A theoretical framework. *Human Resource Management Review*, *27*(4), 678–693. DOI: 10.1016/j.hrmr.2016.12.012

Hoegl, M., & Gemuenden, H. G. (2001). Teamwork quality and the success of innovative projects. *Organization Science*, *12*(4), 435–449. DOI: 10.1287/orsc.12.4.435.10635

Hogan, R. (1996). Personality assessment. In R. S. Barrett (Ed.), *Fair employment strategies in human resource management* (pp. 144–152). Quorum Books/Greenwood Publishing Group.

Ilgen, D. R., Hollenbeck, J. R., Johnson, M., & Jundt, D. (2005). Teams in Organizations: From Input-Process-Output Models to IMOI Models. *Annual Review of Psychology*, *56*, 517–543. DOI: 10.1146/annurev.psych.56.091103.070250 PMID: 15709945

Jackson, S. E., May, K. E., & Whitney, K. (1995). Understanding the dynamics of diversity in decision- making teams. In Guzzo, R. A., & Salas, E. (Eds.), *In Team decision-making effectiveness in organizations* (pp. 204–261). Joey Bass.

Jackson, S. E., & Ruderman, M. N. (Eds.). (1995). *Diversity in work teams: Research paradigms for a changing workplace*. American Psychological Association. DOI: 10.1037/10189-000

Jacques, P. H., Garger, J., Brown, C. A., & Deale, C. S. (2009). Personality and virtual reality team candidates: The roles of personality traits, technology anxiety and trust as predictors of perceptions of virtual reality teams. *Journal of Business and Management, 15*(2), 143–157. DOI: 10.1504/jbm.2009.141174

Jakobwitz, S., & Egan, V. (2006). The dark triad and normal personality traits. *Personality and Individual Differences, 40*(2), 331–339. DOI: 10.1016/j.paid.2005.07.006

Jehn, K. A. (1994). Enhancing effectiveness: An investigation of advantages and disadvantages of value-based intragroup conflict. *International Journal of Conflict Management, 5*(3), 223–238. DOI: 10.1108/eb022744

Jehn, K. A. (1997). A qualitative analysis of conflict types and dimensions in organizational groups. *Administrative Science Quarterly, 40*(2), 530–557. DOI: 10.2307/2393638

Jehn, K. A., Chadwick, C., & Thatcher, S. M. (1997). To agree or not to agree: The effects of value congruence, individual demographic dissimilarity, and conflict on workgroup outcomes. *International Journal of Conflict Management, 8*(4), 287–305. DOI: 10.1108/eb022799

Jehn, K. A., & Mannix, E. A. (2001). The dynamic nature of conflict: A longitudinal study of intragroup conflict and group performance. *Academy of Management Journal, 44*(2), 238–251. DOI: 10.2307/3069453

Jehn, K. A., Northcraft, G. B., & Neale, M. A. (1999). Why differences make a difference: A field study of diversity, conflict and performance in workgroups. *Administrative Science Quarterly, 44*(4), 741–763. DOI: 10.2307/2667054

Jehn, K. A., & Shah, P. P. (1997). Interpersonal relationships and task performance: An examination of mediation processes in friendship and acquaintance groups. *Journal of Personality and Social Psychology, 72*(4), 775–790. DOI: 10.1037/0022-3514.72.4.775

Khodabakhsh, M. R., & Besharat, M. A. (2011). Mediation effect of narcissism on the relationship between empathy and the quality of interpersonal relationships. *Procedia: Social and Behavioral Sciences, 30*, 902–906. DOI: 10.1016/j.sbspro.2011.10.175

Kolb, D. M., & Bartunek, J. M. (1992). *Hidden conflict in organizations: Uncovering behind-the-scenes disputes* (Vol. 141). *Sage (Atlanta, Ga.)*. Advance online publication. DOI: 10.4135/9781483325897

Kolm, A., de Nooijer, J., Vanherle, K., Werkman, A., Wewerka-Kreimel, D., Rachman-Elbaum, S., & van Merriënboer, J. J. (2022). International online collaboration competencies in higher education students: A systematic review. *Journal of Studies in International Education*, *26*(2), 183–201. DOI: 10.1177/10283153211016272

Kozlowski, S. W. J., & Ilgen, D. R. (2006). Enhancing the effectiveness of work groups and teams. *Psychological Science in the Public Interest*, *7*, 77–124. DOI: 10.1111/j.1529-1006.2006.00030.x PMID: 26158912

Lau, D. C., & Murnighan, J. K. (1998). Demographic diversity and faultlines: The compositional dynamics of organizational groups. *Academy of Management Review*, *23*(2), 325–340. DOI: 10.2307/259377

LePine, J. A., Buckman, B. R., Crawford, E. R., & Methot, J. R. (2011). A review of research on personality in teams: Accounting for pathways spanning levels of theory and analysis. *Human Resource Management Review*, *21*(4), 311–330. DOI: 10.1016/j.hrmr.2010.10.004

LePine, J. A., Hollenbeck, J. R., Ilgen, D. R., & Hedlund, J. (1997). Effects of individual differences on the performance of hierarchical decision making teams: Much more than g. *The Journal of Applied Psychology*, *82*(5), 803–811. DOI: 10.1037/0021-9010.82.5.803

Lynch, J., McGregor, A., & Benson, A. J. (2022). My way or the highway: Narcissism and dysfunctional team conflict processes. *Group Processes & Intergroup Relations*, *25*(4), 1157–1171. DOI: 10.1177/1368430221100194

Marcus, D. K., & Zeigler-Hill, V. (2015). A big tent of dark personality traits. *Social and Personality Psychology Compass*, *9*(8), 434–446. DOI: 10.1111/spc3.12185

Mathieu, J. E., Tannenbaum, S. I., Donsbach, J. S., & Alliger, G. M. (2014). A review and integration of team composition models: Moving toward a dynamic and temporal framework. *Journal of Management*, *40*(1), 130–160. DOI: 10.1177/0149206313503014

McCrae, R. R., & Costa, P. T. (1987). Validation of the five-factor model of personality across instruments and observers. *Journal of Personality and Social Psychology*, *52*(1), 81–90. DOI: 10.1037/0022-3514.52.1.81 PMID: 3820081

McGrath, J. (1964). *Social Psychology: A Brief Introduction*. Holt, Rinehart & Winston.

Mesmer-Magnus, J. R., & DeChurch, L. A. (2009). Information sharing and team performance: A meta-analysis. *The Journal of Applied Psychology*, *94*(2), 535–546. DOI: 10.1037/a0013773 PMID: 19271807

Moye, N. A., & Langfred, C. W. (2004). Information sharing and group conflict: Going beyond decision making to understand the effects of information sharing on group performance. *International Journal of Conflict Management*, *15*(4), 381–410. DOI: 10.1108/eb022919

Murmu, S., & Neelam, N. (2022). Impact of emotional intelligence and personality traits on managing team performance in virtual interface. *Asian Journal of Business Ethics*, *11*(Suppl 1), 33–53. DOI: 10.1007/s13520-022-00154-1

Nevicka, B., Ten Velden, F. S., De Hoogh, A. H., & Van Vianen, A. E. (2011). Reality at odds with perceptions: Narcissistic leaders and group performance. *Psychological Science*, *22*(10), 1259–1264. DOI: 10.1177/0956797611417259 PMID: 21931153

O'Neill, T. A., & Allen, N. J. (2014). Team task conflict resolution: An examination of its linkages to team personality composition and team effectiveness outcomes. *Group Dynamics*, *18*(2), 159–173. DOI: 10.1037/gdn0000004

Ong, C. W., Roberts, R., Arthur, C. A., Woodman, T., & Akehurst, S. (2016). The leader ship is sinking: A temporal investigation of narcissistic leadership. *Journal of Personality*, *84*(2), 237–247. DOI: 10.1111/jopy.12155 PMID: 25487857

Paulhus, D. L., Harms, P. D., Bruce, M. N., & Lysy, D. C. (2003). The over-claiming technique: Measuring self-enhancement independent of ability. *Journal of Personality and Social Psychology*, *84*(4), 890–904. DOI: 10.1037/0022-3514.84.4.890 PMID: 12703655

Paulhus, D. L., & Williams, K. M. (2002). The Dark Triad of personality: Narcissism, Machiavellianism and psychopathy. *Journal of Research in Personality*, *36*(6), 556–563. DOI: 10.1016/S0092-6566(02)00505-6

Peeters, M. A., Van Tuijl, H. F., Rutte, C. G., & Reymen, I. M. (2006). Personality and team performance: A meta-analysis. *European Journal of Personality: Published for the European Association of Personality Psychology*, *20*(5), 377–396. DOI: 10.1002/per.588

Prewett, M. S., Brown, M. I., Goswami, A., & Christiansen, N. D. (2018). Effects of team personality composition on member performance: A multilevel perspective. *Group & Organization Management*, *43*(2), 316–348. DOI: 10.1177/1059601116668633

Raskin, R., & Terry, H. (1988). A principal-components analysis of the Narcissistic Personality Inventory and further evidence of its construct validity. *Journal of Personality and Social Psychology*, *54*(5), 890–902. DOI: 10.1037//0022-3514.54.5.890 PMID: 3379585

Roberts, R., & Woodman, T. (2017). Personality and performance: Moving beyond the Big 5. *Current Opinion in Psychology, 16*, 104–108. DOI: 10.1016/j.copsyc.2017.03.033 PMID: 28813330

Robins, R. W., & Beer, J. S. (2001). Positive illusions about the self: Short-term benefits and long-term costs. *Journal of Personality and Social Psychology, 80*(2), 340–352. DOI: 10.1037/0022-3514.80.2.340 PMID: 11220450

Salancik, G. R., & Pfeffer, J. (1978). A social information processing approach to job attitudes and task design. *Administrative Science Quarterly, 23*(2), 224–253. DOI: 10.2307/2392563 PMID: 10307892

Sánchez, J., Zornoza, A., Orengo, V., Peñarroja, V., & Chamakiotis, P. (2018, August). Team feedback intervention and team learning in virtual teams: A moderated mediation model of team cohesion and personality. In *IFIP International Conference on Human Choice and Computers* (pp. 136-148). Cham: Springer International Publishing. https://doi.org/DOI: 10.1007/978-3-319-99605-9_10

Scott, C. P. R., & Wildman, J. L. (2015). Culture, communication, and conflict: A review of the global virtual team literature. In J. L. Wildman & R. L. Griffith (Eds.), *Leading global teams: Translating multidisciplinary science to practice* (pp. 13–32). Springer Science + Business Media. DOI: 10.1007/978-1-4939-2050-1_2

Simons, T. L., & Peterson, R. S. (2000). Task conflict and relationship conflict in top management teams: The pivotal role of intragroup trust. *The Journal of Applied Psychology, 85*(1), 102–111. DOI: 10.1037/0021-9010.85.1.102 PMID: 10740960

Thompson, J. D. (1967). *Organizations in action*. McGraw-Hill. DOI: 10.4324/9781315125930

Turel, O., & Zhang, Y. (2010). Does virtual team composition matter? Trait and problem-solving configuration effects on team performance. *Behaviour & Information Technology, 29*(4), 363–375. DOI: 10.1080/01449291003752922

Wai, M., & Tiliopoulos, N. (2012). The affective and cognitive empathic nature of the dark triad of personality. *Personality and Individual Differences, 52*(7), 794–799. https://doi-org.ezproxy.net.ucf.edu/10.1016/j.paid.2012.01.008

Wallace, H. M., & Baumeister, R. F. (2002). The performance of narcissists rises and falls with perceived opportunity for glory. *Journal of Personality and Social Psychology, 82*(5), 819–834. DOI: 10.1037/0022-3514.82.5.819 PMID: 12003480

Wang, B., Liu, Y., Qian, J., & Parker, S. K. (2021). Achieving effective remote working during the COVID-19 pandemic: A work design perspective. *Applied Psychology, 70*(1), 16–59. DOI: 10.1111/apps.1229 PMID: 33230359

Wang, M. L., & Hsu, B. F. (2012). A study to explore the team virtualization level and team effectiveness from the team personality composition. *Journal of the Knowledge Economy*, *3*, 199–216. DOI: 10.1007/s13132-011-0079-y

Wehrung, J. P. (2017). Displaying narcissism in a virtual team. *Management Review*, *28*(4), 441–460. DOI: 10.5771/0935-9915-2017-4-441

Wilson, J. M., Fletcher, T. D., Pescosolido, T., & Major, D. A. (2021). Extraversion and leadership emergence: Differences in virtual and face-to-face teams. *Small Group Research*, *52*(5), 535–564. DOI: 10.1177/1046496420986620

Xiao, X., Liu, F., Zhou, F., & Chen, S. (2018). Narcissistic leadership and employees' knowledge sharing: Influence of organizational identification and collectivism. *Social Behavior and Personality*, *46*(8), 1317–1329. DOI: 10.2224/sbp.7034

Section 2
Climate

Chapter 6
Maximizing Collaborative Creativity:
Learning and Practices for Instilling an Intentional Team Culture

L. Michelle Bennett
https://orcid.org/0009-0004-4947-8504
LMBennett Consulting, LLC, USA

ABSTRACT

Maximizing creativity in virtual teams requires the intentional integration of key elements. This chapter guides teams in cultivating a collaborative culture by increasing awareness of how members listen and respond to one another. The instructional strategies presented can be incorporated into course curricula, fostering lifelong habits for effectively participating in or leading teams. Through simulations, the chapter provides opportunities for immediate practice in building a team environment rooted in trust, psychological safety, and open communication. It emphasizes active listening across differences and the development of structured agreements that balance flexibility and creativity. Additionally, it highlights the critical role of a collaborative team mindset in sustaining effective teamwork.

INTRODUCTION

The opportunities and challenges of virtual teams in education are numerous and diverse, making them difficult to encapsulate succinctly. Even if they could be enumerated, each team operates within its unique context and dynamic. However, many

DOI: 10.4018/979-8-3373-0375-8.ch006

challenges recur across teams and can be anticipated, allowing for early intervention (Gray, 2008). Teams that are introduced to and practice fundamental collaborative skills from the outset are more likely to integrate them into their collective work. When embedded in the curriculum to develop collaboration skills for team projects, students gain competencies that extend throughout their education and careers. To foster creativity in virtual settings, teams can be equipped with targeted skills explicitly designed to enhance collaboration. This knowledge also aids in recognizing potentially problematic team environments—an invaluable lifelong skill.

A team requires several foundational elements to foster creativity. First, it must have an environment built on trust. Trust is an individual perception, with each member determining whether they can rely on teammates, the team as a whole, or the larger organization. Trust can grow, remain static, or decline over time (Cloud, 2023). Second, effective teams need psychological safety, a group-level phenomenon in which individuals assess their ability to take risks within the team or organization (Edmondson, 1999; A. C. Edmondson, 2019). Psychological safety, like trust, can increase, remain stable, or deteriorate. Third, team members must be willing to voice their thoughts, concerns, and ideas. This aspect is particularly crucial when challenging the status quo, identifying problems, or recognizing opportunities that others may overlook (Morrison et al., 2011; Van Dyne & LePine, 1998). A lack of trust, psychological safety, or voice can negatively impact team dynamics (Argyris, 1991; Cloud, 2023; Edmondson, 2019).

With trust, psychological safety, and voice in place, teams can unite individuals across diverse perspectives, fostering creativity and innovation. Maximizing differences for creativity requires acknowledging, embracing, and treating divergent views as opportunities. Achieving this with mutual respect necessitates a learning environment where team members remain open to new perspectives, embrace vulnerability, and extend the benefit of the doubt—facilitated through advocacy and inquiry (Bennett, 2024; Michalko, 2011). This chapter focuses on guiding teams in intentionally cultivating cultures that support creativity.

USING SIMULATIONS TO TEACH EFFECTIVE TEAM ENGAGEMENT SKILLS

This chapter utilizes simulations and guides teams through practices designed to intentionally cultivate a culture that nurtures both work and relationships. The term cultivate is used deliberately, as fostering relationships differs from completing a checklist of items. It requires ongoing attention, commitment, and adaptation. Like task-related work, relationship-building evolves and must be continually nurtured throughout team engagements.

A key advantage of the simulations in this chapter is that, when implemented explicitly, transparently, and alongside project learning, they become integral to the curriculum and learning outcomes. A common refrain among team members I have worked with is that they can manage their tasks but struggle with team dynamics. Imagine learning how to establish conditions for effective communication and collaboration from the outset and enabling early resolution of challenges. Further, consider the impact of practicing these concepts and applying them throughout your education and career. Would you value the opportunity to develop these strategies, approaches, and tools?

Extensive literature examines the characteristics of successful teams, that outline critical factors for effective team-based collaboration in both in-person and virtual settings (Hackman, 2006). This research defines the *what*—the conditions teams should establish and traits to develop—but offers little guidance on achieving these desired states. The *how* involves understanding what actions to take, how to implement them, and executing them in real-time, regardless of circumstances (Hackman, 2006). This chapter equips teams and those who support them with strategies to foster creativity and innovation.

Individuals, teams, and organizations require guidance in developing the skills necessary for effective collaboration. Key areas include:

- Intentionally evolving from a group of individuals to a cohesive team with shared norms and a collective mindset (Lotrecchiano et al., 2023).
- Transforming unproductive conflict into constructive engagement (Bennett & Gadlin, 2019).
- Responding to unexpected or critical perspectives with curiosity rather than defensiveness (Putnam, 2015).
- Communicating in ways that strengthen relationships and foster mutual understanding (Hubbs et al., 2021).

This chapter introduces key concepts sequentially, culminating in an integrated framework. It begins by distinguishing between the *what* and the *how*, both essential but historically weighted toward the former. To address the *how*, each section presents strategies for developing fundamental collaborative skills—bridging the gap between understanding what needs to be done and executing it effectively. Like any learning process, teams must practice the foundational elements if they want to foster creativity. These include trust, psychological safety, and voice, which support team development and skillful deliberative dialogue, the hallmarks of which are to maximize curiosity and learning about others' perspectives and achieve mutual understanding (Sokolof et al. 2016). Ultimately, these elements can be formalized in a team agreement, providing a structured approach to collaboration.

Launching Teams

Before virtual teams can engage in creative tasks, essential conditions must be established. Whenever possible, teams should convene in person at the outset of an engagement (Olson & Olson, 2014). The subtle yet significant interactions that occur in person, which cannot be replicated virtually, foster collaboration. Face-to-face meetings enable team members to shake hands, make eye contact, and sit together, enhancing interpersonal connections. They can engage in informal conversations, pre- and post-meeting discussions, and spontaneous exchanges that deepen mutual understanding. For instance, sharing a physical space provides a common experience that facilitates idea exchange, reflective discussions, and nonverbal communication through body language and tone. Spontaneous interactions—such as meeting at a coffee bar, sitting together, or conversing during breaks—occur naturally in person but are limited in virtual settings (Olson & Olson, 2014). Although brief, these moments help establish trust and psychological safety, laying the foundation for effective teamwork.

Whether or not an initial in-person meeting or kickoff event is feasible, several strategies can enhance the virtual experience to match the value of face-to-face interactions. Trust develops more slowly in virtual teams but can be strengthened by requiring video participation and adherence to agreed-upon ground rules during synchronous meetings. Structured frameworks provide essential guidelines for productivity, while processes facilitate collaboration. Clear, well-defined communication strategies—such as document sharing, asynchronous engagement, and meeting protocols—help minimize potential stressors in teamwork (Olson & Olson, 2014). Acknowledging challenges explicitly and establishing team-generated ground rules should be a priority, forming the basis of the first practice or simulation in this chapter.

Learning New Skills for Developing and Implementing Team Processes (The *How*)

Effective collaboration across differences often requires individuals to adjust their working styles. However, behavior change is notoriously difficult. Consider the tradition of New Year's resolutions—within days or weeks, most individuals fail to maintain them (Dickson et al., 2021; Norcross & Vangarelli, 1988). Similarly, teams committed to collaboration, a shared vision, and creative outcomes must be willing to modify their approaches.

Behavior change occurs through practice (Argyris & Schön, 1978; Putnam, 2015; Schön, 1991), and sustained practice requires motivation. At the team level, this means teams benefit from discussing and establishing shared values, motivations, and beliefs that will guide their collaboration and relationship dynamics (Lotrecchiano et al., 2023). Once agreed upon, these principles can be documented, such as in a Collaboration Agreement, and put into practice. Developing new skills together requires a willingness to take risks and be vulnerable within the group.

Building trust, psychological safety, and voice is fundamental for team members to learn from one another—whether in perspectives, knowledge, or skill development. But how can these elements be effectively cultivated? Explaining their importance intellectually is one approach but providing teams with direct experience and prompting reflection on their thoughts, emotions, and reactions is far more impactful. Experiential learning, through simulations of collaborative dynamics, enables teams to observe and recognize these processes in real-time.

The *how* offers team members an opportunity to apply both instinctive knowledge and intellectual learning in a simulation, co-creating an experience they can collectively reference (Koppett, 2013; Leonard, 2015). This process elicits reflections on key questions: What does this feel like? What emotions arise? What is effective, and what is not?

Recognizing feelings and emotions through reflection fosters self-awareness. Identifying these internal experiences allows individuals to connect them to the physiological and cognitive processes underlying trust and psychological safety. Working as a team, rather than individually, enhances reflective and reflexive learning, strengthening intentional team development.

Transitioning to How

This chapter presents an approach to help teams collaborate effectively. To develop proficiency, particularly in difficult conversations, teams must adopt new communication strategies and cultivate a habit of practicing together. Humans are unaccustomed to thinking about what they are thinking. Thus, it is useful for team members to become aware of how they are thinking and then decide collectively how those thoughts and beliefs come together as they learn to work together. With a solid understanding of their starting point, they can identify shifts that will enhance the team dynamic.

What does it take to move from knowing *what* to knowing *how*? Understanding *what* an intellectual activity is, whereas *how* is experiential and tied to emotions. Consider learning a new game, practicing a musical piece, setting up technology, or exploring an art form. You likely relied on instructions, sheet music, a manual, or an instructor to first grasp what needed to be done. That step was relatively simple. However, mastering *how* required deeper engagement and practice. Through repetition, you progressed from unskilled to skilled, from discomfort to increasing ease, until the activity became second nature.

As individuals become more competent, they may struggle in particularly challenging situations or when confronted with the unexpected. In teams, this often occurs in difficult conversations, misunderstandings, or moments of judgment. Despite possessing conversational skills, knowing how to respond in real-time can be elusive. This may explain why people acknowledge that teams must prioritize relationships as much as the collaborative project (Bennett et al., 2018). Conceptually, this seems obvious, but when teams attempt to implement it, what initially appeared clear often becomes uncertain and complex.

Weaving Together the Practice of How

This chapter integrates foundational elements into a structured program designed to foster creativity in virtual teams and cultivate intentional collaboration. When applied, these interconnected principles empower teams to explore, discover, and co-create. Each section offers opportunities to develop skills for effective and productive teamwork.

When a team's mood is collegial, members often experience contentment, engagement, and even enjoyment, interacting naturally and authentically without much effort. When teams become skilled enough to handle differences, misunderstandings, or tensions with the same ease, they have co-created environments that promote thoughtful responses and reduce harmful actions and reactions (Argyris & Schön, 1978; Rosenberg, 2015).

The following sections explore facets of the giving-and-receiving dynamic, guiding teams through progressive steps to share experiences, reflect together, and apply insights to their collaboration. Each practice is intentionally unrelated to the team's primary task, instead emphasizing engagement principles. By removing task pressure, this approach creates space for making mistakes, asking questions, retrying, and shared learning. Once these skills are honed in a neutral context, teams can begin applying them to their collaborative work.

Developing Trust and Psychological Safety

According to Edmondson (2019), "psychological safety does not imply ease or comfort … [it] is about candor and willingness to engage in productive conflict to learn from different points of view" (p. 16). Individuals often unconsciously evaluate whether others can be trusted in five key areas (Cloud, 2023). These evaluations include determining whether the other person:

- Genuinely understands them rather than merely claiming to do so;
- Exhibits selfless motives, acting in the team's interest rather than personal gain;
- Demonstrates the skills, abilities, and competence to fulfill their commitments;
- Has personality traits conducive to effective collaboration; and
- Behaves predictably, with past actions reliably indicating future behavior.

Similarly, individuals can gauge their sense of psychological safety and belonging in the team (Edmondson, 2019) by considering whether they feel able to:

- Interact honestly with team members;
- Raise concerns and have them taken seriously;
- Hold others accountable, knowing they will be held accountable in return;
- Exchange direct feedback openly; and
- Propose unconventional or bold ideas without fear of ridicule or retribution.

Trust and psychological safety exist along a continuum, ranging from high to low. Regularly assessing these team dynamics allows teams to track whether they are improving or declining. With this data, teams can identify contributing factors and determine whether intervention is needed (Edmondson, 2019). The team may decide to maintain the status quo if satisfied with the current trend or to make adjustments to improve these critical elements.

Individuals rarely share their thoughts or feelings without trust and a sense of psychological safety. When team members experience belonging, they feel valued for their talents, strengths, and unique qualities (Walton & Cohen, 2011). This sense of appreciation and acceptance can be summarized as: "We accept you for who you are and what you bring to the team." Belonging nurtures creativity and innovation.

Conversely, when team members perceive their ideas or perspectives as unwelcome, they may withdraw. This reaction often arises not from deliberate exclusion but from a combination of instinctive responses to perceived threats and societal conditioning (Greenwald & Banaji, 1995). For example, implicit messages may suggest: "We don't think your ideas are that great and don't really need them." While occasional occurrences might be brushed off, a consistent pattern of such messages leads individuals to stop contributing. Without their input, creative opportunities are missed, and the team's capacity for innovation diminishes.

Trust and psychological safety originate as physiological sensations rather than cognitive processes (Porges, 2004). These sensations, triggered by experiences that your body associates with safety or belonging, originate from the release of the hormone oxytocin into the bloodstream. Often called the "bonding hormone," oxytocin helps reinforce interpersonal connections. In this way, the process of building trust and psychological safety begins in the body rather than the mind. Once initiated, these sensations can be recognized and understood on a cognitive level (Zak, 2008).

This concept matters because when a team aims to intentionally foster trust and psychological safety, they must begin at the physiological level and build from there. Starting small often proves effective. For instance, when a new team forms, members could each share something straightforward and comfortable, such as what brought them to the project or what expertise they bring. This approach involves minimal risk and vulnerability—key components of the process. Once a baseline of trust and psychological safety is established, gradually introducing slightly higher levels of risk and vulnerability can further strengthen the team. Over time, this becomes self-reinforcing, as increased trust leads to greater team productivity (Costa et al., 2001).

Both trust and psychological safety can erode when someone's actions or behaviors have a negative impact. This can happen in several ways, including verbal, physical, moral, or ethical lapses. For example, a team member might fail to follow through on commitments, repeatedly fall short of expectations, act in disappointing ways, or neglect to share credit (Cloud, 2023). When individuals perceive their environment as increasingly untrustworthy and psychologically threatening, stress and anxiety rise, cognitive function declines, and the ability to learn diminishes. In these circumstances, cycles of declining trust and psychological safety can take hold.

In real teams, both positive events and occasional missteps or misunderstandings are inevitable. When challenges arise, it is important to acknowledge them promptly, discuss them as soon as possible, and work through them constructively. This approach prevents issues from escalating and helps the team grow stronger. Being effective at the moment requires team members to be spontaneous—developing through practice the skills and abilities to respond competently and confidently, even under unexpected circumstances. Building trusting and psychologically safe teams is the essential first step toward creating an environment where people feel secure enough to express their perspectives—this will be addressed in the topic that follows the Practices section.

Simulations Designed to Build Trust and Psychological Safety

Practice 1. Establishing Team Ground Rules

Objective: Define clear expectations for team engagement, work processes, and virtual collaboration, ensuring that members understand how to begin working together effectively.

Instructions: The following steps outline a process that encourages team members to reflect on, discuss, and finalize their initial set of ground rules, ensuring everyone's input is considered and that the team starts with clear expectations:

1. Begin by explaining that teams often create a set of common ground rules to guide their interactions.
2. Suggest starting with a provided list of typical ground rules.
3. Have each team member take a moment to consider:
   a. Whether any important items are missing.
   b. Whether any existing items need clarification or raise concerns.
4. Facilitate a group discussion where everyone shares their thoughts. Use a shared whiteboard tool, a document, or a screen-shared slide to record suggestions and concerns in real-time.
   a. Note any additions or adjustments suggested.
   b. Address any items that need clarification.
5. After gathering input, collaborate with the team to finalize the list, acknowledging that it can be updated as needed.
6. Conclude by having the team agree to review the ground rules at the start of every meeting.

The following are ground rules commonly established by teams to ensure effective communication and collaboration:

- Keep the video on and mute yourself when not speaking.
- Maintain confidentiality; what is said in the virtual room stays there, unless the full team agrees otherwise.
- Welcome all input—there are no bad ideas or silly questions.
- Share airtime fairly; agree on a turn-taking method such as using the raised hand function.
- Approach discussions with confidence in your perspective but openness to being wrong.
- Be present, prepared, patient, and caring.
- Ensure every meeting has a clear agenda and objective.

The following debrief and reflection questions are designed to encourage thoughtful analysis and discussion of the exercise:

- What did you find to be the easiest part of this exercise?
- What did you consider the most difficult aspect of the exercise?
- Did you observe any commonalities or differences among the perspectives shared?

Why This Works. Setting expectations for meetings helps build trust within the team. When team members actively participate in creating these expectations, it increases their commitment and motivation to adhere to them. Once a shared list of expectations is established, team members have a common understanding of expected behaviors. They will be able to observe whether others are following these expectations (building trust) or not (diminishing trust) (Bennett et al., 2018). If expectations are not being followed, this can serve as a point for team discussion, which we will explore further.

Ask: Encourage team members to commit to abiding by the agreements the team establishes, both individually and collectively.

The Application: All team meetings should begin with a reminder of the ground rules and an agreement on how to address deviations when they are noticed.

Practice 2. The Story of My Name

Objective: To provide team members with the first opportunity to introduce themselves and share something that most people are unlikely to know about them.

The following instructions outline the steps for guiding participants through the Story of My Name activity:

1. If everyone already knows each other, you can begin directly with the practice of the Story of My Name. If not, start with a round of introductions before proceeding.
2. Inform participants that they can share any story related to their name—whether it's their first or last name, a nickname, or an experience involving their name. The goal is to offer a broad, open space for them to share what feels most comfortable.
3. It may be helpful to model the process, so everyone understands what is being asked.
4. Adjust the timing based on the number of participants. For small groups, one to two minutes per person is sufficient; for larger groups, consider suggesting shorter time limits.

5. Ensure that everyone has a chance to share their story.
6. If someone is hesitant or does not wish to share, ask if there is any aspect of their name they would feel comfortable sharing.

The following debrief and reflection question prompts are designed to encourage thoughtful discussion and personal insight after the activity:

- What surprised you the most about this activity?
- How did it feel to hear others share their stories?
- What emotions did you experience while sharing your own story?
- Is there anything else you'd like to reflect on or discuss regarding the activity?

Why This Works. The exercise encourages participants to take a small risk and be vulnerable with each other by sharing something outside the work context. The topic—related to their name—is a significant part of their story, identity, and often their personal history. As participants share their stories, they experience others actively listening and accepting their words. This fosters a sense of being heard and valued. The experience strengthens connections among participants. Additionally, by focusing on their names, individuals are sharing a meaningful aspect of their identity (Koppett, 2013).

Ask: Encourage participants to reflect on the experience of taking a small risk and being supported by their team members.

The Application: The next step is applying these simulations to team projects. This could involve asking team members to take turns sharing what motivated their interest in the courses they are currently taking, their chosen major and minor, or their initial ideas for the team project.

THE ESSENCE OF RECEIVING MESSAGES FROM OTHERS: FEELING HEARD

According to Koppett (2013), "often we are blind to how much we reject without exploration. By bringing conscious focus to this aspect of their interactions, team members can work to build trust, risk-taking, problem-solving, and a sense of common purpose" (p. 61). Psychological safety is not the sole factor influencing individuals' willingness to take increasing risks within their teams over time. While feeling comfortable speaking up is essential, it is insufficient on its own. People want their voices to matter—to have their contributions acknowledged, concerns taken seriously, and perspectives considered impactful (Sherf et al., 2021). They seek to feel heard (Kerrissey et al., 2022).

How does feeling heard differ from psychological safety? Beyond feeling safe voicing one's views, individuals also receive attention, empathy, and respect from those they engage with. Their input contributes to achieving common ground (Roos, et al., 2023). Someone may feel comfortable speaking up but gradually realize their contributions are ignored or dismissed. They do not experience the intellectual engagement that signals their input is valued or feel appreciated for their contributions. When individuals repeatedly face an environment where they are ignored, they are as likely to withdraw as those who lack trust or psychological safety in their interactions.

Feeling heard does not mean agreement. Creating an environment where all team members feel heard involves fostering a cooperative dialogue that welcomes diverse ideas, opinions, and perspectives. Accepting what another says does not necessitate agreement (Sokoloff et al., 2016). Instead, differing opinions should invite curiosity and encourage individuals to consider alternative perspectives, even when agreement seems unlikely. This requires effort to understand others' viewpoints. Teams should anticipate that differences and concerns will arise and be voiced and focus on ensuring they have the capacity to reach a shared understanding.

Dialogue requires both speaking and active listening. Listeners receive messages while speakers share them, creating a dynamic exchange in which reception matters. Rolling one's eyes conveys a vastly different message than leaning in and nodding. Likewise, sitting back with crossed arms differs from relaxing one's shoulders and making eye contact. Such behavioral cues reveal a person's mindset, reflecting their real-time thoughts and emotions. This occurs because values, beliefs, and feelings shape behavior. The same applies to teams, where shared values, beliefs, and attitudes influence their actions and norms (Argyris, 1991; Argyris & Schön, 1978; Schwarz & Bennett, 2021).

Effective dialogue depends on a collaborative team mindset, beginning with how members collectively perceive one another, their motives, and their approach to communication. Messages may include ideas, constructive or negative criticism, positive feedback, technical knowledge, opinions, or decisions. Teams that intentionally cultivate a collaborative mindset are better equipped to receive messages with curiosity, openness, and a commitment to understanding—including both supportive and challenging exchanges (Steiner & Dick, 1995).

A closer look at the collaborative mindset and its role in team functioning provides valuable insight (Bennett, 2024). The best way to understand this mindset is by comparing it with the unilateral control mindset, recognizing that individuals can adopt either—or both—depending on the situation (Argyris & Schön, 1978).

Consistently operating from a collaborative mindset requires practice, and even then, occasional lapses are inevitable.

Consider a team where members prioritize being right, judge one another, seek to win discussions, assign blame rather than take responsibility, and focus on self-defense. This team operates from a unilateral control mindset, which undermines trust, psychological safety, and a sense of being heard (Argyris, 1977, 1994). Being part of such a team would be challenging, yet these behaviors often emerge when differing opinions arise, misunderstandings occur, or tensions escalate.

Now, imagine a team where members engage transparently, remain inquisitive, demonstrate reliability, make conscious choices, and are fully present with one another. This team exemplifies a collaborative mindset. When interactions feel effortless and productive, this mindset is likely in use.

Teams must intentionally choose the mindset they wish to adopt. They should reflect on how they want to collaborate, identify values that best support their work, and establish actions, norms, and agreements aligned with those values. Through consistent practice, teams build competence, improving their ability to navigate challenges effectively (Senge, 2006, 2014). A collaborative mindset fosters conditions for creativity, risk-taking, constructive challenge, and productive conflict resolution, ultimately advancing the team's progress.

Individual and team mindsets do not change overnight, especially when adopting new actions and norms requires skill development (Senge, 2006, 2014). Learning new skills necessitates practice, patience, feedback, and a shared understanding that everyone is making an effort. This is precisely why teams must practice—progress will include setbacks, but each mistake offers a learning opportunity. Growth occurs through trial, reflection, and extending care and grace to one another. This iterative process is essential for developing a shared team mindset, along with the actions and norms that sustain it. This is how people learn almost anything.

Fostering a trusting, psychologically safe environment allows team members to be fully present, actively listen, and engage meaningfully with one another. The next section will explore these dynamics in relation to practice.

Simulations Designed for Learning How People Feel Heard Using a Collaborative Mindset

Practice 3. What I Like About That

Objective: For team members to practice giving and receiving messages effectively.

Instructions: The following steps guide team members through a structured exercise to practice giving and receiving messages, fostering active listening, acknowledgment, and collaborative communication:

1. This activity can be done with small or large teams. If the team is very large, you may want to use breakout rooms for the exercise, bringing everyone back into the main room for the debrief.
2. Assign each participant a number to establish a sequence for the exercise.
3. The first person (#1) makes a simple statement, such as, "I just made cookies."
4. The next person (#2) acknowledges the statement and adds, "What I like about that is…." For example:
   a. Person 1: "I just got a new job."
   b. Person 2: "You just got a new job! What I like about that is you are making more money and also now we can go out to dinner."
   c. Person 3: "We can go out to dinner! What I like about that is we can go dancing after dinner!"
   d. Person 4: (continues the pattern)
5. Each participant builds on an element of the previous response, continuing for at least two full cycles.
6. Encourage participants to listen actively, be full present, and trust that responses will come naturally to them on their turn. The statements do not need to form a coherent story.
7. The goal is to accept and build upon what the previous person said, allowing for creativity and spontaneity.

The following debrief and reflection questions encourage thoughtful analysis and discussion of the exercise:

- How did you feel during this exercise?
- What thoughts or insights emerged for you?
- Did anything surprise you? If so, what led it to be surprising?

Why This Works: This exercise requires participants to be fully present and attentive, ensuring they actively listen to the previous speaker. It encourages acceptance of others' contributions and builds upon them, reinforcing respect and demonstrating that each idea is valued. By paraphrasing elements of the previous message, participants engage in active listening, while speakers feel acknowledged and heard.

Ask: Encourage team members to observe how they respond to messages in daily interactions. Specifically, focus on the words used after receiving a message and how they contribute to the conversation.

The Application: As a team, track observations of how members respond to messages. Share these examples in a team meeting to promote awareness and enhance shared learning.

Practice 4. Mindset Matters: No-But-And

Objective: This is a three-part simulation designed to give team members real-time experience accepting, receiving, and responding to messages sent in different ways.

Instructions: Parts A, B, and C should be completed in sequence. Please note that if teams have participated in previous exercises using a numbered sequence, take a moment to reorder participants so they interact with different team members.

Part A – No, and ...

1. Assign numbers to participants to establish the sequence for the exercise.
2. The first person suggests an idea, such as, "Let's go for pizza."
3. The next person responds with "No, and..." followed by an alternative suggestion.
4. Each subsequent person continues, responding to the previous statement with "No, and..."

For example:

a. Person 1: "Let's go for Pizza."
b. Person 2: "No, I do not want to go for pizza, and I'd rather go for a walk."
c. Person 3: "No, I don't feel like walking, and I think we should just stay in."
d. Person 4: "No, I don't want to stay in—we did that last night, and I think we should go dancing."
e. Person 5: (continues the pattern)

5. Continue until all participants have responded twice, with the first person closing the cycle.

The following debrief and reflection questions encourage participants to analyze their experience and reflect on the impact of the exercise:

- What was your experience during this exercise?
- How did it feel to say “No” to others' ideas?
- How did it feel when others said “No” to you?

Part B – Yes, but

1. Participants may keep the same order or rearrange it. Please note that changing the sequence allows different individuals to experience both giving and receiving responses from new team members.
2. The first person offers a suggestion, such as, “Let’s go for pizza.”
3. Each participant responds by affirming the previous statement with “Yes,” repeating what they heard, followed by “but” and their reasoning.

For example:

a. Person 1: “Let’s go for pizza.”
b. Person 2: “Yes, let’s go for pizza but I’d rather go walking.”
c. Person 3: “Yes, a walk sounds great, but I’d rather stay inside tonight.”
d. Person 4: “Yes, staying in is a good idea, but I think it would be fun to go dancing.”
e. Person 5: “Yes, … but….”

4. Continue until all participants have responded twice, with the first person closing the cycle.

The following debrief questions encourage participants to analyze their experience and reflect on the impact of the exercise:

- What was your experience during this activity?
- How did it feel to deliver the “Yes, but” response?
- How did it feel to receive a “Yes, but” response?

Part C – Yes, and

1. Participants may keep the same order or rearrange it.
2. The first person offers a suggestion, such as “Let’s go for pizza.”

3. Each participant responds by affirming the previous statement with "Yes," repeating what they heard, followed by "and" to expand on the idea and contribute something new.

For example:

a. Person 1: "Let's go for pizza."
b. Person 2: "Yes, let's go for pizza and maybe we can go for a walk after that."
c. Person 3: "Yes, a walk sounds good, and I would like to go for ice cream at the new place on the corner."
d. Person 4: "Yes, …and"

4. Continue until all participants have responded twice, with the first person closing the cycle.

The following debrief questions encourage participants to analyze their experience and reflect on the impact of the exercise:

- What was your experience during this activity?
- How did you feel when delivering messages??
- How did you feel when receiving them?

The following debrief questions encourage participants to reflect on their overall experience across all three parts (A, B, and C):

- What did you observe as you progressed through the three exercises?
- Did anything surprise you?
- Did you notice any emotions or reactions during any of the exercises?

Why This Works: This exercise simulates three distinct ways of receiving messages. Part A provides the experience of an outright rejection, where the offeror hears a direct "no." Part B simulates a more subtle form of rejection, as the offeror hears "yes, but," which ultimately negates the initial agreement. Part C models full acceptance, where the offeror's idea is acknowledged and expanded upon, leading to a greater sense of being heard. Because communication is a two-way process, each exercise also allows participants to experience both roles—offering and receiving messages (Koppett, 2013; Leonard, 2015).

Ask: Encourage team members to become more aware of how they give and receive messages in daily interactions. Set aside time for discussion: If they were to create a script for how they would like to offer and receive messages, what key elements would they include?

The Application: After practicing the mindset necessary for accepting messages, challenge the team to apply these skills by brainstorming ideas for their project or reflecting on what is working well within the team. Use "yes, and" or "what I like about that is…" as models to build on one another's contributions and foster collaborative problem-solving.

LISTENING FOR UNDERSTANDING BUILDS POTENTIAL FOR EMPATHETIC LISTENING

According to Michalko (2011), "it is no coincidence that the most creative and innovative people throughout history have been experts at forcing new mental connections via the conceptual blending of unrelated subjects" (p. 2). Active listening is a fundamental collaborative skill that requires fully engaging with the speaker to accurately understand and paraphrase their message with the correct nuances (Egan, 2006). It is easy to sense when someone is not truly listening, despite their nods and occasional "uh-huhs." Similarly, we often find ourselves in conversations where our minds drift, only to realize we have missed the last few minutes of what was said. This is a common human tendency.

As explored in the previous section, a receiver can respond to a message in various ways—by dismissing it, accepting it, or ignoring it entirely. These responses can be verbal or conveyed through body language. However, acceptance of a message does not imply agreement. Rather, it signifies that the receiver has truly heard the other person, can paraphrase their message accurately, and can then determine how to respond. When agreement exists, little follow-up may be needed. However, when disagreement or misunderstanding arises, intentional next steps are essential.

Teams should actively monitor for differences of opinion, potential misunderstandings, or unspoken tensions and address them early. If a concern proves irrelevant or can be quickly resolved, no further action is necessary. However, if it holds merit, failing to discuss it may cause escalation. This is when team members should lean into their curiosity, extend the benefit of the doubt, and intentionally adopt a collaborative mindset. They should accept and accurately paraphrase each other's perspectives before formulating genuine, open-ended questions designed to deepen understanding. Authentic questions are not rhetorical or leading but are rooted in a desire to learn (Putnam, 2015).

Effective teamwork thrives on differences among members, and well-managed diversity enhances creativity and innovation (Leroy et al., 2022). Greater differences introduce more possible connections, perspectives, and solutions, providing the team with a wealth of insights. A team operating from a collaborative mindset fosters curiosity, leading to a deeper exploration of both similarities and differences. Creativity emerges in the space between known ideas, where inquiry stimulates discoveries. When team members leverage their unique strengths toward a shared purpose, they unlock their collective potential. However, while differences fuel innovation, poor management of these differences often results in tension and unproductive conflict, ultimately stifling creativity (Michalko, 2011; Van Knippenberg & Hoever, 2017).

Authentic inquiry is the foundation of meaningful dialogue and an essential complement to active listening. The effectiveness of listening increases when the listener understands what they are listening for. What does this mean? In any team interaction—whether engaging with an individual or the entire group—you may need to listen for intellectual understanding to establish common ground and move a project forward. Alternatively, you may need to listen at a deeper, relational level, attuning to the emotions and feelings beneath the surface. This form of deeper listening, known as empathetic listening, helps others feel truly heard, valued, and supported.

At first glance, empathetic listening may not seem essential in project teams. After all, teams come together to accomplish tasks, not to discuss emotions—right? Not exactly. Team members inevitably experience emotions, sometimes intensely, about their ideas and contributions. Every team has both a task component and a relationship component, which cannot be separated. When functioning well, these elements reinforce one another, enhancing creativity, innovation, and impact. Openly acknowledging emotions, needs, and feelings within a team fosters greater cohesion, strengthens trust, sustains psychological safety, and ensures members feel heard.

Successful communication requires listening for understanding and, at times, empathetic listening—the ability to discern unspoken needs embedded in both words and tone (Rosenberg, 2015). While it is impossible to fully know what another person is feeling, this is precisely why dialogue and inquiry are so important. A collaborative mindset allows for listening with openness and care, setting aside judgment, blame, and evaluation. With practice, team members can develop the skills to receive any message with curiosity and intention, leading to deeper learning and stronger connections.

The ability to engage in inquiry during tense, uncomfortable, or awkward situations is essential for fostering a healthy, creative team culture. However, this is only possible when foundational elements—such as trust, psychological safety, and active listening—are in place. Deliberative dialogue, awareness of emerging differences, curiosity about those differences, and the pursuit of common ground are invaluable team skills. The next section will explore how to apply these skills to developing team agreements.

Simulations Designed to Help Team Members Learn How to Listen: For Understanding and Empathetically

Practice 5. The Listening Ladder

Objective: This simulation series provides team members with the opportunity to experience various ways of receiving and responding to messages. It progresses from intentional chaos and non-listening (Parts A and B) to active understanding (Part C), then to meaningful dialogue (Part D), and finally to empathetic connection (Part E). Each step is designed to deepen participants' engagement with the practice of both listening and being listened to. The debriefs encourage reflection on how these skills currently manifest in their interactions and how they can be more intentionally applied within their teams.

Instructions: All simulation sets should be completed in sequence on the same day, with a full group debrief at the end. The first three exercises (Parts A–C) should be done with the same partner, while team members will switch partners before Part D to encourage new interactions. When facilitating this exercise, it is important to provide a high-level overview at the start, as the five-part structure may seem long or complex. While there are multiple components, clearly outlining the process helps participants understand that there is a structured method behind the activity. Detailed instructions should be provided step by step to keep the group engaged. Additionally, unlike many exercises where a debrief follows each section, this simulation is designed to save the debrief for the end. This approach allows participants to fully experience the progression from ignoring each other in the early stages to engaging in deliberative dialogue in the later stages, fostering deeper reflection and awareness. Switching partners after Part C is intentional, as the first three parts focus on building comfort and foundational skills, while Part D integrates these skills in a new dynamic. Working with a different partner at this stage helps reinforce learning in a fresh context. Finally, if empathetic listening (Part E) seems too advanced or risky for the group, facilitators may choose to stop after Part D and conduct the full debrief at that point.

Part A – Restless Noise

1. Explain the logistics and activities so all participants understand the exercise.
2. Logistics:
    a. This practice consists of two parts: Set 1 and Set 2, each lasting 30 seconds.
    b. Participants will work in pairs within breakout rooms.
    c. This exercise requires timing; facilitators can use system features or instruct participants to time themselves.
    d. Each pair will complete both sets before returning to the main room.

3. Activities
   a. Set 1: Alphabet and Counting – One person continuously recites the alphabet, while the other counts numbers aloud simultaneously for 30 seconds.
   b. Set 2: Contact Information – Each participant recites their contact information aloud at the same time for 30 seconds, repeating as needed until time is up.
   c. After completing both sets, participants return to the main room.
   d. No debrief will follow this section. Instead, participants will move directly to Part B with the same pairings.

Part B – Breaking Through

1. Provide a clear explanation of the exercise so all participants understand the process.
2. Logistics:
   a. This exercise consists of two parts: Set 1 and Set 2, each lasting one minute.
   b. Participants will work in breakout rooms with the same pairs from Part A.
   c. The exercise requires timing; facilitators can use system features or instruct participants to track the time themselves.
   d. Each pair will complete both sets before returning to the main room.
3. Activities
   a. Set 1: Listen to Me – Both partners will speak simultaneously about something that interests them, such as their studies or hobbies. Each person should focus entirely on telling their own story, without attempting to listen or respond to their partner. Encourage them to imagine being in a bubble, solely focused on expressing their message.
   b. Set 2: Catching Fragments – Both partners will again speak simultaneously about something that interests them, similar to the previous exercise. However, this time, they should attempt to catch fragments of what their partner is saying. When they hear a keyword or phrase, they should briefly weave it into their own story. For example, if one person hears their partner mention "dogs" while talking about their vacation, they might say, "I saw many dogs on the beach…"—whether or not it is true.
   c. Differences between the two sets:
      i. Set 1: Complete isolation—both individuals speak in parallel with no interaction.
      ii. Set 2: Mostly isolated speaking, but with brief moments of catching and incorporating fragments from the other person.
   d. Ask the pairs to complete both Set 1 and Set 2 before returning to the main room.

e. No debrief will follow this section. Instead, participants will move directly to Part C with the same pairings.

Part C – Finding Focus

1. Set up the exercise so participants understand the process.
2. Logistics:
    a. This practice consists of one exercise, repeated twice so that each participant takes a turn as the asker and the responder.
    b. Participants will continue working in the same pairs as in Parts A and B within breakout rooms.
    c. The exercise requires timing; facilitators can use system features or ask participants to track the time.
    d. Each pair will have two rounds of four minutes, with each person switching roles.
3. Activity

The person starting the conversation is the asker, and the other is the responder.

a. The asker applies active listening by paraphrasing and asking curious, open-ended questions to deepen understanding. (See Table 1 for an example.)
b. The asker selects a question from the list of conversation starters or creates their own and poses it to the responder. (See Table 1 legend for some suggestions.)
c. The responder answers the question genuinely.
d. The asker listens attentively, responds with genuine curiosity, and asks a follow-up question based on what they heard.
e. The Responder answers the follow-up question.
f. Have the pairs do this for four minutes.
g. Pairs continue this exchange until time is up and then switch roles.
h. After both participants have taken a turn, they return to the main room.
i. No debrief will follow this section. Instead, participants will transition to Part D with new pairings.

Curiosity enables team members to engage more deeply in discussions, particularly when seeking to understand different perspectives. When someone expresses a differing view, responding with curiosity fosters open dialogue and deeper insight. Table 1 is an example of what this might sound like between colleagues.

Table 1. Example of Active Listening Method to Use for Part C

Speaker	Conversation Example
Asker	"Do you think ghostwriting (including by artificial intelligence) should be permitted?"
Responder	"Yes, I think it is okay."
Asker	"What leads you to think it's okay?"
Responder	"Well, there are people who have important things to say but don't always have the time to sit down and write it themselves."
Asker	"What leads you to think that having someone with the time to do it instead of them is okay?"
Responder	"Well, the person with the idea has to have conversations with the person writing so it is clear what they really want reflected in the writing. Not to just let them write what they want."
Asker	"So you're thinking there is a difference between engaging with the writer vs. just tossing them a topic to write about. Have I got that right?"
Responder	"Yes, absolutely. Because, if... [continues]"

Note. Possible conversation starters for active listening practice include: What are you doing when you lose all sense of time and are truly in the moment? How would you define [success, expertise, consensus, etc.]? What do you most want to achieve in five years? What is one accomplishment you are very proud of? What mistake did you make that taught you the greatest lesson? Who is one of your role models? If you had to pick one activity—skydiving, scuba diving, or bungee jumping—which one would you choose?

Part D –The Dance

1. Set up the exercise so all participants understand the process.
2. Logistics:
    a. Inform participants that they will be assigned new pairings in the breakout rooms.
    b. This exercise will be completed once, as partners will now engage in a dialogue rather than a structured turn-taking format. They will apply the active listening and inquiry skills practiced in Part C, this time in coordination with their partner.
    c. The exercise requires timing; facilitators can use system features or ask participants to track the time.
    d. Pairs will engage in a five-minute dialogue and return to the main room when finished or when the breakout rooms close.
3. Activity
    a. Ask pairs to apply the active listening and inquiry skills they practiced in the previous exercise to maximize their learning from the other person.
    b. Either participant can initiate the dialogue—they may start with a statement followed by a question or begin directly with a question. The topic is entirely up to them, and they may choose a question from the previous list if needed.
    c. The goal is for each person to maximize learning from their partner, which requires balance and cooperation throughout the conversation.

d. Remind participants to remain fully present and engaged with their partners.
e. Once pairs complete the exercise, they should return to the main room.
f. A debrief of the series so far will take place once everyone has returned.
g. At this point, facilitators may choose to end the session or proceed to the final practice, which introduces the next step: Empathetic listening.

Part E – Between the Lines

1. Set up the exercise so all participants understand the process.
2. Logistics:
   a. Participants will remain in the same pairings as Part D within breakout rooms.
   b. The exercise will be done twice, allowing each person to take turns as the starter and the responder.
   c. The exercise requires timing; facilitators can use system features or ask participants to track the time themselves.
3. Activity
   a. Pairs will alternate roles, with one person as the starter and the other as the responder.
   b. The full exercise lasts eight minutes, with partners switching roles at the halfway mark (four minutes per turn).
   c. The starter begins by expressing a 45-second "storm"—sharing something real that is frustrating, annoying, or bothering them. The topic can be small or significant, depending on their comfort level.
   d. After 45 seconds, the responder will apply the listening skills they have been practicing by paraphrasing what they heard the Starter say. Additionally, they will express what they believe the Starter might be feeling and ask for confirmation, recognizing that their interpretation may not be entirely accurate—which is why they seek clarification. The responder must focus entirely on the starter, resisting the urge to give advice or problem-solve. Instead, they should listen attentively to identify the emotions underlying the Starter's words. The Responder's primary role is to support the Starter in reflecting on their own experience and emotions, creating space for deeper self-awareness. For example:
      i. Starter: "I'm really getting tired of dishes being left in the sink. I feel like it has become my job to always clean everything up..."
      ii. Responder: "I just heard you say you are getting really tired of being the one who has to clean up all the time. I'm thinking you are frustrated and in need of some respect for your time and energy. Am I on track?
      iii. Starter: "Yes... or not quite...or ...."

iv. Responder: "I'm hearing you say not quite, can you help me understand what you are feeling?"

e. Each pair should time themselves and continue the exercise until they feel ready or until four minutes have passed. Once the time is up, they should switch roles and repeat the exercise, ensuring both participants experience being the starter and the responder.

f. Once both participants have taken turns as the Starter and the Responder, instruct them to return to the main room for the final debrief.

The following debrief and reflection questions encourage participants to analyze their experience and reflect on key insights gained throughout the entire exercise series:

- What was your experience participating in this series of exercises (Parts A–E)?
- What insights or realizations did you gain?
- Did anything surprise you? If so, what and why?
- What is a key takeaway for you personally? For your team?

Why This Works: This series of practices immerses team members in social interaction and communication experiences that reflect familiar real-world dynamics, ranging from being ignored to feeling deeply listened to. It offers an experiential journey from superficial exchanges to meaningful connections. Participants often describe debriefing as a moment of realization, highlighting powerful conversations, impactful interactions, and a depth of understanding rarely experienced in a work setting. Additionally, the exercise is frequently noted as a fun and engaging way to learn. With continued practice and the intentional integration of skills from Parts D and E, teams can significantly enhance their ability to collaborate effectively.

Ask: Encourage teams to pause periodically and intentionally apply these skills in their interactions. While it may feel challenging to slow down in a fast-paced environment, recognizing a missed opportunity to use these techniques is itself a success—it signals growing team awareness. Celebrate the act of noticing, as it demonstrates progress in developing more mindful communication. Remind teams that even when moments are missed, they can still revisit the situation to reflect on what happened and consider how a different approach—one that embraces slowing down—might have led to a different outcome.

Application: The skills introduced and practiced in this section can be applied anytime and anywhere a situation calls for deeper engagement. Team members now have a shared language for expressing their needs without judgment, fostering more constructive and open communication. As individuals become more confident in their ability to navigate meaningful conversations, they may be surprised at the various contexts in which they naturally apply these skills. Table 2 outlines some essential characteristics of The Listening Ladder, providing a framework for continued practice and integration into team interactions. The Ladder is designed to guide individuals through progressively deeper levels of attention and awareness toward others. This exercise encourages a shift from surface-level interaction to full presence, fostering greater connection, understanding, and compassion. By engaging in this practice, team members develop the ability to truly listen, acknowledge, and respond in ways that strengthen relationships and enhance collaboration.

Table 2. Essential Characteristics of the Listening Ladder Practices

Stage	Key Features
Part A: Restless Noise	Deliberate noise and chaos; complete disconnect in communication.
Part B: Breaking Through	The focus remains on speaking, not listening; minimal awareness, and listening.
Part C: Finding Focus	Introduces true listening with structured turn-taking; builds inquiry and questioning skills.
Part D: The Dance	Balances speaking and listening, requiring cooperation and mutual understanding.
Part E: Between the Lines	Focuses on emotional understanding, validating feelings, and deepening connection.

BALANCING STRUCTURE (PLANNING AND EXECUTION) WITH FLEXIBILITY (FREEDOM AND PLAY)

According to Hackman (2006), "it is a fantasy – a tempting and pervasive one, but a fantasy nonetheless – that it is possible to have great teams without the bother of creating enabling team structures" (p. 130). While it may seem paradoxical, establishing structures—such as a team mindset, norms, and processes—can significantly enhance collective creativity (Hackman, 2006), which is crucial for innovation and impactful outcomes. Team agreements that define norms, processes, and collaborative structures serve as a scaffold for building trust, fostering psychological safety, and encouraging open communication. The intentional design of a supportive team environment provides the necessary conditions to catalyze creativity (Binyamin & Carmeli, 2017; Rietzschel et al., 2014). Structure establishes boundaries within which teams operate, allowing members to feel secure enough to take risks, experiment, and explore new ideas. When individuals trust that they can propose ideas—no matter how unconventional—without fear of judgment, they become more willing to engage, innovate, and contribute to the team's success.

Social interaction and effective communication are foundational team conditions that foster creativity (Jordanous & Keller, 2016). Like any other team capability that requires nurturing and sustainability, these skills must be developed gradually to create small successes that reinforce themselves, ultimately leading to greater achievements. When teams establish clear social interaction and communication practices, they create an explicit framework that facilitates discussions about both triumphs and challenges. Engaging in open dialogue about accomplishments and areas for improvement cultivates a culture of continuous learning.

This chapter introduced simulations and structured exercises—small, repeatable practices designed to enhance social interaction and communication. These initial steps lay the groundwork for more comprehensive frameworks that support both the task-oriented and relationship-oriented aspects of teamwork. When team norms and agreements are intentionally developed with a collaborative mindset, the team's overall approach will naturally become more collaborative (Schwarz & Bennett, 2021), thereby enabling the foundational elements that catalyze creativity and innovation (Goncalo al., 2019).

Team agreements come in various forms—collaboration agreements, team charters, welcome letters, and management plans, among others. Regardless of the name, they all serve the same purpose: documenting shared expectations. These agreements play a critical role in developing teams, helping them build and reinforce trust, psychological safety, effective communication, and active listening skills. Making expectations explicit provides teams with a mechanism for accountability, ensuring that members hold themselves and each other responsible for upholding the agreed-upon norms. Whether a team is formed for a short-term project or a long-term collaboration, well-defined agreements provide a foundation for intentional maturation and sustained success.

The most effective way for teams to begin developing a collaboration agreement is by identifying the most essential starting elements. Attempting to create a comprehensive document in a single session is neither practical nor efficient. Instead, teams should focus on prioritizing key components, developing a structured plan, outlining foundational agreements, and establishing a schedule for further development. By leveraging both synchronous and asynchronous collaboration, teams can efficiently build out the agreement over time. While not every detail needs to be written collaboratively, every aspect should reflect an integrative process that values and incorporates input from all members. This ensures that the agreement is not only well-structured but also inclusive and representative of the team's collective vision.

Practice for Putting Team Agreements in Place to Maximize Productivity and Innovation

Practice 6. Creating Structure, Releasing Creativity

Objective: Although not a simulation, initiating a structured team agreement document provides a foundational framework for collaboration. This practice integrates key skills from previous sections, fostering discussions on effective teamwork and launching the agreement planning process. By the end, teams will have identified critical areas for agreement and established an implementation timeline.

When disagreements arise during the document's development process, teams should pause and engage in thoughtful inquiry. This is what they have been working towards by intentionally creating trust, psychological safety, and voice. This practical exercise is an integral part of the curriculum, warranting the time necessary for thorough discussion. Milestones may vary depending on the specific course or team duration.

Virtual Materials Needed: A whiteboard platform or similar tool that allows capturing, organizing, and displaying information for all team members.

Instructions: To facilitate the development of structured team agreements, follow these steps:

1. Provide each team with a virtual workspace and two prompts:
   a. What norms and expectations are most essential for this group to establish?
   b. Which initial agreements should the team prioritize?
2. Instruct team members to spend three minutes individually brainstorming and recording each idea on a virtual sticky note, placing them in the shared space.
3. After three minutes, assign teams to breakout groups to share their ideas. Each team member shares one idea at a time, rotating turns until all ideas are presented.
   a. This is not a discussion period; members should focus on sharing, without judgment or reaction.
   b. Those with more ideas continue taking turns until all sticky notes are shared.
   c. The focus is on allowing each participant to share their thoughts and for them to be accepted by the others.
   d. Clarifying questions are permitted as needed.
4. Once all ideas are shared, the team groups similar concepts together.
   a. Encourage teams to explore differing perspectives and learn from each other.
   b. Remind them to slow down, remain curious, and engage in dialogue, as practiced in *The Listening Ladder* simulation.

5. After organizing the sticky notes, teams assign a name to each category that reflects its core theme.
6. The team then establishes a method for prioritizing the list.
   a. Emphasize that this is an essential part of the exercise.
   b. The process should be inclusive and agreed upon by all members.
   c. Encourage the use of deliberative dialogue when differences arise.
7. Once prioritized, the team confirms the top three or four agreements that resonate most.
8. Starting with the highest-priority item, teams begin planning their first collaboration agreements.
9. The duration of this exercise varies based on team size, collaboration timeline, and other factors. The two primary outcomes are:
   a. A clear set of next steps, including assigned responsibilities and deadlines.
   b. A foundational plan outline that can be further developed as needed.

The following debrief and reflection questions provide an opportunity to analyze the experience, explore key insights, and identify important lessons learned:

- What stands out most about this practice?
- Did you find any aspects satisfying, frustrating, or surprising?
- What is your key takeaway?
- What did you learn about yourself and your teammates?
- What did you identify as crucial for your team's success?

Why This Works: When teams begin collaboration planning with topics that matter to them, their motivation to engage increases, as does their accountability in upholding agreements. Many teams initially believe they can work well together without formal planning or written agreements. However, once they begin the exercise, they often recall past team experiences they wish to avoid, and these elements often rise to the top of the list of things to address early in the collaboration. People learn from past experiences what does not work for them and can use that knowledge to help design approaches that are more effective in new situations. This process fosters synergy, leading team members to recognize that explicitly defining certain key elements is both valuable and satisfying.

Ask: Encourage teams to continue implementing their collaboration agreements. As part of their next steps, they should discuss the team values and mindset they want to establish as their foundation. While developing processes, remind them to assess whether their approaches align with these agreed-upon values and mindset. Consider the following questions: Is the process transparent? Does it foster inquiry? Can team members fully commit to being present and engaged? Could a new team member fully understand the norm and/or follow the process by reading your document? You can assign sections, create milestone, and set expectations for a final document.

Application: In the short term, dedicating time to developing a collaboration agreement for their current project team can strengthen working relationships, enhance team dynamics, and improve overall productivity. As they intentionally cultivate a collaborative culture, encourage them to reflect on past exercises and periodically revisit them within their work context. In the mid-to-long term, team members can apply this approach to any future teams they join as their training and careers evolve.

SUMMARY

Virtual teams' success depends on their ability to collaborate effectively, yet many leave this to chance. Practitioners and researchers may want to explore the impact of these strategies in an effort to further define and improve them for their particular contexts and uses. Developing strong teamwork requires effort, sometimes significant effort. The fundamental elements and skill-building processes outlined in this chapter can help teams initiate that journey. When integrated into curricula that encourage students to experience the power of collaborative work, these practices also highlight the importance of relationships and team dynamics. Consistently applying these skills enhances efficiency, fosters creativity, and improves outcomes. Mastering these fundamentals can transform how teams work together now and in the future.

ACKNOWLEDGMENT

I would like to thank Kathrine A. Lawrence for her careful review of the chapter, her insightful reactions, comments, and constructive criticisms, and for the suggestions that strengthened it.

REFERENCES

Argyris, C. (1977). *Double Loop Learning in Organizations*. Retrieved February 19, 2025, from https://hbr.org/1977/09/double-loop-learning-in-organizations

Argyris, C. (1991). Teaching smart people how to learn. *Harvard Business Review*. https://hbr.org/1991/05/teaching-smart-people-how-to-learn

Argyris, C. (1994). Good Communication That Blocks Learning. *Harvard Business Review*, *72*(4), 4.

Argyris, C., & Schön, D. A. (1978). *Organizational learning: A theory of action perspective*. Addison-Wesley.

Bennett, L. M. (2024). Mindset matters for interdisciplinary teams: Choose a collaborative one. *Integration and Implementation Insights*. https://i2insights.org/2024/07/23/collaborative-mindset-for-teamwork/

Bennett, L. M., & Gadlin, H. (2019). Conflict Prevention and Management in Science Teams. In Hall, K. L., Vogel, A. L., & Croyle, R. T. (Eds.), *Strategies for Team Science Success: Handbook of Evidence-Based Principles for Cross-Disciplinary Science and Practical Lessons Learned from Health Researchers* (pp. 295–302). Springer International Publishing. DOI: 10.1007/978-3-030-20992-6_2

Bennett, L. M., Gadlin, H., & Marchand, C. (2018). *Collaboration and team science: A field guide* (2nd ed.). NIH. https://www.lmbennettconsulting.com/_files/ugd/40747d_8058cb6e909242f896721f82beb99801.pdf

Binyamin, G., & Carmeli, A. (2017). Fostering members' creativity in teams: The role of structuring of human resource management processes. *Psychology of Aesthetics, Creativity, and the Arts*, *11*(1), 18–33. DOI: 10.1037/aca0000088

Cloud, H. (2023). *Trust: Knowing when to give it, when to withhold it, how to earn it, and how to fix it when it gets broken*. Worthy Publishing.

Dickson, J. M., Moberly, N. J., Preece, D., Dodd, A., & Huntley, C. D. (2021). Self-regulatory goal motivational processes in sustained new year resolution pursuit and mental wellbeing. *International Journal of Environmental Research and Public Health, 18*(6), 3084. DOI: 10.3390/ijerph18063084 PMID: 33802749

Edmondson, A. (1999). Psychological safety and learning behavior in work teams. *Administrative Science Quarterly, 44*(2), 350–383. DOI: 10.2307/2666999

Edmondson, A. C. (2019). *The fearless organization: Creating psychological safety in the workplace for learning, innovation, and growth.* John Wiley & Sons, Inc.

Egan, G. (2006). *The skilled helper: A problem-management and opportunity development approach to helping* (2nd ed.). Thomson.

Goncalo, J. A., Katz, J. H., & Ellis, L. M. (2019). PIECE Together: How social norms support the process of team creativity. In Paulus, P. B., & Nijstad, B. A. (Eds.), *The Oxford handbook of group creativity and innovation* (pp. 216–230). Oxford University Press. DOI: 10.1093/oxfordhb/9780190648077.013.13

Gray, B. (2008). Enhancing Transdisciplinary Research Through Collaborative Leadership. *American Journal of Preventive Medicine, 35*(2), S124–S132. DOI: 10.1016/j.amepre.2008.03.037 PMID: 18619392

Greenwald, A. G., & Banaji, M. R. (1995). Implicit social cognition: Attitudes, self-esteem, and stereotypes. *Psychological Review, 102*(1), 4–27. DOI: 10.1037/0033-295X.102.1.4 PMID: 7878162

Hackman, J. R. (2006). *Leading teams: Setting the stage for great performances.* Harvard Business School Press.

Hubbs, G., O'Rourke, M., & Orzack, S. H. (Eds.). (2021). *The toolbox dialogue initiative: The power of cross-disciplinary practice* (First edition). CRC Press, Taylor & Francis Group.

Jordanous, A., & Keller, B. (2016). Modelling creativity: Identifying key components through a corpus-based approach. *PLoS One, 11*(10), e0162959. DOI: 10.1371/journal.pone.0162959 PMID: 27706185

Kerrissey, M. J., Hayirli, T. C., Bhanja, A., Stark, N., Hardy, J., & Peabody, C. R. (2022). How psychological safety and feeling heard relate to burnout and adaptation amid uncertainty. *Health Care Management Review, 47*(4), 308–316. DOI: 10.1097/HMR.0000000000000338 PMID: 35135989

Koppett, K. (2013). *Training to imagine: Practical improvisational theatre techniques for trainers and managers to enhance creativity, teamwork, leadership and learning* (2nd ed.). Stylus Pub.

Leonard, K., & Yorton, T. (2015). *Yes, and: How improvisation reverses no, but thinking and improves creativity and collaboration—Lessons from The Second City*. HarperCollins Publishers.

Leroy, H., Buengeler, C., Veestraeten, M., Shemla, M., & Hoever, I. J. (2022). Fostering team creativity through team-focused inclusion: The role of leader harvesting the benefits of diversity and cultivating value-in-diversity beliefs. *Group & Organization Management*, *47*(4), 798–839. DOI: 10.1177/10596011211009683

Lotrecchiano, G. R., Bennett, L. M., & Vovides, Y. (2023). A framework for developing team science expertise using a reflective-reflexive design method (R2DM). *Humanities & Social Sciences Communications*, *10*(1), 810. DOI: 10.1057/s41599-023-02298-2

Michalko, M. (2011). *Creative thinkering: Putting your imagination to work*. New World Library.

Morrison, E. W., Wheeler-Smith, S. L., & Kamdar, D. (2011). Speaking up in groups: A cross-level study of group voice climate and voice. *The Journal of Applied Psychology*, *96*(1), 183–191. DOI: 10.1037/a0020744 PMID: 20718517

Norcross, J. C., & Vangarelli, D. J. (1988). The resolution solution: Longitudinal examination of New Year's change attempts. *Journal of Substance Abuse*, *1*(2), 127–134. DOI: 10.1016/s0899-3289(88)80016-6 PMID: 2980864

Olson, J. R., & Olson, G. M. (Eds.). (2014). *Working together apart: Collaboration over the internet*. Morgan & Claypool.

Porges, S. W. (2004). Neuroception: A subconscious system for detecting threats and safety. *Zero to Three (J)*, *24*(5), 19–24. https://chhs.fresnostate.edu/ccci/documents/07.15.16%20Neuroception%20Porges%202004.pdf

Putnam, R. W. (2015). Recipes and reflective learning, "What would prevent you from saying it that way?" *Action Design*. https://actiondesign.com/resources/readings/recipes-and-reflective-learning

Rietzschel, E. F., Slijkhuis, J. M., & Van Yperen, N. W. (2014). Task structure, need for structure, and creativity. *European Journal of Social Psychology*, *44*(4), 386–399. DOI: 10.1002/ejsp.2024

Roos, C. A., Postmes, T., & Koudenburg, N. (2023). Feeling heard: Operationalizing a key concept for social relations. *PLoS One*, *18*(11), e0292865. DOI: 10.1371/journal.pone.0292865 PMID: 38032901

Rosenberg, M. B. (2015). *Nonviolent communication: A language of life* (3rd ed.). PuddleDancer Press.

Schön, D. A. (Ed.). (1991). *The Reflective turn: Case studies in and on educational practice*. Teachers College Press.

Schwarz, R. M., & Bennett, L. M. (2021). Team effectiveness model for science (TEMS): Using a mutual learning shared mindset to design, develop, and sustain science teams. *Journal of Clinical and Translational Science*, *5*(1), e157. DOI: 10.1017/cts.2021.824 PMID: 34527296

Senge, P. M. (2006). *The fifth discipline: The art and practice of the learning organization*. Currency Doubleday.

Senge, P. M., Kleiner, A., Roberts, C., Ross, R. B., & Smith, B. J. (2014). *The fifth discipline fieldbook: Strategies and tools for building a learning organization*. Crown/Archetype.

Sherf, E. N., Parke, M. R., & Isaakyan, S. (2021). Distinguishing Voice and Silence at Work: Unique Relationships with Perceived Impact, Psychological Safety, and Burnout. *Academy of Management Journal*, *64*(1), 114–148. DOI: 10.5465/amj.2018.1428

Sokoloff, H., Dillon, D., & Dineen, P. (2016). "Debate, discussion, deliberative dialogue"—"3 D's" by Harris Sokoloff, David Dillon, and Patty Dineen. *NIFI*. https://www.nifi.org/en/catalog/product/debate-discussion-deliberative-dialogue-3-ds-harris-sokoloff-david-dillon-and-patty

Steiner, C., & Dick, J. (1995). *Original warm fuzzy tale: Fairytale*. Jalmar Press.

Van Dyne, L., & LePine, J. A. (1998). Helping and voice extra-role behaviors: Evidence of construct and predictive validity. *Academy of Management Journal*, *41*(1), 108–119. DOI: 10.2307/256902

Van Knippenberg, D. L., & Hoever, I. J. (2017). Team diversity and team creativity: A categorization-elaboration perspective. In *Team creativity and innovation* (pp. 41–60). Oxford University Press.

Walton, G. M., & Cohen, G. L. (2011). A Brief Social-Belonging Intervention Improves Academic and Health Outcomes of Minority Students. *Science*, *331*(6023), 1447–1451. DOI: 10.1126/science.1198364 PMID: 21415354

Zak, P. J. (2008). The neurobiology of trust. *Scientific American*. https://www.scientificamerican.com/article/the-neurobiology-of-trust/

Chapter 7
Designing a Supportive Creative Climate for Human-Centered Virtual Teams:
The Role of Rituals

Tracey Rockett
https://orcid.org/0000-0003-1035-9693
Texas Christian University, USA

Stacy Landreth Grau
https://orcid.org/0000-0002-7150-3583
Texas Christian University, USA

ABSTRACT

Fostering a creative environment in virtual teams is possible, but it is more difficult than for traditional face-to-face teams. In order to support creativity in virtual teams we need to deliberately create a human-centered team. The most effective way to do that is to build that is built social connectedness and team cohesion, solid team processes, and psychological safety and trust. This can be done through the creation and use of rituals for a virtual environment. This chapter provides guidance to create rituals for virtual teams that support creativity.

DOI: 10.4018/979-8-3373-0375-8.ch007

INTRODUCTION

Teaching students to work with technology, in addition to teaching core concepts, has become the reality in higher education. Educators must be aware of new technologies and be able to help students use technology effectively to be competitive in today's rapidly changing work environments due to the pace of digital transformation. Digital transformation is defined as the "use of new digital technologies to enable significant business environments" (Fitzgerald et al., 2013; Vuchkovski et al., 2023, p. 1) and has helped to increase the presence and importance of virtual teams in organizations. While virtual teams and remote work have existed for years, these particular ways of doing work saw rapid adoption during and after the COVID-19 pandemic. Existing research on virtual teams describes them based on geographic dispersion and dependence on electronic communication (Bell & Kozlowski, 2002; Gilson et al., 2021; Malhotra et al., 2007; Nemiro, 2004, 2023), and research suggests a series of critical skills needed for team effectiveness in virtual teams (Nemiro, 2004, 2026; Saad & Agogue, 2023). Changing work norms and rapid technological advances require students in higher education and employees to learn these new skills.

While educators have already been working with students to prepare them to work on virtual teams (Hu & Chan, 2024; Ma & Leman, 2023; Nemiro et al., 2023), we propose faculty must be ready to help students learn to work in what we refer to as *human-centered virtual teams* in which students learn how to exhibit collaboration, empathy, and perspective-taking skills (Leman & Mott, 2023: Nemiro, 2026) while working virtually.

In addition, in these human-centered virtual teams, faculty must help students learn how to foster and support team creativity because contemporary organizations are concerned with facilitating creativity and innovation due to their impact on organizational performance. To understand the vital factors needed for creativity in virtual teams, Saad and Agogue (2023) created a framework based on a systematic literature review of virtual teams and creativity that highlighted three areas: (1) the relevant inputs that directly affect a team's creative performance on the individual and team levels, leadership, and technology factors; (2) the general work climate shaping creative conditions such as teamwork and social connectedness; and (3) the virtual collaboration process that guides group interaction and knowledge exchange. Further, Nemiro (2004, 2026) conceptualized a five-component model for ensuring high levels of creativity in virtual teams in business. This model highlighted design, climate, resources, norms and protocols, and continued assessment and learning. Both models have areas of overlap that are important considerations for skill set development.

Virtual teams must focus on several key elements for creating a team climate to maximize the social connections and team climate for creativity to thrive: 1) social connectedness and team cohesion, 2) team processes, and 3) psychological safety and trust. While all of these components are necessary for creativity in traditional, face-to-face teams, they are even more important in virtual teams because the gaps in team distance, time, and culture can reduce psychological safety and cohesion, and create additional challenges when it comes to building team processes and managing conflict. While the virtual aspect necessitates utilizing technology, this is not always seen as a facilitator for creativity. Research shows that increased technology usage, leading to little to no face-to-face time, can seem like an inhibitor to human connection (Lal et al., 2023). However, since technology is required in virtual teams, creating ways to center "humans" in virtual teams is essential. One solution is to embrace the concept of bringing more empathy and connection into virtual teams – what we again refer to as the human centered virtual team. There are ways to connect people using technology that foster humanity. So how might we create conditions that allow people - students and professionals - to connect on a human level but in a virtual space to maximize their creativity and overall performance? And how can we accomplish this given the constraints of technology and potential fatigue and burnout?

One area - rituals - can be an important way to facilitate team social connectedness and cohesion, effective team processes, and psychological safety, especially in virtual environments where face-to-face communication is sacrificed or minimized. This chapter examines the factors that facilitate a favorable climate for creativity in virtual teams, namely team social connectedness and cohesion, team processes, and psychological safety. We aim to provide best practices and practical tools for faculty to help students learn to create human-centered virtual teams with a specific focus on using rituals. As such, the roadmap of our chapter is as follows. First, we define virtual teams, as well as the major concepts associated with creative teams (social connectedness and cohesion, team processes, and psychological safety and trust). We then discuss the principles of human-centered virtual teams, define and discuss the role of rituals, and how these rituals can be positive for the teams. Last, we provide justification and details for several types of rituals associated with social connectedness and cohesion, team processes, and psychological safety and trust. We conclude with considerations on designing rituals for virtual teams.

VIRTUAL TEAMS

Teams are ubiquitous in organizations today. Organizations need teamwork in order to survive and thrive in today's complex, global environment and are looking for employees who are skilled at being good team members and team leaders. Salas et al. (2015) identified the need for teams to perform both taskwork and teamwork. Taskwork is about the tasks teams need to complete to achieve goals, while teamwork is about what team members do to get the job done. It is our belief that faculty can focus on helping students develop both the taskwork for teams as well as the teamwork by helping them develop and use rituals to support those teams.

Virtual teams are teams, first and foremost, and share many of the same opportunities and challenges of traditional teams but also pose additional challenges due to their unique characteristics. Virtual teams have been defined as a "group of individuals with varying degrees of proximity (geographical, temporal, and relational), guided by a common purpose or organizational task who collaborate primarily through technology with minimal face-to-face communication" (Saad & Agogue, 2023, p 119). When team members are distributed geographically, and often culturally, and primarily use technology to communicate and coordinate with one another, it is more difficult to deal with team conflict, and build team psychological safety and trust (Gilson et al., 2021), resulting in work delays and miscommunications (Bell & Kozlowski, 2002; Gilson et al., 2021; Malhotra et al., 2007; Nemiro, 2004, 2023).

Even before the COVID-19 pandemic, there was a rise in the number of organizations that were moving to virtual teams because rapidly developing technology allowed them to communicate and organize successfully across distances (Kimura, 2024). Organizations have been increasing the use of virtual teams to be more competitive globally, reduce the need for travel, and have access to talent that may not be geographically available (DeRosa et al., 2004; Zheng et al., 2024). However, since 2020 we have seen a steep increase in the number of organizations that use technology to work from anywhere, and the rise in virtual teams has risen in concert. Some evidence has suggested that as more people began working on virtual teams, they got better at being on those teams and developed better team processes and conflict management procedures (Klonek et al., 2022).

That said, there are several challenges to virtual teams. Working online can lead to fatigue, a lack of spontaneous interaction, and an overly structured workflow (Bailenson, 2021; Gibson & Gibbs, 2006; Tkalich, 2022; Waizenegger et al., 2020). More seriously, virtual teams often have an environment that is devoid of trust and psychological safety (Edmondson & Lei, 2014; Tkalich, 2022). Some of this happens because of the gaps in distance, time, and even culture. However, much of it is because personal, social, and non-verbal cues are lost in virtual interactions, and they are necessary conditions for building trust and psychological safety. Other commonly cited challenges with virtual teams are the lack of cohesion and connectedness between members (Cai, 2023; Lea & Spears, 1991) and difficulties with relationship communication and trust, including a lack of connection and commitment between members (Morgan, 2018; Tucker, 2023). Therefore, leaders should be strategic about creating conditions to support creativity. There are a variety of ways that one might help build connections between team members to create psychological safety, trust, and community.

Educators must be familiar with ways to create connections in virtual teams and help educate their students in how to do so. Some ways we have had students create connections in their virtual teams include having team members play two truths and a lie, having them share their top five movies, and having them share something about a favorite pet or loved one. Directing students to share personal information online and giving them structure to do so, helps to get them talking and to continue the conversation after the class is finished. In addition, faculty who serve as role models by sharing personal information themselves, also help the process of creating connection.

CLIMATE FOR CREATIVITY

Team creativity is "the process by which team members generate relevant ideas, solutions and working procedures with the potential of turning into innovative outputs," (Saad & Agogue, 2023, p. 119). While current research focuses on creativity in terms of idea generation, this definition is meant to encompass more than ideation. The research shows that creativity can be fostered in virtual teams. Han et al. (2017) argue that virtual work fosters creativity, innovation, and productivity while overcoming space and time limitations. But psychological safety and mutual trust need to be established and nurtured for creativity to thrive (Edmondson, 1999; Han et al., 2017). Saad and Agogue (2023) found that two constructs lead to a productive climate for creativity – a teamwork environment and social connectedness, or cohesion. We would also add that psychological safety is essential for team creativity because in psychologically safe teams, members feel they can take risks, explore new ideas, and make mistakes, all of which are important to the creative process (Edmondson & Mogelof, 2006).

A teamwork environment (Saad & Agogue, 2023) ensures that a communication climate is psychologically safe and supportive because it nurtures trust and promotes informal connections to help mitigate the adverse consequences of virtual work on creativity. Issues to consider include: open discussions, supportive communication, high-risk tolerance (Gibson & Gibbs, 2006), and openly discussing new ideas (Han et al., 2017).

Social connectedness refers to "the extent to which team members share similar abilities to perceive, comprehend and evaluate relevant knowledge" (Saad & Agogue, 2023, p.129). Social connectedness gradually evolves over time as team members get to know one another. In typical virtual teams, this process is slowed even further and may never develop. However, as team members start to feel more socially connected, virtual work becomes more efficient, and exploration is more likely to occur. Ultimately, the level of social connectedness will determine how the creative teamwork will unfold (Saad & Agogue, 2023).

Team cohesion refers to how committed members are to one another and the team, as well as how motivated they are to help the team reach its goals (Kozlowski & Ilgen, 2006). Team cohesion directly supports the feeling of social connectedness through the creation of bonds among members but also indirectly influences the teamwork environment by fostering the bonds that lead to open communication and exploration. Team cohesion is often referred to as a "glue" that holds the team together (Nemiro, 2007; Orazani et al., 2023)

Psychological safety is typically defined as a "shared belief that the team is safe for interpersonal risk taking" (Edmondson, 1999, p 354). Fostering psychological safety will contribute directly to the teamwork environment in that it supports open communication and conflicting ideas and indirectly to the social connections by providing positive interactions that increase trust and liking among team members. When creating a team environment to foster creativity, one needs the ability to experiment and explore in a safe space, along with a strong sense of commitment to the team. That is when working on creative tasks, group members must both feel safe to take risks and feel committed enough to weather the challenges they may face along the way. Psychological safety and cohesion can support the creation of a teamwork environment and foster social connections. But how can we foster this for virtual team members?

HUMAN-CENTERED VIRTUAL TEAMS

A human-centered virtual team refers to a virtual team (remote and/or hybrid) that prioritizes the needs, well-being, and experiences of each team member, focusing on their connection, psychological safety, and overall sense of belonging (IBM, n.d.). This includes ways to foster trust, inclusion, and empathy. A human-centered virtual team applies human-centered design principles to the virtual team dynamic to optimize collaboration, productivity, and creativity. There are several critical aspects of a human-centered virtual team:

- Empathy and understanding through emotional intelligence and support;

- Intentional communication by using multiple channels (video, chat, asynchronous tools) without being overwhelming to ensure that communication norms support diverse needs, working styles, and time zones;
- Technology as an enabler and not a barrier, with tools that enhance human connection rather than create more complications and complexity;
- Trust and connection by creating an environment where team members feel safe to share ideas, ask questions, make mistakes, and question authority;
- Equitable participation and voice by ensuring that all team members are heard and valued by using structured facilitation techniques and rotating leadership roles;
- Flexibility and autonomy by allowing team members to make decisions;
- Purpose driven culture by aligning members along a shared vision and values to reinforce commitment; and
- Focus on well-being by encouraging work-life balance and respect for time, talent, and boundaries to reduce burnout.

Ideally, integrating human-centered principles into virtual teams will also help with feelings of isolation and burnout. Given the ubiquity of virtual teams in higher education, it is meaningful for faculty to teach students how to be good team members and support their teammates by fostering more connection. Additionally, this helps faculty prepare students for virtual teams in the workplace. Some ways we have incorporated human-centered principles into virtual teams in our classes included, having a class session where students do something fun together online that is not related to class work, such as making favorite tacos, doing a virtual escape room together, or sharing photo collages of favorite things.

Overall, this chapter highlights how faculty can help students foster creativity in virtual teams, and we argue that the way to do this is to make teams more "human-centered." This "why" drives the purpose of the chapter. In order to accomplish this, we discussed driving forces to accomplish that - social connectedness and team cohesion, team processes, and psychological safety and trust. These answer the "what." But the devil is in the details. Rituals serve as the "how" to design creative and effective teams in a virtual environment. Figure 1 shows how rituals and the driving forces of team cohesion, team processes, and psychological safety work together to lead to creativity in virtual teams.

Figure 1. Creativity in Virtual Teams

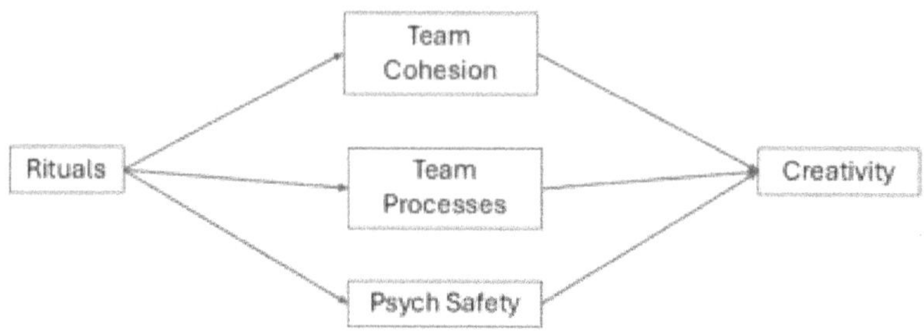

THE ROLE OF RITUALS

Rituals have a long history of academic study (anthropology, sociology, religion, neuroscience, psychology, and organizational behavior). This has helped researchers understand their importance, origins, and historical significance to humans. Rituals describe the most meaningful traditions and cultural practices worldwide - from athletics to religion to marriage. Rituals can be practiced by individuals, groups of people, and entire organizations or cultures. Think about rituals large and small - from rituals associated with Catholic mass service to yoga class. From beach vacations to Burning Man festivals. From sleeping routines for babies to Sunday night dinners. Rituals allow people to connect in the present moment and enable people to turn ordinary activities into something special (Norton, 2024).

As such, rituals have been defined in many ways and there is no consensus on definition. Some of these definitions include that rituals are actions that a person or group does repeatedly, following a similar pattern or script in which they have imbued symbolism and meaning (Ozenc & Hagan, 2019). While examining the psychological foundations of rituals, Hobson et al. (2017) define rituals as "(1) predefined sequences characterized by rigidity, formality, and repetition that are (2) embedded in a larger system of symbolism and meaning, but (3) contain elements that lack direct instrumental purpose" (p. 2). Their definition considers many of the defining features of rituals identified in other works. While all three of these features are present, they may be weighted differently depending on the context (Hobson et al., 2017).

In general, rituals can be characterized by causal opacity, meaning the actions performed do not have a clear physical causal mechanism for achieving their intended effect. Rituals often involve physical movements, props, words, or actions representing something bigger. Rituals have several uses: to identify group members, to ensure commitment to the group, to facilitate cooperation within and between groups, to maintain cohesion, to regulate emotions, including stress and uncertainty, and to impose order (Ozenic & Hagen, 2019).

Recently, rituals for groups and teams have received new research attention (Lepisto, 2022). While there is no definitional consensus, Kim et al. (2021) suggested that group rituals are characterized by three features: physical, psychological, and communal. Physical features include specific types of words and acts, and they argue that group activities that contain specific words and acts that are more repeated, rigid, and tend to be more ritualistic. Consider, for example, a football team that touches a statue before heading out to the field. The psychological features are associated with solidifying a group's values and traditions. Communal features, by definition, involve multiple people and can take on various forms and activities that are shared with others, making them more ritualistic. Kim et al. (2021) also argue that these rituals happen along a continuum - meaning that the more these three features are embedded into group activities, the more ritualistic they become. And they are more meaningful to the group when they become more ritualistic. The researchers found that the ritual meaning can spill over to work tasks, leading members to feel that their work is more meaningful and important overall. Rituals in groups and teams have led to higher levels of cooperation and affiliation, organizational citizenship behaviors, commitment, identification, mimicry, emotional support, and lower anxiety levels (see Kim et al., 2021 for a list of reviewed articles and outcomes).

For the purpose of this chapter, we define rituals as visible and symbolic activities and actions that a team does repeatedly in order to set expectations for what and how the team is to do their work. Specifically, we focus on rituals to support a virtual team's creativity and success. Ultimately rituals are about creating shared meaning and purpose. Rituals can have physical, psychological and communal features (Kim et al., 2021) and can lead to positive outcomes. The power is in the process of rituals - the psychological safety that comes from knowing "what comes next." Rituals are highly contextual and are completed with intent and awareness and help create a better culture for the work - at the organizational, team, or individual level.

According to Ozenc and Hagan (2019), there are rituals for creativity and innovation, performance and flow, conflict and resilience, community bonding, and change and transition that can be important as people work on teams. They can be small and routine (like weekly stand-up meetings), or they can be less frequent and grander, with more elaborate scripts and actions like a graduation ceremony. Rituals can produce intangible benefits important to teams, like a shared purpose, a sense of meaning, and community bonds (Ozenc & Hagan, 2019). Indeed, rituals in organizations follow similar patterns focusing on their role in communication, learning, and group solidarity (Smith & Stewart, 2011).

Rituals are different from routines and habits. Routines are repetitive patterns of interdependent actions involving multiple team members that exist to provide cognitive efficiency and stability (Feldman & Pentland, 2003). For example, a routine can be a weekly 10-minute huddle with team members to prioritize roadblocks. Habits are repetitive activities done almost automatically without any thought (Norton, 2024). For example, a habit might be checking email first thing in the morning. Rituals are more deliberate and have a deeper meaning, like a team chant or cheer when starting a new project (Norton, 2024). People should complete the action in a certain order or specific way. Rituals have elements of routines (e.g., repetition) but are conscious and intentional and often symbolic (Ozenc & Fajardo, 2021).

Rituals are also distinct from team norms, although they can sometimes have overlap. Team norms are shared expectations that inform how team members interact and make decisions (Hackman, 2002). Norms can be explicitly stated and formed deliberately, but they are often implicitly understood and develop and change over time as the team works together (Hackman, 2002). They are basically unwritten rules for how team members are expected to behave. An example of a team norm might be that team members respond to emails from others within 24 hours. Rituals are activities characterized by physical actions, psychological importance, and communality and they typically have more emotional, or even spiritual, resonance than norms (Kim et al., 2021). An example of a team ritual is that the team kicks off Friday meetings with a share-out, where they summarize activities for the week. They are intentional and repeated symbolic acts a team engages in to reinforce shared identity and purpose and unlike norms they are typically explicit and highly visible. Another distinction is that there is a sense of consequences for violating a norm that is not a feature of rituals (Kim et al., 2021). It is noted that rituals can become norms over time, but that at the outset they are a distinct construct (Kim et al., 2021).

Rituals have a few different considerations in virtual environments. Many of the norms and conventions of in-person collaboration do not work well in virtual settings. We saw this during the COVID-19 pandemic when recreating in-person collaboration was ineffective. That led to an explosion of new technology tools like whiteboards and Zoom updates, as well as new ways of interacting and participating. Virtual environments have their own challenges. For example, being online all day does lead to a different type of fatigue and the level of concentration required online is different from in person. People cannot use all senses in a virtual environment, thus overtaxing other senses (e.g., no smell, so visual gets overworked). Social expectations are unclear - it is difficult to know when and how to participate in online meetings. Rituals can help mitigate some of these issues when done well (Ozenc & Fajardo 2021). The design firm IDEO created virtual meeting survival kits during the pandemic to allow people to maintain some semblance of the physical environment.

The kit included a mini whiteboard, sleeping bags for phones and other physical takeaways and members enjoyed "unboxing" their kits (IDEO).

USING RITUALS FOR MAKING TEAMS CREATIVE AND EFFECTIVE

There are many ways to use rituals in virtual teams. Much of this depends on how long the members have been together and whether they know each other outside the virtual context. As such, we have outlined an iterative framework that meets teams where they are. First, if teams are new to each other, it is important to establish a social connection that will deepen into team cohesion. Rituals allow people to get to know each other and establish loose social ties. Some trust takes hold. Second, it is important to provide a foundation for the team's work - the processes and tools for productivity. This includes setting expectations, decision-making frameworks, and ways to address any team conflicts. Last, psychological safety and trust are particularly important for teams pushing the limits of creativity and innovation.

Rituals provide mechanisms for giving and receiving feedback, providing safety for ideation, and celebrating wins and mourning losses. Ozenc and Hagan (2019) outlined important considerations for a ritual rollout listed below (pp. 22-24). Teams can follow this order or they can iterate based on the needs of the team.

- Create a safe space based on openness and transparency among team members. These should be based on the values and needs of the specific team.
- Get buy-in from the team to facilitate ritual design and seed advocates on the team who can assist with this.
- Design rituals from the ground up instead of the top down because there is no way to command people to participate in rituals.
- Keep it cheap and light - and don't call it a ritual. Start scrappy and see what sticks and see if it is a good fit for the team and the situation.
- Know that a ritual does not have to live forever and is not meant to be permanent. As long as it serves the team and is valuable, it is useful. When that stops, it is okay to let it go.
- Design the rituals to feel new but not too new - finding that sweet spot between familiarity and confusion.

A note about the examples we provide below; they are just that - examples. Teams can use these as a starting point but then find ways to make it their own. These may be effective in some situations for some teams and not for others. The value of rituals should be quite personalized for the team and its members.

We believe that rituals will enhance human-centered virtual teams in several ways. First, rituals foster connection and belonging by creating consistent touchpoints to build relationships. Second, rituals enhance psychological safety and trust through repeated practices encouraging open expression and vulnerability. Third, rituals reinforce team culture and identity by shaping and reinforcing values and purpose. Fourth, rituals provide stability and predictability where work-life balance may be blurred or sacrificed. Fifth, rituals help to combat virtual fatigue and burnout by breaking up the monotony of online environments. Sixth, rituals help strengthen accountability by aligning goals and celebrating progress. Last, rituals encourage playfulness and creativity by making work more fun.

In the following sections we will focus on three aspects of team building that are critical to creativity. First, how we create social connectedness and team cohesion - getting to know members on a personal level. Second, how we craft the team environment through processes - how to work together. Third, building psychological safety and trust - how to deepen relationships between members. We will examine how these are greater challenges in virtual teams and suggest rituals that help to build, support, and maintain growth in each of these areas.

SOCIAL CONNECTEDNESS AND TEAM COHESION

Some team researchers consider cohesion the most important component of team functioning (Lott & Lott, 1965). While it has been defined in various ways over the years, we use the definition created by Carron (1982). Carron stated that cohesion is "a dynamic process which is reflected in the tendency for a group to stick together and remain united in the pursuit of its goals and objectives" (1982, p. 124). Cohesion can increase team performance (Cohen & Bailey, 1997; Gully et al., 1995; van der Voet & Steijn, 2021). Further, cohesion has a positive impact on creative tasks as cohesive teams share more information and coordinate activities better (Ooms et al., 2018; Phelps et al., 2012).

We want team members to feel connected socially to one another and the team. When one feels a closeness and attraction within a team based on social relationships between team members, one is experiencing the dimension of social cohesion (Salas et al., 2015). Team cohesion is the ultimate expression of social connectedness in that it is based on a variety of factors such as attraction, perceived similarity, opportunities for interaction, and proximity, all of which serve to bond team members to one another and to the group (Lott & Lott, 1965). Cohesive teams are more likely to want to invest time and effort in sharing information and coordinating with others (Reagans & McEvily, 2003).

Cohesion, particularly socially connected cohesion, can be more difficult for virtual teams to achieve because of the lack of face-to-face interactions which typically allows members to read non-verbal cues and build trust. In virtual teams, there is less sharing of personal information, which is critical to building cohesion (Roth & Doehne, 2024). It is impossible to experience propinquity as virtual team members are geographically dispersed and it is also more difficult to feel attraction or similarity between team members that may have never met in person. However, while virtual teams are not physically proximal, research has suggested that the effects of physical proximity can be achieved virtually if team members are brought together at regular intervals to interact both formally and informally (Leenders et al., 2002). Further, if the team focuses on finding similarities between team members, such as shared values and interests, cohesion can increase (Lott & Lott, 1965; Summer et al., 1988).

While cohesion has been found to be important for general performance, it has a particularly strong impact on creativity. Teams with higher levels of cohesion have higher levels of creativity (Joo et al., 2012; Moore, 1997). Cohesion seems to lead to more creative solutions, in part because cohesive teams supported more feedback between group members (Moore, 1997) and in part because cohesive team members are more engaged in the creative process (Rodriquez-Sanchez et al., 2017). We believe that rituals are critical for teams in that they offer structured interactions that can help individuals find sources of similarity as well as providing opportunities for engagement and feedback. They also offer opportunities to interact socially, outside of the parameters of the work the team is doing.

RITUALS FOR SOCIAL CONNECTEDNESS AND TEAM COHESION

These rituals serve as opportunities to bring teams together, provide ways for them to connect personally and socially, and eventually deepen personal relations. They are all about tapping into the humanity of team members and helping them find places of convergence and common ground. Faculty can help students learn how to use these roles by demonstrating the use of the following in class, as well as encouraging students to come up with their own ideas for rituals to support connectedness and cohesion.

Ritual 1: Mingle, Mingle

In many cases, especially with virtual teams, members have not only never worked together but, in some cases, have not even met each other. So, one of the first issues to consider when developing social connectedness is to find ways to meet and mingle. Methot et al. (2021) found that office chit-chat was an important factor in connection. This can be done in a variety of ways. Depending on the size of the teams, mingle, mingle can be in breakout rooms or on the main platform if working synchronously. When meeting for the first time, keep the questions and prompts light - as if you are at a cocktail party. This can be things like hometown, favorite taco shop, favorite sport, and so forth. Gradually, the prompts can get deeper. Several games and cards include a list of "get to know you" questions.

Ritual 2: Soundtracks of Our Team

People bond over music - what they like and do not like and what connections to music are shared. This serves as a way to deepen the connection for virtual teams. Teams would add their favorite music to a shared playlist that starts each meeting. The playlist can also be played during breaks so that team members learn more about their teammates (and potentially discover some new music). Teams can create playlists for different activities - from brainstorming to reflection. Songs can be selected for specific uses - like a celebration song. Team members can have "walk-on" songs about their identity or purpose (Stanford University D School).

Ritual 3: Check-in Rounds

Check-in Rounds are analogous to "stand up" meetings in person where team members share work tasks. This could extend to what people do in their "outside of work" lives - from hobbies, activities, families, and other adventures. This activity helps build empathy and allows people to bring their full selves to the team environment. This can also be an opportunity to share highs and lows at the end of the week (Ozenic & Fajardo, 2021).

Ritual 4: Ready to Roll

Getting to understand work styles and preferences is important. Creating a poll or template on Miro (miro.com/) or Mural (mural.co/) that places several characteristics on a continuum allows people to highlight their own work styles. Also, it allows the team to see where there is convergence and where conflict may arise. Characteristics can include things such as:

- Early bird - Night owl
- Camera on - Camera off
- Work on it together - Go off alone to think
- Tell me the back story - Cut to the chase
- Need to process with you – Need to move on
- Email me - Text or IM me
- Weekends are downtime - Weekends are catch-up time
- If you are not early, you are late - wait, 30 minutes is not late

Ritual 5: Show and Tell

Sharing something about your personal interests and values helps people get to know you as more than just a coworker. This could be playing a version of MTV's Cribs where you show team members a special place in your home or sharing artifacts from your favorite hobby. This could be done relatively quickly where one person shares at the beginning of each meeting for a few minutes. It is even more impactful if you can get people to be more participative, for example, if you love to cook, sending teammates your favorite recipe, or if you are an artist, sending each member a tiny painting (Ozenic & Fajardo 2021).

TEAM ENVIRONMENT AND PROCESSES

Creating robust team processes is necessary to create a teamwork environment. Team processes are essential to team performance because they help the team collaborate and coordinate to meet team goals (Honts et al., 2012). They help stimulate creativity and innovation and support the building of cohesion and psychological safety. In the book *Leading Teams*, Hackman (2002) cites the importance of creating an enabling structure to create effective teams, in particular through the use of norms. We are interested in a few key team processes that are particularly difficult to manage in virtual teams, specifically coordinating members through norms and roles, fostering open communication, and managing conflict. Faculty can impress upon students the importance of these team processes and demonstrate some ways to do that through the rituals listed below.

Coordinating Members Through Norms and Roles

Two important team processes for providing structure and order to the team are norms and roles. Team norms are shared expectations of team members regarding the behaviors considered important for the team (Hackman, 2002; Taggar & Ellis,

2007) and are critical to team performance in part because they provide structure and a sense of order to team interactions, which can sometimes be quite ambiguous and uncertain (Raven & Rubin, 1976). Norms serve the purpose of helping teams align their expectations about what their goals are, how they might structure work to meet those goals, and what their expected outcomes are (Taggar & Ellis, 2007). Roles also provide structure and order to teams because they provide a set of expectations about the jobs that individuals in the team should be doing and provide a division of labor (Birenbaum, 1984).

Norms in virtual teams are important because they reduce coordination challenges and have a positive effect on task performance (Janicik & Bartel, 2003; Moser & Axtell, 2013). Communication norms in particular play an important role in virtual team performance because they reduce misunderstandings (Henderson et al., 2016; Nemiro, 2026; Verburg et al., 2013). Role clarity is also critical for performance of virtual teams because it reduces confusion about who is doing what and allows the team to get things done (Henderson et al., 2016; Nemiro, 2004, 2026; Rizzo, et al., 1970).

Research suggests that both norms (Du et al., 2021) and roles (Zhang et al., 2022) can be important tools for enhancing creativity in teams. For instance, some research has suggested that teams with strong norms increase the quantity of new ideas (Paulus, 2000; West, 1990). Roles can help teams with creativity because they give structure and a division of labor, which can help individual members focus on different features of the task. Ryssina and Koroleva (1984) suggested that different roles are important at different parts of the creative process. Other research has found that team members who have a creative role identity engage in more creative behaviors (Zhang & Reynolds, 2022). By creating strong norms and roles for virtual teams, the members will be freer to engage in creative behaviors and produce creative ideas.

Fostering Open Communication

Effective teams need to have good communication (Hill, 1982; Iljen et al., 2005). Communication serves a couple of functions in teams. First, it has an informational function, when team members share and exchange information in order to strategize and plan. Second, it serves a social function, when team members share intentions and personal information in order to build trust (Boies et al., 2015).

Virtual teams sometimes struggle with communication, in part, because they lose opportunities for serendipitous or informal communication, and in part, because they tend not to communicate as frequently with one another as face-to-face teams. However, research has shown that virtual teams that use tools and technology that simulate face-to-face meetings, such as video conferencing, are more creative than those that rely on less rich methods (Nemiro, 2002). When using richer communication media, individuals are able to both provide and assess nonverbal and visual cues (Daft & Lengel, 1986). The richer the communication media, the more visual and verbal cues provided in transmitting information between the sender and receivers, which in turn supports both understanding and creativity (Daft & Lengel, 1986).

Open communication is essential for creative teams, in particular, as the creative process needs members to share information with others for success (Monge et al., 1992). Research has found that creative teams need to communicate relatively frequently, and communication should be "decentralized" (Leenders et al., 2003). To support decentralization, Leenders et al. suggested that teams create the role of a 'communication integrator.' These are people who "rather than merely channeling communication between team members, identify those team members who would benefit from joining a particular stream of communication and then use their leadership to bring them into the discussion" (Leenders et al., 2003, p. 85). This increases the frequency of interactions between members and also allows for more individuals to hear and respond to the shared information. In addition, teams that use tools to foster electronic brainstorming, such as Mural or Miro, also see increases in creativity (Maaravi et al., 2021; Muller, 1999) because these tools allow members to mimic in-person creative sessions.

Managing Team Conflict

Conflict can have both positive and negative impacts on team performance. Conflict has been found to be detrimental to teams that are performing routine tasks (Jehn, 1995) and teams that do not have a psychologically safe environment (Bradley et al., 2012). However, when managed effectively, conflict can produce benefits for teams (Jehn & Mannix, 2001). Successful teams are proactive when it comes to conflict resolution (Behfar et al., 2008). Teams that have a process for managing conflict see benefits because they reduce harmful impacts of negative conflict (DeChurch & Marks, 2001; Thomas, 1992).

Virtual teams are potentially more vulnerable to conflict, and specifically the negative impacts of conflict, because misunderstandings are more likely to arise due to lack of non-verbal cues, lower levels of team cohesion and commitment, and greater diversity which is typical in virtual teams. Technology can also play a role in creating conflict because it can lead to information overload and feedback lag (Kankanhalli et al., 2006). Teams operating virtually will likely need a different set of strategies and processes to deal with the conflict, than traditional teams use (Griffith et al, 2003). In addition to developing proactive strategies for managing conflict, virtual teams will need to focus on building trust and psychological safety to produce the best results (Bradley et al., 2012; Griffith et al., 2003).

Creative teams have a tough balance to strike when it comes to conflict. The relationship between team creativity and conflict is complicated by the fact that these teams need conflict to stimulate new ideas but also need to manage the conflict to make sure it does not start to hurt the relationships in and performance of the team. For teams that are engaged in non-routine, or creative tasks, some conflict, particularly task related, can be beneficial (Jehn, 1995). However, creative teams have to balance between the need to generate and effectively use task conflict without having it spill over into relationship conflict (Bolinger et al., 2009). Further, creative teams need to be aware of the timing of conflict and manage the amount of conflict at each stage of the creative process (Chen, 2006).

Building these team processes can be challenging in regular teams, but when dealing with virtual teams, they become even more difficult to create and manage, and it is even more important to get them right from the outset. Virtual teams need to be proactive when it comes to coordinating members through norms and roles, fostering open communication, and managing conflict in order to stimulate creativity. Further, focusing on developing psychological safety and trust in virtual teams has benefits for ameliorating the negative effects of virtuality and stimulating creativity.

RITUALS FOR TEAM ENVIRONMENT AND PROCESSES

The purpose of these rituals is to lay a foundation for work. Teams working in-person establish ways to work, whether kicking off a new project or wrapping up an established project. That said, in virtual environments, it can be trickier to communicate. There is little body language to read and it can be easy to have communication mistakes. Rituals for team processes center on starting and wrapping up projects, facilitating effective communication, mitigating conflicts, and maximizing effective decision-making.

Ritual 1: The Project Kick-Off Canvas

A team contract is a tool that establishes “clarity of roles, responsibilities, and team processes” (Gaspar et al., 2016, p. 14). Team contracts are tools to explicitly craft norms and roles with the team. As Feldman (1984) proposed, norms can be created through explicit statements by group members. When teams have conversations about expectations upfront, whether about norms and roles, how they manage a conflict, or how they will communicate, they are more likely to be on the same page rather than just making assumptions about what others believe is important.

Enter the Project Kick-Off Canvas. This is best used with an online platform like Miro or Mural where teams can co-create in real time. It is important to start with the why - why this team and why this project, so teams should start with areas such as the purpose of the project and the values of the team. From there, the team can create roles and expectations, like how to hold people accountable without hurting autonomy. Roles include who is doing which task for the team (Forsyth & Burnette, 2010). Norms can provide a sense of accountability as one of the components of norms is that team members believe there will be consequences for violating them (Kim et al., 2021). The Kick-Off Canvas also serves as the starting point of the journey of the project. While it does not need to be created each time a team meets, it makes sense to revisit the Kick-Off canvas regularly as a framework to guide discussion.

Ritual 2: The Lucky Shirt

Just like athletes or performers, it makes sense to get ready for high-stress or high-stakes situations. These are small physical actions individuals or teams can perform before something important - say, a big presentation or discussion. These can be as simple or complex as desired, but research shows that these physical actions help regulate emotions and provide a sense of control (Gino, 2018). This can include things like repeating a word three times, touching a spot, or engaging in a secret handshake.

Ritual 3: Repeat After Me

People typically assume that others understand the message that they are trying to communicate with them. However, people can and do interpret things differently than one may have intended. So, when critical information is delivered, one can ask team members to repeat back in their own words what they heard. Making it a ritual and having everyone participate takes away any implied criticism. You may start by saying - "I know this was a lot of information and I may have missed something, so can you "repeat after me"?" This can be shared within the meeting or across meetings, but getting into the habit of checking that you were understood will cut down on miscommunications and conflict.

Ritual 4: The Energy Check-in

Not everyone comes to team engagements with the same level of energy. As such, at the beginning, team members can indicate their level of energy using green (energized), yellow (neutral), and red (struggling). This should cut down on misunderstandings that a team has when engaging synchronously online. The team can also choose fun emojis to communicate this information.

Ritual 5: The Conflict Doctor

When teams have been working together for a while, problems inevitably arise. The Doctor is In (Ozenc & Hagan, 2019) is a ritual for reflecting on team dynamics. Consider it almost like a doctor or therapist - to draw out problems in a structured and neutral way. This can be done by a team member or external team member. This "intervention" or "treatment plan" may involve surfacing interpersonal issues, mapping out and prioritizing issues, building alignment among members, and diagnosing issues. Consider going all in - with a doctor's coat or modifying it as a "team health checkup."

Ritual 6: The Pinning Ceremony

It is important to look at projects like a journey - with a starting point and an ending point. This allows for reflection on the journey as well as an avenue for closure. Stanford's D School has a closing ritual whereby participants get a pin at the end of workshops. It gives a small but clear ending point and special moment that allows team members to bond over their experiences. Even for virtual events, leaders can send along pins and have a brief ceremony online (Stanford University Hasso Plattner Institute of Design).

PSYCHOLOGICAL SAFETY

Psychological safety is critical to creativity because you need safety and security when engaging in creative tasks, which involve taking risks and, sometimes, failing in virtual teams (Lechner & Mortlock, 2022). This need is increased as we lack standard face-to-face interactions and non-verbal cues in virtual teams, which help aid our comfort in taking those risks. Trust has been defined in numerous ways, but for the purposes of this chapter, we are using the definition created by Hakanen and Soudunsaari (2012) in which trust is "considered as faith in others' behaviour and goodwill that can grow or vanish due to interaction and experiences" (p. 39).

When trust is not present, teams will often have difficulty with communication, performance, and creativity (Erdem & Ozen, 2003). Psychological safety exists at the group level while trust is felt between two individuals (Edmondson, 1999). We are not focused on trust itself, but rather the role that trust serves to support an environment for psychological safety to be built (Edmondson, 1999; Erdem & Ozen, 2003).

Virtual teams can struggle with developing psychological safety and trust. In addition to the usual challenges of lack of face-to-face interaction and non-verbal cues, virtual teams suffer from a couple of additional challenges. First, regular team processes, such as getting to know team members personally, asking for help, and talking through problems, take more time and effort, which reduces individuals' motivation to engage in these processes (Lechner & Mortlock, 2022). Second, teams are more likely to develop subgroups as communication "bubbles" occur when people bond with a few team members and create separate communication groups with them (Lechner & Mortlock, 2022). The team becomes imbalanced as psychological safety develops within the bubbles but others outside of the bubble are seen as the outgroup and psychological safety and trust between subgroups is lowered. This is particularly difficult to manage in virtual teams because we do not have the opportunity for spontaneous interactions like in a face-to-face team and subgroups become more deeply invested in their bubbles over time (Lechner & Mortlock, 2022). One suggestion that Lechner and Mortlock (2022) propose to help virtual teams develop psychological safety is to craft a code of conduct, or team contract, together. The team contract then serves to both create structure for the team environment as well as provide a foundation for psychological safety to be built.

Psychological safety is also an important component of creativity in teams. The tasks required of creative teams, from sharing knowledge, to proposing new ideas, to challenging the ideas of others, necessitate psychological safety. One must feel safe taking risks and not be afraid of failure when engaging in the creative process. Creative teams often cite having a psychologically safe environment (Gilson & Shalley, 2004; Liu et al., 2021). In addition, some of the strategies for developing psychological safety in virtual teams can mitigate common complications in virtual teams and can lead to increased creativity and innovation in those teams (Gibson & Gibbs, 2006).

RITUALS FOR PSYCHOLOGICAL SAFETY

In order to help virtual teams avoid challenges with developing psychological safety, Lechner and Mortlock (2022) recommend that these teams engage in connecting as human beings. They suggest three things to help virtual teams build human connections - demonstrating interest in other team members, sharing personal information, and creating new experiences together. Educators can employ these ideas in class in order to help students experience and reflect on what works best for their teams.

As teams learn more about each other and experience working with each other, trust will be built. The key to these rituals is celebrating the "relationship" and "the journey' - the ongoing work being accomplished. Additionally, when teams need to push creative limits, this foundation of trust becomes even more important. These rituals revolve around celebrating longevity and relationships, as well as rituals to maximize creativity, especially through feedback and reflection.

Ritual 1: A Picture is Worth 1,000 Words

Throughout the team's journey, it is important to provide ways to deepen the cohesion of team members. So, this one is simple. Just like music helps people bond, so do photos. This ritual can be used in a variety of ways. First, each team member can share a photo that is special for each meeting or times when teams collaborate. These can be collected and shared as a collage at the end of the project, along with other photos that get added along the way. This serves as a visual "history" of the team's time together (Ozenic & Fajardo, 2021).

Ritual 2: Please and Thank You

While the team is doing its work, it is important to recognize contributions - big and small. As such, there are simple ways to do that with virtual teams. Starting off or ending meetings with small tokens of appreciation or using "reactions" when people do something well affirms people's position on the team. Aim to do this a few times during a session - not so much that the special meaning gets degraded but often enough to make a difference. Small moments jars are also a visual representation of this ritual. Teams can create a "virtual" jar and put post-it notes of appreciation for team members (Ozenic & Hagan, 2019).

Ritual 3: Feedback and Reflection

People tend to like feedback only when it is positive. Few people like to engage in "crucial conversations" (Grenny et al., 2021). There are several ways to give feedback to team members that minimize uncomfortable confrontations. One is Rose/Bud/Thorn, where team members provide things that are working (a rose), things that are not working or are roadblocks or challenges (thorn), and things that have opportunity but need some care (bud). Teams can do this for the project, or they can do this to report how they are feeling about their week or workload. Alternatively, the ritual called I like/I wish was started at the Stanford D School, where team members provide feedback to each team member by stating things that they like about the person's work and things that they wish they would do more or less of regarding the person's work. Making feedback and reflection a regular part of the team's work ensures that problems do not fester and that team members get positive affirmation and credit for things going well.

Ritual 4: Creative Breakthroughs

There are several ways to encourage creativity in virtual teams. To encourage a creative mindset, the team can use exercises such as a divergent thinking warm-up where team members brainstorm unique uses for an ordinary object like a paperclip, brick, or coffee mug. This allows the team to break through rigid thinking patterns. Or, if the team needs to maximize divergent thinking, they can brainstorm ideas on how to make the problem worse in order to break predictable responses.

Design Mad Libs (Ozenc & Hagan, 2019) is an activity used when a virtual team is struggling with routine work and needs a way to switch to creative modes. The team is given a frame - a mad lib - with missing words that they fill in with random words from a stack of cards. Then, they have to create it. The goal is to get the team to create and imagine things together. This can be done using Miro or Mural or just on video conferencing depending on the size of the virtual team. Design Mad Libs serves as a creative prompt that generates a creative spark.

Ritual 5: Failing Forward

Ozenc and Hagan (2019) created the Failure Wake - where teams celebrate the failure of an experiment. It encourages risk and provides a closure for things that fail. Leaders say a few words about what happened; everyone turns their video screen background to black and other team members can choose to say words - just like a wake for a funeral. The point is to affirm that taking risks and sometimes failing is okay and the wake also allows for a debrief of the reasons for that failure.

DESIGNING RITUALS

Virtual teams can and should create their own rituals to address issues of importance. Ozenc and Hagan (2019) and the Ritual Design Lab at Stanford University outlined ideas on how to do this. Using foundations of design thinking, teams can investigate underlying needs, define actionable opportunities, and conduct experiments. They utilize three phases: discovery, design, and deployment. In the discovery phase, teams should explore the moments, inspirations, and inventions that could be the foundation for the ritual. What is the point of the ritual? What problem does it solve? Then, teams find the "hook" or trigger for the ritual. Trigger examples can be project kick-offs, conflicts, and product failures. Design is about ideation about the elements of the ritual and creating symbols and props for it. Then, refine it into a narrative, capitalizing on the sequence. Deployment includes trying it out to see if it works. This framework has been used to create hundreds of rituals for various organizations, teams, and individuals.

Norton (2024) argues that truly effective organizations offer individuals room to design their own rituals for the workplace. This leaves space for individual and team rituals to thrive. In virtual teams and when working from home, individuals create rituals for their work - from "commuting" across the house to "leaving work." Rituals often mark the beginning and end of the day for many virtual teams. Table 1 provides guidance to faculty wanting to help the student teams in their courses create rituals.

Table 1. Guidance for Ritual Design

Section	Guiding Questions
Purpose	Why are you creating this ritual? What behavior, mindset, or value are you reinforcing? What problem are you trying to solve?
Participants	Who is involved? What do they need?
Trigger / Cue	When or how will the ritual begin? What signals that it's time?
Actions	What specifically happens during the ritual? Are there steps, props, or language?
Emotion / Energy	What feeling should this ritual evoke? Calm? Excitement? Reflection? Belonging?
Frequency and Duration	How often will it happen? How long does it take? Daily, weekly, annually?
Artifacts / Symbols	Are there any physical or digital elements involved?
Success Criteria	How will you know if it's working or needs adjustment? What impact should it have?

CONCLUSION

Creating an environment for creativity to flourish can be difficult in traditional teams, but it is ever more complicated in virtual teams. Virtual teams have particular challenges, such as lack of face-to-face interaction, loss of non-verbal cues, geographical distance, communication issues, and lessened cohesion and psychological safety. However, there are ways to overcome these challenges, as we have proposed in this chapter. By creating a human-centered virtual team, and in doing so by being intentional in crafting rituals to improve cohesion, team processes, and psychological safety in the virtual environment, one can achieve an environment for fostering and maintaining creativity in teams.

Faculty, in particular, can be instrumental in helping students learn how to craft human-centered and creative virtual teams using rituals. Exposing students to rituals in the classroom will help students see their utility when working with their own virtual teams. We encourage educators to use, adapt, and create the rituals presented in the chapter as they are engaged with virtual teams in their classes. We also encourage faculty to be creative when creating these rituals. Ask others, including students, about their ideas and feel free to play with them to find rituals that work best for you and your virtual team.

REFERENCES

Bailenson, J. N. (2021). Nonverbal overload: A theoretical argument for the causes of Zoom fatigue. *Technology, Mind, and Behavior*, *2*(1), 1–6.

Behfar, K. J., Peterson, R. S., Mannix, E. A., & Trochim, W. M. (2008). The critical role of conflict resolution in teams: A close look at the links between conflict type, conflict management strategies, and team outcomes. *The Journal of Applied Psychology*, *93*(1), 170. PMID: 18211143

Birenbaum, A. (1984). Toward a theory of role acquisition. *Sociological Theory*, *2*, 315–328.

Bolinger, A. R., Bonner, B. L., & Okhuysen, G. A. (2009). Sticking together: The glue role and group creativity. In Mannix, E., Goncalo, J., & Neale, M. (Eds.), *Creativity in Groups* (Vol. 12, pp. 267–289). Emerald Group Publishing Limited.

Cai, Y. L. (2023). Strengthening perceptions of virtual team cohesiveness and effectiveness in the new normal: A hyperpersonal communication theory perspective. *Asian Business & Management, 22*, 1649-1682. *Article, 1*. Advance online publication. DOI: 10.1057/s41291-023-00225-6 PMID: 40479004

Carron, A. V. (1982). Cohesiveness in sport groups: Interpretations and considerations. *Journal of Sport & Exercise Psychology*, *4*(2), 123–138.

Chamakiotis, P., Dekonick, E. A., & Panteli, N. (2013). Factors influencing creativity in virtual design teams: An interplay between technology, teams, and individuals. *Creativity and Innovation Management*, *22*(3), 265–279.

Chen, M. H. (2006). Understanding the benefits and detriments of conflict on team creativity process. *Creativity and Innovation Management*, *15*(1), 105–116.

DeChurch, L. A., & Marks, M. A. (2001). Maximizing the benefits of task conflict: The role of conflict management. *International Journal of Conflict Management*, *12*(1), 4–22.

DeRosa, D. M., Hantula, D. A., Kock, N., & D'Arcy, J. (2004). Trust and leadership in virtual teamwork: A media naturalness perspective. *Human Resource Management*, *43*(2–3), 219–232. DOI: 10.1002/hrm.20016

Drach-Zahavy, A., & Somech, A. (2001). Understanding team innovation: The role of team processes and structures. *Group Dynamics*, *5*(2), 111–123.

Du, X., Zhang, H., Zhang, S., Zhang, A., & Chen, B. (2021). Creativity and leadership in the creative industry: A study from the perspective of social norms. *Frontiers in Psychology, 12*, 651817. Advance online publication. DOI: 10.3389/fpsyg.2021.651817 PMID: 33889118

Edmondson, A. (1999). Psychological safety and learning behavior in work teams. *Administrative Science Quarterly, 44*(2), 350–383. DOI: 10.2307/2666999

Edmondson, A., & Mogelof, J. P. (2006). Explaining psychological safety in innovation teams: Organizational culture, team dynamics, or personality. In Thompson, L. L., & Choi, H. S. (Eds.), *Creativity and innovation in organizational teams* (pp. 109–138). Lawrence Erlbaum Associates.

Edmondson, A. C., & Lei, Z. (2014). Psychological safety: The history, renaissance, and future of an interpersonal construct. *Annual Review of Organizational Psychology and Organizational Behavior, 1*(1), 23–43. DOI: 10.1146/annurev-orgpsych-031413-091305

Erdem, F., & Ozen, J. (2003). Cognitive and affective dimensions of trust in developing team performance. *Team Performance Management, 9*(5/6), 131–135.

Feldman, M. S., & Pentland, B. T. (2003). Reconceptualizing organizational routines as a source of flexibility and change. *Administrative Science Quarterly, 48*(1), 94–118. DOI: 10.2307/3556620

Fitzgerald, M., Kruschwitz, N., Bonnet, D., & Welch, M. (2014). Embracing digital technology: A new strategic imperative. *MIT Sloan Management Review, 55*(2), 1–12.

Forsyth, D. R., & Burnette, J. (2010). Group processes. In Baumeister, R. F., & Finkel, E. J. (Eds.), *Advanced social psychology: The state of the science* (pp. 495–529). Oxford University Press.

Gaspar, P. M., Catalano, L., & Gaspar, T. M. (2016). Establishing a collaboration contract to facilitate team performance. *Journal of Doctoral Nursing Practice, 9*(1), 13–19. DOI: 10.1891/2380-9418.9.1.13 PMID: 32750998

Gibson, C. B., & Gibbs, J. L. (2006). Unpacking the concept of virtuality: The effects of geographic dispersion, electronic dependence, dynamic structure, and national diversity on team innovation. *Administrative Science Quarterly, 51*(3), 451–495. DOI: 10.2189/asqu.51.3.451

Gilson, L. L., Costa, P., O'Neill, T. A., & Maynard, M. T. (2021). Putting the "TEAM" back into virtual teams. *Organizational Dynamics, 50*(1), 100847. Advance online publication. DOI: 10.1016/j.orgdyn.2021.100847

Gilson, L. L., & Shalley, C. E. (2004). A little creativity goes a long way: An examination of teams' engagement in creative processes. *Journal of Management, 30*(4), 453–470.

Gino, F. (2018, August). Need more self-control? Try a simple ritual. *Scientific American.* https://www.scientificamerican.com/article/need-more-self-control-try-a-simple-ritual/

Grenny, J., Patterson, K., McMillan, R., Switzler, A., & Gregory, E. (2021). *Tools for conversations when stakes are high* (3rd ed.). McGraw Hill.

Griffith, T. L., Mannix, E. A., & Neale, M. A. (2003). Conflict and virtual teams. In Gibson, C. B., & Cohen, S. G. (Eds.), *Virtual teams that work: Creating conditions for virtual team effectiveness* (pp. 335–352). Jossey-Bass.

Gully, S. M., Devine, D. S., & Whitney, D. J. (1995). A meta-analysis of cohesion and performance: Effects of level of analysis and task interdependence. *Small Group Research, 26*(4), 497–520. DOI: 10.1177/1046496495264003

Hackman, J. R., & Hackman, R. J. (2002). *Leading teams: Setting the stage for great performances.* Harvard Business Press.

Hakanen, M., & Soudunsaari, A. (2012). Building trust in high-performing teams. *Technology Innovation Management Review, 2*(6), 38–41. https://timreview.ca/article/562

Han, S. J., Chae, C., Macko, P., Park, W., & Beyerlein, M. (2017). How virtual team leaders cope with creativity challenges. *European Journal of Training and Development, 41*(3), 261–276. DOI: 10.1108/EJTD-10-2016-0073

Henderson, L. S., Stackman, R. W., & Lindekilde, R. (2016). The centrality of communication norm alignment, role clarity, and trust in global project teams. *International Journal of Project Management, 34*(8), 1717–1730. DOI: 10.1016/j.ijproman.2016.09.012

Hobson, N. M., Schroeder, J., Risen, J. L., Xygalatas, D., & Inzlicht, M. (2018). The psychology of rituals: An integrative review and process-based framework. *Personality and Social Psychology Review, 22*(3), 260–284. DOI: 10.1177/1088868317734944 PMID: 29130838

Honts, C., Prewett, M., Rahael, J., & Grossenbacher, M. (2012). The importance of team processes for different team types. *Team Performance Management, 18*(5/6), 312–327.

Hu, W., & Chan, C. K. Y. (2024). Evaluating technological interventions for developing teamwork competency in higher education: A systematic review and meta-ethnography. *Studies in Educational Evaluation*, *83*, 101382. Advance online publication. DOI: 10.1016/j.stueduc.2024.101382

IBM. (n.d.). *Building a human centered organization*. IBM. https://www.ibm.com/design/thinking/page/hco

Islam, G., & Zyphur, M. J. (2009). Rituals in organizations: A review and expansion of current theory. *Group & Organization Management*, *34*(1), 114–139.

Janicik, G. A., & Bartel, C. A. (2003). Talking about time: Effects of temporal planning and time awareness norms on group coordination and performance. *Group Dynamics*, *7*(2), 122–134. DOI: 10.1037/1089-2699.7.2.122

Jehn, K. A. (1992). *The impact of intragroup conflict on effectiveness: A multimethod examination of the benefits and detriments of conflict* [Doctoral dissertation, Northwestern University].

Jehn, K. A. (1995). A multimethod examination of the benefits and detriments of intragroup conflict. *Administrative Science Quarterly*, *40*(2), 256–282. DOI: 10.2307/2393638

Jehn, K. A., & Mannix, E. A. (2001). The dynamic nature of conflict: A longitudinal study of intragroup conflict and group performance. *Academy of Management Journal*, *44*(2), 238–251.

Joo, B. K., Song, J. H., Lim, D. H., & Yoon, S. W. (2012). Team creativity: The effects of perceived learning culture, developmental feedback and team cohesion. *International Journal of Training and Development*, *16*(2), 77–91.

Kankanhalli, A., Tan, B. C. Y., & Wei, K. K. (2006). Conflict and performance in global virtual teams. *Journal of Management Information Systems*, *23*(3), 237–274.

Keswin, E. (2021). *Rituals roadmap: The human way to transform everyday routines into workplace magic*. McGraw Hill.

Kim, T., Sezer, O., Schroeder, J., Risen, J., Gino, F., & Norton, M. (2021). Work group rituals enhance the meaning of work. *Organizational Behavior and Human Decision Processes*, *165*, 197–212.

Kimura, T. (2024). Virtual teams: A smart literature review of four decades of research. *Human Behavior and Emerging Technologies*, *2024*(1), e8373370. Advance online publication. DOI: 10.1155/2024/8373370

Klonek, F. E., Kanse, L., Wee, S., Runneboom, C., & Parker, S. K. (2022). Did the COVID-19 lockdown make us better at working in virtual teams? *Small Group Research, 53*(2), 185–206.

Kozlowski, S. W. J., & Ilgen, D. R. (2006). Enhancing the effectiveness of work groups and teams. *Psychological Science in the Public Interest, 7*(3), 77–124. DOI: 10.1111/j.1529-1006.2006.00030.x PMID: 26158912

Kratzer, J., Gemünden, H. G., & Lettl, C. (2008). Balancing creativity and time efficiency in multi-year R&D projects: The alignment of formal and informal networks. *R & D Management, 38*(5), 538–549. DOI: 10.1111/j.1467-9310.2008.00528.x

Lal, B., Dwivedi, Y. K., & Haag, M. (2023). Working from home during Covid-19: Doing and managing technology-enabled social interaction with colleagues at a distance. *Information Systems Frontiers, 25*(4), 1333–1350. PMID: 34483713

Lea, M., & Spears, R. (1991). Computer-mediated communication, de-individuation and group decision-making. *International Journal of Man-Machine Studies, 34*(2), 283–301. DOI: 10.1016/0020-7373(91)90045-9

Lechner, A., & Mortlock, J. M. T. (2022). How to create psychological safety in virtual teams. *Organizational Dynamics, 51*(2), 100849.

Leenders, R. T. A., Van Engelen, J. M., & Kratzer, J. (2003). Virtuality, communication, and new product team creativity: A social network perspective. *Journal of Engineering and Technology Management, 20*(1–2), 69–92. DOI: 10.1016/S0923-4748(03)00005-5

Leman, A., & Mott, R. (2023). Evaluating the outcomes of human-centered design in a virtual program development higher education course. *Journal of Human Sciences and Extension, 11*(1), 15–30. https://scholarsjunction.msstate.edu/jhse/vol11/iss1/15/

Lepisto, D. A. (2022). Ritual work and the formation of a shared sense of meaningfulness. *Academy of Management Journal, 65*(4), 1327–1352.

Liu, Y., Keller, R. T., & Bartlett, K. R. (2021). Initiative climate, psychological safety and knowledge sharing as predictors of team creativity: A multilevel study of research and development project teams. *Creativity and Innovation Management, 30*(3), 498–510. DOI: 10.1111/caim.12438

Lott, A. J., & Lott, B. E. (1965). Group cohesiveness as interpersonal attraction: A review of relationships with antecedent and consequent variables. *Psychological Bulletin, 64*(4), 259–309. DOI: 10.1037/h0022386 PMID: 5318041

Ma, S., & Leman, A. (2023). Preparing career-ready students by building effective virtual teamwork skills. *NACTA Journal*, *67*(1), 50–56.

Maaravi, Y., Heller, B., Shoham, Y., Mohar, S., & Deutsch, B. (2021). Ideation in the digital age: Literature review and integrative model for electronic brainstorming. *Review of Managerial Science*, *15*(6), 1431–1464. DOI: 10.1007/s11846-020-00400-5

Malhotra, A., Majchrzak, A., & Rosen, B. (2007). Leading virtual teams. *The Academy of Management Perspectives*, *21*(1), 60–70. DOI: 10.5465/amp.2007.24286164

Methot, J. R., Rosado-Solomon, E. H., Downes, P., & Gabriel, A. S. (2021). Office chitchat as a social ritual: The uplifting yet distracting effects of daily small talk. *Academy of Management Journal*, *64*(5), 1445–1471.

Monge, P. R., Cozzens, M. D., & Contractor, N. S. (1992). Communication and motivational predictors of the dynamics of organizational innovation. *Organization Science*, *3*(2), 250–274. DOI: 10.1287/orsc.3.2.250

Moore, R. M. (1997). The positive effects of cohesion on the creativity of small groups. *International Social Science Review*, *72*(3/4), 84–93.

Morgan, N. (2018). *Can you hear me?: How to connect with people in a virtual world*. Harvard Business Press.

Moser, K. S., & Axtell, C. M. (2013). The role of norms in virtual work. *Journal of Personnel Psychology*, *12*(1), 1–6.

Muller, P. C. (1999). *Team-based conceptualization of new products: Creating shared realities using information technological support* (Doctoral dissertation). University of Groningen.

Nemiro, J. (2007). The building blocks for creativity in virtual teams. In MacGregor, S., & Torres, T. (Eds.), *Higher creativity for virtual teams: Developing platforms for co-creation* (pp. 98–121). Information Science Reference.

Nemiro, J. (2023). Virtual teams. In Reiter-Palmon, R., & Hunter, S. (Eds.), *Handbook of organizational creativity: Group and individual influences* (2nd ed., pp. 269–290). Elsevier Publishing.

Nemiro, J. E. (2002). The creative process in virtual teams. *Creativity Research Journal*, *14*(1), 69–83. DOI: 10.1207/S15326934CRJ1401_6

Nemiro, J. E. (2026). *Creativity in virtual teams: Key components for success* (2nd ed.). Cognella Academic Publishing.

Nemiro, J. E., Ayala, A., Lee, J. S., & San Luis, B. (2023). Strategies for managing the challenges of student virtual teams in higher education: A case study. *Quarterly Review of Distance Education*, *24*(1), 55–77.

Norton, M. I. (2024, June 10). Strengthen teams with the power of rituals. *Harvard Business School Faculty Profile*. https://www.exed.hbs.edu/blog/strengthen-teams-with-power-rituals

Norton, M. I. (2024). *The ritual effect: From habit to ritual, harness the surprising power of everyday actions*. Scribner.

Ooms, W., Werker, C., & Caniëls, M. (2018). Personal and social proximity empowering collaborations: The glue of knowledge networks. *Industry and Innovation*, *25*(9), 833–840.

Orazani, S. N., Reynolds, K. J., & Osborne, H. (2023). What works and why in interventions to strengthen social cohesion: A systematic review. *Journal of Applied Social Psychology*, *53*(10), 938–995.

Ozenc, K. (2016, April 24). How do you design a ritual? *Medium – Stanford d.school*. https://medium.com/stanford-d-school/how-do-you-design-a-ritual-e4aeb3e17198

Ozenc, K. (2020, March 2). Designing well-being rituals for preventing workplace burnout. *Medium – Stanford d.school*. https://medium.com/stanford-d-school/designing-well-being-rituals-for-preventing-workplace-burnout-eafa577fe71b

Ozenc, K. (2023, January 4). Human-centered culture design: How to build better organizations. *Medium – Ritual Design Lab*. https://medium.com/ritual-design/human-centered-culture-design-building-better-organizations-70403398283d

Ozenc, K., & Fajardo, G. (2021). *Rituals for virtual meetings*. John Wiley & Sons.

Ozenc, K., & Hagan, M. (2019). *Rituals for work*. John Wiley & Sons.

Paulus, P. B. (2000). Groups, teams, and creativity: The creative potential of idea-generating groups. *Applied Psychology*, *49*(2), 237–262. DOI: 10.1111/1464-0597.00013

Phelps, C., Heidl, R., & Wadhwa, A. (2012). Knowledge, networks, and knowledge networks: A review and research agenda. *Journal of Management*, *38*(4), 1115–1166. DOI: 10.1177/0149206311432640

Pouthier, V. (2017). Griping and joking as identification rituals and tools for engagement in cross-boundary team meetings. *Organization Studies*, *38*(6), 753–774.

Raven, B. H., & Rubin, J. Z. (1976). *Social psychology: People in groups*. Holt, Rinehart & Winston.

Reagans, R., & McEvily, B. (2003). Network structure and knowledge transfer: The effects of cohesion and range. *Administrative Science Quarterly*, *48*(2), 240–267. DOI: 10.2307/3556658

Reiter-Palmon, R., Kramer, W., Allen, J. A., Murugavel, V. R., & Leone, S. (2021). Creativity in virtual teams: A review and agenda for future research. *International Journal of Business Communication*, *8*(1), 166–188.

Ritual Design Lab. (n.d.). *Ritual Design Lab at Stanford University*. https://medium.com/ritual-design

Rizzo, J. R., House, R. J., & Lirtzman, S. I. (1970). Role conflict and ambiguity in complex organizations. *Administrative Science Quarterly*, *15*(2), 150–163. DOI: 10.2307/2391486

Rodríguez-Sánchez, A. M., Devloo, T., Rico, R., Salanova, M., & Anseel, F. (2017). What makes creative teams tick? Cohesion, engagement, and performance across creativity tasks: A three-wave study. *Group & Organization Management*, *42*(4), 521–547.

Roth, P., & Doehne, M. (2024). Cohesion is lower in virtualized collaborations: A comparison of teams' network structure. *Small Group Research*, *55*(4), 560–594.

Ryssina, V. N., & Koroleva, G. N. (1984). Role structures and creative potential of working teams. *R & D Management*, *14*(4), 233–237.

Saad, E., & Agogué, M. (2023). Creativity in virtual teams: Systematic review, synthesis and research agenda. *Creativity and Innovation Management*, *32*(1), 117–140. DOI: 10.1111/caim.12540

Salas, E., Grossman, R., Hughes, A. M., & Coultas, C. W. (2015). Measuring team cohesion: Observations from the science. *Human Factors*, *57*(3), 365–374. DOI: 10.1177/0018720815578267 PMID: 25875429

Salas, E., Shuffler, M. L., Thayer, A. L., Bedwell, W. L., & Lazzara, E. H. (2015). Understanding and improving teamwork in organizations: A scientifically based practical guide. *Human Resource Management*, *54*(4), 599–622. DOI: 10.1002/hrm.21628

Smith, A. C. T., & Stewart, B. (2011). Organizational rituals: Features, functions and mechanisms. *International Journal of Management Reviews*, *13*(2), 113–133. DOI: 10.1111/j.1468-2370.2010.00288.x

Stanford University. (n.d.). *Hasso Plattner Institute of Design (d.school)*. https://dschool.stanford.edu/

Stein, D. H., Schroeder, J., Hobson, N., Gino, F., & Norton, M. I. (2022). When alterations are violations: Moral outrage and punishment in response to (even minor) alterations to rituals. *Journal of Personality and Social Psychology: Interpersonal Relations and Group Processes, 123*(1), 123–153. PMID: 33492153

Summers, I., Coffelt, T., & Horton, R. E. (1988). Work-group cohesion. *Psychological Reports, 63*(2), 627–636. DOI: 10.2466/pr0.1988.63.2.627 PMID: 3406279

Taggar, S., & Ellis, R. (2007). The role of leaders in shaping formal team norms. *The Leadership Quarterly, 18*(2), 105–120. DOI: 10.1016/j.leaqua.2007.01.002

Thomas, K. W. (1992). Conflict and negotiation processes in organizations. In Dunnette, M. D., & Hough, L. M. (Eds.), *Handbook of industrial and organizational psychology* (Vol. 3, pp. 651–717). Consulting Psychologists Press.

Tkalich, A., Šmite, D., Andersen, N. H., & Moe, N. B. (2022). What happens to psychological safety when going remote? *IEEE Software, 41*(1), 113–122.

Tucker, C., Olsen, B., & Hale, R. T. (2023). Trust and commitment: A comparative study of virtual team communication across industries. *Team Performance Management, 29*(1/2), 152–165. DOI: 10.1108/TPM-04-2022-0032

Verburg, R. M., Bosch-Sijtsema, P., & Vartiainen, M. (2013). Getting it done: Critical success factors for project managers in virtual work settings. *International Journal of Project Management, 31*(1), 68–79. DOI: 10.1016/j.ijproman.2012.04.005

Vuchkovski, D., Zalaznik, M., Mitręga, M., & Pfajfar, G. (2023). A look at the future of work: The digital transformation of teams from conventional to virtual. *Journal of Business Research, 163*, 113912. DOI: 10.1016/j.jbusres.2023.113912

Waizenegger, L., McKenna, B., Cai, W., & Bendz, T. (2020). An affordance perspective of team collaboration and enforced working from home during COVID-19. *European Journal of Information Systems, 29*(4), 429–442. DOI: 10.1080/0960085X.2020.1800417

Watson-Jones, R. E., & Legare, C. H. (2016). The social functions of group rituals. *Current Directions in Psychological Science, 25*(1), 42–46. DOI: 10.1177/0963721415618486

West, M. A. (1990). The social psychology of innovation in groups. In West, M. A., & Farr, J. L. (Eds.), *Innovation and creativity at work: Psychological and organizational strategies* (pp. 309–333). Wiley.

Zhang, H., Li, F., & Reynolds, K. J. (2022). Creativity at work: Exploring role identity, organizational climate and creative team mindset. *Current Psychology (New Brunswick, N.J.)*, *41*(6), 3993–4000.

Zheng, S., Yan, M., Liang, Y., Chen, Y., Wei, Q., & Li, S. (2024). Understanding the positive and negative effects of team virtuality: A theoretical review and research agenda. *Human Resource Management Review*, *34*(2), 101013. Advance online publication. DOI: 10.1016/j.hrmr.2024.101013

Chapter 8
Information Sharing and Psychological Safety in Virtual Teams

Joshua Fairchild
https://orcid.org/0000-0003-0049-0137
Creighton University, USA

Addison LeGrand
Creighton University, USA

Jaelyn Rose Bentzinger
Creighton University, USA

Katie Pfeiffer
Creighton University, USA

ABSTRACT

Virtual teamwork has become a regular part of life for student teams. However, there is still much that is unknown about the factors that contribute to effective collaboration among virtual teams. Research has shown that psychological safety is essential for team performance, but virtual teamwork creates additional psychological distance between team members that may make developing this vital climate factor challenging. As newly formed virtual teams navigate challenging tasks, they may feel compelled to focus more on tackling the task than developing social relations needed to support psychological safety. This can impair the development of team climate factors that support long-term team success. This chapter investigates how virtual teams may navigate challenging tasks while still supporting the development of group dynamics such as psychological safety, collective efficacy, and team

DOI: 10.4018/979-8-3373-0375-8.ch008

viability. To illustrate and further investigate these topics, this chapter describes a recent empirical study in which teams faced tasks of varying difficulty using a virtual reality paradigm.

INTRODUCTION

Communication, information exchange, and knowledge sharing are the keys to success in all forms of teamwork. In education, team-based projects are growing increasingly popular as a learning tool and are widely used in experiential learning. However, when the 2020 COVID-19 pandemic hit, and the world shut down, all of these exchanges of information had to occur virtually. This created a "digital divide," with the ability to communicate and collaborate gated based on communities' unequal access to technology (Sosa Diaz, 2021). This digital divide created additional challenges in which some students, such as students of a lower socio-economic status, first generation students, and those from marginalized racial groups, are less prepared for virtual collaboration than others (Bonfadelli, 2002; van Dijk, 2017; Cotten & Jelenewicz, 2006). For instance, a Pew Research Center (Pew Research, 2021a) study identified that 80% of white adults own a computer or have broadband internet access, whereas only 69% of African American adults and 67% of Hispanic adults do. Access is further stratified based on income; among households earning less than $30,000 annually, only 57% have broadband internet access, and only 59% have a home computer. Among households earning $100,000 or more, these statistics increase to 93% and 92%, respectively (Pew Research Center, 2021b).

Since the pandemic, students' varying familiarity with online learning tools, and the integration of remote or online e-learning platforms in brick-and-mortar classrooms have outpaced our knowledge of how to best support students in higher education (Cobo-Rendón et al., 2022). This effect is particularly salient for students collaborating in virtual teams. Since team-based, project-focused learning in the classroom is a vital tool for encouraging active learning and teaching teamwork skills, it is crucial to understand how to best support teamwork among students who may be collaborating remotely. Nemiro (2004), for instance, describes several factors necessary for successful creativity and performance in virtual teams, including the vital role of team climate. This chapter examines some of the key challenges associated with remote collaboration, specifically those that can predict information sharing among team members.

In particular, the chapter will explore several team climate factors that predict such information sharing and performance, using a recent empirical study involving the use of virtual reality technology to examine team interactions in distributed teams, where members have differential access to information. Such a situation is similar to what often occurs in student virtual teams, where team members may have different knowledge and skills, as well as different understandings of the task, and different proficiency and comfort with collaborative technology. The chapter will utilize this combination of a review of theory and practice, coupled with empirical data, to make recommendations for how to enhance collaboration, information sharing, and team learning in student virtual teams.

Background Rationale

Teamwork is crucial for success in organizations, and so has become the norm in many workplaces (Cirella, 2021; Khawam, DiDona, & Hernandez, 2017; Hartenian, 2003). At the same time, team-based learning is also increasingly common in the classroom, where educators recognize the potential value of encouraging active learning through team-based projects (Burgess, van Diggele, Roberts, & Mellis, 2020; Cabrera et al., 2002), both as an educational tool, and for preparing students for work in team-based organizations (e.g., Sisk, 2011). In a study from 2019 (predating the COVID-19 pandemic), 60% of undergraduate participants reported they often engaged in collaborative projects in school (Fardous & Karim, 2019).

Today, such teamwork is often at least partially remote, with one or more members being located apart from one another using technology as the basis of communication and collaboration (Morrison-Smith & Ruiz, 2020). Trends toward remote collaboration and virtual teamwork have been on the rise for several years (Deem et al., 2020), and such practices have become far more common since the COVID-19 pandemic. By the end of 2021, 75% of employees were working remotely in some capacity (Matney, 2022). Accordingly, many students seek out and engage with e-learning opportunities, as these mirror the kinds of work experiences they will likely have post-college (Bashir & Lapshun, 2024).

Even in traditional college courses, online document sharing platforms such as Google Docs and Microsoft SharePoint have encouraged remote collaboration among students and student teams. Furthermore, institutions for higher education have reflected this shift towards remote learning, increasing the quantity of online classes offered and increasing distance learning technology for opportunities such as studying abroad (Bevins et al., 2020). As in the workplace, the COVID-19 pandemic accelerated these changes, with additional remote collaboration tools such as Zoom and Microsoft Teams having been installed by over a million organizations globally (Warren, 2020) and are likewise prevalent in many educational settings.

Although most schools have returned to primarily in-person learning in the wake of the pandemic, virtual teamwork and remote collaboration have remained a central part of teamwork in classrooms and in the workplace. That said, there is still much that is unknown about how teams effectively collaborate and share information when working apart from one another. Collaboration in virtual teams introduces challenges that are less present in wholly face-to-face teams.

Namely, even if virtual team members are able to communicate in real time (such as with phone calls or video chat), perceived psychological distance likely remains an impediment. When team members are not physically located together and collaborating in person, it is more difficult to develop shared referent points for the task, as well as for one another (Axtell, Fleck, & Turner, 2004). That is, when team members are not working together in real-time, face-to-face, it is more challenging to understand what each person is working on, who knows what, and the personality characteristics, skills, and work styles of each team member (Oshri, Van Fenema, & Kotlarsky, 2008; Yoo & Kanawattanachai, 2001; Yoon & Zhu, 2004).

Thus, successful virtual teams need to overcome these barriers in order to support more effective collaboration. In context of Nemiro (2004)'s recognition that climate is a critical supporting factor for creative virtual team success, it is crucial that virtual teams develop a climate that supports information sharing. This will enable team members to develop a shared sense of the task at hand, and of one another (Andeson & West, 1998; Hülsheger, Anderson, & Salgado, 2009). That is, clear shared mental models (Mathieu, Heffner, Goodwin, Salas, & Cannon-Bowers, 2001; Mohammed & Dumville, 2001) and strong transactive memory systems (Lewis, 2003) are crucial for successful performance (Kim, Kim, & Jo, 2021; Lewis, 2003; Wang, Huang, Davison, & Yang, 2018). Mental models are defined as the knowledge a person holds of a system, its purpose, function, and the ability to predict the system's behavior; thus, a shared mental model (SMM) refers to a *team* in which people share knowledge of a system, its function, purpose, and relevant behaviors (Jonker et al., 2011).

Transactive memory systems (TMS) are defined as knowledge possessed by all group members, along with a shared understanding of how to access that knowledge. In other words, transactive memory systems involve knowing "who knows what" (Hertel et al., 1985). These critical processes have been studied in the traditional (i.e., in-person) workplace (e.g., Hu, Erdogan, Jiang, Bauer, & Liu, 2018; Uitdewilligen & Waller, 2018), but remote work and virtual teams create additional hurdles for successful collaboration, particularly among student teams in educational settings. Being able to develop shared team mental models gives team members the upper hand in improvised adaptation, giving team members the ability to anticipate one another's actions in a context where there is no time to plan ahead. In order to achieve this, team members need to identify and understand that each person not only may have different knowledge and skills. In virtual teams, members may not have access to the same information and may have a harder time figuring out "who knows what" (Mesmer-Magnus, DeChurch, Jimenez-Rodriguez, Wildman, & Shuffler, 2011). Therefore, successful teamwork involves not just achieving a high level of performance, but exhibiting effective team learning behaviors (Edmondson, 1999; Edmondson, Dillon, & Roloff, 2007). This is especially crucial in academic settings, where learning may be as (or more) important than performance.

Team Learning Behavior and Information Sharing

Edmondson and colleagues (Edmondson, 1999; Edmondson et al., 2007) argue that team learning is not just the sum of individual members' acquired knowledge and skill, but their shared experiences are a vital form of learning as well. It is not just a matter of learning what is needed to complete a task but learning about one another and developing group dynamics that support longer-term success (Edmondson, 1999; Edmondson, Winslow, Bohmer, & Pisano, 2003). In particular, team learning behavior involves not just developing shared codified knowledge of the team's work, but tacit knowledge of group norms, expectations, and member attitudes (Edmondson et al., 2003).

Though vitally important, developing team learning behavior becomes more challenging in virtual or otherwise distributed teams. Sole and Edmondson (2002), for instance, examined the role of situated knowledge in team learning. Such knowledge is a product not just of facts learned, but of the learner and the context in which they have acquired the knowledge. When team members are dispersed, it can be exceptionally difficult to share such site-specific knowledge. Doing so requires that team members take the time and effort to develop a climate that is fully supportive of information sharing, and willing to examine and learn from failures and errors that will inevitably occur along the way (MacPhail & Edmondson, 2011; Sole & Edmondson, 2002). That is, psychological safety is essential for information sharing and team learning in virtual teams, and it may greatly influence the development of transactive memory systems among team members.

More specifically, there are three dimensions that work in tandem to develop transactive memory systems, all of which can be influenced by team learning in a psychologically safe environment: 1) developing a shared sense of the task, 2) gaining awareness of members' expertise, and 3) developing a shared understanding of team members' roles. The development of transactive memory systems (Lewis, 2003) is a delicate and complex process, made more challenging when teamwork is at least partially remote. However, research by Yoon and Zhou (2021) suggests that the perceived utility of the virtual communication tools (such as Microsoft Teams, Slack, or Google Docs) may positively influence the development of each of these three dimensions of transactive memory systems, potentially enhancing virtual team effectiveness.

Specifically, Yoon and Zhou (2021) indicate that successfully using communication technologies can enhance a team's shared understanding of their task, of one another's areas of expertise, and of who is responsible for what parts of the task. Likewise, Lewis (2003) indicates that strong transactive memory systems involve an awareness of the specialization of each member's knowledge, faith in one another's expertise, and a belief that team members are able to coordinate their efforts on the task at hand.

When teams are working remotely, challenges with communication and information sharing can arise, since members may not have simultaneous access to the same information. This challenge raises the question of what can be done to better prepare students for effective collaboration and information sharing when working in virtual teams. That is, when team members are not all physically in the same space, and may not have access to the same information, they may perceive a greater degree of psychological distance (Trope & Liberman, 2010), which can make it extremely difficult to develop a shared understanding of one another and of the task at hand. Thus, using communication tools that facilitate information sharing and help provide a common referent point may be quite valuable.

In the classroom, although members of a student team may share an overall goal (such as "getting a good grade on their project"), each member likely has their own expectations, workstyles, knowledge, and skills. Developing applicable team norms, figuring out who knows what, and who has the skills and motivation to tackle various parts of a project is a challenge for any student team, but one that is magnified by the psychological distance often implicit in virtual teamwork. For instance, a study of the Covid-19 shift to student virtual teams (Valente & MacMahon, 2020) found that asynchronous communication in student virtual teams was associated with less in-depth critical analysis and overall less effective team communication. Similarly, student virtual teams may experience a weaker sense of shared identity and task commitment than face-to-face teams (Mayfield & Valenti, 2024).

Thus, it is critical to understand how teams can successfully navigate the challenges associated with this increasingly prevalent form of teamwork. Specifically, successful performance in virtual or otherwise distributed teams requires effective information sharing (Aissa et al., 2022; House, 2019). Effective information and knowledge sharing associated with team learning is crucial for facilitating the transfer of individual knowledge into collective (team) knowledge without information loss or misinterpretation (Yang, 2007). In student teams, where learning (not just "performance") is a critical goal, such knowledge transfer is especially valuable, as it supports not just task success, but student learning overall (e.g., Hansen, 2006). Additionally, information sharing can evoke creativity and encourage complex problem solving that is beneficial for all forms of teamwork (Castaneda & Cueller, 2020), including student teams.

Despite the critical nature of information sharing in virtual teams, the capacity for such information sharing is often impacted by the degree to which members of a virtual team are separated. With regard to student virtual teams, such separation may involve geographic differences (members located in different places), temporal differences (members accessing information or communicating at different times), or technological separation (members differing in their access to or familiarity with technology) (Prasad, DeRosa, & Beyerlein, 2017; Siebdrat, Hoegl, & Ernst, 2009). In such circumstances, information sharing can easily become restricted, particularly if team members do not feel sufficiently confident in their relationships with one another (Edmondson, 1999; Guchait et al., 2014).

Overcoming Perceived Separation: The Role of Psychological Safety

In psychologically safe teams, members feel comfortable sharing their ideas and conveying information even in confusing, ambiguous situations, or challenging (Edmondson, 1999; Edmondson & Brandsby, 2023; Edmondson & Lei, 2014; Frazier, Fainschmidt, Klinger, Pezeshkan, & Vracheva, 2017). Psychological safety involves a shared perception that members of a team feel a collaborative climate, where reflection and learning is encouraged. When team members share a high level of psychological safety, then psychological safety goes beyond individual beliefs, forming a collaborative climate within each group, where members believe that everyone wants what is best for the team. This includes a willingness to disclose personal errors (Edmondson, 1999), viewing others' errors as learning opportunities (Edmondson, 2011; Van Dyck, Frese, Baer, & Sonnentag (2005), and seeking and providing feedback (London, Volmer, Zyberaj, & Kluger, 2023).

Indeed, psychological safety is associated with positive perceptions of involvement and information sharing in teams, as well as critical improvements in team learning behavior. Thus, in any collective task, psychological safety is a critical driver of team learning and thus, group success. In academic settings, team learning itself is especially critical, as performance is likely not the only outcome of importance; pedagogically speaking, learning (not exceptional performance) is the ultimate goal. Building a sense of psychological safety is perhaps even more critical for students working in virtual teams, since team members may feel disconnected from one another, due to perceived psychological distance (Morrison-Smith & Ruiz, 2020).

Team members' perceived level of psychological safety is heavily influenced by a team's processes and other resultant cognitive and affective states (e.g., Ilgen, Hollenbeck, Johnson, & Jundt, 2005). Poor interactions, including communication challenges, can undermine team psychological safety (Dusenberry & Robinson, 2020).

In addition, research has made it clear that trust and psychological safety are two sides of the same coin, with trust positively predicting psychological safety for hybrid, remote and in-person teams (Edmondson, 1999; Santos, 2023). Moreover, in a survey reflective of remote work implementation during the Covid-19 pandemic, Aguillion and Cronin-Gilmore (2024) identified five central concerns from employee's responses regarding remote communication, one of which was trust concerns. Likewise, Majid and Wey (2011) found there is a significant effect of trust on technological based information sharing, which is developed from repeated remote information exchanges (Okeoma & Chinwe, 2024). Thus, the role of psychological safety plays an important part in remote information exchange in order to achieve successful collaboration, present task success, and continued team learning (Zhang, Fang, Wei, & Chen, 2010).

In contrast, information sharing is not the only construct affected by trust. Research suggests that for emergence of normative actions to occur, trust is imperative. Specifically, when team members do not come from the same social settings and thus have diverse ideas of cultural norms (Chatman & Flynn, 2001; Hertel et al., 2013). In a longitudinal study by Crisp and Jarvenpaa (2013) to investigate swift trust (trust that is formed within temporary situations), college students were asked to virtually devise a business plan while geographically separated across four continents. Through this, Crisp and Jarvenpaa (2013) found that early trusting beliefs significantly affected participants' confidence to engage in normative actions, which in turn influenced trust (and ultimately outcomes) later in the process.

Therefore, psychological safety (and associated trust) are vital for developing the confidence to collaborate and succeed as a team, as well as the comfort and social satisfaction needed to want to keep working together throughout the task and into the future. In light of this, it is important to examine some of these team climate factors that can develop as a result of psychological safety.

Communication Challenges in Virtual Teams

Additional climate factors can create further challenges though; a present example can be seen in intergenerational normative communication styles. Generation Y, known as millennials, may prefer video calls and instantaneous communication; whereas Generation Z, the generation now filling colleges, prefer asynchronous, short communication strategies using visual cues such as emojis (Choudhary et al., 2024). Thus, student virtual teams may face additional collaboration challenges, as they may struggle to develop clear communication norms among group members. The consequence of limited adherence to group norms can act as an additional barrier within student virtual teams. A lack of face-to-face contact, verbal cues, or task initiation cues are defined as 'cue deprivation', and can impair effective virtual collaboration (Morrison-Smith & Ruiz, 2020). That is, lacking face-to-face communication cues, student teams may struggle to develop the norms they need to coalesce as a cohesive unit, able to learn and perform as a group. As an antithesis, Reeve and Tseng (2011) describe agentic engagement in terms of how students collaboratively engage with the assignments they are given (versus passively absorbing material). Virtual teamwork poses a risk to such agentic engagement, due to the potential for cue deprivation that might undermine collaborative action. Almusharraf and Bailey (2021) tested this theory on college students using videoconferencing to explore the effects of agentic engagement on collaborative learning. They found that, in such virtual team contexts, a student's *inclination* to make the environment more psychologically safe for themselves, by interacting and engaging virtually, can lead to a higher rate of success.

However, developing norms for information sharing and collaboration take time and effort (DiMaggio & Van Alstyne, 2013), a challenge made more difficult in student virtual teams, where psychological distance is greater (Johnson, Suriya, Yoon, Berrett, & La Fleur, 2002; Teh, Baniassad, Van Rooy, & Boughton, 2011), and members likely have competing priorities outside of the classroom (such as work or social obligations, other courses, and extracurriculars). As previously discussed, such an increase in psychological safety can enhance positive group dynamics associated with team success, including information sharing among team members (Edmondson, 1999; Lee, Swink, & Pandejpong, 2011). Namely, developing a sense of collective efficacy and team viability are likely essential.

The Role of Collective Efficacy in Team Performance and Team Learning

Bandura (1997) describes collective efficacy as a team's shared perception that they are able to succeed at a particular task. Such a belief is essential for success on the task at hand (such as a class group project), but also more broadly valuable as an instrument to strengthen the team's sense of agency; the idea that they are in control of their outcomes (Tasa, Taggar, & Seijts, 2007). Illustrative of this, a longitudinal study by Tasa and colleagues (2007) found that developing a sense of collective efficacy for a present task influenced future collective efficacy, as well as the development of teammates' teamwork-oriented behaviors. As further illustration of the value of this construct, Tao and colleagues (Tao, Wang, Robson, & Hughes, 2025) found that high levels of collective efficacy improved teams' abilities to learn from their failures. That is, team learning was strengthened in the presence of collective efficacy.

Collective efficacy is task-specific (Bandura, 1997). That is, a team's belief in their ability to succeed at a particular task may not generalize to their belief to succeed at future tasks. However, as discussed previously, collective efficacy for a particular task *does* influence the development of teamwork-oriented behaviors (Tasa & colleagues, 2007) as well as enhancing team learning (Tao et al., 2025). Therefore, collective efficacy has the potential to have long-term benefits, if the team is able to keep working together effectively.

The Impact of Team Viability on Team Success

Often, it is not sufficient for a team to succeed at their present task; they must also remain willing to keep working together in the future. In the classroom, students often collaborate on semester-long projects, which may have multiple tasks associated with them. In such contexts, succeeding at an early task, but burning out or becoming overly frustrated with one's teammates is a recipe for long-term disaster. That is, team viability is likewise essential.

In a review and synthesis of the literature on team viability, Bell and Marentette (2011) describe the construct as "the team's capacity for the sustainability and growth required for success in future performance episodes" (Bell and Marentette, 2011, p. 279). That is, it is the degree to which team members share a belief that the team is on a positive trajectory and cannot just succeed at the current task (i.e., collective efficacy), but that they can, and want to, remain successful together long-term. Such attitudes are beneficial for enabling a team to continue functioning through potential setbacks (e.g., Bell & Marentette, 2011; Foo, Sin, & Yiong, 2006).

Together, it is expected that collective efficacy and team viability will create a feedback loop, improving confidence and encouraging team learning by enhancing information sharing among team members. However, developing this positive climate requires that the team dedicate at least part of their time and effort to developing strong social relations, a task that (as previously discussed) poses unique challenges for virtual teams. This matter becomes further complicated, as the nature of the team's task itself may impair the development of such positive relationships. Namely, when new virtual teams face tasks that are particularly challenging, they may struggle to develop the positive climate (i.e., psychological safety, collective efficacy, and team viability) needed to facilitate information sharing and team learning. This may prove doubly problematic for student virtual teams, where worry over excessively challenging tasks may induce procrastination among team members, limiting task-related communication and harming performance and learning (Van Hooft & Van Mierlo, 2018).

The Impact of Task Difficulty on Psychological Safety and Team Climate

Psychological distance reduces a team's shared understanding of the task (Axtell et al., 2004), and so when the task at hand appears complex or challenging, teams are likely to spend a greater proportion of time and effort spent making sense of a task. By necessity then, these teams are therefore not spending as much time developing strong social relationships that are needed for long-term team success and team learning. This becomes especially likely when the cost of failure is particularly high; team members are likely less willing to take risks, admit needing assistance, or suggest unconventional solutions if such things might increase vulnerability for failure – all factors that would negatively impact the development of psychological safety (Edmondson, 2011).

Furthermore, a growing body of research suggests that sensemaking is a critical task for teams, involving developing an understanding of the task at hand, as well as understanding the role(s) that oneself and their teammates play in accomplishing that task (Klein, Wiggins, & Dominguez, 2010). As with many group dynamics factors, this becomes both more critical and more challenging in virtual teams (Rafaeli, Ravid, & Cheshin, 2009). Sensemaking is cognitively demanding, requiring juggling many factors (Klein et al., 2010). When the task at hand is complex or appears very challenging, it can occupy an inordinately large portion of a team's sensemaking capabilities.

According to Baumeister's theory of ego depletion (e.g., Baumeister & Vohs, 2007), self-control is a limited resource. Extrapolating from this, if team members need to focus much of their cognitive control on making sense of a difficult task, they will be less able to exercise self-control over their interactions with one another. Again, this is likely compounded in virtual teams, where developing social relations is already cognitively demanding (e.g., Serrat & Serrat, 2017). Difficult tasks also raise pressure on the team to not make mistakes, raising the psychological cost of errors (e.g., Edmondson, 2004). Therefore, there is likely more pressure on team members to be "correct," reducing idea sharing and willingness to listen to less conventional ideas, further impairing information sharing and team learning. Thus, in the face of a difficult task, virtual teams likely benefit from some factor that can reduce this cognitive load.

The Potential Moderating Role of Team Cohesion

In group dynamics literature, cohesion refers to the extent to which team members collaborate as they pursue the team's goals (cf., Mach, Dolan, & Tzafrir, 2010). In addition to the actual degree of collaboration, as a climate factor, team cohesion involves a shared perception that the team is on the same page regarding their collaboration. That is, it is not just the actual level of interdependence exercised among team members, but a perception of members desire to work interdependently. Expanding from this, Mach and colleagues (2010) note that interdependent tasks require developing a great deal of trust. Therefore, it is expected that, when teams develop a climate of cohesion and are working on an interdependent task, they may feel more inclined to trust one another. As previously mentioned, trust is closely related to psychological safety.

Moreover, a sufficiently high level of cohesion may assist with the team's sensemaking. Developing a shared sense of a complex task is cognitively demanding, but if the team already has a clear perception that they will be closely coordinating their efforts, that becomes one fewer matter to process. Reducing this cognitive burden may enhance team information sharing and performance. In fact, a study by Paul and colleagues (Paul, Drake, & Liang, 2011) found that there is a reciprocal relationship between team trust, cohesion, and performance; cultivating cohesion increased feelings of trust, which improved performance, and such improved performance further enhanced cohesion. As further evidence, a recent meta-analysis by Chaudhary and colleagues (Chaudhary, Chopra, & Kaur, 2022) found that team cohesion is a critical predictor of performance for virtual teams.

With specific regard to educational settings, when student virtual teams are approaching a complex task, it is important to be sensitive to the fact that they may feel overwhelmed as they juggle task-related sensemaking and developing social relationships. Helping them to build a climate high in team cohesion may prove to be a useful intervention. However, research on how newly formed teams navigate such tasks while also getting to know one another is not well-studied. Therefore, this chapter will now review a recent empirical study that aims to shed light on some less-studied relationships between task difficulty and team climate in virtual teams. This examination is intended to shed light on some of the team climate-related challenges student virtual teams may face, and also to help identify some potential interventions.

AN EMPIRICAL STUDY OF THE EFFECTS OF TASK DIFFICULTY ON PSYCHOLOGICAL SAFETY AND TEAM CLIMATE

The recent empirical investigation described here aims to fill some of the gaps in existing literature regarding collaboration in virtual teams. Namely, this study involves manipulating the difficulty of an initial task, then examining how it affects the development of team climate factors such as psychological safety, collective efficacy, and team viability. These findings are intended to offer potential solutions to the collaborative challenges faced by student virtual teams in higher education.

Participants

There were 333 participants in this study, who completed the study in groups of 3 or 4, resulting in a total of 89 teams. The young adult participants were primarily college undergraduates (Mean age = 19.03, $SD = 1.44$) at a United States Midwestern Private University who received course credit in exchange for their participation. Of these students, 39.06% reported having used a virtual reality headset before.

Materials

Virtual Teamwork Induction

This study induced perceived psychological distance and disparate access to information similar to what students encounter when working in virtual teams. One team member was isolated in a virtual reality headset and tasked with completing a task they could only solve by collaborating with their teammates, who they could not see. Specifically, teams engaged with the game *Keep Talking and Nobody Explodes* (Steel Crate Games, 2015) throughout this task. In this game, team members need to collaborate and communicate to defuse a virtual bomb, which only the person in virtual reality can see or interact with. The other team members have a "manual" that describes the steps needed to defuse the bomb (by solving a series of puzzles). Furthermore, this study utilized a modification for this game developed by the research team using the *Unity* programming language. This modification let the researchers specify and hold constant the attributes of the bombs that each team was tasked with defusing, ensuring consistency across teams. It also enabled the "task difficulty" experimental manipulation, as described below.

Success requires the entire team developing a shared mental model (Mohammed & Dumville, 2001) for the task, and effectively sharing information and problem solving as a group.

Task Difficulty

The researchers manipulated the perceived difficulty of the task by providing each team with a practice trial to orient them to the task. In actuality, there were two versions of the practice trial; one in which the practice task was extremely difficult, and one in which the practice task was extremely simple. In both cases, teams were told that this practice trial was a good indicator of the type of task they would be facing. As a result, teams who undertook the difficult practice trial would likely perceive the ensuing task as very difficult, and teams who undertook the easy practice trial would likely perceive the ensuing task as very easy.

Group Dynamics Factors

Team cohesion was measured using a four-item scale from the Group Environment Questionnaire (Carron, Widmeyer, & Brawley, 1985). This scale asked questions such as: "Our team is united in trying to reach its goals for performance," "I'm unhappy with my team's level of commitment to the task," and "Our team members have conflicting aspirations for the team's performance".

Similarly, Edmondson's (1990) seven-item scale was used to measure psychological safety. This scale asks participants to respond to statements such as: "If you make a mistake on this team, it is often held against you," "It is safe to take a risk on this team," and "It is difficult to ask other members of this team for help."

Team viability was assessed using a seven-item scale from Bushe and Coetzer (2007), which asked questions such as: "Being a member of this team has been personally satisfying?" "The members of this team could work a long time together?" and "I would choose this team to work with on similar tasks in the future?" Lastly, collective efficacy was measured using a ten-item scale adapted from Paskevich and colleagues (Paskevich, Brawley, Dorsch, & Widmeyer, 1999), which asks questions such as, "My team is able to reach agreement about what needs to get done," "My team members communicate well with one another despite any differences in cultural background," and "My team members work well together even in challenging situations." Each scale was formatted as a 7-point scale and used the same scale labels (1= *Strongly Disagree*, 2=*Moderately Disagree*, 3=*Disagree a Little*, 4=*Neither Agree nor Disagree*, 5=*Agree a Little*, 6=*Moderately Agree*, 7=*Strongly Agree*).

Procedure

Upon arrival at the study, participants drew one of four cards labeled numerically, "1-4". This indicated where they would be seated at a table with four chairs which were also labeled numerically. When they sat down, there was a printed QR code presented that directed them to an online consent document which was followed by a demographic questionnaire (hosted on the Qualtrics survey platform). In some cases, not every participant arrived at the lab at the same time, so completing the pre-experiment questionnaire acted as a buffer in the participants getting to speak to each other, allowing participants a few minutes to introduce themselves to one another if they so chose. Once the demographic survey was completed, it was explained that the person who drew the card with a "3" was the person who wore the virtual reality headset (an Oculus Rift headset). Participants were then oriented to the task, and the remaining two to three participants were assigned to use the manual containing the potential solutions to defuse the bomb.

Next, the researchers placed the headset on the selected person, handed out a printed copy of the manual to the remaining team members, and began the practice trial. In this trial, teams were given five minutes to solve a single puzzle to defuse the bomb. As previously stated, this puzzle was either designed to be exceptionally difficult or extremely easy. The task would end in success if the team solved the puzzle within the time limit and would end in failure if the team ran out of time or made three mistakes.

After the practice trial concluded in either success or failure, team members completed a second survey, which assessed perceived psychological safety and team cohesion. After everyone completed this survey, the team was instructed to begin their main task, in which they were given 15 minutes to defuse a bomb consisting of three puzzles. Once again, they would succeed at the task if they solved all puzzles within the allotted time and would fail if they ran out of time or made three mistakes.

After the task ended in either success or failure, team members completed a final survey assessing perceptions of collective efficacy and team viability on the team's main task.

RESULTS

This study predicted that collective efficacy would have a positive effect on likelihood of succeeding at a task that required coordination and information sharing. A logistic regression analysis was conducted to test this hypothesized effect. This analysis showed a modest trend toward significance, in which teams high in collective efficacy were more likely to succeed at the task *($e^B = 2.88$, $p = .12$).*

Additionally, the study also predicted that difficult tasks would impair the development of psychological safety, which would in turn hinder the emergent states of team viability and collective efficacy. A pair of moderated mediation analyses were conducted in SPSS using Model 7 of Hayes' (2022) PROCESS Macro. Specifically, psychological safety was tested as a mediator between task difficulty and both collective efficacy and team viability, as moderated by team cohesion.

In the first moderated mediation analysis, the overall model explained significant variance in collective efficacy ($R^2 = .326$, $F\,(2,86) = 20.79$, $p < .001$). Psychological safety positively predicted collective efficacy ($b = 0.637$, $t(85) = 5.589$, $p <.001$), but the direct effect of task difficulty on collective efficacy was not significant ($b = -.125$, $t(85) = -0.97$, $p = .336$. Instead, there was the conditional indirect effect of task difficulty on collective efficacy was significant at low levels of team cohesion

(b = -0.181, 95% CI [-.367, -.021], but not at moderate or high levels of cohesion. The index of moderated mediation was significant (b = 0.148, 95% CI [.020, .290], indicating that cohesion moderates the indirect effect of task difficulty on collective efficacy through psychological safety.

In the second moderated mediation analysis, the overall model explained significant variance in team viability (R^2 = .407, F (2,86) = 29.47, p < .001). Psychological safety positively predicted team viability (b = .753, t(86) = 6.22, p < .001. There was a marginally significant negative direct effect of task difficulty on team viability (b = -.266, t(86) = -1.94, p = .056). The conditional indirect effect of task difficulty on viability through psychological safety was significant at low levels of cohesion (b = -.214, 95% CI [-.428, -.022], but not at moderate or high levels of cohesion. The index of moderated mediation was significant (b = .174, 95% CI p.020, .349], indicating that cohesion moderates the indirect effect of task difficulty on team viability through psychological safety.

For diagrams of these results, please see Figures 1 and 2.

Figure 1. Moderated mediation effects of task difficulty and team cohesion on collective efficacy, acting through psychological safety.

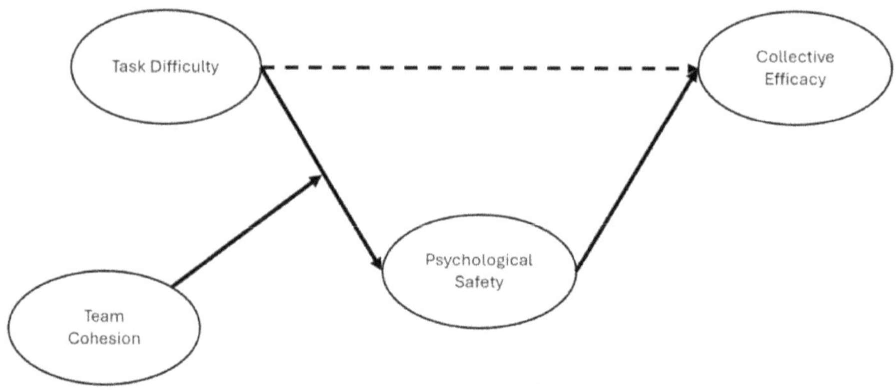

Figure 2. Moderated mediation effects of task difficulty and team cohesion on team viability, acting through psychological safety.

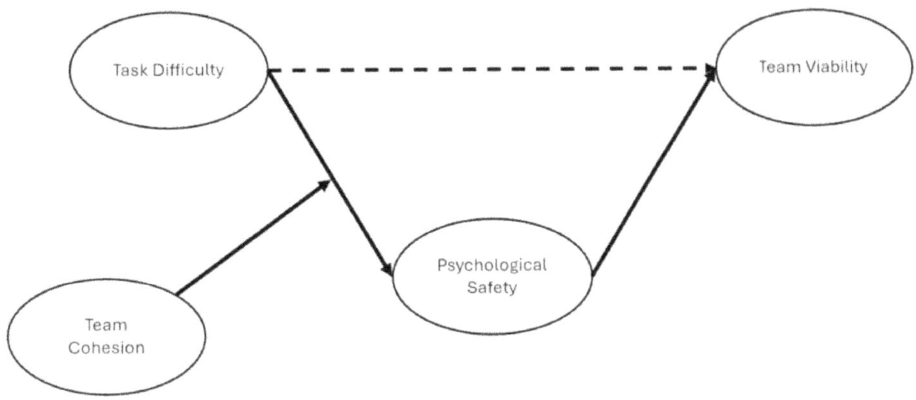

DISCUSSION AND IMPLICATIONS

This chapter reviewed several challenges associated with virtual teamwork that may affect student teams. Namely, developing a psychologically safe climate is essential for effective team learning and performance, and such a climate further enhances collective efficacy and psychological safety. However, facing a very challenging task may tax the limits of a team's sensemaking abilities (Klein et al., 2010; Rafaeli et al., 2009), and may likewise strain their capacity to focus on developing social relationships (e.g., Baumeister & Vohl, 2007).

The experimental study described in this chapter represents a preliminary attempt to understand some of these group dynamics factors that influence team climate and performance in virtual teams, including possible ways to mitigate the challenges. Specifically, it examines how the difficulty of a task undertaken by remote teams can affect the critical dynamics of team viability and collective efficacy within the team, through its effects on psychological safety.

Interpreting and Integrating the Empirical Findings

First, this study examined the potential effect of collective efficacy on immediate task performance. This relationship showed something of a trend, indicating that teams higher in collective efficacy may be more likely to succeed than teams with lower collective efficacy. Admittedly, this relationship did not reach the conventional level of statistical significance; however, from a practical perspective, it does appear that raising collective efficacy may have a positive effect on performance. Beyond that, in the classroom, education involves much more than just "success" or "failure." Ultimately, learning is the most important outcome (Klein, Kuh, Chun, Hamilton, & Shavelson, 2005), and collective efficacy appears to play an important role in team learning (Tao et al., 2025; Wang & Lin, 2007). Indeed, collective efficacy appears to serve as a mediator between psychological safety and the quality of team performance (Kim, Lee, & Connerton, 2020).

Looking further, this empirical study examined how the perceived difficulty of a team's task influenced the development of psychological safety, a crucial factor for information sharing and team learning, as well as the development of other climate factors necessary for long-term team success. Teams that experienced an inordinately difficult initial task developed a weaker sense of psychological safety, in turn impairing the development of both collective efficacy and team viability. That is, teams that faced an extremely challenging task likely focused primarily on making sense of this challenge and avoiding mistakes, preventing them from developing crucial team climate factors. In such contexts, members may feel pressure to be correct, rather than to learn and grow. The reduction in unique information sharing associated with low psychological safety (Edmondson, 2011) also likely impairs the development of a strong transactive memory system (Lewis, 2003; Yoo & Kanawattanachai, 2001).

However, if teams develop a sense of cohesion early on, they feel like they are on the same page, and united in their goal of tackling the challenging task. This may blunt the negative effects of task difficulty on psychological safety, because more cohesive teams can handle the potential disruptions of sharing risky ideas or proposing unconventional solutions, knowing that, ultimately, they are on the same page.

Practical Implications for Student Virtual Teams

Synthesizing the previous points, building social relations in virtual teams is an inherently challenging undertaking (e.g., Ahuja & Galvin, 2003; Morrison-Smith & Ruiz, 2020). In particular, the psychological distance between team members of student virtual teams may act as an additional barrier to developing social relationships. Thus, building a strong, positive climate that can support information sharing and learning requires a great deal of cognitive effort from group members.

As such, strong socialization, and developing a shared understanding of the group, likely will not happen if the team is immediately presented with a challenging task that they have to collaboratively understand. Instead, they would need to divert their limited cognitive resources to addressing the task at hand (Baumeister

& Vohl, 2007). This ultimately would be counterproductive, as a virtual team that has not developed a positive climate supportive of information sharing and team learning will struggle to succeed at such challenging tasks.

Bolstering Cohesion and Psychological Safety in Student Virtual Teams

In courses where students will be working in virtual teams, faculty should consider implementing some form of early intervention to encourage the development of some level of team cohesion, prior to assigning the team a challenging task. These interventions do not necessarily need to be directly related to the students' eventual task; any activity that requires collaboration and communication can shift team members' referent point from "I" to "we," ultimately contributing to seeing the team as a single entity, rather than a collection of individuals (Friedley & Manchester, 2005).

Cultivating a baseline level of team cohesion will help build a sense of unity among team members (Forsyth, 2021). In turn, this can bolster a team's capacity to develop psychological safety and share information effectively (Kakar, 2018). This will enable the development of psychological safety, which can further facilitate collective efficacy and team viability, setting the team up for success throughout a longer-term project.

Furthermore, since students likely face many competing pressures and are under substantial stress, academic and otherwise (e.g., Jenkins, Weeks, & Hard, 2021), educators should consider taking a more active role in fostering a climate of psychological safety. This could involve actively engaging students in developing pedagogical processes for the course (Cook-Sather, 2016), and addressing student performance issues as "teachable moments," rather than opportunities to punish (Verduzco-Baker, 2018).

However, it is important to recognize that psychological safety is not the same thing as complacency. A psychologically safe team should feel comfortable not just being in one another's presence (i.e., confident that nothing unpleasant will come up), but confident that, should challenging issues or disagreements arise, the team will be able to successfully and safely navigate them together.

In essence, psychologically safe student teams (and the classes they are embedded within) are akin to "brave spaces," as defined by Arao and Clemens (2013). In a brave space, individuals do not feel sheltered from unpleasantness, but instead feel as though their peers will support them in navigating challenging circumstances. With regard to student virtual teams, the course instructor likely plays a critical role in helping to develop such a brave space. As a shared referent point for potentially psychologically distant team members, the instructor should actively model bravery; that is, they should openly acknowledge their own limitations, and express their willingness to collaborate with their students in order to grow and learn. Furthermore, if the instructor is operating on invalid assumptions (such as those regarding students' access to or familiarity with technology), they should be open to being corrected by their students, emphasizing that admitting mistakes is crucial to learning. (Arao & Clemens, 2013; Cook-Sather, 2016; Verduzco-Baker, 2018). According to social learning theory (e.g., Hill, Song, & West, 2009), such modeling is often a highly effective means of facilitating learning and behavior change for students.

In the present context, this modeling can lead to learning that the classroom environment (and the teams formed within it), are psychologically safe. By extension, student teams in which members feel psychologically safe may be more inclined to take interpersonal risks and share personal or controversial ideas. Such open information sharing contributes to team learning through the development of shared mental models.

On the whole, the extant literature, as well as the empirical study discussed here, underscore the importance of cohesion and psychological safety as critical factors contributing to beneficial team outcomes. Namely, psychological safety facilitates increased levels of team viability and collective efficacy, which may create a feedback loop to further enhance intrateam information sharing, mental model development, and transactive memory system formation.

Managing Conflict in "Safe" Teams

The potential benefits of a cohesive, psychologically safe team do not necessarily make a case for "more is better." In fact, research has consistently demonstrated that too much team cohesion can in fact harm information sharing and performance. Research shows that highly cohesive teams that remain together for an extended period report feeling that they are performing better and becoming more innovative, but in actuality, the converse is often true (Skilton & Dooley, 2010). Essentially, team members begin to develop an illusion of invulnerability, conflating their smooth social interactions with task success. This can lead to instances of groupthink, as team members may fail to notice or point out shortcomings in the team's decision-making processes (Janis, 2008; McAvoy & Butler, 2008).

Groupthink may be particularly problematic for student teams, as students vary in terms of their commitment to the task, the degree to which they may value their grade, or their motivation to learn. This can lead to some students acquiescing or going along with a majority opinion, rather than engaging in the more challenging process of critically evaluating the team's performance so far (Fransen, Kirschner, & Erkens, 2011).

Furthermore, cohesion as a climate factor involves a shared perception that all team members are on the same page. However, if members of the team all believe they are already in alignment regarding the task at hand, they may feel less compelled to share information. A reduction in information sharing can drastically impair team learning (Edmondson, 2011), and reduce team adaptability and reflexivity (Schippers, West, & Dawson, 2015). Likewise, a meta-analysis by Beal and colleagues (Beal, Cohen, Burke, & McLendon, 2003) found that excessive cohesion could undermine team performance. In virtual teams specifically, although a moderate level of cohesion is beneficial for information sharing and performance, too much cohesion was found to impair knowledge sharing (Kakar, 2018).

In theory, a climate of psychological safety should help to reduce the risk of such issues. However, some emerging research suggests potential boundary conditions to be aware of. Specifically, although psychological safety is crucial for team learning and team success, it is a "necessary but not sufficient" condition. Namely, research by Fairchild and Hunter (2014) examined student engineering teams over the course of a semester and found that teams high in psychological safety produced fewer creative products than teams lower in psychological safety, unless the teams also experienced a substantial level of task conflict. This suggests that not only do teams need to perceive that everyone feels comfortable sharing their ideas and speaking freely; but they must also engage in those behaviors. That is, teams need to actually engage in facing tough issues and debating solutions when necessary. This may prove especially challenging for student teams collaborating virtually; when communication is more challenging, teams may resort to communicating about more superficial things, such as common interests, inside jokes, or nicknames, rather than addressing more difficult issues necessary to learn and grow as a team (Kim, Magnusen, & Andrew, 2016).

Thus, instructors play a crucial role in not just creating a psychologically safe environment for learning, but also an environment where students will not shy away from meaningful engagement with difficult concepts and civil, task-focused disagreement. Therefore, particularly in courses that will involve virtual teamwork, instructors should clearly communicate expectations for civil communication (Arao & Clemens, 2013). Furthermore, educators should consider collaborating with their students to develop ground rules for sharing information and expressing dissent (Cook-Sather, 2016; Verduzco-Baker, 2018).

Not only will such collaboration enhance student buy-in for these rules, in accordance with Social Learning Theory (e.g., Hill et al., 2009; Pritchard & Woollard, 2013), if the instructor takes such an approach, it effectively models for students that it is okay to not personally have all the answers, and encourages engaging in productive discussion, even if everyone is not immediately on the same page (Cook-Sather, 2016). Expanding on this collaborative approach, Cook-Sather (2016) further emphasizes the value in student-faculty partnerships, in which students can voice not only their ideas, but also their concerns or critiques about the class, its goals, or its projects. This modeling helps to create an inclusive environment that can extend to student interactions with one another as they navigate work in virtual teams.

Faculty should also consider implementing activities that encourage some level of task-focused conflict within teams. This may include exercises like requiring members to share their most unconventional idea, or to anonymously write out constructive critiques of the group's chosen solution. However, it is important to find the correct balance, and to make sure that any disagreements remain task-focused, rather than spilling into interpersonal feuds (de Wit, Greer, & Jehn, 2012). Once again, inviting students to participate in constructing the guidelines for managing such interactions will give them agency over the process (Arao &Clemens, 2013) and can help ensure that conflict stays productive and task focused.

LIMITATIONS AND FINAL THOUGHTS

The primary goal of this chapter was to investigate the social processes that may contribute to positive climate factors associated with information sharing and team learning in student virtual teams. On the whole, the extant literature underscores the importance of cohesion and psychological safety as critical factors contributing to beneficial team outcomes. However, if not managed properly, student virtual teams may not be able to harness these benefits, and may experience lower levels of learning and performance instead. The goal of presenting the empirical study described in this chapter was to elucidate some of these benefits and challenges. However, there are some potential limitations to this study that should be addressed.

First, this chapter posits that some baseline level of cohesiveness is necessary for the development of other positive team dynamics. However, this is not a condition that could be assessed through the empirical study described here, as the researchers did not measure cohesion at the outset of the task (only at the midpoint and endpoint). The study likewise did not account for the fact that some students may have known each other or worked together previously, nor did the researchers code for how much team members socialized or otherwise interacted prior to beginning the task. Given what this chapter proposes about the benefits of early cohesiveness for virtual teamwork, this would be a worthwhile factor to be examined in future research.

Additionally, the empirical study perhaps did not account for the notably higher stakes for student team performance in the classroom. Although the task at hand (defusing a "bomb") was intended to be high pressure, there was ultimately no consequence for failure; naturally, this is not the case for students working on a class project, where grades may be at stake. This means the study was unable to examine how psychological safety may affect team members' perceptions of mistakes that might impact the group as a whole. That is, are mistakes or critiques still viewed as opportunities to learn if they might harm someone's grade?

Finally, this study was a relatively brief set of performance episodes. Over the course of 45 minutes, teams attempted two tasks. Although the multiple surveys used were intended to capture changes in attitudes and climate as the team continued to work together, this is still a very short span of time compared to the weeks or months that a student virtual team may collaborate in a college course. Therefore, future research should investigate how team climate factors such as cohesion, psychological safety, and information sharing may affect learning and performance over a longer time span.

In closing, student virtual teams present unique collaborative challenges. The psychological distance present in such teams can make it more difficult to get on the same page (developing shared mental models and transactive memory systems), and this can be compounded when teams need to determine how to approach a challenging task. However, if teams are adequately supported and are able to build a sufficiently (though not excessively) cohesive climate, they can manage the cognitive load associated with such tasks. As a result, they can develop a climate of psychological safety, leading to more effective information sharing and, eventually, greater levels of collective efficacy and team viability. When managed effectively, student virtual teams can cultivate a climate that enables them to learn and perform as well as face-to-face teams, as long as special attention is paid to their unique characteristics.

REFERENCES

Ågerfalk, P. J., Fitzgerald, B., & Slaughter, S. A. (2009). Introduction to the special issue—flexible and distributed information systems development: State of the art and research challenges. *Information Systems Research*, *20*(3), 317–328.

Aguillon, S., & Cronin-Gilmore, J. (2024). How Remote Work Changes Communication in Organizations. *Journal of Behavioral and Applied Management*, *24*(3), 173–185.

Ahuja, M. K., & Galvin, J. E. (2003). Socialization in virtual groups. *Journal of Management*, *29*(2), 161–185.

Aissa, N. B., Gurău, C., Psychogios, A., & Somsing, A. (2022). Transactional memory systems in virtual teams: Communication antecedents and the impact of TMS components on creative processes and outcomes. *Technological Forecasting and Social Change*, *174*, 1–14.

Almusharraf, N. M., & Bailey, D. (2021). Online engagement during COVID-19: Role of agency on collaborative learning orientation and learning expectations. *Journal of Computer Assisted Learning*, *37*(5), 1285–1295. PMID: 34226784

Anderson, N. R., & West, M. A. (1998). Measuring climate for work group innovation: Development and validation of the team climate inventory. *Journal of Organizational Behavior*, *19*(3), 235–258.

Arao, B., & Clemens, K. (2013). From safe spaces to brave spaces: A new way to frame dialogue around diversity and social justice. In Landreman, L. M. (Ed.), *The art of effective facilitation* (pp. 135–150). Routledge.

Axtell, C. M., Fleck, S. J., & Turner, N. (2004). Virtual teams: Collaborating across distance. *International Review of Industrial and Organizational Psychology*, *19*, 205–248.

Bandura, A. (1997). *Self-efficacy: The exercise of control*. W. H. Freeman.

Bashir, S., & Lapshun, A. L. (2025). E-learning future trends in higher education in the 2020s and beyond. *Cogent Education*, *12*(1), 2445331.

Baumeister, R. F., & Vohs, K. D. (2007). Self-Regulation, ego depletion, and motivation. *Social and Personality Psychology Compass*, *1*(1), 115–128.

Beal, D. J., Cohen, R. R., Burke, M. J., & McLendon, C. L. (2003). Cohesion and performance in groups: A meta-analytic clarification of construct relations. *The Journal of Applied Psychology*, *88*(6), 989. PMID: 14640811

Bell, S. T., & Marentette, B. J. (2011). Team viability for long-term and ongoing organizational teams. *Organizational Psychology Review, 1*(4), 275–292.

Bevins, F., Bryant, J., Krishnan, C., & Law, J. (2020). Coronavirus: How should US higher education plan for an uncertain future? In *The path to the next normal* (pp. 120-125). McKinsey & Company.

Bonfadelli, H. (2002). The Internet and Knowledge Gaps: A Theoretical and Empirical Investigation. *European Journal of Communication, 17*(1), 65–84.

Burgess, A., van Diggele, C., Roberts, C., & Mellis, C. (2020). Facilitating small group learning in the health professions. *BMC Medical Education, 20*, 1–6. PMID: 33272270

Bushe, G. R., & Coetzer, G. H. (2007). Group development and team effectiveness: Using cognitive representations to measure group development and predict task performance and group viability. *The Journal of Applied Behavioral Science, 43*(2), 184–212.

Cabrera, A. F., Crissman, J. L., Bernal, E. M., Nora, A., Terenzini, P. T., & Pascarella, E. T. (2002). Collaborative learning: Its impact on college students' development and diversity. *Journal of College Student Development, 43*(1), 20–34.

Carron, A. V., Widmeyer, W. N., & Brawley, L. R. (1985). The development of an instrument to assess cohesion in sport teams: The Group Environment Questionnaire. *Journal of Sport & Exercise Psychology*, *7*(3), 244–266.

Casteneda, D. I., & Cuellar, S. (2020). Knowledge sharing and innovation: A systematic review. *Knowledge and Process Management*, *27*(3), 159–173.

Chatman, J. A., & Flynn, F. J. (2001). The influence of demographic heterogeneity on the emergence and consequences of cooperative norms in work teams. *Academy of Management Journal*, *44*, 956–974.

Chaudhary, M., Chopra, S., & Kaur, J. (2022). Cohesion as a cardinal antecedent in virtual team performance: A meta-analysis. *Team Performance Management*, *28*(5/6), 398–414.

Choudhary, R., Shaik, Y. A., Yadav, P., & Rashid, A. (2024). Generational differences in technology behavior: A systematic literature review. *Journal of Infrastructure. Policy and Development*, *8*(9), 6755.

Cirella, S. (2021). Managing collective creativity: Organizational variables to support creative teamwork. *European Management Review*, *18*(4), 404–417.

Cohen, T. N., Griggs, A. C., Kanji, F. F., Cohen, K. A., Lazzara, E. H., Keebler, J. R., & Gewertz, B. L. (2021). Advancing team cohesion: Using an escape room as a novel approach. *Journal of Patient Safety and Risk Management, 26*(3), 126–134.

Cook-Sather, A. (2016). Creating brave spaces within and through student-faculty pedagogical partnerships. *Teaching and Learning Together in Higher Education, 1*(18), 1.

Cotten, S. R., & Jelenewicz, S. M. (2006). A Disappearing Digital Divide Among College Students? Peeling Away the Layers of the Digital Divide. *Social Science Computer Review, 24*(4), 497–506.

Crisp, C. B., & Jarvenpaa, S. L. (2013). Swift Trust in Global Virtual Teams: Trusting Beliefs and Normative Actions. *Journal of Personnel Psychology, 12*(1), 45–56.

De Wit, F. R., Greer, L. L., & Jehn, K. A. (2012). The paradox of intragroup conflict: A meta-analysis. *The Journal of Applied Psychology, 97*(2), 360. PMID: 21842974

Deem, J., Beyer, S., Dana, H., Chicone, R., Ringler, I., Ferebee, S., & Strouble, D. (2020). Increasing Student Success with Team Projects in the Virtual Classroom. *Online Journal of Distance Learning Administration, 23*(3).

Di Maggio, M., & Van Alstyne, M. W. (2013). Information sharing, social norms and performance. *Social Norms and Performance (July 9, 2013).*

Dusenberry, L., & Robinson, J. (2020). Building psychological safety through training interventions: Manage the team, not just the project. *IEEE Transactions on Professional Communication, 63*, 207–226.

Edmondson, A. (1999). Psychological safety and learning behavior in work teams. *Administrative Science Quarterly, 44*(2), 350–383.

Edmondson, A. C. (2004). Learning from failure in health care: Frequent opportunities, pervasive barriers. *BMJ Quality & Safety, 13*(suppl 2), ii3–ii9. PMID: 15576689

Edmondson, A. C. (2011). Strategies for learning from failure. *Harvard Business Review, 89*(4), 48–55. PMID: 21510518

Edmondson, A. C., & Bransby, D. P. (2023). Psychological safety comes of age: Observed themes in an established literature. *Annual Review of Organizational Psychology and Organizational Behavior, 10*(1), 55–78.

Edmondson, A. C., Dillon, J. R., & Roloff, K. S. (2007). 6 three perspectives on team learning: Outcome improvement, task Mastery, and group process. *The Academy of Management Annals, 1*(1), 269–314.

Edmondson, A. C., & Lei, Z. (2014). Psychological safety: The history, renaissance, and future of an interpersonal construct. *Annual Review of Organizational Psychology and Organizational Behavior, 1*(1), 23–43.

Edmondson, A. C., Winslow, A. B., Bohmer, R. M., & Pisano, G. P. (2003). Learning how and learning what: Effects of tacit and codified knowledge on performance improvement following technology adoption. *Decision Sciences, 34*(2), 197–224.

Fairchild, J., & Hunter, S. T. (2014). "We've Got Creative Differences": The effects of task conflict and participative safety on team creative performance. *The Journal of Creative Behavior, 48*(1), 64–87.

Ferdous, T., & Karim, A. (2019). Working in Groups outside the Classroom: Affective Challenges and Probable Solutions. *International Journal of Instruction, 12*, 341–358.

Foo, M. D., Sin, H. P., & Yiong, L. P. (2006). Effects of team inputs and intrateam processes on perceptions of team viability and member satisfaction in nascent ventures. *Strategic Management Journal, 27*(4), 389–399.

Forsyth, D. R. (2021). Recent advances in the study of group cohesion. *Group Dynamics, 25*(3), 213.

Fransen, J., Kirschner, P. A., & Erkens, G. (2011). Mediating team effectiveness in the context of collaborative learning: The importance of team and task awareness. *Computers in Human Behavior, 27*(3), 1103–1113.

Frazier, M. L., Fainshmidt, S., Klinger, R. L., Pezeshkan, A., & Vracheva, V. (2017). Psychological safety: A meta-analytic review and extension. *Personnel Psychology, 70*(1), 113–165.

Friedley, S. A., & Manchester, B. B. (2005). Building team cohesion: Becoming" We" instead of. *Me. National Forensic Journal, 23*(1), 95–100.

Gosling, S. D., Rentfrow, P. J., & Swann, W. B.Jr. (2003). A Very Brief Measure of the Big Five Personality Domains. *Journal of Research in Personality, 37*, 504–528.

Guchait, P., Paşamehmetoğlu, A., & Dawson, M. (2014). Perceived supervisor and co-worker support for error management: Impact on perceived psychological safety and service recovery performance. *International Journal of Hospitality Management, 41*, 28–37.

Hansen, R. S. (2006). Benefits and problems with student teams: Suggestions for improving team projects. *Journal of Education for Business, 82*(1), 11–19.

Hartenian, L. S. (2003). Team member acquisition of team knowledge, skills, and abilities. *Team Performance Management*, *9*, 23–30.

Hill, J. R., Song, L., & West, R. E. (2009). Social learning theory and web-based learning environments: A review of research and discussion of implications. *American Journal of Distance Education*, *23*(2), 88–103.

House, C. (2019). Distributed teams—Challenges and opportunities. *Research Technology Management*, *62*(5), 11–13.

Hu, J., Erdogan, B., Jiang, K., Bauer, T. N., & Liu, S. (2018). Leader humility and team creativity: The role of team information sharing, psychological safety, and power distance. *The Journal of Applied Psychology*, *103*(3), 313. PMID: 29094959

Hülsheger, U. R., Anderson, N., & Salgado, J. F. (2009). Team-level predictors of innovation at work: A comprehensive meta-analysis spanning three decades of research. *The Journal of Applied Psychology*, *94*(5), 1128. PMID: 19702361

Ilgen, D. R., Hollenbeck, J. R., Johnson, M., & Jundt, D. (2005). Teams in organizations: From input-process-output models to IMOI models. *Annual Review of Psychology*, *56*, 517–543. PMID: 15709945

Janis, I. L. (2008). Groupthink. *IEEE Engineering Management Review*, *36*(1), 36.

Jenkins, A., Weeks, M. S., & Hard, B. M. (2021). General and specific stress mindsets: Links with college student health and academic performance. *PLoS One*, *16*(9), e0256351. PMID: 34495976

Johnson, S. D., Suriya, C., Yoon, S. W., Berrett, J. V., & La Fleur, J. (2002). Team development and group processes of virtual learning teams. *Computers & Education*, *39*(4), 379–393.

Jonker, C.M., van Riemsdijk, M.B., Vermeulen, B. (2011). Shared Mental Models: A Conceptual Analysis. *Springer Nature, 6541.*

Keoma, E., & Chinwe, A. (2024). Reciprocity and Trust as Predictors of Technology-Enabled Knowledge Sharing among Library and Information Science Professionals in Public Universities of South-East, Nigeria. *International Journal of Knowledge Dissemination*, *4*, 1–17.

Khawam, A. M., DiDona, T., & Hernandez, B. S. (2017). Effectiveness of Teamwork in the Workplace. *International Journal of Sciences, Basic and Applied Research*, *32*, 267–286.

Kim, S., Lee, H., & Connerton, T. P. (2020). How psychological safety affects team performance: Mediating role of efficacy and learning behavior. *Frontiers in Psychology*, *11*, 1581. PMID: 32793037

Kim, S., Magnusen, M. J., & Andrew, D. P. (2016). Divided we fall: Examining the relationship between horizontal communication and team commitment via team cohesion. *International Journal of Sports Science & Coaching*, *11*(5), 625–636.

Kim, S. M., Kim, M. J., & Jo, S. J. (2021). The relationships between perceived team psychological safety, transactive memory system, team learning behavior and team performance among individual team members. *Leadership and Organization Development Journal*, *42*(6), 958–975.

Klein, G., Wiggins, S., & Dominguez, C. O. (2010). Team sensemaking. *Theoretical Issues in Ergonomics Science*, *11*(4), 304–320.

Klein, S. P., Kuh, G., Chun, M., Hamilton, L., & Shavelson, R. (2005). An approach to measuring cognitive outcomes across higher education institutions. *Research in Higher Education*, *46*, 251–276.

Krumm, S., Terwiel, K., & Hertel, G. (2013). Challenges in norm formation and adherence: The knowledge, skills, and ability requirements of virtual and traditional cross-cultural teams. *Journal of Personnel Psychology*, *12*(1), 33–44.

Lee, J. Y., Swink, M., & Pandejpong, T. (2011). The roles of worker expertise, information sharing quality, and psychological safety in manufacturing process innovation: An intellectual capital perspective. *Production and Operations Management*, *20*(4), 556–570.

Lewis, K. (2003). Measuring transactive memory systems in the field: Scale development and validation. *The Journal of Applied Psychology*, *88*(4), 587. PMID: 12940401

London, M., Volmer, J., Zyberaj, J., & Kluger, A. N. (2023). Gaining feedback acceptance: Leader-member attachment style and psychological safety. *Human Resource Management Review*, *33*(2), 100953.

Mach, M., Dolan, S., & Tzafrir, S. (2010). The differential effect of team members' trust on team performance: The mediation role of team cohesion. *Journal of Occupational and Organizational Psychology*, *83*(3), 771–794.

MacPhail, L. H., & Edmondson, A. C. (2011). Learning domains: The importance of work context in organizational learning from error. In Hofmann, D. A., & Frese, M. (Eds.), *Errors in organizations* (pp. 177–198). Routledge.

Majid, S., & Wey, S. M. (2011). Knowledge sharing behavior of graduate students. In Murray, E. J. (Ed.), *Global aspects and cultural perspectives on knowledge management: emerging dimensions* (pp. 113–125). Information Science Reference/ IGI Global.

Mathieu, J. E., Heffner, T. S., Goodwin, G. F., Salas, E., & Cannon-Bowers, J. A. (2000). The influence of shared mental models on team process and performance. *The Journal of Applied Psychology*, *85*(2), 273. PMID: 10783543

Matney, M. (2022). 2022 Global Virtual Teams Survey Report. RW3 Culture Wizard Global Inclusion Experts. www.rw-3.com/blog/global-virtual-teams-survey-report -2022

Mayfield, C. O., & Valenti, A. (2024). Team satisfaction, identity, and trust: A comparison of face-to-face and virtual student teams. *Active Learning in Higher Education*, *25*(2), 213–226.

McAvoy, J., & Butler, T. (2008). The desire for cohesion in virtual teams: Be careful what you wish for. In Koch, N. (Ed.), *E-collaboration in modern organizations: Initiating and managing distributed projects* (pp. 220–241). Information Science Reference/IGI Global.

Mehmood, M. S., Jian, Z., Akram, U., Akram, Z., & Tanveer, Y. (2022). Entrepreneurial leadership and team creativity: The roles of team psychological safety and knowledge sharing. *Personnel Review*, *51*(9), 2404–2425.

Mesmer-Magnus, J. R., DeChurch, L. A., Jimenez-Rodriguez, M., Wildman, J., & Shuffler, M. (2011). A meta-analytic investigation of virtuality and information sharing in teams. *Organizational Behavior and Human Decision Processes*, *115*(2), 214–225.

Mohammed, S., & Dumville, B. C. (2001). Team mental models in a team knowledge framework: Expanding theory and measurement across disciplinary boundaries. *Journal of Organizational Behavior*, *22*(2), 89–106.

Morrison-Smith, S., & Ruiz, J. (2020). Challenges and barriers in virtual teams: A literature review. *SN Applied Sciences*, *2*(6), 1–33.

Nemiro, J. (2007). The building blocks for creativity in virtual teams. In MacGregor, S., & Torres, T. (Eds.), *Higher creativity for virtual teams: Developing platforms for co-creation* (pp. 98–121). Information Science Reference/IGI Global.

Nemiro, J. (2023). Virtual teams. In R. Reiter-Palmon & S. Hunter's (Eds.), *Handbook of organizational creativity: Group and individual influences,* 2nd edition (pp. 269–290). Elsevier Publishing.

Obo-Rendón, R., Bruna Jofre, C., Lobos, K., Cisternas San Martin, N., & Guzman, E. (2022). Return to University Classrooms with Blended Learning: A Possible Post-pandemic COVID-19 Scenario. *Frontiers in Education*, *7*, 957175.

Oshri, I., Van Fenema, P., & Kotlarsky, J. (2008). Knowledge transfer in globally distributed teams: The role of transactive memory. *Information Systems Journal*, *18*(6), 593–616.

Paskevich, D. M., Brawley, L. R., Dorsch, K. D., & Widmeyer, W. N. (1999). Relationship between collective efficacy and team cohesion: Conceptual and measurement issues. *Group Dynamics*, *3*(3), 210.

Paul, R., Drake, J. R., & Liang, H. (2016). Global virtual team performance: The effect of coordination effectiveness, trust, and team cohesion. *IEEE Transactions on Professional Communication*, *59*(3), 186–202.

Pew Research Center. (2021a, July 22). *Digital divide persists even as Americans with lower incomes make gains in tech adoption* [Report]. https://www.pewresearch.org/short-reads/2021/06/22/digital-divide-persists-even-as-americans-with-lower-incomes-make-gains-in-tech-adoption/

Pew Research Center. (2021b, July 16). *Home broadband adoption, computer ownership vary by race, ethnicity in the U.S.* [Report]. https://www.pewresearch.org/short-reads/2021/07/16/home-broadband-adoption-computer-ownership-vary-by-race-ethnicity-in-the-u-s/

Prasad, A., DeRosa, D., & Beyerlein, M. (2017). Dispersion beyond miles: Configuration and performance in virtual teams. *Team Performance Management*, *23*(3), 186–204.

Pritchard, A., & Woollard, J. (2013). *Psychology for the classroom: Constructivism and social learning*. Routledge.

Rafaeli, A., Ravid, S., & Cheshin, A. (2009). Sensemaking in virtual teams: The impact of emotions and support tools on team mental models and team performance. *International Review of Industrial and Organizational Psychology*, *24*, 151–181.

Reeve, J. M., & Tseng, C. (2011). Agency as a Fourth Aspect of Students' Engagement During Learning Activities. *Contemporary Educational Psychology*, *36*(4), 257–267.

Schippers, M. C., West, M. A., & Dawson, J. F. (2015). Team reflexivity and innovation: The moderating role of team context. *Journal of Management*, *41*(3), 769–788.

Schwarzer, R., & Jerusalem, M. (1995). *General Self-Efficacy Scale (GSE)* [Database record]. APA PsychTests.

Serrat, O., & Serrat, O. (2017). Managing virtual teams. In *Knowledge solutions: Tools, methods, and approaches to drive organizational performance*, 619-625.

Setkhumbong, T., Na-Songkhla, J., & Tantrarungroj, P. (2020). A Literature Perspective of Key Factors Influencing Creativity and Conceptual Model for Virtual Learning Team Work. *Humanities, Arts and Social Sciences Studies*, 427-460.

Siebdrat, F., Hoegl, M., & Ernst, H. (2009). How to manage virtual teams. *MIT Sloan Management Review*, *50*(4), 63–68.

Sisk, R. J. (2011). Team-based learning: Systematic research review. *The Journal of Nursing Education*, *50*(12), 665–669. PMID: 22007709

Skilton, P. F., & Dooley, K. J. (2010). The effects of repeat collaboration on creative abrasion. *Academy of Management Review*, *35*(1), 118–134.

Sole, D., & Edmondson, A. (2002). Situated knowledge and learning in dispersed teams. *British Journal of Management*, *13*(S2), S17–S34.

Sosa Díaz, M. J. (2021). Emergency remote education, family support and the digital divide in the context of the COVID-19 lockdown. *International Journal of Environmental Research and Public Health*, *18*(15), 7956. PMID: 34360248

Steel Crate Games. (2015). *Keep Talking and Nobody Explodes*. Quest VR Games.

Tao, X., Wang, C. L., Robson, P. J., & Hughes, M. (2025). How does team learning from failure facilitate new product performance? The double-edged moderating effect of collective efficacy. *Small Business Economics*, *64*(1), 133–155.

Tasa, K., Taggar, S., & Seijts, G. H. (2007). The development of collective efficacy in teams: A multilevel and longitudinal perspective. *The Journal of Applied Psychology*, *92*(1), 17. PMID: 17227148

Teh, A., Baniassad, E., Van Rooy, D., & Boughton, C. (2011). Social psychology and software teams: Establishing task-effective group norms. *IEEE Software*, *29*(4), 53–58.

Trope, Y., & Liberman, N. (2010). Construal-level theory of psychological distance. *Psychological Review*, *117*(2), 440. PMID: 20438233

Uitdewilligen, S., & Waller, M. J. (2018). Information sharing and decision-making in multidisciplinary crisis management teams. *Journal of Organizational Behavior*, *39*(6), 731–748.

Valente, M. & MacMahon, M. E. (2020). Virtual communication for student group projects: The COVID-19 effect. *All Ireland Journal of Higher Education, 12*(3).

Van Dijk, J. A. (2017). Digital Divide: Impact of Access. *The International Encyclopedia of Media Effects*, 1-11.

Van Dyck, C., Frese, M., Baer, M., & Sonnentag, S. (2005). Organizational error management culture and its impact on performance: A two-study replication. *The Journal of Applied Psychology*, *90*(6), 1228. PMID: 16316276

Van Hooft, E. A., & Van Mierlo, H. (2018). When teams fail to self-regulate: Predictors and outcomes of team procrastination among debating teams. *Frontiers in Psychology*, *9*, 464. PMID: 29674991

Verduzco-Baker, L. (2018). Modified brave spaces: Calling in brave instructors. *Sociology of Race and Ethnicity (Thousand Oaks, Calif.)*, *4*(4), 585–592.

Wang, S. L., & Lin, S. S. (2007). The effects of group composition of self-efficacy and collective efficacy on computer-supported collaborative learning. *Computers in Human Behavior*, *23*(5), 2256–2268.

Wang, Y., Huang, Q., Davison, R. M., & Yang, F. (2018). Effect of transactive memory systems on team performance mediated by knowledge transfer. *International Journal of Information Management*, *41*, 65–79.

Warren, T. (2020, March 26). Slack breaks user records as demand surges for remote working. *The Verge*. https://www.theverge.com/2020/3/26/21195092/slack-new-user-records-coronavirus-pandemic-remote-working-growth-concurrent-users

Watson, D., Clark, L. A., & Tellegen, A. (1988). Development and validation of brief measures of positive and negative affect: The PANAS scales. *Journal of Personality and Social Psychology*, *54*, 1063–1070. PMID: 3397865

Wegner, D. M., Giuliano, T., & Hertel, P. T. (1985). Cognitive interdependence in close relationships. In Ickes, W. J. (Ed.), *Compatible and incompatible relationships* (pp. 253–276). Springer-Verlag.

Wilson, J., Oleary, M., Metiu, A., & Jett, Q. R. (2008). Perceived Proximity in Virtual Work: Explaining the Paradox of Far-But-Close. *Organization Studies*, *29*, 979–1002.

Yang, J. (2007). The impact of knowledge sharing on organizational learning and effectiveness. *Journal of Knowledge Management*, *11*, 83–90.

Yoo, Y., & Kanawattanachai, P. (2001). Developments of transactive memory systems and collective mind in virtual teams. *The International Journal of Organizational Analysis*, *9*(2), 187–208.

Yoon, K., & Zhu, Y. (2022). Social Media Affordances and Transactive Memory Systems in Virtual Teams. *Management Communication Quarterly*, *36*(2), 235–260.

Zhang, Y., Fang, Y., Wei, K., & Chen, H. (2010). Exploring the role of psychological safety in promoting the intention to continue sharing knowledge in virtual communities. *International Journal of Information Management*, *30*(5), 425–436.

Chapter 9
Teamwork in Action:
Harnessing Sports to Boost Creative Collaboration in Virtual Teams

Amitava Pal
https://orcid.org/0009-0007-8934-2718
ICFAI University, India

Kavita Mathad
https://orcid.org/0000-0002-0058-9084
Presidency University, Bangalore, India

M. Rajkumar
https://orcid.org/0000-0002-7606-0152
ICFAI University, India

ABSTRACT

This study investigates the field of sports entrepreneurship, specifically examining the process of incubation and its impact on innovation. Sports companies have a significant role in fostering economic growth and community development. However, achieving success in this field necessitates strategic support and access to resources. Business incubation offers a well-organized setting for ambitious sports entrepreneurs to enhance their ideas, develop robust strategies, and attain sustainable success. Conducting qualitative research with sports entrepreneurs offered valuable insights for entrepreneurs and incubation practitioners, shedding light on effective strategies and the typical obstacles.

DOI: 10.4018/979-8-3373-0375-8.ch009

INTRODUCTION

In today's interconnected world, working in virtual teams has become essential for students. Whether collaborating on school projects, internships, or future careers, communicating and working effectively online is crucial. Students frequently engage with peers from different locations, cultural backgrounds, and time zones, making effective communication and organization vital for success. However, virtual teamwork presents challenges such as miscommunication, lack of engagement, and difficulties establishing trust. Without face-to-face interactions, students may feel disconnected, misunderstand each other, or struggle to stay focused. These obstacles can hinder productivity and make teamwork frustrating. To overcome these challenges, students must develop key skills, including clear communication, trust-building, and adaptability—fundamental skills in sports teams.

Sports provide an excellent model for teamwork. On the field, athletes work together toward a common goal, trusting each other and understanding their roles within the team. Each player contributes their strengths, and success is achieved through collective effort. These same principles can be applied to virtual teams, where defining roles, maintaining strong communication, and fostering mutual trust can significantly enhance collaboration (McEwan & Beauchamp, 2014). This chapter explores how students can apply lessons from sports to improve their virtual teamwork skills. It offers practical strategies to enhance communication, engagement, and efficiency in online collaborations. By embracing sports-inspired teamwork techniques, students can navigate virtual environments more confidently in academic settings or future professional endeavours. Teamwork is a universal skill—valuable in sports, classrooms, and digital workspaces. With the right mindset and strategies, students can transform virtual teamwork into an opportunity for growth, preparing them for a highly connected and collaborative future.

While much has been written about sports psychology and virtual teamwork, this chapter uniquely bridges the two by proposing structured, sports-inspired strategies to enhance creative collaboration in virtual academic and professional teams. It not only draws parallels but also offers practical frameworks and exercises rooted in real sports practices and tailored for digital collaboration environments.

LITERATURE REVIEW

Effective teamwork is a critical factor influencing overall team performance, cohesion, and adaptability in various settings, including sports, organizational contexts, and high-stakes environments. Tannenbaum, Beard, and Salas (1992) highlighted the importance of structured team-building interventions in enhancing team effectiveness.

Research by Carron, Colman, Wheeler, and Stevens (2002) further established a positive correlation between team cohesion and performance, reinforcing the significance of psychological bonds among members. Zaccaro, Rittman, and Marks (2001) emphasized the role of leadership in shaping team dynamics, suggesting that effective leadership fosters trust, coordination, and shared goals. Moreover, Burke et al. (2006) proposed a conceptual model explaining team adaptation, illustrating how teams respond to evolving challenges. Mathieu et al. (2008) extended this framework, reviewing key advancements in team effectiveness and offering insights into future research directions. Hackman (2002) emphasized that leadership and structural conditions are pivotal in setting the stage for high-performing teams. West (2012) also provided practical lessons on fostering teamwork, focusing on organizational research findings. Meta-analytical studies by Gully, Devine, and Whitney (1995) and Morgan et al. (1986) reinforced that cohesive teams exhibit higher performance, particularly in environments requiring high interdependence. Stajkovic, Lee, and Nyberg (2009) investigated the influence of collective efficacy and group potency on performance, finding strong predictive relationships. Similarly, Bell (2007) explored deep-level composition variables as predictors of team success. DeChurch and Mesmer-Magnus (2010) examined the cognitive underpinnings of teamwork, confirming that shared mental models significantly enhance team performance. Nahrgang, Morgeson, and Hofmann (2011) linked job demands, burnout, and engagement to workplace safety outcomes, demonstrating broader implications of team functioning. Tannenbaum and Cerasoli (2013) further analyzed the impact of team debriefs on performance, confirming their effectiveness in refining team strategies. Research by LePine et al. (2008) tested a multidimensional model of teamwork processes, linking them to various team effectiveness criteria. Chiocchio and Essiembre (2009) examined disparities in cohesion and performance across different team types, revealing nuanced differences between project, production, and service teams. Schaubroeck, Lam, and Peng (2011) found that cognition-based and affect-based trust mediates leadership effects on team performance. Hülsheger, Anderson, and Salgado (2009) explored team-level predictors of workplace innovation, identifying collaboration as a key driver. Mesmer-Magnus and DeChurch (2009) confirmed that information sharing is crucial to team success. Salas et al. (2008) synthesized findings on team training, concluding that structured interventions significantly enhance team outcomes. Finally, Mathieu et al. (2000) highlighted the influence of shared mental models on teamwork processes and performance, reinforcing the critical role of cognitive alignment in achieving collective success.

Collectively, the literature highlights that effective teamwork is a comprehensive construct influenced by cohesion, leadership, shared mental models, collective efficacy, and structured interventions. These studies consistently emphasize that encouraging psychological bonds, trust, coordination, cognitive alignment, and adaptive processes significantly enhances team performance across varied contexts. This foundation informs the next section, which outlines the specific objectives guiding the present study.

OBJECTIVE OF THE CHAPTER

This chapter explores the key factors influencing teamwork effectiveness, including cohesion, leadership, communication, and shared mental models. The chapter provides insights into how team dynamics impact performance, adaptation, and innovation across various settings by examining theoretical models and empirical research. Also, it highlights the role of structured interventions, trust, and information sharing in fostering high-performing teams.

SPORTS AS A BLUEPRINT FOR STUDENT TEAMWORK

Sports teams serve as an effective model for demonstrating how teamwork leads to success. By examining how athletes collaborate, students can gain valuable insights into setting shared goals, defining roles, and fostering mutual trust (McEwan & Beauchamp, 2014). These principles can be applied to academic group projects, classroom activities, and future professional environments (Maslen, 2015). Research from the University of Kansas indicates that over 97% of high school student-athletes graduate, a rate 10% higher than their non-athlete peers. Additionally, student-athletes tend to achieve higher GPA outcomes than those who do not participate in sports (Maslen, 2015). Beyond the playing field, team sports cultivate essential communication, decision-making, teamwork, and time management skills. They also contribute to personal development by enhancing self-esteem, fostering meaningful connections, and building character. Likewise, sports' cognitive and emotional benefits, including improved focus, creativity, and problem-solving abilities, extend beyond athletics, positively influencing academic performance and long-term career success. The following table draws parallels between traditional sports teams and virtual teams, illustrating how key practices in sports can be adapted to enhance collaboration, communication, and performance in virtual settings.

Table 1. Link Between Sports and Virtual Teams

Sports Team Principal	Virtual Team Parallel	Example Application
Clear roles and positions	Defined responsibilities	Assigning tasks early in a project
Pre-game huddles	Team check-ins/huddles	Weekly syncs to clarify goals
Practice and drills	Simulation or warm-ups	Roleplays or draft reviews
Halftime adjustment	Mid-project feedback loop	Reflect and adjust the strategy
Coach and captain leadership	Distributed peer leadership	Peer-led retrospectives

What Students Can Learn From Sports Teams

Shared Goals and Collective Accountability

In sports, every team operates with a shared objective—winning a game, achieving a high score, or enhancing overall performance. This collective focus encourages players to collaborate, support each other, and maintain accountability (McEwan & Beauchamp, 2014). For instance, a volleyball team preparing for a championship match must rely on every player's commitment during practice and on the court. The team's overall performance suffers if one player skips practice or fails to focus during drills. Similarly, during the match, a player missing a crucial serve can cost the team valuable points, highlighting the impact of individual responsibility on collective success (Maslen, 2015).

This principle extends to academic settings, particularly in group projects. Consider a team of students working on a presentation about climate change. They divide responsibilities—one student conducts research, another student designs slides, and a third prepares the delivery. If the researcher fails to complete their task, the entire project lacks depth, potentially resulting in a lower grade for the group. By drawing lessons from sports, students can better understand the importance of accountability, ensuring that their contributions support the overall success of their team (Maslen, 2015).

Role Clarity and Trust in Achieving Success

In any successful sports team, each player has a clearly defined role that aligns with their strengths. For instance, in football (soccer), the goalkeeper's primary responsibility is to defend the goal, while forwards concentrate on scoring. Midfielders bridge the gap between defense and offense, ensuring smooth transitions in play.

If a goalkeeper abandons their defensive duties to attempt scoring goals, the team becomes vulnerable and risks losing the match (McEwan & Beauchamp, 2014).

A similar principle applies to academic teamwork. Consider a group of students working on a school magazine. One student is responsible for writing articles, another designs the layout, and a third oversees printing. If the writer suddenly takes over the layout without expertise in design software, the project may become disorganized. Likewise, if the designer lacks confidence in the writer's ability to produce quality content, they may micromanage, causing unnecessary delays. Establishing clear roles and trusting teammates to fulfil their responsibilities is essential for efficiency and success (Maslen, 2015). Like in sports, effective teamwork in academic and professional settings relies on individuals leveraging their strengths while trusting others to perform their designated roles.

Intentional Practice in Virtual Teams

Just as sports teams rely on regular practice sessions to build muscle memory, teamwork habits, and strategic awareness, virtual teams also benefit from deliberate and repeated practice. In sports, practice is not just about physical drills—it is about rehearsing roles, refining coordination, and mentally preparing for unexpected challenges. The same mindset can be applied to digital collaboration.

For virtual teams, this kind of "team training" might include dry runs before major presentations, brainstorming sprints to simulate creative problem-solving, or peer review cycles for refining drafts. These intentional moments provide opportunities to develop shared language, build trust, and align on expectations. They also allow teams to experiment safely, reflect on what worked, and make adjustments before final delivery, much like a scrimmage in sports.

Crucially, these sessions should be seen not as add-ons but as core components of collaboration, helping teams build fluency in their roles and confidence under pressure. Over time, just like practiced athletes, virtual team members can respond more intuitively and cohesively to fast-changing scenarios, enhancing performance and creativity.

ADAPTING TO CHALLENGES TOGETHER

In sports, teams frequently encounter unforeseen challenges, such as player injuries, formidable opponents, or adverse weather conditions. For instance, in basketball, if a key player sustains an injury during a crucial game, the team must quickly adapt its strategy. The team often relies on effective teamwork, communication, and problem-solving to compensate for the setback. Rather than assigning blame, it focuses on collective efforts to navigate the challenge (McEwan & Beauchamp, 2014).

A similar dynamic applies in academic settings. Consider a group of students working on a science fair project. They must reassess their approach if their experiment unexpectedly fails just days before the deadline. Instead of panicking or blaming one another, they can regroup, brainstorm alternative solutions, and redistribute tasks efficiently. As in sports, these situations teach students the importance of remaining composed under pressure, adapting to change, and working collaboratively to overcome obstacles (Maslen, 2015).

CELEBRATING SUCCESS AND LEARNING FROM FAILURE

Sports teams celebrate victories collectively and analyse defeats to improve their performance. For example, after winning a tournament, a cricket team acknowledges each player's contributions, from the bowler who took crucial wickets to the batter who scored key runs. Following a loss, the team reviews areas that need improvement, such as communication lapses or lack of focus, and works on these weaknesses in subsequent training sessions (McEwan & Beauchamp, 2014). This reflective process helps teams grow and perform better in future competitions (Cotterill, 2017).

For students, adopting a similar approach can enhance their teamwork experiences. If a group wins a school debate competition, they can celebrate together, recognizing the speaker's preparation, the researcher's efforts, and the strategist's planning. Conversely, if they lose, they can reflect on shortcomings—whether insufficient evidence in arguments or a lack of confidence in delivery—and make improvements for the next opportunity (Maslen, 2015). This self-assessment and continuous learning process, inspired by sports teams, fosters resilience and skill development in academic and professional settings (Fletcher & Sarkar, 2012).

Drawing Parallels

Teamwork in sports closely mirrors the dynamics of virtual student teams. Both environments require collaboration, clear communication, and trust to achieve shared goals (Salas et al., 2005). By studying how sports teams operate, students can apply similar strategies to navigate challenges in virtual teamwork, such as disengagement and role confusion (Klein et al., 2009). Structured roles, effective communication strategies, and mutual accountability—fundamental in sports—can significantly enhance the success of virtual teams (Edmondson, 1999).

How Sports Teamwork Mirrors Virtual Team Dynamics

Diverse Skills and Roles

Sports teams consist of players with specialized skills and clearly defined roles. For example, in basketball, some players excel at scoring points (forwards), while others specialize in defense (guards) or playmaking (point guards). The team's success depends on each player executing their role while trusting teammates to fulfill theirs (McEwan & Beauchamp, 2014). Similarly, in virtual student teams, members bring unique strengths such as research, writing, design, or presentation skills. A well-structured team ensures that each person contributes effectively to the outcome. However, when roles are unclear or one person tries to take on too many tasks, the team may struggle with efficiency and quality (Klein et al., 2009). For instance, during online debate preparation, one student may focus on gathering research, another on structuring arguments, and a third on refining delivery. Without clear task delegation, duplicated efforts or missing key information can hinder the team's performance (Salas et al., 2005).

Reliance on Communication

Effective and timely communication is a key factor in sports team success. In soccer, players rely on verbal cues, hand signals, and quick decision-making to coordinate strategies and respond to dynamic game situations (Cotterill, 2017). Without such communication, even skilled players may fail to function as a cohesive unit. Likewise, virtual teams depend on digital communication tools such as video calls, chat platforms, and collaborative software to stay connected (Mesmer-Magnus & DeChurch, 2009). However, virtual settings introduce challenges such as delayed responses, misinterpretations, and disengagement. Drawing inspiration from sports teams, virtual teams can implement structured "team talk" strategies, such as regular check-ins, clear task updates, and concise feedback loops, to maintain clarity and connection (Edmondson, 1999). For example, a virtual team working on a digital poster for an event can use a shared document where each member updates their progress. If a team member encounters an issue, such as difficulty sourcing high-quality images, timely communication ensures that others can help or adjust the timeline accordingly.

Why Sports Strategies Are Suited to Virtual Team Challenges

Addressing Disengagement

Athletes remain engaged in sports because they see the direct impact of their contributions. A cricket bowler, for instance, understands that their performance influences the team's success, which motivates them to stay focused even during long matches (Fletcher & Sarkar, 2012). Coaches and captains are crucial in maintaining team morale through encouragement, constructive feedback, and recognition of individual efforts (Cotterill, 2017). In virtual student teams, disengagement often occurs when individuals do not see the immediate effects of their work or lack recognition. By applying sports strategies, virtual team leaders can foster engagement by celebrating small wins, such as completing a draft or resolving a technical issue, and reinforcing the team's larger goal (Salas et al., 2005). For instance, a team designing a virtual science experiment can hold weekly progress meetings where each member presents their contributions, keeping everyone motivated to participate.

Clarifying Roles to Avoid Confusion

Successful sports teams operate efficiently because each player understands their role. In volleyball, for example, the setter positions the ball for the hitter, while the libero focuses on defense. Role confusion can lead to missed plays and decreased performance (McEwan & Beauchamp, 2014). Similarly, virtual teams benefit from clearly defined roles at the outset of a project. Assigning tasks based on individual strengths helps prevent overlap and miscommunication (Klein et al., 2009). For instance, in an online marketing project, one member might oversee content creation, another manages social media outreach, and another analyzes audience engagement. Regular status updates ensure that every team member understands their responsibilities and how their work contributes to their success (Edmondson, 1999).

Building Trust and Team Spirit

Trust is a cornerstone of sports team dynamics. Players build trust through shared experiences such as training sessions, strategy discussions, and celebrating victories. This trust enables athletes to rely on one another, especially in high-pressure situations (Fletcher & Sarkar, 2012). Virtual teams can foster a similar sense of camaraderie through intentional team-building activities. For example, scheduling informal video calls, conducting brainstorming sessions, or dedicating time for non-work-related discussions can strengthen relationships and improve collaboration (Salas et al., 2005). For instance, a student team organizing an online fundraiser can begin each meeting by sharing personal updates or discussing creative ideas unrelated to the project. These interactions build rapport, making collaboration smoother and more effective (Mesmer-Magnus & DeChurch, 2009).

KEY LESSONS FROM SPORTS FOR STUDENT VIRTUAL TEAMS

Sports and Virtual Teamwork: Collaboration, Trust, and Adaptability

Success in sports and virtual teamwork hinges on effective collaboration, trust, and adaptability. Just as athletes unite to achieve shared goals, students in virtual teams can employ similar strategies to enhance efficiency and navigate challenges. By integrating key lessons from sports, such as strong leadership, trust-building, and resilience under pressure, students can develop essential teamwork skills and thrive in digital environments (McEwan & Beauchamp, 2014; Salas et al., 2005).

Leadership and Peer Collaboration- Sports Captains as Leaders

In sports, the captain serves as more than just a symbolic leader; they are the team's driving force. Captains set the tone for performance and attitude, inspiring teammates to maintain focus and determination. For example, during a cricket match, if the team is rapidly losing wickets, an effective captain remains composed, uplifts team morale, and adapts the game plan to recover (Cotterill, 2017). Similarly, in virtual teams, student leaders play a crucial role in maintaining direction. If deadlines are missed, a team leader can reassess the workflow, delegate tasks strategically, and motivate team members to stay engaged (Edmondson, 1999). Proactive leadership fosters trust and respect, strengthening team dynamics (Klein et al., 2009).

Applying Leadership in Virtual Teams

Leadership in virtual environments involves motivating teammates, resolving conflicts, and ensuring seamless communication. For example, if a team member struggles with a technical task, the leader can provide direct assistance or delegate another teammate with relevant expertise to help. This mirrors a sports captain assigning responsibilities based on individual strengths, maximizing team efficiency (Salas et al., 2005).

Collaboration Through Peer Leadership

Successful sports teams thrive on mutual support rather than relying solely on a single leader. In football, players anticipate each other's moves, passing strategically to create scoring opportunities. Similarly, in virtual teams, students can collaborate by leveraging each other's strengths. If one member excels in research and another in design, they can divide tasks accordingly while providing mutual assistance, creating a balanced and productive team environment (Fletcher & Sarkar, 2012).

Trust and Team Spirit - Building Trust in Sports

Trust in sports is often cultivated through repeated interactions, drills, and team-building exercises. A typical example is the "trust fall" exercise, where a teammate falls backward, relying on others to catch them. This fosters confidence in teammates and strengthens relationships. Similarly, in basketball, trust is demonstrated when a player passes the ball to a teammate in a crucial moment, believing in their ability to score (McEwan & Beauchamp, 2014).

Building Trust in Virtual Teams

Trust is built through transparency and consistent communication in virtual environments. Regular updates, progress reports, and shared decision-making ensure that all team members remain aligned and accountable. This process mirrors passing the baton in a relay race—each member relies on others to execute their responsibilities effectively (Mesmer-Magnus & DeChurch, 2009).

Creating a Supportive Team Environment

Sports teams are renowned for their camaraderie and support systems. For example, if a teammate misses a critical shot in volleyball, others offer encouragement rather than criticism, fostering resilience and confidence. This positive reinforcement helps teams maintain high morale and collective focus (Cotterill, 2017).

Similarly, in virtual teams, students can cultivate a supportive atmosphere by constructively celebrating achievements and addressing mistakes. If a teammate submits an incomplete draft, instead of assigning blame, the group can collaborate to improve it and offer constructive feedback. Small gestures, such as acknowledging a well-executed presentation with a simple "Great job!", can significantly enhance team morale and motivation (Edmondson, 1999).

Adaptability Under Pressure- Staying Flexible in Sports

Athletes often encounter unexpected challenges that require quick thinking and adaptability. For instance, in football, a sudden change in weather may prompt a team to shift its strategy from an offensive to a defensive approach. This ability to adjust tactics on the spot is crucial for success in competitive sports (Fletcher & Sarkar, 2012).

Adapting to Virtual Teams

Virtual teams frequently face their own set of challenges, such as technical issues or sudden changes in project requirements. For example, if the designated presenter in an online group project experiences an internet outage, another team member must step in to deliver the presentation. Developing the ability to adapt quickly ensures that the team continues to function smoothly and meets its objectives (Salas et al., 2005).

Activities for Adaptability

To build adaptability skills, virtual teams can engage in simulations or dynamic exercises that require quick adjustments. For instance, a team might be asked to prepare a presentation on a specific topic, only to be instructed halfway through the exercise to pivot to a completely different subject. This practice helps students remain calm under pressure, refine critical thinking skills, and develop resilience—just as athletes must modify strategies mid-game to secure victory (Mesmer-Magnus & DeChurch, 2009).

ENCOURAGING CREATIVITY IN VIRTUAL STUDENT TEAMS THROUGH SPORTS PRACTICES

Fostering Creativity in Virtual Teams Through Sports Strategies

Creativity is a critical factor in the success of any virtual team. Sports provide valuable lessons in thinking outside the box, pushing boundaries, and learning from both victories and setbacks (Cotterill, 2017). By integrating sports-inspired strategies into virtual teamwork, students can enhance their creativity, collaboration, and problem-solving skills (Klein et al., 2009). Below are some ways these principles can be applied effectively.

While competition can be a powerful motivator and driver of high performance, it must be balanced with collaboration to truly foster creativity—especially in team settings. In many sports, success does not come from individual brilliance alone but from seamless coordination, mutual trust, and team discipline. A winning team often succeeds because its members understand each other's strengths, anticipate each other's moves, and adapt collectively under pressure.

The same principles apply to virtual teams, particularly in academic and professional settings where innovation and problem-solving are key. When individuals compete for recognition or dominance, it can lead to silos, miscommunication, or hesitation to share ideas. In contrast, when teams focus on shared goals, emphasize peer-led feedback, and engage in cooperative brainstorming, creativity flows more freely.

Team rituals such as joint ideation sessions, reflection circles, and rotating leadership can replace competitive energy with constructive interdependence, allowing diverse ideas to surface and evolve. Moreover, these non-competitive environments are more inclusive, ensuring that all voices—especially those of quieter team members—are heard and valued.

By consciously designing collaboration spaces that celebrate collective intelligence over individual performance, virtual teams can replicate the best aspects of sports teamwork and unlock deeper levels of creative synergy.

Game-Like Challenges: Encouraging Innovative Thinking

Sports often require players to devise quick strategies to overcome unexpected challenges, an approach that can inspire virtual teams (Fletcher & Sarkar, 2012). For example, a team leader or educator can introduce a "game challenge" where students work together to solve a fictional problem using their unique skills. Consider a scenario where a virtual team is assigned a budget to plan a sports event. Each student assumes a role, such as marketing, logistics, or ticket sales, and they brainstorm innovative ways to ensure the event's success. Just like in sports, every participant must contribute their strengths to achieve a common goal (Salas et al., 2005).

Constructive Competition: Driving Creativity and Innovation

Healthy competition in sports motivates athletes to push their limits, perform at their best, and continuously improve. The same principle can be applied to virtual teams (McEwan & Beauchamp, 2014). Setting up challenges where students compete in small groups can inspire creativity and innovation. For instance, an educator could ask two virtual teams to create the most engaging presentation on a topic such as "The Future of Sports." Each team strives to outperform the other by incorporating unique visuals, compelling storytelling, and innovative ideas. Ultimately, both teams benefit from the creative process and gain valuable skills for future projects (Klein et al., 2009).

Celebrating Wins and Learning From Failures

In sports, teams celebrate victories together—whether through a group huddle or a post-game debrief—while also analysing losses to identify areas for improvement. Virtual teams can adopt this practice by holding debrief sessions after completing a project (Edmondson, 1999). During these sessions, team members can discuss what went well and explore ways to improve. For instance, after completing a major project, a virtual team could schedule a "celebration call" where they acknowledge each member's contributions and reflect on the experience. Similar to how sports teams review match footage to refine their techniques, virtual teams can analyse past challenges and apply those lessons to future collaborations (Salas et al., 2005).

STUDENT ROLES: APPLYING SPORTS TEAM STRUCTURES IN VIRTUAL TEAMS

Sports teams thrive because every player has a clear role and understands their responsibilities. This structured approach can also be applied to virtual student teams, ensuring that tasks are efficiently managed, and individual strengths are optimized (McEwan & Beauchamp, 2014).

Defining Roles and Responsibilities

In sports, every player has a specific role that contributes to the team's success. A striker in football focuses on scoring goals, defenders protect their side of the field, and the goalkeeper prevents the opposition from scoring (Cotterill, 2017). Similarly, virtual teams function best when roles are clearly defined. For example, a student skilled in organization can assume the role of team leader, ensuring deadlines are met and tasks are distributed efficiently. Another student with strong research skills can be designated as the researcher, responsible for gathering critical data. A confident speaker might take on the role of presenter, ensuring the team's work is communicated effectively.

For instance, in a virtual project focused on climate change solutions, roles could be divided as follows: one student researches scientific data, another collects statistical evidence, a third designs presentation slides, and the final member delivers the presentation. Just as in sports, defining clear roles ensures that every participant understands their responsibilities, leading to smoother collaboration and improved outcomes (Klein et al., 2009).

Rotating Roles: Enhancing Adaptability and Skill Development

Athletes sometimes switch positions during training to gain a broader understanding of team dynamics and develop new skills. For example, a football defender might practice as a striker to improve their offensive awareness (Fletcher & Sarkar, 2012). Similarly, virtual teams can benefit from role rotation, allowing members to experience different responsibilities over time.

For example, in a group designing a website, the usual researcher could take on the layout design role, while the leader might focus on gathering and organizing data for the first time. This approach helps students develop new competencies, fosters empathy for different roles, and uncovers hidden talents. Additionally, role rotation enhances team adaptability—if a member becomes unavailable, another can step in, ensuring that progress continues uninterrupted (Mesmer-Magnus & DeChurch, 2009).

By defining and rotating roles, virtual student teams can improve efficiency, strengthen relationships, and cultivate essential skills that will benefit them in both academic and professional settings (Edmondson, 1999). Just as in sports, fostering flexibility and collaboration leads to a more dynamic and resilient team.

COMMUNICATION AND INCLUSIVITY: LESSONS FROM SPORTS FOR DIVERSE STUDENT TEAMS

Sports teams unite individuals from diverse backgrounds, fostering essential lessons in communication and inclusivity. These lessons are particularly valuable for virtual student teams, where differences in culture, language, and personality can create challenges. By drawing from sports practices, students can develop stronger connections, improve teamwork, and create more inclusive virtual environments (Cotterill, 2017; Salas et al., 2005).

Breaking the Ice: Building Team Camaraderie

Sports teams often begin with warm-up exercises or playful drills to help players relax and bond. Similarly, virtual student teams can use icebreakers to build rapport and create a comfortable working environment. Research suggests that engaging in informal, team-building activities fosters trust and collaboration, leading to improved performance (Edmondson, 1999). For instance, virtual team members can participate in quick trivia games or share interesting personal facts, mirroring the locker-room banter and pre-game rituals that strengthen bonds among athletes (Klein et al., 2009).

If students from different countries are collaborating on a project, an icebreaker such as sharing their favourite local dish or holiday tradition can help them feel more at ease. These small moments of connection promote camaraderie, making teamwork more enjoyable and productive (Mesmer-Magnus & DeChurch, 2009).

Managing Conflict: Lessons from the Locker Room

Conflict is a natural part of any high-performing team—on the field or online. In sports, high-pressure environments often give rise to tensions, disagreements, and moments of miscommunication. However, successful teams have structured ways to navigate these challenges. Captains mediate between players, coaches facilitate clear expectations, and team meetings provide space to air concerns and recalibrate group dynamics. These practices not only resolve immediate issues but also strengthen team trust and cohesion over time.

Virtual teams can adopt similar conflict resolution strategies by creating an environment of psychological safety, where all members feel comfortable expressing concerns without fear of judgment. Structured feedback sessions, rotating leadership roles, and open forums for discussion can mirror the locker room's role in de-escalating tensions. Just as a strong team talk can reset a struggling sports squad, a well-facilitated virtual check-in can realign objectives and restore positive collaboration. Normalizing conflict as a growth opportunity, rather than a setback, is key to fostering creative and resilient virtual teams.

Bridging Cultural and Communication Gaps

Sports teams frequently consist of players who speak different languages or come from diverse cultural backgrounds. To overcome these challenges, teams rely on shared signals, visual cues, and simplified communication methods. For example, in soccer, hand gestures and concise phrases like "pass" or "goal!" facilitate communication regardless of language barriers (Fletcher & Sarkar, 2012).

Virtual teams can adopt similar strategies to ensure clear communication. Establishing simple communication rules, such as using visual aids like diagrams or slides, can improve understanding for all members. Studies show that structured communication methods, including shared glossaries and translation tools, help bridge linguistic gaps in multicultural teams (McEwan & Beauchamp, 2014). For instance, a diverse virtual team working on a business proposal can use color-coded charts or emojis during discussions to clarify their points and reduce misunderstandings (Salas et al., 2005).

Ensuring Equal Participation

Inclusive sports practices ensure that every player has the opportunity to contribute, even those who may not take center stage. Coaches often encourage newer or quieter players by assigning them specific roles or soliciting their input during strategy discussions (Cotterill, 2017). Research indicates that inclusive leadership and role distribution increase team engagement and performance (Klein et al., 2009).

Virtual student teams can apply similar strategies to empower all members. For example, a team leader can actively seek input from quieter participants during meetings or assign them tasks that showcase their strengths. Additionally, rotating roles—such as having different members lead discussions or summarize key points—ensures that everyone feels valued and engaged (Edmondson, 1999).

Consider a scenario where a student in a virtual team excels in visual design but rarely speaks up. By recognizing their skill and assigning them the role of the team's graphic designer, the group not only ensures equal participation but also boosts the student's confidence and overall contribution. Research supports that role recognition and structured participation strategies significantly enhance collaboration and team success (Mesmer-Magnus & DeChurch, 2009).

FEEDBACK AND GROWTH: COACHING STUDENTS FOR SUCCESS IN VIRTUAL TEAMS

In sports, feedback and continuous improvement are essential for success, and these principles are equally valuable in virtual student teams. Coaches provide guidance on technique, while teammates analyse game strategies, helping athletes refine their performance (Cotterill, 2017). Similarly, virtual teams can benefit from constructive feedback, progress tracking, and self-reflection to enhance collaboration and achieve their goals (Edmondson, 1999).

The Role of Feedback in Sports

In sports, coaches and teammates deliver immediate feedback during practice or competition. For instance, a coach might correct a football player's positioning or a tennis player's swing technique, enabling real-time adjustments for better performance (McEwan & Beauchamp, 2014). Virtual student teams can adopt a similar approach by implementing structured peer feedback. Research suggests that peer evaluations improve work quality and enhance group collaboration (Klein et al., 2009).

For example, if a team member is responsible for creating a presentation, others can provide feedback on its clarity, structure, and visual appeal. Constructive feedback should focus on actionable improvements rather than merely identifying flaws (Salas et al., 2005). One effective model adapted from sports involves three steps:

- Highlight what was done well.
- Identify areas for improvement.
- Offer specific, actionable suggestions.

For instance, after a virtual team meeting, feedback might include: "You explained your research clearly, but adding more examples would make it more relatable. Perhaps you could include one or two case studies?" Applying structured feedback mechanisms fosters growth and team cohesion (Mesmer-Magnus & DeChurch, 2009).

Tracking Progress and Reflecting on Outcomes

Sports teams often analyse performance metrics to identify strengths and areas for development. For example, a basketball team might track shooting accuracy and turnovers to assess their progress and make data-driven improvements (Fletcher & Sarkar, 2012). Similarly, virtual teams can utilize project management tools and progress trackers to evaluate their work. A marketing team, for instance, could use a shared tracker listing tasks, deadlines, and project milestones. At each stage, comparing actual outcomes to initial goals helps teams recognize where they excel and where adjustments are needed (Klein et al., 2009).

Self-reflection is another fundamental component of sports training. Athletes often review their performances to determine what worked well and what needs refinement. Virtual teams can incorporate debrief sessions after completing projects, discussing lessons learned and strategies for improvement. Structured reflection questions—such as "What went well?" and "What could we have done differently?"—encourage critical thinking and continuous learning (Edmondson, 1999).

Encouraging Self-Reflection and Team Evaluation

Self-reflection is a powerful tool in sports, allowing athletes to assess their individual contributions. A swimmer, for example, might evaluate how their breathing technique influenced their performance, while a runner could analyse their pacing strategy (McEwan & Beauchamp, 2014). Virtual teams can foster similar habits by encouraging members to reflect on their roles and learning experiences.

After completing a virtual science fair project, students could individually document their insights:

- What did I learn from this experience?
- What challenges did I face, and how did I overcome them?
- What can I improve in future collaborations?

Additionally, team-wide evaluations can assess group dynamics, communication effectiveness, and problem-solving strategies. Research shows that teams that engage in structured self-evaluation develop a culture of openness, trust, and continuous improvement (Mesmer-Magnus & DeChurch, 2009). By integrating sports-based feedback and reflection strategies, virtual teams can enhance both their collaboration and performance.

CASE STUDY: COLLABORATIVE ENGINEERING IN THE EUROPEAN AUTOMOTIVE INDUSTRY

As part of a large-scale European research initiative, engineering teams from multiple countries collaborated virtually to redesign a component for a commercial vehicle (May et al., 2001). Despite working across geographies and time zones, these teams employed a suite of digital collaboration tools—video conferencing, shared whiteboards, and CAD annotation platforms—that functioned much like a well-coordinated sports team executing rehearsed plays.

Crucially, the teams adopted sports-inspired principles: regular strategy huddles, clearly defined roles, and a shared commitment to goals. The structured digital interactions allowed them to identify design flaws early, iteratively co-create new solutions, and drastically cut down review cycles.

The impact was significant: the team reported time savings of up to 20% for modified components and projected 50% savings for entirely new designs, thanks to reduced delays, real-time feedback, and minimal rework. This virtual collaboration success mirrors the effectiveness of team sports models—where preparation, communication, and trust enable high performance under pressure (May et al., 2001).

PRACTICAL EXERCISES FOR STUDENTS: TURNING LESSONS INTO ACTION

Applying teamwork lessons in a virtual environment can be challenging, but incorporating practical exercises inspired by sports can help students build essential skills such as communication, collaboration, and problem-solving. Research suggests that experiential learning activities enhance engagement and team cohesion (Salas et al., 2005). These activities bring virtual teams together, simulate the dynamics of sports teams, and promote growth through hands-on learning (McEwan & Beauchamp, 2014).

Virtual Warm-Up Drills: Warm-up drills in sports energize players and foster team spirit, and similar activities in virtual settings can help students break the ice and build strong relationships. Team-building exercises improve trust and cooperation, which are critical for effective teamwork (Edmondson, 1999).

Facilitator Note:

- **Objective:** Build psychological safety and encourage informal connection.
- **When to Use:** At the **beginning** of the team's formation or project kick-off.
- **Debrief:** Ask students, *"What surprised you during this warm-up?"* or *"What did you learn about your teammates?"*

Two Truths and a Lie: In this activity, each team member shares two true statements and one false statement about themselves, and the team guesses which statement is the lie. For instance, a virtual team working on a digital marketing plan might use this exercise during their first meeting. A student might say, "I love baking, I've travelled to three countries, and I'm a night owl." The team then discusses and makes their guesses, learning surprising details about each other, such as who might be creative or detail oriented. Studies indicate that such informal interactions foster interpersonal trust and collaboration (Mesmer-Magnus & DeChurch, 2009).

Facilitator Note:

- **Objective:** Promote interpersonal trust, curiosity, and engagement.
- **When to Use:** During the **team's first or second meeting**.
- **Debrief:** Ask, *"Did you find it easy to relate to others?"* or *"How did this affect your comfort level with the team?"*

Tip: Use this with care. Provide context and clear facilitation to avoid discomfort or unintended judgments.

Virtual Scavenger Hunt: Students are assigned to find items or digital resources that represent specific themes. For example, a team working on a climate change presentation might be asked to share an object symbolizing sustainability. One student might hold up a reusable water bottle, prompting a discussion on sustainable living. This activity fosters creativity, introduces diverse perspectives, and enhances engagement, similar to team-building drills used in sports training (Klein et al., 2009).

Facilitator Note:

- **Objective:** Spark creativity, surface personal values, and encourage diverse perspectives.
- **When to Use: Early to mid-phase**, especially after initial rapport has been built.
- **Debrief:** Discuss, *"How did each item reflect your interpretation of the theme?"* and *"What new ideas or perspectives did this bring to your thinking?"*

Simulated Sports Scenarios: Simulations allow students to practice teamwork strategies commonly used in sports to solve problems, helping them develop key skills applicable to virtual team projects (Fletcher & Sarkar, 2012).

Facilitator Note:

- **Objective:** Practice decision-making under pressure and explore collaborative problem-solving.
- **When to Use:** In the **mid-phase** of the project, when roles are established.
- **Debrief:** Ask, *"How did each role contribute to the outcome?" "What dynamics did you notice that helped or hindered problem-solving?"*

Role-Playing as a Sports Team: Students are assigned roles such as captain, strategist, or analyst and must resolve a sports-related scenario, such as devising a strategy for an underdog cricket team in a fictional league. The strategist develops a game plan, the captain motivates the team, and the analyst studies the opponent's strengths and weaknesses. This exercise mirrors real-world leadership and decision-making scenarios, helping students improve delegation, critical thinking, and leadership—skills essential for virtual team success (McEwan & Beauchamp, 2014).

Facilitator Note:

- **Objective:** Enhance role clarity, leadership, and group coordination.
- **When to Use:** During the **midpoint** or as part of leadership development.

- **Debrief:** Reflect on, *"What was challenging about your role?" "How did the team's structure affect your performance?"*

Problem-Solving Case Study: Students analyse a real-world sports conflict and propose solutions as a team. For example, they might evaluate a case where two football players clash over leadership roles. Through structured discussion, they explore conflict resolution strategies, such as rotating leadership roles or setting clearer team objectives. Research highlights that collaborative problem-solving foster accountability and enhances decision-making abilities in group settings (Salas et al., 2005).

Facilitator Note:

- **Objective:** Explore conflict resolution, active listening, and team negotiation.
- **When to Use:** At the **mid to late phase**, when team dynamics are clear.
- **Debrief:** Ask, *"What strategies worked for resolving the conflict?" "How can these approaches help in our real team setting?"*

Team Huddles and Post-Game Analysis: Just as sports teams regroup during huddles to reassess strategies, boost morale, and communicate clearly under pressure, virtual teams can hold structured, recurring meetings to realign on shared goals, troubleshoot issues, and maintain team energy (Cotterill, 2017).

This is relevant because it ensures that all members stay connected and on track, even without physical proximity

Team Huddles: Before starting a new project, students conduct a "huddle" to discuss goals, roles, and challenges. For example, a team preparing for a virtual hackathon might outline their strategy: one member handles coding, another focuses on design, and another manages the presentation. The huddle concludes with a motivational discussion to ensure all members feel confident in their roles. Research supports that structured team discussions enhance clarity and prevent misunderstandings, fostering greater team commitment (Edmondson, 1999).

Facilitator Note:

- **Objective:** Strengthen coordination and motivation before starting tasks.
- **When to Use:** At the **beginning** of a new phase or task.
- **Debrief:** Ask, *"Was everyone clear on their role today?" "What could make our huddles more effective?"*

Post-Project Analysis: Once a project is completed, teams gather for a structured review to reflect on their performance. A research team, for instance, might analyse what contributed to their success, such as meeting deadlines, and what challenges they faced, such as unclear communication. One member might suggest implementing project management tools to improve workflow. Studies show that post-project analysis helps teams identify strengths, address weaknesses, and develop actionable strategies for future collaborations (Klein et al., 2009).

Facilitator Note:

- **Objective:** Encourage accountability, learning from experience, and future planning.
- **When to Use:** At the **end** of a project or major milestone.
- **Debrief:** Guide the team with questions like, *"What are our key takeaways?" "What systems should we keep or improve?"*

Celebrating Wins: Acknowledging achievements is an essential aspect of team building. In sports, players celebrate victories together, which reinforces positive behaviour and strengthens team morale. Virtual teams can adopt this practice by holding a "celebration call" after completing a task. For instance, a student team that successfully hosted a webinar can share positive feedback from attendees, exchange virtual high-fives, and discuss how their collaboration contributed to success. Research indicates that recognizing achievements enhances motivation and fosters a culture of encouragement within teams (Mesmer-Magnus & DeChurch, 2009).

Facilitator Note:

- **Objective:** Boost morale, reinforce team identity, and foster positive reinforcement.
- **When to Use:** After **key achievements or project wrap-up**.
- **Debrief:** Invite reflections such as, *"What part of the team's success are you proud of?"* or *"How did celebrating together impact your connection with the group?"*

DISCUSSION POINTS AND FUTURE DIRECTIONS

Research has consistently shown a strong connection between team cohesion and performance, with variations based on task type and interdependence. Effective leadership plays a crucial role in fostering cohesion, trust, and overall team effectiveness, requiring a balance between directive and participative styles. As teams operate in dynamic environments, their ability to adapt and build resilience through shared experiences and mental models becomes essential. The cognitive and behavioral aspects of teamwork, such as shared mental models, collective efficacy, and trust, continue to shape team success, yet more research is needed on how these factors evolve over time. Additionally, structured team training and debriefing have been found to enhance performance, but the effectiveness of different training methodologies requires further exploration. Open and structured communication is another critical factor influencing decision-making and overall performance, particularly in an era of digital transformation where virtual collaboration tools are becoming increasingly prevalent. Looking ahead, technology-driven teamwork presents new challenges and opportunities as AI-assisted and remote teams become more common. Longitudinal studies are necessary to understand how team processes and effectiveness develop over time, rather than relying solely on cross-sectional analyses. Cultural and contextual factors significantly impact team dynamics, making it essential to examine how diversity and organizational environments influence cohesion, leadership, and adaptability. Psychological safety has also emerged as a key driver of innovation and team learning, warranting further investigation. Finally, adopting a multidisciplinary approach that integrates insights from sports psychology, business management, and organizational behavior can provide a more comprehensive understanding of team effectiveness and innovation. Addressing these areas will offer deeper insights into optimizing virtual team performance across various industries and disciplines.

KEY TAKEAWAYS

- Sports provide a powerful metaphor for building trust, role clarity, and communication in virtual teams.
- Creativity thrives when teams balance structure (plays) and flexibility (freedom to adapt).
- Intentional practice, peer leadership, and reflection loops strengthen virtual collaboration.
- Conflict, when managed constructively, can drive innovation.
- Facilitated exercises inspired by sports rituals can foster engagement, adaptability, and group cohesion.

CONCLUSION: BECOMING VIRTUAL TEAM CHAMPIONS

The sports-inspired strategies we have discussed provide valuable tools and lessons for virtual student teams. These principles are not just about improving teamwork in the classroom, they are skills that can be applied throughout life and in any professional setting. Let's break down the key takeaways: The sports teamwork strategies we have covered—such as setting shared goals, building trust, clear communication, role clarity, and fostering creativity—mirror the dynamics of a successful sports team. Just like in a game, virtual teams can benefit from everyone working towards a common purpose and having a clear understanding of their individual roles. Applying these strategies helps create a more cohesive team that can navigate challenges together, much like athletes do on the field.

The ability to collaborate effectively, communicate clearly, and adapt under pressure is essential in almost every career. In the workplace, just like in sports, employees often work in teams to achieve complex goals. The skills students develop from virtual teamwork—such as leadership, problem-solving, and adaptability—are crucial when they enter the job market. By practicing these skills in a virtual setting, students are preparing themselves for the collaborative, fast-paced, and often high-pressure environments they will face in their professional lives. Just as athletes approach every match with focus, resilience, and a willingness to learn from mistakes, students can adopt the same mindset to enhance their performance in both virtual teams and real-world situations. By embracing the principles of teamwork, trust, and continuous improvement, students are more likely to succeed in their academic work and beyond. The key is to treat every challenge as an opportunity to grow, to be flexible in the face of adversity, and to always strive for improvement. In essence, becoming a virtual team champion is about taking on every task with the mindset of an athlete: committed, resilient, and driven by a passion for excellence. By applying these lessons from sports, students will not only excel in their virtual teams but will also be well-equipped to tackle the challenges of any collaborative environment they encounter in the future. The power of teamwork is universal—whether you are on a sports field or collaborating virtually in a team, success is built on trust, communication, and a shared sense of purpose.

ACKNOWLEDGMENT

We would like to extend our warmest gratitude to those who have supported us through this work. We are especially grateful for the continuous support, patience, and understanding from our family members while we do this project. Their love and support are priceless. We also appreciate the efforts of people who gave some kind of insight, advice, and resources that have made this work more meaningful.

REFERENCES

Bell, S. T. (2007). Deep-level composition variables as predictors of team performance: A meta-analysis. *The Journal of Applied Psychology*, *92*(3), 595–615. DOI: 10.1037/0021-9010.92.3.595 PMID: 17484544

Burke, C. S., Stagl, K. C., Salas, E., Pierce, L., & Kendall, D. (2006). Understanding team adaptation: A conceptual analysis and model. *The Journal of Applied Psychology*, *91*(6), 1189–1207. DOI: 10.1037/0021-9010.91.6.1189 PMID: 17100478

Carron, A. V., Colman, M. M., Wheeler, J., & Stevens, D. (2002). Cohesion and performance in sport: A meta-analysis. *Journal of Sport & Exercise Psychology*, *24*(2), 168–188. DOI: 10.1123/jsep.24.2.168

Chiocchio, F., & Essiembre, H. (2009). Cohesion and performance: A meta-analytic review of disparities between project teams, production teams, and service teams. *Small Group Research*, *40*(4), 382–420. DOI: 10.1177/1046496409335103

Christian, M. S., Bradley, J. C., Wallace, J. C., & Burke, M. J. (2009). Workplace safety: A meta-analysis of the roles of person and situation factors. *The Journal of Applied Psychology*, *94*(5), 1103–1127. DOI: 10.1037/a0016172 PMID: 19702360

Cotterill, S. T. (2017). *Team Psychology in Sports: Theory and Practice*. Routledge.

DeChurch, L. A., & Mesmer-Magnus, J. R. (2010). The cognitive underpinnings of effective teamwork: A meta-analysis. *The Journal of Applied Psychology*, *95*(1), 32–53. DOI: 10.1037/a0017328 PMID: 20085405

Edmondson, A. C. (1999). Psychological safety and learning behavior in work teams. *Administrative Science Quarterly*, *44*(2), 350–383. DOI: 10.2307/2666999

Fletcher, D., & Sarkar, M. (2012). A grounded theory of psychological resilience in Olympic champions. *Psychology of Sport and Exercise*, *13*(5), 669–678. DOI: 10.1016/j.psychsport.2012.04.007

Gully, S. M., Devine, D. J., & Whitney, D. J. (1995). A meta-analysis of cohesion and performance: Effects of level of analysis and task interdependence. *Small Group Research, 26*(4), 497–520. DOI: 10.1177/1046496495264003

Hackman, J. R. (2002). *Leading Teams: Setting the Stage for Great Performances.* Harvard Business Press.

Hülsheger, U. R., Anderson, N., & Salgado, J. F. (2009). Team-level predictors of innovation at work: A comprehensive meta-analysis spanning three decades of research. *The Journal of Applied Psychology, 94*(5), 1128–1145. DOI: 10.1037/a0015978 PMID: 19702361

Klein, C., DiazGranados, D., Salas, E., Le, H., Burke, C. S., Lyons, R., & Goodwin, G. F. (2009). Does team building work? *Small Group Research, 40*(2), 181–222. DOI: 10.1177/1046496408328821

LePine, J. A., Piccolo, R. F., Jackson, C. L., Mathieu, J. E., & Saul, J. R. (2008). A meta-analysis of teamwork processes: Tests of a multidimensional model and relationships with team effectiveness criteria. *Personnel Psychology, 61*(2), 273–307. DOI: 10.1111/j.1744-6570.2008.00114.x

Mathieu, J. E., Heffner, T. S., Goodwin, G. F., Salas, E., & Cannon-Bowers, J. A. (2000). The influence of shared mental models on team process and performance. *The Journal of Applied Psychology, 85*(2), 273–283. DOI: 10.1037/0021-9010.85.2.273 PMID: 10783543

Mathieu, J. E., Maynard, M. T., Rapp, T., & Gilson, L. (2008). Team effectiveness 1997-2007: A review of recent advancements and a glimpse into the future. *Journal of Management, 34*(3), 410–476. DOI: 10.1177/0149206308316061

May, A., & Carter, C., & HUSAT Research Institute. (2001). A case study of virtual team working in the European automotive industry. *International Journal of Industrial Ergonomics, 27*, 171–186.

McEwan, D., & Beauchamp, M. R. (2014). The effectiveness of teamwork in sports settings: A meta-analytic review. *Journal of Applied Sport Psychology, 26*(2), 200–217. DOI: 10.1080/10413200.2013.785887

Mesmer-Magnus, J. R., & DeChurch, L. A. (2009). Information sharing and team performance: A meta-analysis. *Journal of Applied Psychology, 94*(2), 535-546. DOI: 10.1177/001872088602800404

Nahrgang, J. D., Morgeson, F. P., & Hofmann, D. A. (2011). Safety at work: A meta-analytic investigation of the link between job demands, job resources, burnout, engagement, and safety outcomes. *The Journal of Applied Psychology*, *96*(1), 71–94. DOI: 10.1037/a0021484 PMID: 21171732

Salas, E., DiazGranados, D., Klein, C., Burke, C. S., Stagl, K. C., Goodwin, G. F., & Halpin, S. M. (2008). Does team training improve team performance? A meta-analysis. *Human Factors*, *50*(6), 903–933. DOI: 10.1518/001872008X375009 PMID: 19292013

Salas, E., Sims, D. E., & Burke, C. S. (2005). Is there a "big five" in teamwork? *Small Group Research*, *36*(5), 555–599. DOI: 10.1177/1046496405277134

Schaubroeck, J., Lam, S. S. K., & Peng, A. C. (2011). Cognition-based and affect-based trust as mediators of leader behavior influences on team performance. *The Journal of Applied Psychology*, *96*(4), 863–871. DOI: 10.1037/a0022625 PMID: 21299271

Stajkovic, A. D., Lee, D. S., & Nyberg, A. J. (2009). Collective efficacy, group potency, and group performance: Meta-analyses of their relationships, and test of a mediation model. *The Journal of Applied Psychology*, *94*(3), 814–828. DOI: 10.1037/a0015659 PMID: 19450017

Tannenbaum, S. I., Beard, R. L., & Salas, E. (1992). Team building and its influence on team effectiveness: An examination of conceptual and empirical developments. *Advances in Psychology*, *82*, 117–153. DOI: 10.1016/S0166-4115(08)62386-6

Tannenbaum, S. I., & Cerasoli, C. P. (2013). Do team and individual debriefs enhance performance? A meta-analysis. *Human Factors*, *55*(1), 231–245. DOI: 10.1177/0018720812448394 PMID: 23516804

West, M. A. (2012). *Effective teamwork: Practical lessons from organizational research*. BPS Blackwell.

Zaccaro, S. J., Rittman, A. L., & Marks, M. A. (2001). Team leadership. *The Leadership Quarterly*, *12*(4), 451–483. DOI: 10.1016/S1048-9843(01)00093-5

Chapter 10
Creative Collaborative Applications for Virtual Language Learning Experiences

Başak Eda Hancı-Azizoglu
https://orcid.org/0000-0001-6937-5925
Mediterranean (Akdeniz) University, Turkey

Abdullah Özgel
https://orcid.org/0009-0003-2799-7090
Mediterranean (Akdeniz) University, Turkey

Şevket Tekin
https://orcid.org/0009-0000-4720-9213
Mediterranean (Akdeniz) University, Turkey

Eşref Can Yılmaz
Mediterranean (Akdeniz) University, Turkey

Hüseyin Kafes
Mediterranean (Akdeniz) University, Turkey

ABSTRACT

The advent of the digital age has transformed the virtual learning environment. Virtual learning environments are fast becoming one of the quintessential elements of modern teaching methodologies. More specifically, the ability to interact and cooperate through digital media opens up new horizons for intercultural dialogue and competence building in language acquisition. In parallel, the vital norms and

DOI: 10.4018/979-8-3373-0375-8.ch010

protocols that enable student teams to excel in virtual contexts are examined within the context of this study,

INTRODUCTION

The advent of the digital age has transformed the virtual learning environment (Bellemare et al., 2013). Virtual learning environments are fast becoming one of the quintessential elements of modern teaching methodologies. More specifically, the ability to interact and cooperate through digital media opens up new horizons for intercultural dialogue and competence building in language acquisition. Moving to virtual collaboration comes with challenges in preserving interpersonal relationships by ensuring active engagement in activities and fostering creativity in the digital environment. Because the practice of language acquisition requires solid inter-relational commitments to achieve language performance successfully, it is a sense of friendship and trust between participants that improves collaboration and language proficiency significantly (Chatterjee, 2005). Moreover, task engagement is important to keep learners motivated, while creativity can make them navigate strange linguistic structures and cultural contexts efficiently. Hence, educators are now urged to have an intentional approach to designing, managing, and maintaining online learning environments that holistically account for these elements (Jacobs, 2023). For this purpose, this chapter discusses challenges and strategies for improving interpersonal relationships in virtual teams through task engagement and creativity within virtual teams of language acquisition. Combining views from theories of education, technological development, and group dynamics, this chapter offers an overall framework for educators and learners in effective digital collaborations.

First of all, most modern academic and professional environments contain virtual teams which can be defined as online-enabled groups that are working across space and time boundaries (Nemiro, 2023). The virtual teams are then dynamic and inclusive in nature; thus, learners can overcome different barriers related to time, distance, and resource availability while developing their competencies of creativity, flexibility, and collaboration. Their successful incorporation into learning environments requires organizational readiness, specific training, and well-developed mechanisms for evaluating collaboration skills. Students must be provided with the tools and strategies necessary to successfully face all challenges of virtual collaboration: maintaining engagement, handling conflicts, and breeding creativity. It is discussed that the basic aspects of preparing and assessing students for virtual teamwork are institutional readiness, faculty and student training, and ways of evaluation. The ultimate aim is to equip students with the skills necessary to become competent in the digital era.

In this way, the shift toward digital interfaces in the work environment has dramatically changed how virtual teams function, mainly in educational and professional settings (Jacobs, 2023). The rapid growth of virtual teams, driven by the advances in technology and the changes that COVID-19 brought into society, has transformed the world of education and work (Greimel et al., 2023). Virtual teams in a higher education context are therefore relevant in improving collaboration, developing essential skills, and preparing students for remote and hybrid work arrangements.

While increasing in prevalence, virtual teams face challenges related to trust building, motivation, and encouragement of teamwork. Unlike traditional in-person teamwork, virtual collaboration often lacks immediate feedback, physical presence, and non-verbal cues—precisely those elements that help build trust and motivation (Mulye et al., 2023). Effective communication is one of the basic elements of team success, although it requires developing specific norms and rules in virtual settings. In contrast to face-to-face interactions, online communication necessitates intentional approaches to address obstacles through hardships of the absence of real-time feedback, the limitation of non-verbal signals, and the constraints imposed by geographical or cultural differences. With that goal in mind, this chapter discusses the vital methodologies, tools, and strategies that enable student teams in higher education to excel in virtual contexts. The specific strategies discussed include the following:

1. Strategies for building and maintaining relationships in student virtual teams, including a) how to build communication and trust, b) how to build a learning community, c) how to foster collaborative creativity within the team, d) the role that teachers play in building student skills, and d) required competencies for students to build effective virtual teams;
2. Strategies for effective virtual collaboration, including the appropriate use of communication tools and team charters; and
3. Strategies for maintaining productivity and engagement in student virtual teams.

STRATEGIES FOR BUILDING AND MAINTAINING RELATIONSHIPS IN VIRTUAL TEAMS

Building Communication and Trust

The efficient exchange of information constitutes a fundamental aspect of successful virtual language-learning teams. Clear and transparent communication cultivates trust and engagement, thereby establishing a setting in which collaboration can flourish. In this context, educators assume a critical responsibility in fostering such openness by employing organized activities and utilizing digital tools (Josué et al., 2023). For example, initiatives such as collaborative storytelling and group brainstorming allow students to consolidate their linguistic resources and develop a collective sense of purpose.

Similarly, icebreakers like "Two Truths and a Lie" or cultural presentations allow the students to get to know each other and bring mutual understanding while working together. Digital tools such as Google Docs or Padlet allow real-time collaboration where participants can actively participate and feel connected (Nguyen, 2023). Academic collaboration cultivates personal connections that do wonders for team cohesion. Virtual social spaces—like group chats or virtual lounges—replicate the informality of physical classrooms and alleviate feelings of isolation. Peer mentorship programs match more advanced learners with novices in an attempt to get mutual growth and trust flowing. Moreover, the introductions in multimedia form with videos, voice notes, or pictures make online teammates more personal and connected by the feeling of being involved in a community (Israilova, 2021).

Trust is critical in effective virtual collaboration at times when non-verbal communication is absent (Vidolov, 2022). Instructors should build trust by explicitly stating goals and roles through collaborative initial planning, which would help in achieving cohesiveness and responsibility among group members. Just as important is creating a safe space for making errors which helps to encourage students to view mistakes as a learning opportunity. This flexible and safe learning environment develops confidence in students by reducing anxiety.

Another positive component for building trust in a digital learning environment is consistency. Consistency in instructor behavior—through balanced recognition of contributions—sets a standard for constructive and respectful interaction in the team. Therefore, effective interpersonal relationships among virtual teams require constant assessment and proactive intervention. During this phase, diagnostic tools, immediate intervention strategies, and reflective practices may be useful for educators to supervise and develop team cohesion for monitoring interpersonal relationships by considering the challenges of monitoring relationships on digital platforms (Thenuwara et al. 2023). To illustrate, regular surveys and polls provide critical avenues for gauging team dynamics and identifying areas of improvement. Observation logs help bring comprehensive insight into participation patterns and potential conflicts through the monitoring of exchanges during online meetings. Data analytics from Slack or Microsoft Teams give an empirical view of engagement rates, allowing timely interventions to solve anticipated digital communication problems.

In addition to early intervention strategies, role rotations ensure balanced participation by preventing dominance and encouraging diverse contributions among team members. Conflict resolution training, including techniques of active listening and "I-statements," equips students to handle disagreements constructively by promoting harmony and productivity. Reflection fosters awareness and personal growth; thus it is an important aspect of virtual team collaboration. The use of journals supports self-awareness among students and allows them to document their learning experiences (Flanagan et al., 2021). Moreover, guided group conversations about team dynamics support mutual understanding and open channels for shared improvement.

Games can also be quite effective in implementing these digital strategies. Gamification features, such as leaderboards, badges, and team challenges, sustain excitement and motivation among students. Cultural immersion activities, in the form of virtual exchanges or real-world simulations such as job interviews or travel dialogues, also offer a wealth of meaningful and authentic engagement opportunities that bring improvement both linguistically and culturally. Long-term collaborative projects of class blogs or dialogue journals continue to sustain interaction through a sense of ownership and shared goals for language learners (Kanso & Monette, 2014).

Building a Learning Community

Cultivating a robust sense of community among virtual teams contributes to increased motivation and retention through the establishment of significant connections that extend beyond task-oriented interactions. Collective practices, including weekly coffee meetings, language-focused film viewings, or themed conversations, provide informal avenues for bonding that introduce consistency and familiarity within the team. Acknowledging achievements, irrespective of whether they are minor successes or significant milestones, serves to reinforce affirmative behaviors and enhance team morale. No doubt, and quite importantly, recognizing accomplishments during virtual meetings motivates team members and reinforces their sense of collective unity (Widiyanto et al., 2023). In the first place, it seems clear that task engagement refers to the affective and cognitive effort that learners invest in their tasks. In the case of second language learners, promoting task engagement is important to ensure that collaboration leads to both content learning and language acquisition (Mohtar & Yunus, 2022). In this way, stimulating and challenging tasks keep students engaged and active in online environments. Activities involving role-play, such as interviewing, debating on current issues, or acting out cultural interactions, give students a chance to actively use the real-life language. These kinds of activities promote participation while developing teamwork with classmates. More engagement is ensured by incorporating game-based learning strategies, where tools like quizzes, puzzles, or escape-room simulations make language acquisition fun and interactive. Furthermore, intercultural understanding is realized through activities on cultural exchange. For instance, the exploration and presentation of cultural festivals or food traditions in the target language are great ideas to build a safe and fun learning environment for language learners.

Regular review is needed in order to work through problems and maintain consistency. Individual sessions provide personalized feedback and guidance, while group sessions give a sense of collective progress and help build individual relationships (Carby, 2023). Such conversations foster collaborative problem-solving and keep teams focused on their objectives. Setting up clarity in expectations and task goals is essential in developing a strong commitment to the assignments in virtual teams (Afrouzi et al., 2023; Govender & Arnedo-Moreno, 2021). If students understand what the tasks are meant for and are provided with clear expectations, then they are likely to be fully committed to the project. Clear instructions, such as detailed rubrics and descriptions of the tasks, enable the alignment of goals, objectives, and assessment criteria. The efficient observation of task interrelationships is important in assessing student involvement and cooperative efforts. Mechanisms for automated feedback, such as those represented by Google Workspace and Microsoft Teams, provide instant information on participation rates, task fulfillment, and individual contributions. On the other hand, peer review systems bring accountability, where students are supposed to comment on the contributions of other members of their group to foster critical thinking and deeper engagement. One-on-one check-ins, led by a facilitator, during synchronous meetings or individually, open the way for specific feedback and real-time goal or plan adjustments while addressing any arising concerns by keeping the team motivated (Fischer et al., 2019).

Fostering Collaborative Creativity in Language Acquisition

Language learning activities provide a built-in structure for creative exploration, combining both linguistic and cultural elements (Zacharaki & Sebastian-Galles, 2021). In this sense, creativity is a powerful motivator and factor for involvement in virtual teams (Lisovska et al., 2019). It allows learners to explore new ideas, take risks, and interact with language learning through creative approaches. If designed carefully, virtual spaces can provide an ideal environment for collaborative creativity. What seems obvious is that creativity thrives in virtual teams when members feel their input is valued. A psychologically safe environment needs to be created where students feel comfortable at sharing their thoughts without fear of judgment. Tools, including Padlet or Jamboard, allow for anonymous ideation, which encourages equal participation. Constructive conflict—disagreements that challenge assumptions—often leads to creative solutions. In this way, teachers can help students navigate through conflict by framing it as an opportunity for growth and encouraging activities like debates or scenario-based discussions. These approaches facilitate effective management of tension while simultaneously enhancing linguistic abilities.

From another perspective, enabling learners to exercise autonomy in their educational pursuits enhances both motivation and creativity (Raginsky, 2023). The provision of flexible project alternatives empowers students to select their own topics, roles, and presentation methods, thereby fostering a sense of ownership. Asynchronous learning affords students the flexibility to incorporate tasks into their personal schedules, thus accommodating various learning rhythms and preferences. This methodology acknowledges individual needs while simultaneously ensuring substantive contributions. Conversely, it is equally hard to implement creativity in the digital language teaching process because creativity needs time and resources. Access to user-friendly platforms like Trello, Canva, and Google Docs makes it easy for a team to collaborate and allows creativity to flow (Makruf & Tejaningsih, 2023). Providing adequate time for brainstorming, iteration, and refinement enables students to fully shape their ideas and achieve the project's objectives (Madaan et al., 2023). Despite challenges in the design process, these approaches nurture creativity while developing planning and self-organization skills.

For instance, game design nurtures language acquisition through engaging interactive activities (Ha et al., 2023). Learners construct quiz games focused on revising vocabulary or grammar; design virtual escape rooms for testing problem-solving skills or craft interactive stories where participant choices are informed by the linguistic input. Therefore, these activities can help to enhance creativity and collaboration among learners while upping their language skills. Another effective and creative tool for language learners for digital learning practices is digital narrative initiatives. Digital storytelling allows students to weave both language and culture into dynamic narratives: using Adobe Spark, Canva, or Google Slides to create a story with their own multimedia resources of text, audio, or even video. Along with presenting linguistic skills, language learners represent a coalescence of culture in the class. Groups can create cultural narrative projects based on holiday customs or historical events. Collaborative writing in digital storytelling really encourages teamwork and fluency in using creative language as the students negotiate ideas, create dialogues, and integrate idiomatic expressions into their narratives (Zahra & Febria, 2023). Similarly, role-playing scenarios allow students to engage in authentic contexts that help them acquire language in a practical way. Situations akin to business discussions, cultural encounters, or problem-solving exercises promote the development of communication skills, critical thinking, and collaboration competencies. By taking on roles that require active participation, students enhance their ability to handle linguistic and cultural nuances, which builds their confidence in real-life communication (Ibrahim et al., 2023).

The following summary describes the specific strategies just reviewed that educators can use to build and maintain relationships in student virtual teams in language acquisition and in other academic disciplines as well.

Summary of Strategies for Building and Maintaining Relationships

For Building Communication and Trust

- Collaborative storytelling and group brainstorming activities
- Icebreakers like "Two Truths and a Lie"
- Cultural presentations allowing students to develop mutual understanding
- Digital tools such as Google Docs or Padlet for real-time collaboration
- Virtual social spaces—like group chats or virtual lounges
- Peer mentorship programs matching advanced learners with novices
- Online student introductions through multimedia (videos, voice notes, or pictures)
- Clear team goals and roles, possibly rotation of roles as well
- Creating a safe space for students to make errors
- Consistency and balanced recognition of team members' contributions
- Team dynamic assessment and proactive intervention, with the use of diagnostic tools (polls, surveys, observation logs, data analytics)
- Conflict resolution training
- Reflection journals
- Guided group conversations
- Games (such as leaderboards, badges, and team challenges)
- Cultural immersion activities (virtual exchanges or real-world simulations such as job interviews or travel dialogues)
- Long-term collaborative projects of class blogs or dialogue journals

For Building a Learning Community:

- Collective practices such as weekly coffee meetings, language-focused film viewings, or themed conversations
- Acknowledging achievements, whether minor successes or significant milestones
- Activities involving role-play, such as interviewing, debating on current issues, or acting out cultural interactions
- Game-based learning strategies, like quizzes, puzzles, or escape-room simulations
- Cultural exchange, such as exploration and presentation of cultural festivals or food traditions
- Individual sessions to provide personalized feedback and guidance and/or group progress review sessions

- Clear goals and instructions, such as detailed rubrics and descriptions of the tasks
- Assessment through observation, use of mechanisms for automated feedback, such as participation rates, peer review systems, or one-on-one check-ins, led by instructor

For Fostering Collaborative Creativity:

- Tools that allow for anonymous ideation like Padlet or Jamboard
- Constructive conflict
- Learner autonomy through flexible project alternatives
- User-friendly platforms like Trello, Canva, and Google Docs
- Sufficient time for brainstorming, iteration, and development of ideas
- Engaging interactive activities and games
- Digital storytelling
- Role-playing scenarios

The Role of Teachers in Virtual Teams

Technology plays a main role in the effectiveness of virtual teams; that is, advanced tools and platforms will help streamline collaboration, augment communication, and optimize task management. As technological advances continue, virtual collaboration will most likely retain its significance in the area of language learning. Emerging innovations, such as artificial intelligence-based language resources, personalized learning environments, and game-like assessment techniques, are now changing the way learners interact and collaborate (Arrieta et al., 2019). Educators are the key to establishing a creative and collaborative environment of this sort. They set the stage for effective virtual learning experiences by guiding the students and by providing them with resources, for supportive team dynamics. Educators must also be adaptable and open to new technologies and pedagogical approaches. This can be done through constant professional development and collaboration with colleagues. Educators can design activities and goal-setting tasks to foster mutual understanding and camaraderie among the team. Regular check-ins, conducted in group formats or one-on-one sessions, build on that trust by letting students know that their input and challenges are valued. By this definition, the development of trust among virtual teams requires focused efforts (Antwi-Amoabeng et al., 2021). Giving constructive criticism is also crucial, and feedback is a critical element in nurturing creativity and collaboration in the digital learning environment. Constructive and actionable feedback allows students to improve their ideas while, at the same time, building confidence in their abilities. It is important that educators establish a feedback loop using peer-to-peer assessment, instructor feedback, and iterative project evaluations for continuous improvement. Data-driven insights from analytics tools can help educators monitor engagement and performance. By identifying participation patterns, educators can proactively address challenges by ensuring that all team members remain actively involved and committed to the given task (Lim et al., 2023).

In one sense, collaborative platforms like Trello, Slack, or Microsoft Teams allow for the facilitation of coordination and communication. Students can, therefore, share ideas and manage projects with their fellow members while being updated on the progress made by teams (Stahl, 2023). Real-time collaboration elements within tools like Google Workspace encourage active participation and engagement. Specifically, virtual teams bring with them the unique opportunity to connect with peers across the world. By fostering global connections, educators can create enriched learning experiences that better prepare students for success in a multicultural and interconnected world (Emberson et al., 2021). Thus, virtual reality (VR) and augmented reality (AR) are the great transformers in the virtual education field (Al-Ansi et al., 2023). VR technologies can indeed simulate real-life environments, whether cultural or professional and provide learners with highly interactive experiences that improve linguistic skills and cultural awareness. Educators can nurture inclusivity by acknowledging and valuing the cultural differences among members of the team. Fostering open conversations about cultural norms and expectations leads to mutual respect and a better learning environment altogether (Oktavia et al., 2022). Cultural competence in working within virtual teams is important for effective collaboration among diverse populations (Mayer et al., 2023). The inclusion of cultural awareness in language learning activities promotes inclusivity and mutual respect. With this in mind, students can explore different cultures by engaging in projects that focus on cultural traditions, customs, or historical settings. This fosters cross-cultural understanding while developing language skills (Oktavia et al., 2022). Perhaps most obviously, it would also include dialects, idiomatic phrases, and cultural references in some activities to make the students appreciate linguistic diversity and develop practical communication skills in different language contexts.

Educators should also plan to develop in students fundamental skills that enable successful cooperation in a virtual setting. Those skills include:

- ***Communication Skills:*** Students must develop clear and effective communication strategies in virtual settings (Zhang et al., 2023). Educators should model and encourage best practices for virtual communication by making sure that students express their ideas clearly while listening to others attentively.
- ***Conflict Resolution:*** Virtual teams may experience miscommunication or delays. Instructors should provide learners with means by which they can resolve conflicts so that they may work in a positive environment (Greimel et al., 2023).

- ***Creative Problem-Solving:*** Virtual teamwork in language learning requires students to think creatively while overcoming the challenges—whether the challenge is linguistic or collaborative. (Horning & Brown, 1981). Teachers can foster creativity by means of brainstorming sessions, collaborative tasks, and problem-solving exercises.
- ***Self-Regulation:*** Time management and motivation are important within an asynchronous or hybrid learning environment (Mnih et al., 2016). Educators can help students develop self-regulation strategies so they will stay organized and engaged throughout the project.

Required Competencies for Building Effective Virtual Teams

Apart from knowledge and skills, the students must have appropriate specific abilities in order to be successful in virtual teamwork by developing subtle aspects of digital-age interpersonal and adaptive competencies (Erdős et al., 2023). First of all, the establishment of trust and rapport is acknowledged as one of the critical competencies in virtual team environments (Basilotta-Gómez-Pablos et al., 2022). In the absence of traditional face-to-face interaction, students are expected to develop sophisticated communication skills that foster genuine relationships. This involves the acquisition of the ability to communicate information clearly, actively listen, demonstrate reliability, and show empathy through electronic media. This means students need to become competent in building meaningful relationships through text, video, and collaborative tools while understanding that trust is earned through regular and honest interactions, regardless of the physical distance (Fussell, 2020).

The other important ability in conducting virtual collaboration is the adaptation to changes in technology. In this age of rapid digital transformation, learners need to develop flexible learning mindsets that will accommodate the evolution of technology (Martínez-Peláez et al., 2023). It means developing the capacity to understand, learn, and integrate new digital tools quickly into their collaborative practices. This kind of adaptability requires not only technical competency but also a sense of curiosity, openness to change, and willingness to try new technologies that could improve the productivity and communication of a learning team. This approach is also applicable to digital language learning environments.

Integration of knowledge, skills, and abilities (KSAs) into language learning practices is important for both students and educators to be able to succeed in virtual teamwork. To do so, educators can create learning environments where both collaboration and language proficiency are nurtured simultaneously (Liu et al., 2022). Within this process, engagement is a collective responsibility of both teachers and students in online learning environments (Kujala et al., 2022). This skill requires creativity, initiative, and a deep understanding of the subtleties of virtual communication. Students should learn how to initiate and maintain their own motivation (Ryan & Deci, 2020) by creating engaging experiences and techniques for how to keep group members connected and focused on common goals (Mengoni et al., 2021). This surely includes the development of these skills: initiating conversations, proposing new ways of collaboration, giving and receiving effective feedback, and thinking of ways to make virtual interactions more engaging and meaningful. Virtual language acquisition is a practice that faces many challenges, such as lack of engagement, misunderstanding, technological problems, and isolation (Zhao & Liu, 2022). It is essential to implement the right strategies to overcome these barriers and set up the ideal learning environment. Virtual environments often suffer from poor communication, especially for learners who may lack confidence in their use of the language (Chandra et al., 2022).

An engaging and interactive virtual classroom is one where the students can become active participants. The intuitive interfaces of services such as Zoom breakout rooms, Google Classroom discussion boards, and Microsoft Teams are designed in a way that makes navigation easy. Obstacles from technology would not prevent the students from engaging in a class if the teachers strive to create an environment that allows for communication, creativity, and teamwork skills. Such avenues ensure that the virtual classroom environment is always structured, friendly, and accommodating to teamwork. Interactive elements in the form of polls, quizzes, and collaborative documents can also help to keep students engaged by making passive learning experiences active (Fadiyah et al., 2023). This will allow for different styles of learning and provide channels for synchronous and asynchronous collaboration by letting students participate at their own pace while fostering a sense of shared engagement. Additionally, introductory activities like icebreakers and informal group discussions are key to creating a positive and inclusive atmosphere (Fu et al., 2022). Such activities reduce the sense of isolation often associated with virtual environments by fostering relationships between individuals by making students feel more at ease as part of the group. Collaborative tools are a critical element of effective virtual collaboration by enabling students to work together on shared assignments through improving their problem-solving skills (Biró et al., 2023).

In addition, project management tools such as Trello, Slack, and Asana give broad organizational frameworks that help teams assign tasks, track progress, and manage deadlines. These kinds of tools foster transparency and equal participation through aligning personal contributions with group objectives. Currently, real-time applications, such as Google Docs and Jamboard, boost engagement greatly by letting learners collaborate on content creation while providing timely feedback to each other (Elsheikh, 2023). Such tools are better for language learning because they support more activities related to collaborative writing, peer assessments, and group exercises in languages that dismantle the walls of asynchronous learning.

Language-specific platforms, such as Duolingo for Schools and Babbel for Teams, assist in enhancing these collaborative tools by focusing on customized material targeted toward vocabulary and grammar (Arora et al., 2021). All these tools will enable the development of linguistic competence both individually and cooperatively with others. Hence, these platforms also provide the benefit of personalized learning experiences while tracking one's progress by successfully developing an integration of personal development and collaborative tasks.

On the other hand, it is important to establish socio-emotional connections in virtual environments for language learners. Casual exchanges, such as group discussions or forums based on common interests, allow students to practice their language skills in both relaxed and authentic situations (Delahunty et al., 2013). These aid in developing interpersonal relations and alleviate the anxiety often associated with online communication. Moreover, peer mentorship programs are helpful in this respect. These programs not only support language learning but also foster a sense of community and shared growth among the participants. With the judicious incorporation of KSAs into virtual language learning, educators can construct dynamic environments that will allow for fostering collaboration and language proficiency (Al-Husban & Tawalbeh, 2023).

One of the major hurdles in virtual learning environments is the lack of immediate feedback, especially in asynchronous formats, which can lead to frustration and disengagement (Simmermeyer et al., 2022). Without timely responses, students often feel disconnected from both their instructors and their peers. To overcome this, educators can use automated tools in the form of grammar checkers and language assessment programs that give immediate corrections and insights into student progress. Peer feedback mechanisms significantly augment this process by allowing students to assess one another's work, thereby fostering accountability by facilitating a more profound learning experience. Additionally, organized interactions with instructors offer a chance for individualized feedback by warranting that students perceive a sense of support and involvement throughout their educational progression.

Misunderstandings are more likely to occur without the non-verbal clues of facial expressions and body language. Tutors can ease these problems by providing structured communication templates for emails, chat messages, or project updates (Turaev et al., 2023). These can help reduce anxiety while increasing clarity. Although tools like Google Translate may offer some initial support for groups of students with differing levels of proficiency, the ultimate goal remains the same: to promote students' independence in using the target language (Parovic et al., 2023). Moreover, setting clear expectations for communication, like respect in interaction, cuts the possibility of confusion and makes collaboration easier.

Considering language learners, isolation and anxiety are the top challenges for learners whose confidence in speaking and writing has not yet developed fully. Building a supportive community in class can mitigate that and enhance student engagement through creating group discussions and informal social spaces to connect and collaborate with others. In addition, peer mentorship programs, in which more experienced learners lead the newcomers, provide linguistic and emotional support that is beneficial for both the mentor and the mentee. The creation of low-anxiety activities—such as language games, conversation circles, and writing prompts—provides students with safe spaces to practice their skills by building their confidence over time. Peer and self-evaluations, as well as observations by facilitators, offer additional perspectives on such dynamics. The assessment of creativity and problem-solving abilities is of paramount importance, with an emphasis on how students recognize challenges and collaboratively devise solutions. Tools such as Trello and Miro help educators monitor the processes of brainstorming and project execution. Furthermore, automated feedback mechanisms reveal trends in students' critical thinking and creativity, thereby permitting focused assistance for their growth. Collectively, these methodologies guarantee that students attain the requisite skills and competencies essential for success in languages through virtual team contexts.

Organizational readiness is another critical factor in making virtual collaboration work. A solid technological infrastructure is necessary with tools like Zoom, Slack, and Microsoft Teams to ensure seamless communication, resource allocation, and project management. The implementation of cloud-based systems increases accessibility and data security and thus helps in efficient collaboration among diverse teams. This would require continuous technical support to resolve any issues that might arise and to ensure the users' trust in these resources. With respect to building trust among learners, policies specifically designed for the learning of virtual teams hold significant importance. Establishing clear protocols for respectful communication, safeguarding data privacy, and protecting intellectual property contributes to fostering a positive and secure online environment (Garrido et al., 2023). Mechanisms for performance evaluation that are equitable and transparent, which are tailored to virtual contexts, support the maintenance of motivation and accountability among team members.

The evaluation of virtual collaboration skills is carried out by using both qualitative and quantitative methods. For instance, communication may be evaluated in terms of participation in discussions and reaction to feedback given. Some analytics on platforms like Zoom and Microsoft Teams will also be helpful in gauging students' engagement. This covers aspects such as contributions to group efforts, adherence to roles, and the development of trust within the team. Accordingly, a wide array of tools and methodologies must be utilized to thoroughly evaluate virtual collaboration competencies. The collaborative platforms of Google Workspace and Asana provide important insights into the dynamics of a team, where educators can observe individual participation and assess overall group engagement. Peer and self-assessments promote accountability and encourage self-reflection by enabling students to appraise their contributions and realize areas of improvement. Automated platforms, such as Grammarly and Edmodo, provide instant feedback on the quality of communication and collaboration through enabling educators to collect valuable data to single out areas that need improvement. Simulated virtual projects, such as role-playing activities and replicating real-life challenges can allow students to put their problem-solving skills into action in controlled learning settings (Tipmontree & Tasanameelarp, 2021).

There can be no doubt that both teachers and students require training in order for virtual classrooms to be successful (Ouyang et al., 2022). The training of teachers focuses on pedagogical changes, such as reconfiguring their teaching methods to online environments and using active learning methods for group tasks. It also includes technical skills that are abilities for involving the use of learning management systems and troubleshooting. Teachers will also have to develop positive interactions through rapport-building competencies to overcome conflicts within group dynamics. Students also benefit from instruction that acclimates them to collaborative tools and online behavioral norms. Orientation activities may introduce digital platforms and establish norms for active participation in digital classes. In a like manner, instruction in time management, conflict resolution strategies, and task organization prepare students to be successful in both asynchronous and synchronous environments (Vizeshfar et al., 2022). Activities that build confidence, such as gamified activities and peer mentoring, also promote engagement and help students navigate the virtual classroom with ease.

Summary of Required Competencies and Strategies for Building Effective Virtual Teams

For Developing Digital-Age Interpersonal and Adaptive Competencies:

- Ability to build trust and rapport without face-to-face interaction
- Effective communication skills through digital media (clarity, empathy, active listening)
- Consistent and honest virtual interactions to earn trust
- Comfort with communicating via text, video, and collaborative tools
- Establishing socio-emotional connections through informal exchanges or interest-based forums
- Peer mentorship programs to support language learning
- Structured communication templates for emails, chats, and updates
- Protocols promoting respectful communication and data protection

- Performance evaluations designed for virtual transparent and equitable environments

For Fostering Technological Adaptability and Tool Integration:

- Capacity to learn and adopt new digital tools quickly
- Openness to innovation and flexible learning mindsets
- Use of project management tools like Trello, Asana, and Slack
- Utilization of real-time collaboration tools like Google Docs and Jamboard
- Integration of language-specific platforms like Duolingo for Schools and Babbel
- Cloud-based systems for seamless resource sharing and accessibility
- Continuous tech support to maintain confidence in digital platforms

For Enhancing Collaboration, Motivation, and Engagement:

- Initiating conversations and proposing new collaborative strategies
- Effective feedback exchange among peers
- Creating interactive and engaging learning experiences
- Use of polls, quizzes, breakout rooms, and collaborative documents
- Establishing clear goals, group roles, and communication expectations
- Low-anxiety activities such as conversation circles, language games, and writing prompts
- Peer and self-evaluation to monitor contribution and foster accountability
- Orientation sessions for digital tools and virtual class norms
- Training in time management and conflict resolution
- Gamified activities to build confidence and increase participation

For Creating an Inclusive and Productive Virtual Learning Environment:

- Instructor-student interactions for personalized feedback
- Automated feedback tools (e.g., Grammarly, Edmodo) for real-time corrections
- Collaborative writing, peer assessment, and shared exercises to support language learning
- Simulated real-life tasks (e.g., role-play) to apply problem-solving skills
- Observation and analytics tools (Zoom, Microsoft Teams) to monitor engagement
- Designing structured, friendly, and inclusive virtual spaces
- Facilitator observations to support student creativity and group dynamics

STRATEGIES FOR EFFECTIVE VIRTUAL COLLABORATION

Communication Tools

Virtual collaboration requires flexible communication instruments that can deliver benefits in both synchronous and asynchronous environments. These tools help to establish good rapport and trust among the team members through activities such as icebreakers or gamified interactions, and they can also boost engagement and a feeling of togetherness. With the right uses of technologies and strategies, both teachers and students can overcome barriers and maximize the benefits of virtual collaboration. To illustrate, Microsoft Teams and Zoom allow immediate brainstorming and even decision-making strategies for learners, and therefore language learners may find the opportunity to exchange ideas. Virtual whiteboards like Miro encourage creativity by allowing students to visually arrange their ideas and collaborate during these brainstorming efforts. In addition, tools like Trello and Google Docs boost asynchronous interactions and allow students to collaborate with one another, even from different time zones, while ensuring equal participation despite differences in scheduling (Petrescu et al., 2022).

On the other hand, these communication tools have their drawbacks. Technological disparities impede students' access to participation without a reliable device or internet connection; thus, in this case institutionally founded subsidies would help. Virtual settings also lack non-verbal cues, and this may lead to possible misunderstandings. This can be mitigated through the promotion of video conferencing and the integration of expressive elements like emojis to bring out emotions and nuances, since virtual communication is not natural in the sense of building a social relationship that is possible with eye contact and in-person interaction. Tool fatigue is another interesting concern, and it occurs as a result of juggling multiple platforms which may lead to confusion or burnout. Strategic selection of user-friendly, effective tools, combined with adequate training, can streamline the experience to maintain student engagement.

Team Charters

Team charters encourage virtual collaboration since they provide structure and clarity in an environment that lacks face-to-face interaction. With clear definitions of project objectives, roles, and responsibilities of individual members, as well as schedules, these charters avoid ambiguities that usually arise in virtual collaboration. They ensure that each member understands what they contribute to the team's shared success, thus reducing the chances of misunderstanding. Another major advantage is accountability since the structured format of charters helps to alleviate free-riding tendencies (Johnson et al., 2021). When responsibilities and deadlines are clearly articulated, it is more likely that team members will stick to their assigned tasks and meet expected standards.

Furthermore, the fact that the charter includes mechanisms for conflict resolution makes it easier to handle conflicts constructively; and this preserves the harmony and productivity of members. Additionally, evaluation metrics, such as progress tracking and feedback sessions, contribute toward continuous improvement while working together to achieve their set goals. In this context, team charters provide a number of advantages. They provide a structured pattern that allows students to focus on creativity and problem-solving without diversions into issues related to logistics. With the creation of the charter, inclusiveness is achieved, where a range of views can shape the purpose and norms of the team. This helps build cohesiveness and develops ownership among members. Moreover, the use of team charters prepares students for the professional workplace, where such documents are frequently used in managing remote and hybrid projects. By acquainting students with these methodologies, educators facilitate the acquisition of critical competencies necessary for their prospective professional endeavors.

Despite the numerous benefits of team charters, there are also several challenges associated with their applications. A common obstacle is resistance to formalization because both students and professionals may view the structured approach as too rigid or bureaucratic. This resistance can hinder full engagement in the process by lowering the overall effectiveness of the charter. Moreover, the time needed to create an all-inclusive charter may be perceived as a drawback, especially in high-tempo environments where those involved may prefer urgent action to strategic planning. Another challenge comes from the fact that virtual teams are dynamic; as structures, roles, and project goals change, keeping a relevant and up-to-date charter requires ongoing dedication. One other factor is flexibility; provisions for periodic review should be included so the charter grows with the team. Gamification will help in making the process more interesting and turn the development into an activity that brings about more participation and ownership. Yet another critical dimension in virtual teamwork is laying up proper foundations of communication. Clear and shared objectives will guide and direct all members' efforts toward common outcomes. Ground rules for communication are necessary for navigating the complexities that go along with virtual interactions, and these could include response time expectations, preferred platforms, or guidelines for giving constructive feedback.

Regardless of the feedback provided, virtual teams face some unique challenges, including variable levels of digital literacy and a lack of experience in working collaboratively in a team (Morrison-Smith & Ruiz, 2020). For example, employing systematic strategies such as the "sandwich approach" when providing feedback can preserve an affirmative ambiance while simultaneously tackling aspects that require enhancement (Prochazka et al., 2020). These established conventions facilitate communication, reduce disputes, and foster a cooperative online setting. In virtual teams, effective use of technology is important to ensure inclusive and seamless communication. Microsoft Teams or Google Workspace platforms allow for both real-time and delayed interactions with tools that fit all possible needs. Features such as live captions, support for multiple languages, and user-friendly interfaces ensure accessibility for all team members, regardless of their technical abilities or language barriers. Moreover, setting up clear channels of communication builds trust and creates a sense of community.

Trust and cohesion, elements that frequently pose challenges in virtual environments, can be cultivated through the implementation of team charters. By defining communication protocols and outlining decision-making procedures, charters promote transparency and establish a basis for successful collaboration. This framework mitigates the limitations imposed by the lack of non-verbal signals and informal exchanges, which are essential in conventional teamwork, thereby enabling virtual teams to prosper even in the absence of physical proximity. There exist a few major components of an effective team charter to direct collaboration: a shared vision and common goals of the team will inspire its members and strengthen their sense of belonging within the team. Clearly defined roles and responsibilities will prevent duplication and ensure that everything gets done. Communication protocols will determine how and when to communicate in order to minimize misunderstanding and improve the functionality of a team.

In sum, educators will find the following tools useful for building effective virtual collaboration in student language acquisition virtual teams:

- Synchronous communication tools, like Microsoft Teams, Zoom, and Miro for immediate brainstorming and decision-making,
- Asynchronous communication tools, like Trello and Google Docs, to encourage asynchronous interactions and collaboration, and
- Team charters that outline clear definitions of project objectives, roles, and responsibilities of individual members, schedules, and conflict resolution mechanisms.

STRATEGIES FOR MAINTAINING PRODUCTIVITY AND ENGAGEMENT IN VIRTUAL TEAMS

Virtual teams face the usual challenges around issues of time zones, miscommunication, and accountability (Morrison-Smith & Ruiz, 2020). Educators and team leaders play a vital role in affecting communication strategies through virtual teams (Liao, 2017). Additionally, educators provide support and training on digital etiquette and thereby equip students with the necessary skills to succeed in their online interactions. Preliminary team-building activities include icebreakers and group challenges that bring trust to its members. Initiatives of such nature ensure that the students participating in them are empowered with all the knowledge relevant for adequate communication during academic and professional activities conducted over virtual spaces. In addition, virtual icebreakers, informal check-ins, and casual engagements in the form of online coffee breaks replicate the unplanned interactions that are typical with face-to-face teams. Moreover, the use of anonymous surveys or suggestion boxes makes it possible to raise any concerns without judgment and thus encourage honest feedback for continued betterment. By this definition, feedback mechanisms are important to raise the level of activity and performance among virtual teams. Feedback also facilitates effective communication and enhances team dynamics. Peer review, where members appraise each other's contributions anonymously, brings out crucial aspects of individual strengths and areas of improvement. Peer review promotes teamwork and mutual responsibility by enabling group members to review and improve each other's input. Equally important are protocols for conflict resolution since conflicts are an inherent part of any team setting. Strategies like conflict mapping help identify underlying issues while assigning a neutral mediator can prevent disputes from escalating. Automated feedback tools, such as Grammarly or Turnitin, provide immediate and objective assessments that also help team members polish their work while reducing the workload for instructors.

On the other hand, overcoming common challenges in virtual teamwork requires further proactive strategies. For example, feelings of isolation can be overcome by arranging regular video calls that simulate face-to-face interactions and give a sense of community. Another major challenge is that of handling different working styles, which can be accomplished through personality profiling. One needs to know the strengths and preferences of each team member so that the team can adapt its interaction style for comfort to maximize productivity within the team. Consistent engagement can also be achieved through the use of gamification strategies, such as rewarding milestone achievements. This will create a fun environment that will keep the team motivated and focused on delivering or attaining their set or desired goals (Muñoz et al., 2020). Well-defined roles and responsibilities are one of the basic pillars of any effective virtual collaboration. Identifying specific roles—such as project manager, content creator, or editor—ensures that every team member understands their role and contributes constructively. Roles may be rotated every now and then, so it is not only a question of shifting responsibilities but also of acquiring new competencies by team members and fostering a much deeper understanding of the team's dynamics. This approach breeds cooperation and strengthens the group's overall cohesion. Accordingly, increasing accountability via shared task boards or automated progress reports—thus making contributions visible and encouraging transparency— is one way of making sure that all members are involved and working toward team goals.

It is important for time management that virtual teams set clear, specific, and attainable goals for the team to be focused and motivated. In this respect, the SMART objective framework—Specific, Measurable, Achievable, Relevant, and Time-bound—ensures clear and attainable goals (Ogbeiwi, 2017). This approach helps team members understand their objectives and track their progress effectively. Additional tools, such as Microsoft Teams or Zoom, improve team efforts by providing an integrated environment for communication, sharing of files, and live brainstorming. Tools such as shared whiteboards and collaborative documents nurture creativity and engage the solving of problems proactively. Time management in virtual settings is most important since virtual teams usually multitask on several projects. The Work Breakdown Structure (Tausworthe, 1979) creates smaller, manageable components from bigger tasks and ensures that the workloads are balanced so that deadlines are met. Project management tools like Slack, Trello, or Asana simplify task assignments and progress tracking by keeping the team organized on schedule. For teams that work internationally, tools like World Time Buddy help manage time zone differences and make it fair to schedule meetings so that everyone can participate without much hassle. Scheduled team reflections allow for dialogues across the organization on effective practices and areas that need change by creating an environment of transparency.

Moreover, time zone conflicts can be handled through schedule rotation of meetings that fairly distribute inconvenience or through tools like Doodle to identify times agreeable to all. Miscommunication caused by ambiguous language or differences in culture can be minimized through an emphasis on clear and concise communication and training in techniques of conflict resolution. Effective virtual team management is based on clear communication strategies and well-defined frameworks (Swart et al., 2022). So, it is important to set protocols in place for communications. Teams should decide on appropriate tools for synchronous and asynchronous communication, like video calls for brainstorming and discussion boards for updates. Regular check-ins, either weekly or biweekly, maintain alignment and provide opportunities to reassess goals and address challenges. Writing down important decisions, action items, and deadlines ensures that critical information is still on hand for later reference by reducing the chances of misunderstandings. For instance, active listening and empathy are critical elements of effective communication in virtual settings. The lack of physical cues makes miscommunication more likely, so it becomes important for the team members to confirm understanding and acknowledge contributions. The simple practice of paraphrasing a colleague's points or showing engagement through emojis can bridge the gap that distance creates. With empathy, teams can understand the differences in culture and the individual, thus creating a work environment that is inclusive, where every member knows and feels their worth.

Overall, trust is a critical ingredient for the success of virtual teams, and it needs to be developed purposefully. At an individual level, relationships can be built by doing virtual icebreakers, introductory videos, or personality assessments, which create an opportunity for team members to connect with each other on a personal level. Moreover, work process transparency, enhanced by collaborative platforms such as Google Drive or Trello, keeps every team member aware of others' progress and accountable for their work. Sustained involvement, evidenced through proactive contributions to dialogues and assignments, bolsters confidence and dedication among the group members. The fact remains that a constructive team culture is essential to maintain motivation and reduce anxiety in online environments (Hilliard et al., 2019). A supportive atmosphere can be created through socio-emotional ties, including informal conversations that emulate "water-cooler" discussions. Virtual lounges or discussion boards provide forums for informal interaction, allowing team members to feel valued and connected. Emphasis on diversity and inclusion strengthens teamwork by bringing together a variety of perspectives, which fuels creativity and innovation.

Below is a list of the strategies just reviewed that educators may utilize to maintain productivity and engagement in student virtual teams in language acquisition and other academic areas of study in higher education as well:

Strategies for Maintaining Productivity and Engagement

- Providing support and training in digital etiquette, conflict resolution, active listening, and the use of empathy
- Preliminary team-building activities, such as icebreakers and group challenges to build initial team trust
- Informal virtual check-ins, and casual engagements like online coffee breaks
- Anonymous surveys or suggestion boxes to encourage honest feedback for continued improvement
- Peer reviews, where members appraise each other's contributions anonymously
- Automated feedback tools, such as Grammarly or Turnitin, to provide immediate and objective assessments
- Developing protocols for conflict resolution and strategies like conflict mapping to identify underlying issues
- Regular video calls to give a sense of community and overcome team members' feelings of isolation.

- Personality profiling, outlining each team member's strengths and preferences
- The use of gamification strategies, such as rewarding milestone achievements, to maintain consistent engagement
- Well-defined team member roles and responsibilities and rotating those roles as well
- Shared task boards or automated progress reports to ensure transparency and accountability
- Developing SMART (Specific, Measurable, Achievable, Relevant, and Time-bound) team goals
- Using a Work Breakdown Structure in which teamwork is divided into smaller, manageable components
- Project management tools like Slack, Trello, or Asana to simplify task assignments and progress tracking
- Using tools like World Time Buddy to schedule team meetings when members are dispersed across various time zones. Meetings times can be rotated to fairly distribute inconvenience or tools like Doodle can be used to identify times agreeable to all.
- Appropriate use of synchronous and asynchronous communication tools, like video calls for brainstorming and discussion boards for updates
- Regular check-ins (weekly or biweekly) to maintain alignment, reassess goals and address challenges
- Documenting and writing down important decisions, action items, and deadlines to ensure that critical information is available for later reference
- Creating an overall supportive atmosphere by developing socio-emotional ties through informal conversations in virtual lounges and/or in discussion boards

In summary, student virtual teams are capable of attaining significant success by implementing effective communication strategies, utilizing team charters, and maintaining a dedication to continuous improvement. By proactively addressing challenges and cultivating a culture characterized by trust and inclusion, virtual teams can optimize their capabilities and establish a positive, productive atmosphere that is conducive to collaboration.

CONCLUSION

Technology continues to evolve, and so must our approaches to virtual learning to ensure both students and educators are adaptable and equipped to rise to the challenges and opportunities presented by digital collaboration. The primary aim of educators must be to enable students to achieve fluency in the target language while developing their interpersonal and cognitive skills necessary for them to function effectively in a globalized and technologically interdependent world. Virtual teams within the higher education realm are a significant shift towards increased interconnectivity and adaptability in the educational system. Within this framework, educators may find ways to address obstacles, use resources, and promote participation in dynamic environments that would better prepare students for the expectations of a largely digital era (Dumford & Miller, 2018). The new landscape in higher education brings forth intricacies in managing online learning.

For this reason, virtual collaboration in language education opens significant possibilities for the enhancement of cooperation and innovation within the process of language learning. In this respect, educators working with language learners can help students succeed in online learning environments by establishing interpersonal relationships, keeping learners engaged with clearly thought-out assignments, and by creating a context that allows for creativity. With a combination of well-planned strategies, effective tools, and the development of essential KSAs, language learners may acquire not only linguistic skills but also the collaborative and creative communication skills needed for success in today's technology driven world. Effective communication is indeed the foundation of successful virtual teams, especially in the higher education environment, where collaboration is a key component of both learning and innovation. By adhering to important norms and protocols in setting goals clearly, being inclusive, and creating a culture of feedback, students will be better prepared to handle the unique challenges that come with virtual collaboration (McLarnon et al., 2019). Within this global learning process, educators can nurture students' confidence, encourage meaningful relationships, and assure success in academic and professional settings. By investing in resources to improve technological capabilities, fostering an environment of flexibility, and providing comprehensive training programs, educational institutions can effectively prepare learners to succeed in remote and hybrid professional environments.

Thus, designing creative and culturally sensitive digital practices that will keep up with student preparation outside just academia and into the new employment landscape becomes much more important for the role of educators. Having that skill in communication underpinned by technology mastery—virtual teams are gaining authority in the modern, high-tech world—such remote or hybrid environments call on the necessity of working efficiently toward individual and common targets for the well-being of the planet. Doing as such, these methodologies not only prepare students for success in school but also equip them with crucial skills needed to navigate through an increasingly digital workplace. As virtual teamwork becomes part of education and the workforce, learning these norms and protocols is no longer enough—they must be mastered (Mogavi et al., 2024). This chapter has provided a framework of strategies to enable educators and students to practice virtual collaboration with an impact on productivity, creativity, and sustained motivation within the dynamically changing remote world. Strong assessment methods, coupled with the effective use of communication technologies, ensure that students will gain fundamental competencies in teamwork, innovative thinking, and the solving of complex problems. What is more, the effective management of tasks and projects in virtual student teams requires a blend of effective communication, clear role allocations, and adaptability of processes. A supportive environment, use of digital tools, and compliance with given guidelines can enable a team to overcome the inherent challenges embedded in virtual collaboration.

REFERENCES

Afrouzi, H., Kwon, S. Y., Landier, A., Ma, Y., & Thesmar, D. (2023). Overreaction in expectations: Evidence and theory. *The Quarterly Journal of Economics, 138*(3), 1713–1764. DOI: 10.1093/qje/qjad009

Al-Ansi, A. M., Jaboob, M., Garad, A., & Al-Ansi, A. (2023). Analyzing augmented reality (AR) and virtual reality (VR) recent development in education. *Social Sciences & Humanities Open*, *8*(1), 100532. DOI: 10.1016/j.ssaho.2023.100532

Al-Husban, N. A., & Tawalbeh, M. (2023). EFL teachers' practices and perspectives on learner autonomy in virtual language learning environments in Jordan. *International Journal of Language Education*, *1*(1), 1. DOI: 10.26858/ijole.v1i1.36156

Antwi-Amoabeng, D., Beutler, B. D., Chahal, G., Mahboob, S., Gullapalli, N., Tedja, R., Madhani-Lovely, F., & Rowan, C. (2021). Ensuring trust in COVID-19 data. *Medicine*, *100*(35), e26972. DOI: 10.1097/md.0000000000026972 PMID: 34477127

Arora, A., Nakov, P., Hardalov, M., Sarwar, S. M., Nayak, V., Dinkov, Y., Zlatkova, D., Dent, K., Bhatawdekar, A., Bouchard, G., & Augenstein, I. (2021). Detecting harmful content on online platforms: What platforms need vs. where research efforts go. *arXiv (Cornell University)*. /arxiv.2103.00153DOI: 10.48550

Arrieta, A. B., Díaz-Rodríguez, N., Del Ser, J., Bennetot, A., Tabik, S., Barbado, A., Garcia, S., Gil-Lopez, S., Molina, D., Benjamins, R., Chatila, R., & Herrera, F. (2019). Explainable Artificial Intelligence (XAI): Concepts, taxonomies, opportunities and challenges toward responsible AI. *Information Fusion*, *58*, 82–115. DOI: 10.1016/j.inffus.2019.12.012

Basilotta-Gómez-Pablos, V., Matarranz, M., Casado-Aranda, L., & Otto, A. (2022). Teachers' digital competencies in higher education: A systematic literature review. *International Journal of Educational Technology in Higher Education*, *19*(1). Advance online publication. DOI: 10.1186/s41239-021-00312-8

Bellemare, M. G., Naddaf, Y., Veness, J., & Bowling, M. (2013). The Arcade Learning Environment: An evaluation platform for general agents. *Journal of Artificial Intelligence Research*, *47*, 253–279. DOI: 10.1613/jair.3912

Biró, A., Cuesta-Vargas, A. I., Martín-Martín, J., Szilágyi, L., & Szilágyi, S. M. (2023). Synthetized multilanguage OCR using CRNN and SVTR models for real-time collaborative tools. *Applied Sciences (Basel, Switzerland)*, *13*(7), 4419. DOI: 10.3390/app13074419

Carby, N. (2023). Personalized feedback in a virtual learning environment. *Journal of Educational Supervision*, *6*(1), 36–44. DOI: 10.31045/jes.6.1.3

Chandra, A. N. R., Jamiy, F. E., & Reza, H. (2022). A systematic survey on cybersickness in virtual environments. *Computers*, *11*(4), 51. DOI: 10.3390/computers11040051

Chatterjee, S. (2005). Children's friendship with place: A conceptual inquiry. *Children, Youth and Environments*, *15*(1), 1–26. DOI: 10.1353/cye.2005.0057

Delahunty, J., Verenikina, I., & Jones, P. (2013). Socio-emotional connections: Identity, belonging and learning in online interactions. A literature review. *Technology, Pedagogy and Education*, *23*(2), 243–265. DOI: 10.1080/1475939x.2013.813405

Dumford, A. D., & Miller, A. L. (2018). Online learning in higher education: Exploring advantages and disadvantages for engagement. *Journal of Computing in Higher Education*, *30*(3), 452–465. DOI: 10.1007/s12528-018-9179-z

Elsheikh, A. H. (2023). Applications of machine learning in friction stir welding: Prediction of joint properties, real-time control and tool failure diagnosis. *Engineering Applications of Artificial Intelligence*, *121*, 105961. DOI: 10.1016/j.engappai.2023.105961

Emberson, R., Kirschbaum, D., & Stanley, T. (2021). Global connections between El Nino and landslide impacts. *Nature Communications*, *12*(1). Advance online publication. DOI: 10.1038/s41467-021-22398-4 PMID: 33859185

Erdős, F., Németh, R., & Firuza, B. (2023). Virtual teamwork in gamified 3D environment. *Híradástechnika/Infocommunications Journal, 15*(Special Issue), 15–20. DOI: 10.36244/icj.2023.si-iodcr.3

Fadiyah, F., Fuadi, A., Nurjannah, N., Irmayanti, I., & Lita, W. (2023). QUIZIZZ Application-Based Interactive Learning Media Development Workshop for Junior High School Teacher. *Pengabdian Jurnal Abdimas*, *1*(2), 59–65. DOI: 10.55849/abdimas.v1i2.157

Fischer, J., Alpert, A., & Rao, P. (2019). Promoting intern resilience: Individual chief wellness check-ins. *MedEdPORTAL: the Journal of Teaching and Learning Resources*. Advance online publication. DOI: 10.15766/mep_2374-8265.10848 PMID: 31921994

Flanagan, E. W., Beyl, R. A., Fearnbach, S. N., Altazan, A. D., Martin, C. K., & Redman, L. M. (2021). The impact of COVID-19 stay-at-home orders on health behaviors in adults. *Obesity (Silver Spring, Md.)*, *29*(2), 438–445. DOI: 10.1002/oby.23066 PMID: 33043562

Fu, S., Yu, Y., Chen, J., Han, B., & Wu, Z. (2022). Towards a probabilistic approach for risk analysis of nuclear-powered icebreakers using FMEA and FRAM. *Ocean Engineering*, *260*, 112041. DOI: 10.1016/j.oceaneng.2022.112041

Fussell, R. D. (2020). Gather us in: Building meaningful relationships in Catholic schools amid a COVID-19 context. *Journal of Catholic Education*, *23*(1). Advance online publication. DOI: 10.15365/joce.2301102020

Garrido, G. M., Nair, V., & Song, D. (2023). SOK: Data privacy in virtual reality. *Proceedings on Privacy Enhancing Technologies. Privacy Enhancing Technologies Symposium*, *2024*(1), 21–40. DOI: 10.56553/popets-2024-0003

Govender, T., & Arnedo-Moreno, J. (2021). An analysis of game design elements used in Digital Game-Based Language Learning. *Sustainability*, *13*(12), 6679. DOI: 10.3390/su13126679

Greimel, N. S., Kanbach, D. K., & Chelaru, M. (2023). Virtual teams and transformational leadership: An integrative literature review and avenues for further research. *Journal of Innovation & Knowledge*, *8*(2). Advance online publication. DOI: 10.1016/j.jik.2023.100351

Ha, N. T. N., Spittle, M., Watt, A., & Van Dyke, N. (2023). A systematic literature review of micro-credentials in higher education: A non-zero-sum game. *Higher Education Research & Development*, *42*(6), 1527–1548.

Hilliard, J., Kear, K., Donelan, H., & Heaney, C. (2019). Students' experiences of anxiety in an assessed, online, collaborative project. *Computers & Education*, *143*. Advance online publication. DOI: 10.1016/j.compedu.2019.103675

Horning, A. S., & Brown, H. D. (1981). Principles of language learning and teaching. *Modern Language Journal*, *65*(4), 417. DOI: 10.2307/327392

Ibrahim, M., & Aydoğmuş, M. (2023). Examining ESL preservice teachers' personal factors that best predict their confidence to integrate technology in future classrooms. *Journal of Education and Recreation Patterns*, *4*(1), 134–152.

Israilova, I. (2021). "telegram" as a modern simplified and rapid means of distance learning using multimedia form. *ACADEMICIA an International Multidisciplinary Research Journal*, *11*(1), 1037–1044. DOI: 10.5958/2249-7137.2021.00183.x

Jacobs, D. (2023). Taking an intentional approach to technology. *Childhood Education*, *99*(4), 72–75. DOI: 10.1080/00094056.2023.2232285

Johnson, W. H., Baker, D. S., Dong, L., Taras, V., & Wankel, C. (2021). Do team charters help team-based projects? The effects of team charters on performance and satisfaction in global virtual teams. *Academy of Management Learning & Education, 21*(2), 236–260. DOI: 10.5465/amle.2020.0332

Josué, N. A., Bedoya-Flores, M. C., Mosquera-Quiñonez, E. F., Mesías-Simisterra, Á. E., & Bautista-Sánchez, J. V. (2023). Educational platforms: Digital tools for the teaching-learning process in education. *Ibero-American Journal of Education & Society Research, 3*(1), 259–263. DOI: 10.56183/iberoeds.v3i1.626

Kanso, A., & Monette, D. (2014). Foundations for long-term collaborative research. *In Proceedings of the 2014 International Workshop on Long-term Industrial Collaboration on Software Engineering*, 43–48. DOI: 10.1145/2647648.2647654

Kujala, J., Sachs, S., Leinonen, H., Heikkinen, A., & Laude, D. (2022). Stakeholder engagement: Past, present, and future. *Business & Society, 61*(5), 1136–1196. DOI: 10.1177/00076503211066595

Liao, C. (2017). Leadership in virtual teams: A multilevel perspective. *Human Resource Management Review, 27*(4), 648–659. DOI: 10.1016/j.hrmr.2016.12.010

Lim, W. M., Gunasekara, A., Pallant, J. L., Pallant, J. I., & Pechenkina, E. (2023). Generative AI and the future of education: Ragnarök or reformation? A paradoxical perspective from management educators. *International Journal of Management Education, 21*(2), 100790. DOI: 10.1016/j.ijme.2023.100790

Lisovska, L., Terebukh, A., & Hatsuk, M. (2019). Grounds of modern models and systems of organizational creativity support. *Journal of Lviv Polytechnic National University Series of Economics and Management Issues, 6*(3), 99–112. DOI: 10.23939/semi2019.03.099

Liu, T., Wu, Q., Chang, L., & Gu, T. (2022). A review of deep learning-based recommender system in e-learning environments. *Artificial Intelligence Review, 55*(8), 5953–5980. DOI: 10.1007/s10462-022-10135-2

Madaan, A., Tandon, N., Gupta, P., Hallinan, S., Gao, L., Wiegreffe, S., Alon, U., Dziri, N., Prabhumoye, S., Yang, Y., Welleck, S., Majumder, B. P., Gupta, S., Yazdanbakhsh, A., & Clark, P. (2023). Self-Refine: Iterative refinement with self-feedback. *arXiv (Cornell University)*. /arxiv.2303.17651DOI: 10.48550

Makruf, I., & Tejaningsih, E. (2023). Overcoming online learning challenges in the COVID-19 pandemic by user-friendly platform. *Journal of Education and Learning, 17*(2), 307–316. DOI: 10.11591/edulearn.v17i2.20513

Martínez-Peláez, R., Ochoa-Brust, A., Rivera, S., Félix, V. G., Ostos, R., Brito, H., Félix, R. A., & Mena, L. J. (2023). Role of digital transformation for achieving sustainability: Mediated role of stakeholders, key capabilities, and technology. *Sustainability, 15*(14), 11221. DOI: 10.3390/su151411221

Mayer, C., Sivatheerthan, T., Mütze-Niewöhner, S., & Nitsch, V. (2023). Sharing leadership behaviors in virtual teams: Effects of shared leadership behaviors on team member satisfaction and productivity. *Team Performance Management, 29*(1/2), 90–112. DOI: 10.1108/tpm-07-2022-0054

McLarnon, M. J. W., O'Neill, T. A., Taras, V., Law, D., Donia, M. B. L., & Steel, P. (2019). Global virtual team communication, coordination, and performance across three peer feedback strategies. *Canadian Journal of Behavioural Science/Revue Canadienne. Science et Comportement, 51*(4), 207–218. DOI: 10.1037/cbs0000135

Mengoni, M., Ceccacci, S., Giraldi, L., & Montanari, R. (2021). How to create engaging experiences from human emotions. *DIID, 74*(74). Advance online publication. DOI: 10.30682/diid7421b

Mnih, V., Badia, A. P., Mirza, M., Graves, A., Harley, T., Lillicrap, T. P., Silver, D., & Kavukcuoglu, K. (2016). Asynchronous methods for deep reinforcement learning. *arXiv (Cornell University).* /arxiv.1602.01783DOI: 10.48550

Mogavi, R. H., Deng, C., Kim, J. J., Zhou, P., Kwon, Y. D., Metwally, A. H. S., Tlili, A., Bassanelli, S., Bucchiarone, A., Gujar, S., Nacke, L. E., & Hui, P. (2023). ChatGPT in education: A blessing or a curse? A qualitative study exploring early adopters' utilization and perceptions. *Computers in Human Behavior Artificial Humans, 2*(1), 100027. DOI: 10.1016/j.chbah.2023.100027

Mohtar, M., & Md Yunus, M. (2022). A systematic review of online learning during COVID 19: Students' motivation, task engagement and acceptance. *Arab World English Journal (AWEJ) 2nd Special Issue on COVID-19.*

Morrison-Smith, S., & Ruiz, J. (2020). Challenges and barriers in virtual teams: A literature review. *SN Applied Sciences, 2*(6). Advance online publication. DOI: 10.1007/s42452-020-2801-5

Mulye, A., Bhasin, A., Borger, B., & Fant, C. (2023). Virtual immediate feedback with POCUS in Belize. *Frontiers in Digital Health, 5.* Advance online publication. DOI: 10.3389/fdgth.2023.1268905 PMID: 38026838

Muñoz, M., Negrón, A. P. P., & Hernández, L. (2020). Gamification in virtual reality environments for the integration of highly effective teams. In A. Negrón, G. López, & H. Aguirre (Eds.), *Virtual reality designs* (pp. 151–175). CRC Press eBooks. DOI: 10.1201/9781003019589-7

Nemiro, J. (2023). Virtual teams. In R. Reiter-Palmon & S. Hunter's (Eds.), *Handbook of organizational creativity: Group and individual influences,* 2nd edition (pp. 269–290). Elsevier Publishing.

Nguyen, T. H. (2023). Students' perceptions and practice of the blended learning approach to writing skills: Using Google Docs. *ICTE Conference Proceedings, 3,* 52–67. DOI: 10.54855/ictep.2335

Ogbeiwi, O. (2017). Why written objectives need to be really SMART. *British Journal of Health Care Management, 23*(7), 324–336. DOI: 10.12968/bjhc.2017.23.7.324

Oktavia, S., & Abdulkarim, A. (2022, January). The Use of the VCT Model in Civic Education to Build the Moral Awareness of Students in the Global Era. In *Annual Civic Education Conference (ACEC 2021)* (pp. 412-416). Atlantis Press.

Ouyang, L., Wu, J., Jiang, X., Almeida, D., Wainwright, C. L., Mishkin, P., Zhang, C., Agarwal, S., Slama, K., Ray, A., Schulman, J., Hilton, J., Kelton, F., Miller, L., Simens, M., Askell, A., Welinder, P., Christiano, P., Leike, J., & Lowe, R. (2022). Training language models to follow instructions with human feedback. *arXiv (Cornell University).* /arxiv.2203.02155DOI: 10.48550

Parović, M., Ansell, A., Vulić, I., & Korhonen, A. (2023). Cross-lingual transfer with target language-ready task adapters. *arXiv preprint arXiv:2306.02767.*

Petrescu, D., Enache, D., & Duta, L. (2022). Collaborative decision-making in online education. *Procedia Computer Science, 199,* 1090–1094. DOI: 10.1016/j.procs.2022.01.138

Prochazka, J., Ovcari, M., & Durinik, M. (2020). Sandwich feedback: The empirical evidence of its effectiveness. *Learning and Motivation, 71,* 101649. DOI: 10.1016/j.lmot.2020.101649

Raginsky, M. (2023). Biological autonomy. *Biological Theory, 18*(4), 303–308.

Ryan, R. M., & Deci, E. L. (2020). Intrinsic and extrinsic motivation from a self-determination theory perspective: Definitions, theory, practices, and future directions. *Contemporary Educational Psychology, 61,* 101860. DOI: 10.1016/j.cedpsych.2020.101860

Simmermeyer, E., Walsh, S., & Karcher, E. (2022). Associating Synchronous and Asynchronous Remote Teaching Formats with Student Situational Interest and Motivation. *NACTA Journal*. Advance online publication. DOI: 10.56103/4shou

Stahl, G. (2023). *Computer support for collaborative learning: Foundations for a Cscl Community (cscl 2002 Proceedings)*. Routledge eBooks. DOI: 10.4324/9781315045467

Swart, K., Bond-Barnard, T., & Chugh, R. (2022). *Challenges and critical success factors of digital communication, collaboration and knowledge sharing in project management virtual teams: A review*. AIS Electronic Library (AISeL). https://aisel.aisnet.org/ijispm/vol10/iss4/5/

Tausworthe, R. C. (1979). The work breakdown structure in software project management. *Journal of Systems and Software*, *1*, 181–186. DOI: 10.1016/0164-1212(79)90018-9

Thenuwara, D., Sanjani, L. K. K., & Anuththara, K. (2023). The Digital Transformation of Higher Education in Sri Lanka due to COVID-19. *KDU Institutional Repository,* 224-232. http://ir.kdu.ac.lk/handle/345/7051

Tipmontree, N. S., & Tasanameelarp, N. A. (2021). Using role playing activities to improve Thai EFL students' oral English communication skills. *International Journal of Business and Society*, *21*(3), 1215–1225. DOI: 10.33736/ijbs.3345.2020

Turaev, S., Al-Dabet, S., Babu, A., Rustamov, Z., Rustamov, J., Zaki, N., Mohamad, M. S., & Loo, C. K. (2023). Review and analysis of patients' body language from an artificial intelligence perspective. *IEEE Access : Practical Innovations, Open Solutions*, *11*, 62140–62173. DOI: 10.1109/access.2023.3287788

Vidolov, S. P. (2022). Virtual collaboration as co-enacting intercorporeality. *European Journal of Information Systems*, *33*(2), 244–266. DOI: 10.1080/0960085x.2022.2152743

Vizeshfar, F., Rakhshan, M., Shirazi, F., & Dokoohaki, R. (2022). The effect of time management education on critical care nurses' prioritization: A randomized clinical trial. *Acute and Critical Care*, *37*(2), 202–208. DOI: 10.4266/acc.2021.01123 PMID: 35545237

Widiyanto, A., Pujiarto, B., Prabowo, N. A., Hanafi, M., Widyanto, R. A., Avizenna, M. H., Rodito, J., & Fadhilla, N. M. (2023). Influence of blockchain implementation for virtual meetings at Home Learning Indonesia. [iJET]. *International Journal of Emerging Technologies in Learning*, *18*(06), 220–227. DOI: 10.3991/ijet.v18i06.37255

Zacharaki, K., & Sebastian-Galles, N. (2021). The ontogeny of early language discrimination: Beyond rhythm. *Cognition*, *213*, 104628. PMID: 33618839

Zahra, A., & Febria, D. (2023). Online collaborative writing to enhance students' writing motivation and writing ability. *ENGGANG Jurnal Pendidikan Bahasa Sastra Seni Dan Budaya, 3*(2), 132–144. DOI: 10.37304/enggang.v3i2.9120

Zhang, R., Duan, W., Flathmann, C., McNeese, N., Freeman, G., & Williams, A. (2023). Investigating AI teammate communication strategies and their impact in Human-AI teams for effective teamwork. *Proceedings of the ACM on Human-Computer Interaction, 7*(CSCW2), 1–31. DOI: 10.1145/3610072

Zhao, Y., & Liu, S. (2022). A Deep Learning Model with Virtual Reality Technology for Second Language Acquisition. *Mobile Information Systems*, *2022*, 1–7. DOI: 10.1155/2022/9686725

Compilation of References

Aaron De Smet, B. D. (2021, July 9). It's Time for Leaders to Get Real About Hybrid. *The McKinsey Quarterly*.

Afrouzi, H., Kwon, S. Y., Landier, A., Ma, Y., & Thesmar, D. (2023). Overreaction in expectations: Evidence and theory. *The Quarterly Journal of Economics*, *138*(3), 1713–1764. DOI: 10.1093/qje/qjad009

Ågerfalk, P. J., Fitzgerald, B., & Slaughter, S. A. (2009). Introduction to the special issue—flexible and distributed information systems development: State of the art and research challenges. *Information Systems Research*, *20*(3), 317–328.

Aguillon, S., & Cronin-Gilmore, J. (2024). How Remote Work Changes Communication in Organizations. *Journal of Behavioral and Applied Management*, *24*(3), 173–185.

Ahuja, M. K., & Galvin, J. E. (2003). Socialization in virtual groups. *Journal of Management*, *29*(2), 161–185.

Aissa, N. B., Gurău, C., Psychogios, A., & Somsing, A. (2022). Transactional memory systems in virtual teams: Communication antecedents and the impact of TMS components on creative processes and outcomes. *Technological Forecasting and Social Change*, *174*, 1–14.

Alam, A., & Mohanty, A. (2022, December). Facial analytics or virtual avatars: Competencies and design considerations for student-teacher interaction in AI-powered online education for effective classroom engagement. In *International Conference on Communication, Networks and Computing* (pp. 252-265). Springer Nature Switzerland. DOI: 10.1007/978-3-031-43145-6_21

Al-Ansi, A. M., Jaboob, M., Garad, A., & Al-Ansi, A. (2023). Analyzing augmented reality (AR) and virtual reality (VR) recent development in education. *Social Sciences & Humanities Open*, *8*(1), 100532. DOI: 10.1016/j.ssaho.2023.100532

Alenezi, M. (2023). Digital learning and digital institution in higher education. *Education Sciences*. Advance online publication. DOI: 10.3390/educsci13010088

Al-Husban, N. A., & Tawalbeh, M. (2023). EFL teachers' practices and perspectives on learner autonomy in virtual language learning environments in Jordan. *International Journal of Language Education, 1*(1), 1. DOI: 10.26858/ijole.v1i1.36156

Almusharraf, N. M., & Bailey, D. (2021). Online engagement during COVID-19: Role of agency on collaborative learning orientation and learning expectations. *Journal of Computer Assisted Learning, 37*(5), 1285–1295. PMID: 34226784

Alsharo, M., Gregg, D., & Ramirez, R. (2017). Virtual team effectiveness: The role of knowledge sharing and trust. *Information & Management, 54*, 479–490. DOI: 10.1016/j.im.2016.10.005

Amankwah-Amoah, J., Abdalla, S., Mogaji, E., Elbanna, A., & Dwivedi, Y. K. (2024). The impending disruption of creative industries by generative AI: Opportunities, challenges, and research agenda. *International Journal of Information Management, 102759*. Advance online publication. DOI: 10.1016/j.ijinfomgt.2024.102759

Anderson, N. R., & West, M. A. (1998). Measuring climate for work group innovation: Development and validation of the team climate inventory. *Journal of Organizational Behavior, 19*(3), 235–258.

Antwi-Amoabeng, D., Beutler, B. D., Chahal, G., Mahboob, S., Gullapalli, N., Tedja, R., Madhani-Lovely, F., & Rowan, C. (2021). Ensuring trust in COVID-19 data. *Medicine, 100*(35), e26972. DOI: 10.1097/md.0000000000026972 PMID: 34477127

Arao, B., & Clemens, K. (2013). From safe spaces to brave spaces: A new way to frame dialogue around diversity and social justice. In Landreman, L. M. (Ed.), *The art of effective facilitation* (pp. 135–150). Routledge.

Argyris, C. (1977). *Double Loop Learning in Organizations*. Retrieved February 19, 2025, from https://hbr.org/1977/09/double-loop-learning-in-organizations

Argyris, C. (1991). Teaching smart people how to learn. *Harvard Business Review*. https://hbr.org/1991/05/teaching-smart-people-how-to-learn

Argyris, C. (1994). Good Communication That Blocks Learning. *Harvard Business Review, 72*(4), 4.

Argyris, C., & Schön, D. A. (1978). *Organizational learning: A theory of action perspective*. Addison-Wesley.

Aron, A., Melinat, E., Aron, E. N., Vallone, R. D., & Bator, R. J. (1997). The experimental generation of interpersonal closeness: A procedure and some preliminary findings. *Personality and Social Psychology Bulletin, 23*(4), 363–377. DOI: 10.1177/0146167297234003

Arora, A., Nakov, P., Hardalov, M., Sarwar, S. M., Nayak, V., Dinkov, Y., Zlatkova, D., Dent, K., Bhatawdekar, A., Bouchard, G., & Augenstein, I. (2021). Detecting harmful content on online platforms: What platforms need vs. where research efforts go. *arXiv (Cornell University)*. /arxiv.2103.00153DOI: 10.48550

Arrieta, A. B., Díaz-Rodríguez, N., Del Ser, J., Bennetot, A., Tabik, S., Barbado, A., Garcia, S., Gil-Lopez, S., Molina, D., Benjamins, R., Chatila, R., & Herrera, F. (2019). Explainable Artificial Intelligence (XAI): Concepts, taxonomies, opportunities and challenges toward responsible AI. *Information Fusion, 58*, 82–115. DOI: 10.1016/j.inffus.2019.12.012

Auernhammer, J., & Roth, B. (2021). The origin and evolution of Stanford University's design thinking: From product design to design thinking in innovation management. *Journal of Product Innovation Management, 38*(6), 623–644. DOI: 10.1111/jpim.12594

Axtell, C. M., Fleck, S. J., & Turner, N. (2004). Virtual teams: Collaborating across distance. *International Review of Industrial and Organizational Psychology, 19*, 205–248.

Babbar, M., & Gupta, T. (2022). Response of educational institutions to COVID-19 pandemic: An inter-country comparison. *Policy Futures in Education*. Advance online publication. DOI: 10.1177/14782103211021937 PMID: 40478015

Back, M. D. (2018). The narcissistic admiration and rivalry concept. In Hermann, A. D., Brunell, A., & Foster, J. D. (Eds.), *Handbook of trait narcissism: Key advances, research methods, and controversies* (pp. 57–67). Springer. DOI: 10.1007/978-3-319-92171-6_6

Bailenson, J. N. (2021). Nonverbal overload: A theoretical argument for the causes of Zoom fatigue. *Technology, Mind, and Behavior, 2*(1), 1–6.

Balthazard, P., Potter, R. E., & Warren, J. (2004). Expertise, extraversion and group interaction styles as performance indicators in virtual teams: How do perceptions of IT's performance get formed? *The Data Base for Advances in Information Systems, 35*(1), 41–64. DOI: 10.1145/968464.968469

Bandura, A. (1997). *Self-efficacy: The exercise of control*. W. H. Freeman.

Banerjee, A., Taylor, D., Stranz, A., & Wahl, A. (2021). Facilitated reflection meetings as a relational approach to problem-solving within long-term care facilities. *Journal of Aging Studies*. Advance online publication. DOI: 10.1016/j.jaging.2021.100965 PMID: 34794710

Barrick, M. R., & Mount, M. K. (1991). The Big Five personality dimensions and job performance: A meta-analysis. *Personnel Psychology*, *44*(1), 1–26. DOI: 10.1111/j.1744-6570.1991.tb00688.x

Barron, T., Friend, M., Dieker, L., & Kohnke, S. (2022). Co-teaching in uncertain times: Using technology to improve student learning and manage today's complex educational landscape. *Journal of Special Education Technology*, *37*(3), 439–446. DOI: 10.1177/01626434211033579

Baruah, J., & Green, K. (2023). Innovation in virtual teams: The critical role of anonymity across divergent and convergent thinking processes. *The Journal of Creative Behavior*. Advance online publication. DOI: 10.1002/jocb.603

Bashir, S., & Lapshun, A. L. (2025). E-learning future trends in higher education in the 2020s and beyond. *Cogent Education*, *12*(1), 2445331.

Basilotta-Gómez-Pablos, V., Matarranz, M., Casado-Aranda, L., & Otto, A. (2022). Teachers' digital competencies in higher education: A systematic literature review. *International Journal of Educational Technology in Higher Education*, *19*(1). Advance online publication. DOI: 10.1186/s41239-021-00312-8

Baumeister, R. F., & Vohs, K. D. (2007). Self-Regulation, ego depletion, and motivation. *Social and Personality Psychology Compass*, *1*(1), 115–128.

Beal, D. J., Cohen, R. R., Burke, M. J., & McLendon, C. L. (2003). Cohesion and performance in groups: A meta-analytic clarification of construct relations. *The Journal of Applied Psychology*, *88*(6), 989. PMID: 14640811

Behfar, K. J., Peterson, R. S., Mannix, E. A., & Trochim, W. M. (2008). The critical role of conflict resolution in teams: A close look at the links between conflict type, conflict management strategies, and team outcomes. *The Journal of Applied Psychology*, *93*(1), 170. PMID: 18211143

Bell, B. S., & Kozlowski, S. W. J. (2002). A typology of virtual teams: Implications for effective leadership. *Group & Organization Management*, *27*(1), 14–49. DOI: 10.1177/1059601102027001003

Bellemare, M. G., Naddaf, Y., Veness, J., & Bowling, M. (2013). The Arcade Learning Environment: An evaluation platform for general agents. *Journal of Artificial Intelligence Research*, *47*, 253–279. DOI: 10.1613/jair.3912

Bell, S. T. (2007). Deep-level composition variables as predictors of team performance: A meta-analysis. *The Journal of Applied Psychology*, *92*(3), 595–615. DOI: 10.1037/0021-9010.92.3.595 PMID: 17484544

Bell, S. T., Brown, S. G., Colaneri, A., & Outland, N. (2018). Team composition and the ABCs of teamwork. *The American Psychologist*, *73*(4), 349–362. DOI: 10.1037/amp0000305 PMID: 29792453

Bell, S. T., & Marentette, B. J. (2011). Team viability for long-term and ongoing organizational teams. *Organizational Psychology Review*, *1*(4), 275–292.

Benhelal, E., Shamsaei, E., & Rashid, M. I. (2021). Challenges against CO2 abatement strategies in cement industry: *A review. Journal of Environmental Sciences (China)*. Advance online publication. DOI: 10.1016/j.jes.2020.11.020 PMID: 33985750

Bennett, L. M. (2024). Mindset matters for interdisciplinary teams: Choose a collaborative one. *Integration and Implementation Insights*. https://i2insights.org/2024/07/23/collaborative-mindset-for-teamwork/

Bennett, E. E., & McWhorter, R. R. (2021). Virtual HRD's role in crisis and the post Covid-19 professional lifeworld: Accelerating skills for digital transformation. *Advances in Developing Human Resources*, *23*(1), 5–25. DOI: 10.1177/1523422320973288

Bennett, L. M., & Gadlin, H. (2019). Conflict Prevention and Management in Science Teams. In Hall, K. L., Vogel, A. L., & Croyle, R. T. (Eds.), *Strategies for Team Science Success: Handbook of Evidence-Based Principles for Cross-Disciplinary Science and Practical Lessons Learned from Health Researchers* (pp. 295–302). Springer International Publishing. DOI: 10.1007/978-3-030-20992-6_2

Bennett, L. M., Gadlin, H., & Marchand, C. (2018). *Collaboration and team science: A field guide* (2nd ed.). NIH. https://www.lmbennettconsulting.com/_files/ugd/40747d_8058cb6e909242f896721f82beb99801.pdf

Bevins, F., Bryant, J., Krishnan, C., & Law, J. (2020). Coronavirus: How should US higher education plan for an uncertain future? In *The path to the next normal* (pp. 120-125). McKinsey & Company.

Binyamin, G., & Carmeli, A. (2017). Fostering members' creativity in teams: The role of structuring of human resource management processes. *Psychology of Aesthetics, Creativity, and the Arts*, *11*(1), 18–33. DOI: 10.1037/aca0000088

Birenbaum, A. (1984). Toward a theory of role acquisition. *Sociological Theory*, *2*, 315–328.

Biró, A., Cuesta-Vargas, A. I., Martín-Martín, J., Szilágyi, L., & Szilágyi, S. M. (2023). Synthetized multilanguage OCR using CRNN and SVTR models for real-time collaborative tools. *Applied Sciences (Basel, Switzerland)*, *13*(7), 4419. DOI: 10.3390/app13074419

Blay, T., Froese, F. J., Taras, V., & Gunkel, M. (2023). Convergence of collaborative behavior in virtual teams: The role of external crises and implications for performance. *The Journal of Applied Psychology*, *109*(4), 469–489. DOI: 10.1037/apl0001133 PMID: 37917493

Bolinger, A. R., Bonner, B. L., & Okhuysen, G. A. (2009). Sticking together: The glue role and group creativity. In Mannix, E., Goncalo, J., & Neale, M. (Eds.), *Creativity in Groups* (Vol. 12, pp. 267–289). Emerald Group Publishing Limited.

Bomström, H., Kelanti, M., Annanperä, E., Liukkunen, K., Kilamo, T., Sievi-Korte, O., & Systä, K. (2023). Information needs and presentation in agile software development. *Information and Software Technology*, *162*, 107265. DOI: 10.1016/j.infsof.2023.107265

Bonfadelli, H. (2002). The Internet and Knowledge Gaps: A Theoretical and Empirical Investigation. *European Journal of Communication*, *17*(1), 65–84.

Borg, M. E., Butterfield, K. M., Wood, E., Zhang, H. H., & Pinto, S. (2021). Investigating the impacts of personality on the use and perceptions of online collaborative platforms in higher education. *SN Social Sciences*, *1*(40), 1–22. DOI: 10.1007/s43545-020-00053-x PMID: 34693305

Boser, U. (2017). *Learn Better: Mastering the Skills for Success in Life, Business, and School, or How to Become an Expert in Just about Anything*. Rodale Publishing.

Boulter, M. W., Roberts, R., & Hardy, J. (2022). Upsetting the apple cart: Within-team profiles of intragroup conflict and their associations with narcissism. *Psychology of Sport and Exercise*, *63*, 102291. DOI: 10.1016/j.psychsport.2022.102291

Bremner, S., Peirson-Smith, A., Jones, R., & Bhatia, V. (2014). Task design and interaction in collaborative writing: The students' story. *Business and Professional Communication Quarterly*, *77*(2), 150–168. DOI: 10.1177/2329490613514598

Breuer, C., Hüffmeier, J., & Hertel, G. (2016). Does trust matter more in virtual teams? A meta-analysis of trust and team effectiveness considering virtuality and documentation as moderators. *The Journal of Applied Psychology*, *101*(8), 1151–1177. DOI: 10.1037/apl0000113 PMID: 27228105

Brew, M. (2025). *Microlearning: A Beginner's Guide*. Retrieved from EduMe: https://www.edume.com/blog/what-is-microlearning

Brown, R. P., Budzek, K., & Tamborski, M. (2009). On the meaning and measure of narcissism. *Personality and Social Psychology Bulletin, 35*(7), 951–964. DOI: 10.1177/0146167209335461 PMID: 19487486

Brown, S. A., Sparapani, R., Osinski, K., Zhang, J., Blessing, J., Cheng, F., & Olson, J. (2023). Team principles for successful interdisciplinary research teams. *American Heart Journal Plus : Cardiology Research and Practice, 32*, 100306. DOI: 10.1016/j.ahjo.2023.100306 PMID: 38510201

Burgess, A., van Diggele, C., Roberts, C., & Mellis, C. (2020). Facilitating small group learning in the health professions. *BMC Medical Education, 20*, 1–6. PMID: 33272270

Burke, C. S., Stagl, K. C., Salas, E., Pierce, L., & Kendall, D. (2006). Understanding team adaptation: A conceptual analysis and model. *The Journal of Applied Psychology, 91*(6), 1189–1207. DOI: 10.1037/0021-9010.91.6.1189 PMID: 17100478

Burt, B. A., Stone, B.Jr, Perkins, T., Polk, A., Ramirez, C., & Rosado, J. (2022). Team culture of community: Cultural practices for scientific team cohesion and productivity. *Small Group Research, 53*(6), 855–890. DOI: 10.1177/10464964221097699

Bushe, G. R., & Coetzer, G. H. (2007). Group development and team effectiveness: Using cognitive representations to measure group development and predict task performance and group viability. *The Journal of Applied Behavioral Science, 43*(2), 184–212.

Bush-Evans, R. (2020). *There's no I in team but there is a me: The influence of narcissism on team processes and organisational outcomes* (Doctoral dissertation, University of Southampton).

Cabrera, A. F., Crissman, J. L., Bernal, E. M., Nora, A., Terenzini, P. T., & Pascarella, E. T. (2002). Collaborative learning: Its impact on college students' development and diversity. *Journal of College Student Development, 43*(1), 20–34.

Cai, Y. L. (2023). Strengthening perceptions of virtual team cohesiveness and effectiveness in the new normal: A hyperpersonal communication theory perspective. *Asian Business & Management, 22*, 1649-1682. *Article, 1.* Advance online publication. DOI: 10.1057/s41291-023-00225-6 PMID: 40479004

Campbell, W. K., Brunell, A. B., & Finkel, E. J. (2006). Narcissism, Interpersonal Self-Regulation, and Romantic Relationships: An Agency Model Approach. In Vohs, K. D., & Finkel, E. J. (Eds.), *Self and relationships: Connecting intrapersonal and interpersonal processes* (pp. 57–83). The Guilford Press.

Campbell, W. K., Goodie, A. S., & Foster, J. D. (2004). Narcissism, confidence, and risk attitude. *Journal of Behavioral Decision Making*, *17*(4), 297–312. DOI: 10.1002/bdm.475

Campbell, W. K., Rudich, E. A., & Sedikides, C. (2002). Narcissism, self-esteem, and the positivity of self-views: Two portraits of self-love. *Personality and Social Psychology Bulletin*, *28*(3), 358–368. DOI: 10.1177/0146167202286007

Campion, M. A., Medsker, G. J., & Higgs, A. C. (1993). Relations between work group characteristics and effectiveness: Implications for designing effective work groups. *Personnel Psychology*, *46*(4), 823–847. DOI: 10.1111/j.1744-6570.1993.tb01571.x

Carby, N. (2023). Personalized feedback in a virtual learning environment. *Journal of Educational Supervision*, *6*(1), 36–44. DOI: 10.31045/jes.6.1.3

Carnevale, P. J., & Probst, T. M. (1998). Social values and social conflict in creative problem solving and categorization. *Journal of Personality and Social Psychology*, *74*(5), 1300–1309. DOI: 10.1037/0022-3514.74.5.1300 PMID: 9866189

Carron, A. V. (1982). Cohesiveness in sport groups: Interpretations and considerations. *Journal of Sport & Exercise Psychology*, *4*(2), 123–138.

Carron, A. V., Colman, M. M., Wheeler, J., & Stevens, D. (2002). Cohesion and performance in sport: A meta-analysis. *Journal of Sport & Exercise Psychology*, *24*(2), 168–188. DOI: 10.1123/jsep.24.2.168

Carron, A. V., Widmeyer, W. N., & Brawley, L. R. (1985). The development of an instrument to assess cohesion in sport teams: The Group Environment Questionnaire. *Journal of Sport & Exercise Psychology*, *7*(3), 244–266.

Casteneda, D. I., & Cuellar, S. (2020). Knowledge sharing and innovation: A systematic review. *Knowledge and Process Management*, *27*(3), 159–173.

Chamakiotis, P., Dekonick, E. A., & Panteli, N. (2013). Factors influencing creativity in virtual design teams: An interplay between technology, teams, and individuals. *Creativity and Innovation Management*, *22*(3), 265–279.

Chan, C. K. Y. (2023). A comprehensive AI policy education framework for university teaching and learning. *International Journal of Educational Technology in Higher Education*, *20*(1), 38. DOI: 10.1186/s41239-023-00408-3

Chandra, A. N. R., Jamiy, F. E., & Reza, H. (2022). A systematic survey on cybersickness in virtual environments. *Computers*, *11*(4), 51. DOI: 10.3390/computers11040051

Charlier, S. D., Stewart, G. L., Greco, L. M., & Reeves, C. J. (2016). Emergent leadership in virtual teams: A multilevel investigation of individual communication and team dispersion antecedents. *The Leadership Quarterly*, *27*(5), 745–764. DOI: 10.1016/j.leaqua.2016.05.002

Chatman, J. A., & Flynn, F. J. (2001). The influence of demographic heterogeneity on the emergence and consequences of cooperative norms in work teams. *Academy of Management Journal*, *44*, 956–974.

Chatterjee, S. (2005). Children's friendship with place: A conceptual inquiry. *Children, Youth and Environments*, *15*(1), 1–26. DOI: 10.1353/cye.2005.0057

Chaudhary, M., Chopra, S., & Kaur, J. (2022). Cohesion as a cardinal antecedent in virtual team performance: A meta-analysis. *Team Performance Management*, *28*(5/6), 398–414.

Chen, M. H. (2006). Understanding the benefits and detriments of conflict on team creativity process. *Creativity and Innovation Management*, *15*(1), 105–116.

Chiocchio, F., & Essiembre, H. (2009). Cohesion and performance: A meta-analytic review of disparities between project teams, production teams, and service teams. *Small Group Research*, *40*(4), 382–420. DOI: 10.1177/1046496409335103

Choudhary, R., Shaik, Y. A., Yadav, P., & Rashid, A. (2024). Generational differences in technology behavior: A systematic literature review. *Journal of Infrastructure. Policy and Development*, *8*(9), 6755.

Chrimes, N., Higgs, A., Hagberg, C. A., Baker, P. A., Cooper, R. M., Greif, R., & Cook, T. M. (2022). Preventing unrecognised oesophageal intubation: A consensus guideline from the Project for Universal Management of Airways and international airway societies. *Anaesthesia*, *77*(12), 1395–1415. DOI: 10.1111/anae.15817 PMID: 35977431

Christian, M. S., Bradley, J. C., Wallace, J. C., & Burke, M. J. (2009). Workplace safety: A meta-analysis of the roles of person and situation factors. *The Journal of Applied Psychology*, *94*(5), 1103–1127. DOI: 10.1037/a0016172 PMID: 19702360

Cirella, S. (2021). Managing collective creativity: Organizational variables to support creative teamwork. *European Management Review*, *18*(4), 404–417.

Cloud, H. (2023). *Trust: Knowing when to give it, when to withhold it, how to earn it, and how to fix it when it gets broken*. Worthy Publishing.

Cogliser, C. C., Gardner, W. L., Gavin, M. B., & Broberg, J. C. (2012). Big five personality factors and leader emergence in virtual teams: Relationships with team trustworthiness, member performance contributions, and team performance. *Group & Organization Management, 37*(6), 752–784. DOI: 10.1177/1059601112464266

Cohen, E. G. (1994). Restructuring the classroom: Conditions for productive small groups. *Review of Educational Research, 64*(1), 1–35.

Cohen, T. N., Griggs, A. C., Kanji, F. F., Cohen, K. A., Lazzara, E. H., Keebler, J. R., & Gewertz, B. L. (2021). Advancing team cohesion: Using an escape room as a novel approach. *Journal of Patient Safety and Risk Management, 26*(3), 126–134.

Cook-Sather, A. (2016). Creating brave spaces within and through student-faculty pedagogical partnerships. *Teaching and Learning Together in Higher Education, 1*(18), 1.

Cotten, S. R., & Jelenewicz, S. M. (2006). A Disappearing Digital Divide Among College Students? Peeling Away the Layers of the Digital Divide. *Social Science Computer Review, 24*(4), 497–506.

Cotterill, S. T. (2017). *Team Psychology in Sports: Theory and Practice*. Routledge.

Cox, P. L., & Bobrowski, P. E. (2016). The team charter assignment: Improving the effectiveness of classroom teams. *Journal of Behavioral and Applied Management, 1*(2), 789–805.

Crisp, C. B., & Jarvenpaa, S. L. (2013). Swift Trust in Global Virtual Teams: Trusting Beliefs and Normative Actions. *Journal of Personnel Psychology, 12*(1), 45–56.

Cronin, M. A., & Weingart, L. R. (2007). Representational gaps, information processing, and conflict in functionally diverse teams. *Academy of Management Review, 32*(3), 761–773. DOI: 10.5465/amr.2007.25275511

Dallimore, E.J., J. H. (2016). Creating a Community of Learning Through Classroom Discussion: Student Perceptions of the Relationships Among Participation Learning, Comfort and Preparation. *Journal on Excellence in College Teaching, 27*(3), 137–171.

Daraojimba, E. C., Nwasike, C. N., Adegbite, A. O., Ezeigweneme, C. A., & Gidiagba, J. O. (2024). Comprehensive review of agile methodologies in project management. *Computer Science & IT Research Journal, 5*(1), 190–218. DOI: 10.51594/csitrj.v5i.717

Day, D. V., Riggio, R. E., Tan, S. J., & Conger, J. A. (2021). Advancing the science of 21st-century leadership development: Theory, research, and practice. *The Leadership Quarterly*. Advance online publication. DOI: 10.1016/j.leaqua.2021.101557

De Dreu, C. K. W., Evers, A., Beersma, B., Kluwer, E. S., & Nauta, A. (2001). A theory-based measure of conflict management strategies in the workplace. *Journal of Organizational Behavior*, *22*(6), 645–668. DOI: 10.1002/job.107

De Dreu, C. K., & Weingart, L. R. (2003). Task versus relationship conflict, team performance, and team member satisfaction: A meta-analysis. *The Journal of Applied Psychology*, *88*(4), 741–749. DOI: 10.1037/0021-9010.88.4.741 PMID: 12940412

De Jong, B. A., Dirks, K. T., & Gillespie, N. (2016). Trust and team performance: A meta-analysis of main effects, moderators, and covariates. *The Journal of Applied Psychology*, *101*(8), 1134–1150. DOI: 10.1037/apl0000110 PMID: 27123697

De Wit, F. R., Greer, L. L., & Jehn, K. A. (2012). The paradox of intragroup conflict: A meta-analysis. *The Journal of Applied Psychology*, *97*(2), 360. PMID: 21842974

DeChurch, L. A., & Marks, M. A. (2001). Maximizing the benefits of task conflict: The role of conflict management. *International Journal of Conflict Management*, *12*(1), 4–22.

DeChurch, L. A., & Mesmer-Magnus, J. R. (2010). The cognitive underpinnings of effective teamwork: A meta-analysis. *The Journal of Applied Psychology*, *95*(1), 32–53. DOI: 10.1037/a0017328 PMID: 20085405

DeChurch, L. A., Mesmer-Magnus, J. R., & Doty, D. (2013). Moving beyond relationship and task conflict: Toward a process-state perspective. *The Journal of Applied Psychology*, *98*(4), 559–578. DOI: 10.1037/a0032896 PMID: 23731027

Deem, J., Beyer, S., Dana, H., Chicone, R., Ringler, I., Ferebee, S., & Strouble, D. (2020). Increasing Student Success with Team Projects in the Virtual Classroom. *Online Journal of Distance Learning Administration*, *23*(3).

Delahunty, J., Verenikina, I., & Jones, P. (2013). Socio-emotional connections: Identity, belonging and learning in online interactions. A literature review. *Technology, Pedagogy and Education*, *23*(2), 243–265. DOI: 10.1080/1475939x.2013.813405

Dennis, A. R., Fuller, R. M., & Valacich, J. S. (2008). Media, tasks, and communication processes: A theory of media synchronicity. *Management Information Systems Quarterly*, *32*, 575–600.

Dennis, A. S., Barlow, J. B., & Dennis, A. R. (2022). The power of introverts: Personality and intelligence in virtual teams. *Journal of Management Information Systems, 39*(1), 102–129. DOI: 10.1080/07421222.2021.2023408

DeRosa, D. M., Hantula, D. A., Kock, N., & D'Arcy, J. (2004). Trust and leadership in virtual teamwork: A media naturalness perspective. *Human Resource Management, 43*(2–3), 219–232. DOI: 10.1002/hrm.20016

DeShon, R. P., Kozlowski, S. W. J., Schmidt, A. M., Milner, K. R., & Wiechmann, D. (2004). A multiple-goal, multilevel model of feedback effects on the regulation of individual and team performance. *The Journal of Applied Psychology, 89*(6), 1035–1056. DOI: 10.1037/0021-9010.89.6.1035 PMID: 15584840

Devdas, D. (2024). *The human equation: Penta factor.* Notion Press.

Devine, D. J., Habig, J. K., Martin, K. E., Bott, J. P., & Grayson, A. L. (2004). Tinsel Town: A top management simulation involving distributed expertise. *Simulation & Gaming, 35*(1), 94–134. DOI: 10.1177/1046878103258I

Deželak, Z., Zabukovšek, S. S., & Bobek, S. (2023). Changes of Collaboration Platforms' Use Perceived by Users Because of COVID: A Research Study of Changes in User Experience of Microsoft Teams Platform. In Birdie, A. K., & Joshi, R. (Eds.), *Reshaping the business world post-COVID-19: Management strategies for sustainable behavior change* (pp. 93–125). Apple Academic Press. DOI: 10.1201/9781003372424

Di Maggio, M., & Van Alstyne, M. W. (2013). Information sharing, social norms and performance. *Social Norms and Performance (July 9, 2013).*

Dickson, J. M., Moberly, N. J., Preece, D., Dodd, A., & Huntley, C. D. (2021). Self-regulatory goal motivational processes in sustained new year resolution pursuit and mental wellbeing. *International Journal of Environmental Research and Public Health, 18*(6), 3084. DOI: 10.3390/ijerph18063084 PMID: 33802749

Dincă, M., Lu trea, A., Oni iu, A., Cra ovan, M., & Berge, T. (2021). The effects of disciplinary composition on virtual learning group process dynamics: Students' perspectives. *Sustainability*. Advance online publication. DOI: 10.3390/su13158493

Donate, M. J., González-Mohíno, M., Appio, F. P., & Bernhard, F. (2022). Dealing with knowledge hiding to improve innovation capabilities in the hotel industry: The unconventional role of knowledge-oriented leadership. *Journal of Business Research, 144*, 572–586. DOI: 10.1016/j.jbusres.2022.02.001

Donelan, H., & Kear, K. (2024). Online group projects in higher education: Persistent challenges and implications for practice. *Journal of Computing in Higher Education*. Advance online publication. DOI: 10.1007/s12528-023-09360-7 PMID: 37359044

Donia, M. B. L., O'Neill, T. A., & Brutus, S. (2018). The longitudinal effects of peer feedback in the development and transfer of student teamwork skills. *Learning and Individual Differences*, *61*, 87–98. DOI: 10.1016/j.lindif.2017.11.012

Douglas, H., Bore, M., & Munro, D. (2012). Distinguishing the dark triad: Evidence from the five-factor model and the Hogan development survey. *Psychology (Irvine, Calif.)*, *3*(3), 237–242. DOI: 10.4236/psych.2012.33033

Drach-Zahavy, A., & Somech, A. (2001). Understanding team innovation: The role of team processes and structures. *Group Dynamics*, *5*(2), 111–123.

Dulebohn, J. H., & Hoch, J. E. (2017). Virtual teams in organizations. *Human Resource Management Review*, *27*(4), 569–574. DOI: 10.1016/j.hrmr.2016.12.004

Dumford, A. D., & Miller, A. L. (2018). Online learning in higher education: Exploring advantages and disadvantages for engagement. *Journal of Computing in Higher Education*, *30*(3), 452–465. DOI: 10.1007/s12528-018-9179-z

Dusenberry, L., & Robinson, J. (2020). Building psychological safety through training interventions: Manage the team, not just the project. *IEEE Transactions on Professional Communication*, *63*, 207–226.

Du, T. V., Miller, J. D., & Lynam, D. R. (2022). The relation between narcissism and aggression: A meta-analysis. *Journal of Personality*, *90*(4), 574–594. DOI: 10.1111/jopy.12684 PMID: 34689345

Du, X., Zhang, H., Zhang, S., Zhang, A., & Chen, B. (2021). Creativity and leadership in the creative industry: A study from the perspective of social norms. *Frontiers in Psychology*, *12*, 651817. Advance online publication. DOI: 10.3389/fpsyg.2021.651817 PMID: 33889118

Edirisinghe, G. S., Trindade, M. A., & Luo, L. (2024). Game changer: Cloud-based classroom interactions powered by Google Sheets. *Decision Sciences Journal of Innovative Education*, *22*(3), 197–211. DOI: 10.1111/dsji.12316

Edmondson, A. (1999). Psychological safety and learning behavior in work teams. *Administrative Science Quarterly*, *44*(2), 350–383. DOI: 10.2307/2666999

Edmondson, A. C. (2004). Learning from failure in health care: Frequent opportunities, pervasive barriers. *BMJ Quality & Safety*, *13*(suppl 2), ii3–ii9. PMID: 15576689

Edmondson, A. C. (2011). Strategies for learning from failure. *Harvard Business Review*, *89*(4), 48–55. PMID: 21510518

Edmondson, A. C. (2019). *The fearless organization: Creating psychological safety in the workplace for learning, innovation, and growth.* John Wiley & Sons, Inc.

Edmondson, A. C., & Bransby, D. P. (2023). Psychological safety comes of age: Observed themes in an established literature. *Annual Review of Organizational Psychology and Organizational Behavior, 10*(1), 55–78.

Edmondson, A. C., Dillon, J. R., & Roloff, K. S. (2007). 6 three perspectives on team learning: Outcome improvement, task Mastery, and group process. *The Academy of Management Annals, 1*(1), 269–314.

Edmondson, A. C., & Lei, Z. (2014). Psychological safety: The history, renaissance, and future of an interpersonal construct. *Annual Review of Organizational Psychology and Organizational Behavior, 1*(1), 23–43. DOI: 10.1146/annurev-orgpsych-031413-091305

Edmondson, A. C., Winslow, A. B., Bohmer, R. M., & Pisano, G. P. (2003). Learning how and learning what: Effects of tacit and codified knowledge on performance improvement following technology adoption. *Decision Sciences, 34*(2), 197–224.

Edmondson, A., & Mogelof, J. P. (2006). Explaining psychological safety in innovation teams: Organizational culture, team dynamics, or personality. In Thompson, L. L., & Choi, H. S. (Eds.), *Creativity and innovation in organizational teams* (pp. 109–138). Lawrence Erlbaum Associates.

Egan, G. (2006). *The skilled helper: A problem-management and opportunity development approach to helping* (2nd ed.). Thomson.

Eisman, A. B., Kim, B., Salloum, R. G., Shuman, C. J., & Glasgow, R. E. (2022). Advancing rapid adaptation for urgent public health crises: Using implementation science to facilitate effective and efficient responses. *Frontiers in Public Health, 10*, 959567. DOI: 10.3389/fpubh.2022.959567 PMID: 36091566

Eklund, M., & Isotalus, P. (2024). Having it both ways: Learning communication skills in face-to-face and online environments. *Frontiers in Education*. Advance online publication. DOI: 10.3389/feduc.2024.1270164

Elforgani, M. S. A., Alabsi, A. A. N., & Alwarafi, A. (2024). Strategic Approaches to Design Teams for Construction Quality Management and Green Building Performance. *Buildings (Basel, Switzerland)*. Advance online publication. DOI: 10.3390/buildings14072020

Ellis, S., & Davidi, I. (2005). After-event reviews: Drawing lessons from successful and failed experience. *The Journal of Applied Psychology, 90*(5), 857–871. DOI: 10.1037/0021-9010.90.5.857 PMID: 16162059

Ellis, S., Mendel, R., & Nir, M. (2006). Learning from successful and failed experience: The moderating role of kind of after-event review. *The Journal of Applied Psychology*, *91*(3), 669–680. DOI: 10.1037/0021-9010.91.3.669 PMID: 16737362

Elsheikh, A. H. (2023). Applications of machine learning in friction stir welding: Prediction of joint properties, real-time control and tool failure diagnosis. *Engineering Applications of Artificial Intelligence*, *121*, 105961. DOI: 10.1016/j.engappai.2023.105961

Emberson, R., Kirschbaum, D., & Stanley, T. (2021). Global connections between El Nino and landslide impacts. *Nature Communications*, *12*(1). Advance online publication. DOI: 10.1038/s41467-021-22398-4 PMID: 33859185

Emich, K. J., Lu, L., Ferguson, A., Peterson, R. S., & McCourt, M. (2022). Team composition revisited: A team member attribute alignment approach. *Organizational Research Methods*, *25*(4), 642–672. DOI: 10.1177/10944281211042388

Emich, K. J., McCourt, M., Lu, L., Ferguson, A., & Peterson, R. (2024). Team composition revisited: Expanding the team member attribute alignment approach to consider patterns of more than two attributes. *Organizational Research Methods*, *27*(2), 329–348. DOI: 10.1177/10944281231166656

Engineers Canada. (2021). *Trends in engineering enrolment and degrees awarded in 2016–2020*. https://engineerscanada.ca/reports/enrolment-and-degrees-awarded-report/canadian-engineers-for-tomorrow-2020

Erdem, F., & Ozen, J. (2003). Cognitive and affective dimensions of trust in developing team performance. *Team Performance Management*, *9*(5/6), 131–135.

Erdős, F., Németh, R., & Firuza, B. (2023). Virtual teamwork in gamified 3D environment. *Híradástechnika/Infocommunications Journal, 15*(Special Issue), 15–20. DOI: 10.36244/icj.2023.si-iodcr.3

Fadiyah, F., Fuadi, A., Nurjannah, N., Irmayanti, I., & Lita, W. (2023). QUIZIZZ Application-Based Interactive Learning Media Development Workshop for Junior High School Teacher. *Pengabdian Jurnal Abdimas*, *1*(2), 59–65. DOI: 10.55849/abdimas.v1i2.157

Fairchild, J., & Hunter, S. T. (2014). "We've Got Creative Differences": The effects of task conflict and participative safety on team creative performance. *The Journal of Creative Behavior*, *48*(1), 64–87.

Feldman, M. S., & Pentland, B. T. (2003). Reconceptualizing organizational routines as a source of flexibility and change. *Administrative Science Quarterly*, *48*(1), 94–118. DOI: 10.2307/3556620

Felty, R., Whitaker, B. G., Bergman, S. M., & Bergman, J. Z. (2015). The longitudinal influence of narcissism in the team context. *International Journal of Organization Theory and Behavior, 18*(2), 147–176. DOI: 10.1108/IJOTB-18-02-2015-B001

Ferdous, T., & Karim, A. (2019). Working in Groups outside the Classroom: Affective Challenges and Probable Solutions. *International Journal of Instruction, 12*, 341–358.

Fischer, J., Alpert, A., & Rao, P. (2019). Promoting intern resilience: Individual chief wellness check-ins. *MedEdPORTAL: the Journal of Teaching and Learning Resources*. Advance online publication. DOI: 10.15766/mep_2374-8265.10848 PMID: 31921994

Fitzgerald, M., Kruschwitz, N., Bonnet, D., & Welch, M. (2014). Embracing digital technology: A new strategic imperative. *MIT Sloan Management Review, 55*(2), 1–12.

Flanagan, E. W., Beyl, R. A., Fearnbach, S. N., Altazan, A. D., Martin, C. K., & Redman, L. M. (2021). The impact of COVID-19 stay-at-home orders on health behaviors in adults. *Obesity (Silver Spring, Md.), 29*(2), 438–445. DOI: 10.1002/oby.23066 PMID: 33043562

Flavián, C., Guinaliu, M., & Jordan, P. (2022). Virtual teams are here to stay: How personality traits, virtuality and leader gender impact trust in the leader and team commitment. *European Research on Management and Business Economics, 28*(2), 100193. DOI: 10.1016/j.iedeen.2021.100193

Fletcher, D., & Sarkar, M. (2012). A grounded theory of psychological resilience in Olympic champions. *Psychology of Sport and Exercise, 13*(5), 669–678. DOI: 10.1016/j.psychsport.2012.04.007

Foo, M. D., Sin, H. P., & Yiong, L. P. (2006). Effects of team inputs and intrateam processes on perceptions of team viability and member satisfaction in nascent ventures. *Strategic Management Journal, 27*(4), 389–399.

Forsyth, D. R. (2021). Recent advances in the study of group cohesion. *Group Dynamics, 25*(3), 213.

Forsyth, D. R., & Burnette, J. (2010). Group processes. In Baumeister, R. F., & Finkel, E. J. (Eds.), *Advanced social psychology: The state of the science* (pp. 495–529). Oxford University Press.

Foster, J. D., & Twenge, J. M. (2010). Narcissism and relationships: From light to dark. In *The dark side of close relationships II* (pp. 401-428). Routledge/Taylor & Francis Group.

Fransen, J., Kirschner, P. A., & Erkens, G. (2011). Mediating team effectiveness in the context of collaborative learning: The importance of team and task awareness. *Computers in Human Behavior*, *27*(3), 1103–1113.

Frazier, M. L., Fainshmidt, S., Klinger, R. L., Pezeshkan, A., & Vracheva, V. (2017). Psychological safety: A meta-analytic review and extension. *Personnel Psychology*, *70*(1), 113–165.

Friedley, S. A., & Manchester, B. B. (2005). Building team cohesion: Becoming" We" instead of. *Me. National Forensic Journal*, *23*(1), 95–100.

Frost, M., & Duan, S. X. (2020). Rethinking the role of technology in virtual teams in light of COVID-19. *Charles Sturt University Research Output*, 1–7. https://researchoutput.csu.edu.au/en/publications/rethinking-the-role-of-technology-in-virtual-teams-in-light-of-co

Furumo, K., de Pillis, E., & Green, D. (2009). Personality influences trust differently in virtual and face-to-face teams. *International Journal of Human Resources Development and Management*, *9*(1), 36–58. DOI: 10.1504/IJHRDM.2009.021554

Fu, S., Yu, Y., Chen, J., Han, B., & Wu, Z. (2022). Towards a probabilistic approach for risk analysis of nuclear-powered icebreakers using FMEA and FRAM. *Ocean Engineering*, *260*, 112041. DOI: 10.1016/j.oceaneng.2022.112041

Fussell, R. D. (2020). Gather us in: Building meaningful relationships in Catholic schools amid a COVID-19 context. *Journal of Catholic Education*, *23*(1). Advance online publication. DOI: 10.15365/joce.2301102020

Garrido, G. M., Nair, V., & Song, D. (2023). SOK: Data privacy in virtual reality. *Proceedings on Privacy Enhancing Technologies. Privacy Enhancing Technologies Symposium*, *2024*(1), 21–40. DOI: 10.56553/popets-2024-0003

Garro-Abarca, V., Palos-Sanchez, P., & Aguayo-Camacho, M. (2021). Virtual teams in times of pandemic: Factors that influence performance. *Frontiers in Psychology*, *12*, 624637. DOI: 10.3389/fpsyg.2021.624637 PMID: 33679543

Gaspar, P. M., Catalano, L., & Gaspar, T. M. (2016). Establishing a collaboration contract to facilitate team performance. *Journal of Doctoral Nursing Practice*, *9*(1), 13–19. DOI: 10.1891/2380-9418.9.1.13 PMID: 32750998

Gersick, C. J. G. (1988). Time and transition in work teams: Toward a new model of group development. *Academy of Management Journal*, *31*(1), 9–41. DOI: 10.2307/256496

Gibson, C. B., & Gibbs, J. L. (2006). Unpacking the concept of virtuality: The effects of geographic dispersion, electronic dependence, dynamic structure, and national diversity on team innovation. *Administrative Science Quarterly*, *51*(3), 451–495. DOI: 10.2189/asqu.51.3.451

Gifford, J. (2022). Remote working: Unprecedented increase and a developing research agenda. *Human Resource Development International*. Advance online publication. DOI: 10.1080/13678868.2022.2049108

Gilson, L. L., Costa, P., O'Neill, T. A., & Maynard, M. T. (2021). Putting the "TEAM" back into virtual teams. *Organizational Dynamics*, *50*(1), 100847. Advance online publication. DOI: 10.1016/j.orgdyn.2021.100847

Gilson, L. L., Maynard, M. T., Jones Young, N. C., Vartiainen, M., & Hakonen, M. (2015). Virtual teams research: 10 years, 10 themes, and 10 opportunities. *Journal of Management*, *41*(5), 1313–1337. DOI: 10.1177/0149206314559946

Gilson, L. L., & Shalley, C. E. (2004). A little creativity goes a long way: An examination of teams' engagement in creative processes. *Journal of Management*, *30*(4), 453–470.

Gino, F. (2018, August). Need more self-control? Try a simple ritual. *Scientific American*. https://www.scientificamerican.com/article/need-more-self-control-try-a-simple-ritual/

Gokhale, A. A. (1995). Collaborative learning enhances critical thinking. *Journal of Technology Education*, *7*(1), 22–30.

Goldberg, L. R. (2013). An alternative "description of personality": The Big-Five factor structure. In *Personality and Personality Disorders* (pp. 34–47). Routledge. DOI: 10.1037/0022-3514.59.6.1216

Goldberg, L. R., Johnson, J. A., Eber, H. W., Hogan, R., Ashton, M. C., Cloninger, C. R., & Gough, H. G. (2006). The international personality item pool and the future of public-domain personality measures. *Journal of Research in Personality*, *40*(1), 84–96. DOI: 10.1016/j.jrp.2005.08.007

Goncalo, J. A., Katz, J. H., & Ellis, L. M. (2019). PIECE Together: How social norms support the process of team creativity. In Paulus, P. B., & Nijstad, B. A. (Eds.), *The Oxford handbook of group creativity and innovation* (pp. 216–230). Oxford University Press. DOI: 10.1093/oxfordhb/9780190648077.013.13

Goodyear, P., Carvalho, L., & Yeoman, P. (2021). Activity-Centred Analysis and Design (ACAD): Core purposes, distinctive qualities and current developments. *Educational Technology Research and Development*, *69*, 445–464. DOI: 10.1007/s11423-020-09926-7 PMID: 33456288

Gosling, S. D., Rentfrow, P. J., & Swann, W. B.Jr. (2003). A Very Brief Measure of the Big Five Personality Domains. *Journal of Research in Personality*, *37*, 504–528.

Gotian, R. (2022). *The success factor: Developing the mindset and skillset for peak business performance*. Kogan Page.

Govender, T., & Arnedo-Moreno, J. (2021). An analysis of game design elements used in Digital Game-Based Language Learning. *Sustainability*, *13*(12), 6679. DOI: 10.3390/su13126679

Gray, B. (2008). Enhancing Transdisciplinary Research Through Collaborative Leadership. *American Journal of Preventive Medicine*, *35*(2), S124–S132. DOI: 10.1016/j.amepre.2008.03.037 PMID: 18619392

Greenwald, A. G., & Banaji, M. R. (1995). Implicit social cognition: Attitudes, self-esteem, and stereotypes. *Psychological Review*, *102*(1), 4–27. DOI: 10.1037/0033-295X.102.1.4 PMID: 7878162

Greimel, N. S., Kanbach, D. K., & Chelaru, M. (2023). Virtual teams and transformational leadership: An integrative literature review and avenues for further research. *Journal of Innovation & Knowledge*, *8*(2). Advance online publication. DOI: 10.1016/j.jik.2023.100351

Grenny, J., Patterson, K., McMillan, R., Switzler, A., & Gregory, E. (2021). *Tools for conversations when stakes are high* (3rd ed.). McGraw Hill.

Griffith, T. L., Mannix, E. A., & Neale, M. A. (2003). Conflict and virtual teams. In Gibson, C. B., & Cohen, S. G. (Eds.), *Virtual teams that work: Creating conditions for virtual team effectiveness* (pp. 335–352). Jossey-Bass.

Griffith, T. L., & Neale, M. A. (2001). Information processing in traditional, hybrid, and virtual teams: From nascent knowledge to transactive memory. *Research in Organizational Behavior*, *23*, 379–421. DOI: 10.1016/S0191-3085(01)23009-3

Grijalva, E., & Newman, D. A. (2015). Narcissism and counterproductive work behavior (CWB): Meta-analysis and consideration of collectivist culture, Big Five personality, and narcissism's facet structure. *Applied Psychology*, *64*(1), 93–126. DOI: 10.1111/apps.12025

Grosskopf, S., & Barmeyer, C. (2021). Learning from multi-paradigmatic sensitivity in cross-cultural management? Empirical and theoretical considerations. *International Journal of Cross Cultural Management, 21*(2), 181–202. DOI: 10.1177/14705958211019437

Guchait, P., Paşamehmetoğlu, A., & Dawson, M. (2014). Perceived supervisor and co-worker support for error management: Impact on perceived psychological safety and service recovery performance. *International Journal of Hospitality Management, 41*, 28–37.

Gully, S. M., Devine, D. S., & Whitney, D. J. (1995). A meta-analysis of cohesion and performance: Effects of level of analysis and task interdependence. *Small Group Research, 26*(4), 497–520. DOI: 10.1177/1046496495264003

Gupta, S., Pathak, G. S., & Biswas, B. (2023). The roles of conflict management and psychological empowerment in virtual teams. *Information Technology & People, 37*(8), 66–108. DOI: 10.1108/ITP-04-2022-0265

Hackman, J. R. (1987). The design of work teams. In *Handbook of Organizational Behavior* (pp. 315-342).

Hackman, J. R. (2002). *Leading Teams: Setting the Stage for Great Performances.* Harvard Business Press.

Hackman, J. R., Brousseau, K. R., & Weiss, J. A. (1976). The interaction of task design and group performance strategies in determining group effectiveness. *Organizational Behavior and Human Performance, 16*(2), 350–365. DOI: 10.1016/0030-5073(76)90021-0

Hackman, J. R., & Hackman, R. J. (2002). *Leading teams: Setting the stage for great performances.* Harvard Business Press.

Hackman, J. R., & Oldham, G. R. (1975). Development of the job diagnostic survey. *The Journal of Applied Psychology, 60*(2), 159–170. DOI: 10.1037/h0076546

Hackman, J. R., & Oldham, G. R. (1976). Motivation through the design of work: Test of a theory. *Organizational Behavior and Human Performance, 16*(2), 250–279. DOI: 10.1016/0030-5073(76)90016-7

Hackman, J. R., & Oldham, G. R. (1980). *Work redesign.* Addison-Wesley.

Hakanen, M., & Soudunsaari, A. (2012). Building trust in high-performing teams. *Technology Innovation Management Review, 2*(6), 38–41. https://timreview.ca/article/562

Haleem, A., Javaid, M., Qadri, M. A., & Suman, R. (2022). Understanding the role of digital technologies in education: A review. *Sustainable Operations and Computers, 3*, 275–285. DOI: 10.1016/j.susoc.2022.05.004

Ha, N. T. N., Spittle, M., Watt, A., & Van Dyke, N. (2023). A systematic literature review of micro-credentials in higher education: A non-zero-sum game. *Higher Education Research & Development, 42*(6), 1527–1548.

Handke, L., Klonek, F., O'Neill, T. A., & Kerschreiter, R. (2022). Unpacking the role of feedback in virtual team effectiveness. *Small Group Research, 53*(1), 41–87. DOI: 10.1177/10464964211057116

Handy, C. (2006). Managing the dream. Learning organizations. In J. Renesch & S. Chawla (Eds.), *Learning organizations: Developing cultures for tomorrow's workplace.* Productivity Print. DOI: 10.4324/9781003578840

Han, S. J., Chae, C., Macko, P., Park, W., & Beyerlein, M. (2017). How virtual team leaders cope with creativity challenges. *European Journal of Training and Development, 41*(3), 261–276. DOI: 10.1108/EJTD-10-2016-0073

Han, S. J., & Stieha, V. (2020). Growth mindset for human resource development: A scoping review of the literature with recommended interventions. *Human Resource Development Review, 19*(3), 309–331. DOI: 10.1177/1534484320939739

Hansen, R. S. (2006). Benefits and problems with student teams: Suggestions for improving team projects. *Journal of Education for Business, 82*(1), 11–19.

Hao, Q., Yang, W., & Shi, Y. (2019). Characterizing the relationship between conscientiousness and knowledge sharing behavior in virtual teams: An interactionist approach. *Computers in Human Behavior, 91*, 42–51. DOI: 10.1016/j.chb.2018.09.035

Harrison, D. A., Mohammed, S., McGrath, J. E., Florey, A. T., & Vanderstoep, S. W. (2003). Time matters in team performance: Effects of member familiarity, entrainment, and task discontinuity on speed and quality. *Personnel Psychology, 56*(3), 633–669. DOI: 10.1111/j.1744-6570.2003.tb00753.x

Harrison, D. A., Price, K. H., & Bell, M. P. (1998). Beyond relational demography: Time and the effects of surface-and deep-level diversity on work group cohesion. *Academy of Management Journal, 41*(1), 96–107. DOI: 10.2307/256901

Hartenian, L. S. (2003). Team member acquisition of team knowledge, skills, and abilities. *Team Performance Management, 9*, 23–30.

Harvey, J.-F., Johnson, K. J., Roloff, K. S., & Edmondson, A. C. (2019). From orientation to behavior: The interplay between learning orientation, open-mindedness, and psychological safety in team learning. *Human Relations*, *72*(11), 1726–1751. DOI: 10.1177/0018726718817812

Hastings, E. M., Ojha, V., Austriaco, B. V., Karahalios, K., & Bailey, B. P. (2023). Composing team compositions: An examination of instructors' current algorithmic team formation practices. *Proceedings of the ACM on Human-Computer Interaction, 7*(CSCW2), 1–24. https://doi.org/DOI: 10.1145/3610096

Heilporn, G., Lakhal, S., & Bélisle, M. (2021). An examination of teachers' strategies to foster student engagement in blended learning in higher education. *International Journal of Educational Technology in Higher Education*, *18*(1), 25. DOI: 10.1186/s41239-021-00260-3 PMID: 34805484

Henderson, L. S., Stackman, R. W., & Lindekilde, R. (2016). The centrality of communication norm alignment, role clarity, and trust in global project teams. *International Journal of Project Management*, *34*(8), 1717–1730. DOI: 10.1016/j.ijproman.2016.09.012

Herriott, H. L., & McNulty, M. A. (2022). Virtual learning impacts communication and teamwork. *The Clinical Teacher*. Advance online publication. DOI: 10.1111/tct.13514 PMID: 35851567

Hertel, G., Geister, S., & Konradt, U. (2005). Managing virtual teams: A review of current empirical research. *Human Resource Management Review*, *15*(1), 69–95. DOI: 10.1016/j.hrmr.2005.01.002

Hilliard, J., Kear, K., Donelan, H., & Heaney, C. (2019). Students' experiences of anxiety in an assessed, online, collaborative project. *Computers & Education*, *143*. Advance online publication. DOI: 10.1016/j.compedu.2019.103675

Hill, J. R., Song, L., & West, R. E. (2009). Social learning theory and web-based learning environments: A review of research and discussion of implications. *American Journal of Distance Education*, *23*(2), 88–103.

Hincapie, M. X., & Hill, N. S. (2024). The Impact of Team Virtuality on the Performance of On-Campus Student Teams. *Academy of Management Learning & Education*, *23*(1), 158–175. DOI: 10.5465/amle.2022.0397

Hinds, P. J., & Mortensen, M. (2005). Understanding conflict in geographically distributed teams: The moderating effects of shared identity, shared context, and spontaneous communication. *Organization Science*, *16*(3), 290–307. DOI: 10.1287/orsc.1050.0122

Hobson, N. M., Schroeder, J., Risen, J. L., Xygalatas, D., & Inzlicht, M. (2018). The psychology of rituals: An integrative review and process-based framework. *Personality and Social Psychology Review*, *22*(3), 260–284. DOI: 10.1177/1088868317734944 PMID: 29130838

Hoch, J. E., & Dulebohn, J. H. (2017). Team personality composition, emergent leadership and shared leadership in virtual teams: A theoretical framework. *Human Resource Management Review*, *27*(4), 678–693. DOI: 10.1016/j.hrmr.2016.12.012

Hodges, C. B., & Fowler, D. J. (2020). The covid-19 crisis and faculty members in higher education: From emergency remote teaching to better teaching through reflection. *International Journal of Multidisciplinary Perspectives in Higher Education*, *5*(1), 118–122.

Hoefling, T. (2017). *Working Virtually: Transforming the Mobile Workplace* (2nd ed.). Stylus Publishing.

Hoegl, M., & Gemuenden, H. G. (2001). Teamwork quality and the success of innovative projects. *Organization Science*, *12*(4), 435–449. DOI: 10.1287/orsc.12.4.435.10635

Hogan, R. (1996). Personality assessment. In R. S. Barrett (Ed.), *Fair employment strategies in human resource management* (pp. 144–152). Quorum Books/Greenwood Publishing Group.

Hollenbeck, J. R., DeRue, D. S., & Guzzo, R. (2004). Bridging the gap between I/O research and HR practice: Improving team composition, team training, and team task design. *Human Resource Management*, *43*(4), 353–366. DOI: 10.1002/hrm.20029

Honts, C., Prewett, M., Rahael, J., & Grossenbacher, M. (2012). The importance of team processes for different team types. *Team Performance Management*, *18*(5/6), 312–327.

Hopko, S., Wang, J., & Mehta, R. (2022). Human factors considerations and metrics in shared space human-robot collaboration: A systematic review. *Frontiers in Robotics and AI*. Advance online publication. DOI: 10.3389/frobt.2022.799522 PMID: 35187093

Horning, A. S., & Brown, H. D. (1981). Principles of language learning and teaching. *Modern Language Journal*, *65*(4), 417. DOI: 10.2307/327392

House, C. (2019). Distributed teams—Challenges and opportunities. *Research Technology Management*, *62*(5), 11–13.

Hubbs, G., O'Rourke, M., & Orzack, S. H. (Eds.). (2021). *The toolbox dialogue initiative: The power of cross-disciplinary practice* (First edition). CRC Press, Taylor & Francis Group.

Hu, J., Erdogan, B., Jiang, K., Bauer, T. N., & Liu, S. (2018). Leader humility and team creativity: The role of team information sharing, psychological safety, and power distance. *The Journal of Applied Psychology, 103*(3), 313. PMID: 29094959

Hülsheger, U. R., Anderson, N., & Salgado, J. F. (2009). Team-level predictors of innovation at work: A comprehensive meta-analysis spanning three decades of research. *The Journal of Applied Psychology, 94*(5), 1128. PMID: 19702361

Hu, W., & Chan, C. K. Y. (2024). Evaluating technological interventions for developing teamwork competency in higher education: A systematic review and meta-ethnography. *Studies in Educational Evaluation, 83*, 101382. Advance online publication. DOI: 10.1016/j.stueduc.2024.101382

IBM. (n.d.). *Building a human centered organization*. IBM. https://www.ibm.com/design/thinking/page/hco

Ibrahim, M., & Aydoğmuş, M. (2023). Examining ESL preservice teachers' personal factors that best predict their confidence to integrate technology in future classrooms. *Journal of Education and Recreation Patterns, 4*(1), 134–152.

Ilgen, D. R., Hollenbeck, J. R., Johnson, M., & Jundt, D. (2005). Teams in organizations: From input-process-output models to IMOI models. *Annual Review of Psychology, 56*(1), 517–543. DOI: 10.1146/annurev.psych.56.091103.070250 PMID: 15709945

Imel, S. (1992). *Reflective Practice in Adult Education. ERIC Digest #122*. Retrieved from ERIC Clearinghouse on Adult, Career, and Vocational Education: https://eric.ed.gov/?id=ED346319

Islam, G., & Zyphur, M. J. (2009). Rituals in organizations: A review and expansion of current theory. *Group & Organization Management, 34*(1), 114–139.

Ismail, A., Hidajat, T., Dora, Y. M., Prasatia, F. E., & Pranadani, A. (2023). *Leading the digital transformation: Evidence from Indonesia*. Independently published.

Israilova, I. (2021). "telegram" as a modern simplified and rapid means of distance learning using multimedia form. *ACADEMICIA an International Multidisciplinary Research Journal, 11*(1), 1037–1044. DOI: 10.5958/2249-7137.2021.00183.x

Itzchakov, G., Weinstein, N., Vinokur, E., & Yomtovian, A. (2023). Communicating for workplace connection: A longitudinal study of the outcomes of listening training on teachers' autonomy, psychological safety, and relational climate. *Psychology in the Schools*, *60*(4), 1279–1298. DOI: 10.1002/pits.22835

Jackson, S. E., May, K. E., & Whitney, K. (1995). Understanding the dynamics of diversity in decision- making teams. In Guzzo, R. A., & Salas, E. (Eds.), *In Team decision-making effectiveness in organizations* (pp. 204–261). Joey Bass.

Jackson, S. E., & Ruderman, M. N. (Eds.). (1995). *Diversity in work teams: Research paradigms for a changing workplace*. American Psychological Association. DOI: 10.1037/10189-000

Jacobs, D. (2023). Taking an intentional approach to technology. *Childhood Education*, *99*(4), 72–75. DOI: 10.1080/00094056.2023.2232285

Jacques, P. H., Garger, J., Brown, C. A., & Deale, C. S. (2009). Personality and virtual reality team candidates: The roles of personality traits, technology anxiety and trust as predictors of perceptions of virtual reality teams. *Journal of Business and Management*, *15*(2), 143–157. DOI: 10.1504/jbm.2009.141174

Jakobwitz, S., & Egan, V. (2006). The dark triad and normal personality traits. *Personality and Individual Differences*, *40*(2), 331–339. DOI: 10.1016/j.paid.2005.07.006

Jancovich, L., & Stevenson, D. (2021). Failure seems to be the hardest word to say. *International Journal of Cultural Policy*. Advance online publication. DOI: 10.1080/10286632.2021.1879798

Janicik, G. A., & Bartel, C. A. (2003). Talking about time: Effects of temporal planning and time awareness norms on group coordination and performance. *Group Dynamics*, *7*(2), 122–134. DOI: 10.1037/1089-2699.7.2.122

Janis, I. L. (2008). Groupthink. *IEEE Engineering Management Review*, *36*(1), 36.

Jarvenpaa, S. L., & Leidner, D. E. (1999). Communication and trust in global virtual teams. *Organization Science*, *10*(6), 791–815. DOI: 10.1287/orsc.10.6.791

Javed, H. (2024). Creating a positive workplace culture: diversity, equity, and inclusion initiatives. *Innovative Human Resource Management for SMEs*. DOI: 10.4018/979-8-3693-0972-8.ch020

Jehn, K. A. (1992). *The impact of intragroup conflict on effectiveness: A multimethod examination of the benefits and detriments of conflict* [Doctoral dissertation, Northwestern University].

Jehn, K. A. (1994). Enhancing effectiveness: An investigation of advantages and disadvantages of value-based intragroup conflict. *International Journal of Conflict Management*, *5*(3), 223–238. DOI: 10.1108/eb022744

Jehn, K. A. (1997). A qualitative analysis of conflict types and dimensions in organizational groups. *Administrative Science Quarterly*, *40*(2), 530–557. DOI: 10.2307/2393638

Jehn, K. A., Chadwick, C., & Thatcher, S. M. (1997). To agree or not to agree: The effects of value congruence, individual demographic dissimilarity, and conflict on workgroup outcomes. *International Journal of Conflict Management*, *8*(4), 287–305. DOI: 10.1108/eb022799

Jehn, K. A., & Mannix, E. A. (2001). The dynamic nature of conflict: A longitudinal study of intragroup conflict and group performance. *Academy of Management Journal*, *44*(2), 238–251. DOI: 10.2307/3069453

Jehn, K. A., Northcraft, G. B., & Neale, M. A. (1999). Why differences make a difference: A field study of diversity, conflict and performance in workgroups. *Administrative Science Quarterly*, *44*(4), 741–763. DOI: 10.2307/2667054

Jehn, K. A., & Shah, P. P. (1997). Interpersonal relationships and task performance: An examination of mediation processes in friendship and acquaintance groups. *Journal of Personality and Social Psychology*, *72*(4), 775–790. DOI: 10.1037/0022-3514.72.4.775

Jenkins, A., Weeks, M. S., & Hard, B. M. (2021). General and specific stress mindsets: Links with college student health and academic performance. *PLoS One*, *16*(9), e0256351. PMID: 34495976

Johnson, J. A. (2014). Measuring thirty facets of the Five Factor Model with a 120-item public domain inventory: Development of the IPIP-NEO-120. *Journal of Research in Personality*, *51*, 78–89. DOI: 10.1016/j.jrp.2014.05.003

Johnson, S. D., Suriya, C., Yoon, S. W., Berrett, J. V., & La Fleur, J. (2002). Team development and group processes of virtual learning teams. *Computers & Education*, *39*(4), 379–393.

Johnson, W. H., Baker, D. S., Dong, L., Taras, V., & Wankel, C. (2022). Do team charters help team-based projects? The effects of team charters on performance and satisfaction in global virtual teams. *Academy of Management Learning & Education*, *21*, 236–260.

Jonathan, H., & Westover, P. F. (2024, November 26). *Cultivating Community and Connection: A New Playbook for the Hybrid Workforce*. Retrieved from Forbes Coaches Council: https://www.forbes.com/councils/forbescoachescouncil/2024/11/26/cultivating-community-and-connection-a-new-playbook-for-the-hybrid-workforce/

Jonker, C.M., van Riemsdijk, M.B., Vermeulen, B. (2011). Shared Mental Models: A Conceptual Analysis. *Springer Nature, 6541.*

Joo, B. K., Song, J. H., Lim, D. H., & Yoon, S. W. (2012). Team creativity: The effects of perceived learning culture, developmental feedback and team cohesion. *International Journal of Training and Development*, *16*(2), 77–91.

Jordanous, A., & Keller, B. (2016). Modelling creativity: Identifying key components through a corpus-based approach. *PLoS One*, *11*(10), e0162959. DOI: 10.1371/journal.pone.0162959 PMID: 27706185

Josué, N. A., Bedoya-Flores, M. C., Mosquera-Quiñonez, E. F., Mesías-Simisterra, Á. E., & Bautista-Sánchez, J. V. (2023). Educational platforms: Digital tools for the teaching-learning process in education. *Ibero-American Journal of Education & Society Research*, *3*(1), 259–263. DOI: 10.56183/iberoeds.v3i1.626

Kankanhalli, A., Tan, B. C. Y., & Wei, K. K. (2006). Conflict and performance in global virtual teams. *Journal of Management Information Systems*, *23*(3), 237–274.

Kanso, A., & Monette, D. (2014). Foundations for long-term collaborative research. *In Proceedings of the 2014 International Workshop on Long-term Industrial Collaboration on Software Engineering*, 43–48. DOI: 10.1145/2647648.2647654

Karl, K. A., Peluchette, J. V., & Aghakhani, N. (2022). Virtual work meetings during the COVID-19 pandemic: The good, bad, and ugly. *Small Group Research.* Advance online publication. DOI: 10.1177/10464964211015286 PMID: 38603094

Kauffeld, S., & Lehmann-Willenbrock, N. (2012). Meetings matter: Effects of team meetings on team and organizational success. *Small Group Research*, *43*(2), 130–158. DOI: 10.1177/1046496411429599

Keoma, E., & Chinwe, A. (2024). Reciprocity and Trust as Predictors of Technology-Enabled Knowledge Sharing among Library and Information Science Professionals in Public Universities of South-East, Nigeria. *International Journal of Knowledge Dissemination*, *4*, 1–17.

Kerrissey, M. J., Hayirli, T. C., Bhanja, A., Stark, N., Hardy, J., & Peabody, C. R. (2022). How psychological safety and feeling heard relate to burnout and adaptation amid uncertainty. *Health Care Management Review*, *47*(4), 308–316. DOI: 10.1097/HMR.0000000000000338 PMID: 35135989

Kerzner, H., Zeitoun, A., & Vargas, R. V. (2022). *Project management next generation: The pillars for organizational excellence*. Wiley.

Keswin, E. (2021). *Rituals roadmap: The human way to transform everyday routines into workplace magic*. McGraw Hill.

Khamis, T., Naseem, A., Khamis, A., & Petrucka, P. (2021). The COVID-19 pandemic: A catalyst for creativity and collaboration for online learning and work-based higher education systems and processes. *Journal of Work-Applied Management, 13*(2), 184–196. DOI: 10.1108/JWAM-01-2021-0010

Khan, M. T., & Ullah, S. (2025). Balancing innovation: The role of paradoxical leadership and ambidexterity in fostering team creativity. *International Journal of Innovation Science*. Advance online publication. DOI: 10.1108/IJIS-07-2024-0206

Khawam, A. M., DiDona, T., & Hernandez, B. S. (2017). Effectiveness of Teamwork in the Workplace. *International Journal of Sciences, Basic and Applied Research, 32*, 267–286.

Khodabakhsh, M. R., & Besharat, M. A. (2011). Mediation effect of narcissism on the relationship between empathy and the quality of interpersonal relationships. *Procedia: Social and Behavioral Sciences, 30*, 902–906. DOI: 10.1016/j.sbspro.2011.10.175

Kiely, G., Butler, T., & Finnegan, P. (2022). Global virtual teams coordination mechanisms: Building theory from research in software development. *Behaviour & Information Technology*. Advance online publication. DOI: 10.1080/0144929X.2021.1909141

Kim, J., Lee, H., & Cho, Y. H. (2022). Learning design to support student-AI collaboration: Perspectives of leading teachers for AI in education. *Education and Information Technologies*. Advance online publication. DOI: 10.1007/s10639-021-10831-6

Kim, S. M., Kim, M. J., & Jo, S. J. (2021). The relationships between perceived team psychological safety, transactive memory system, team learning behavior and team performance among individual team members. *Leadership and Organization Development Journal, 42*(6), 958–975.

Kim, S., Lee, H., & Connerton, T. P. (2020). How psychological safety affects team performance: Mediating role of efficacy and learning behavior. *Frontiers in Psychology, 11*, 1581. PMID: 32793037

Kim, S., Magnusen, M. J., & Andrew, D. P. (2016). Divided we fall: Examining the relationship between horizontal communication and team commitment via team cohesion. *International Journal of Sports Science & Coaching, 11*(5), 625–636.

Kim, T., Sezer, O., Schroeder, J., Risen, J., Gino, F., & Norton, M. (2021). Work group rituals enhance the meaning of work. *Organizational Behavior and Human Decision Processes*, *165*, 197–212.

Kimura, T. (2024). Virtual teams: A smart literature review of four decades of research. *Human Behavior and Emerging Technologies*, *2024*(1), e8373370. Advance online publication. DOI: 10.1155/2024/8373370

Klein, C., DiazGranados, D., Salas, E., Le, H., Burke, C. S., Lyons, R., & Goodwin, G. F. (2009). Does team building work? *Small Group Research*, *40*(2), 181–222. DOI: 10.1177/1046496408328821

Klein, G., Wiggins, S., & Dominguez, C. O. (2010). Team sensemaking. *Theoretical Issues in Ergonomics Science*, *11*(4), 304–320.

Klein, S. P., Kuh, G., Chun, M., Hamilton, L., & Shavelson, R. (2005). An approach to measuring cognitive outcomes across higher education institutions. *Research in Higher Education*, *46*, 251–276.

Klonek, F. E., Kanse, L., Wee, S., Runneboom, C., & Parker, S. K. (2022). Did the COVID-19 lockdown make us better at working in virtual teams? *Small Group Research*, *53*(2), 185–206.

Kolb, D. M., & Bartunek, J. M. (1992). *Hidden conflict in organizations: Uncovering behind-the-scenes disputes* (Vol. 141). *Sage (Atlanta, Ga.)*. Advance online publication. DOI: 10.4135/9781483325897

Kolditz, T. A., Gill, L., Brown, R. P., & Collins, J. (2021). *Leadership reckoning: Can higher education develop the leaders we need?* Monocle Press.

Kolm, A., de Nooijer, J., Vanherle, K., Werkman, A., Wewerka-Kreimel, D., Rachman-Elbaum, S., & van Merriënboer, J. J. (2022). International online collaboration competencies in higher education students: A systematic review. *Journal of Studies in International Education*, *26*(2), 183–201. DOI: 10.1177/10283153211016272

Koppett, K. (2013). *Training to imagine: Practical improvisational theatre techniques for trainers and managers to enhance creativity, teamwork, leadership and learning* (2nd ed.). Stylus Pub.

Kozlowski, S. W. J., & Bell, B. S. (2003). Work groups and teams in organizations. In Borman, W. C., Ilgen, D. R., & Klimoski, R. J. (Eds.), Handbook of psychology: Vol. 12. *Industrial and organizational psychology* (pp. 333–375). John Wiley & Sons, Inc. DOI: 10.1002/0471264385.wei1214

Kozlowski, S. W. J., & Ilgen, D. R. (2006). Enhancing the effectiveness of work groups and teams. *Psychological Science in the Public Interest, 7*, 77–124. DOI: 10.1111/j.1529-1006.2006.00030.x PMID: 26158912

Kozlowski, S. W., Gully, S. M., Nason, E. R., & Smith, E. M. (1999). Developing adaptive teams: A theory of compilation and performance across levels and time. In Ilgen, D. R., & Pulakos, E. D. (Eds.), *The changing nature of work performance: Implications for staffing, personnel actions, and development* (pp. 240–292). Jossey-Bass.

Kratzer, J., Gemünden, H. G., & Lettl, C. (2008). Balancing creativity and time efficiency in multi-year R&D projects: The alignment of formal and informal networks. *R & D Management, 38*(5), 538–549. DOI: 10.1111/j.1467-9310.2008.00528.x

Krumm, S., Terwiel, K., & Hertel, G. (2013). Challenges in norm formation and adherence: The knowledge, skills, and ability requirements of virtual and traditional cross-cultural teams. *Journal of Personnel Psychology, 12*(1), 33–44.

Kujala, J., Sachs, S., Leinonen, H., Heikkinen, A., & Laude, D. (2022). Stakeholder engagement: Past, present, and future. *Business & Society, 61*(5), 1136–1196. DOI: 10.1177/00076503211066595

Kyambade, M., Namuddu, R., Mugambwa, J., & Namatovu, A. (2024). I can't express myself at work: Encouraging socially responsible leadership and psychological safety in higher education setting. *Cogent Education, 11*(1), 2373560. DOI: 10.1080/2331186X.2024.2373560

Lacerenza, C. N., Marlow, S. L., Tannenbaum, S. I., & Salas, E. (2018). Team development interventions: Evidence-based approaches for improving teamwork. *The American Psychologist, 73*(4), 517–531. DOI: 10.1037/amp0000295 PMID: 29792465

Lal, B., Dwivedi, Y. K., & Haag, M. (2023). Working from home during Covid-19: Doing and managing technology-enabled social interaction with colleagues at a distance. *Information Systems Frontiers*. Advance online publication. DOI: 10.1007/s10796-021-10182-0 PMID: 34483713

Lantz, A., Ulber, D., & Friedrich, P. (2019). Why work in teams, and for what are teams effective? In A. Lantz, D. Ulber, & P. Friedrich, *The Problems with Teamwork, and How to Solve Them* (1st ed., pp. 1–29). Routledge. https://doi.org/DOI: 10.4324/9780429056024-1

Larson, N. L., McLarnon, M. J. W., & O'Neill, T. A. (2020). Challenging the "static" quo: Trajectories of engagement in team processes toward a deadline. *The Journal of Applied Psychology*, *105*(10), 1145–1163. DOI: 10.1037/apl0000479 PMID: 31985237

Lau, D. C., & Murnighan, J. K. (1998). Demographic diversity and faultlines: The compositional dynamics of organizational groups. *Academy of Management Review*, *23*(2), 325–340. DOI: 10.2307/259377

Lea, M., & Spears, R. (1991). Computer-mediated communication, de-individuation and group decision-making. *International Journal of Man-Machine Studies*, *34*(2), 283–301. DOI: 10.1016/0020-7373(91)90045-9

Lechner, A., & Tobias Mortlock, J. (2022). How to create psychological safety in virtual teams. *Organizational Dynamics*, *51*(2), 100849. DOI: 10.1016/j.orgdyn.2021.100849

Lee, J. Y., Swink, M., & Pandejpong, T. (2011). The roles of worker expertise, information sharing quality, and psychological safety in manufacturing process innovation: An intellectual capital perspective. *Production and Operations Management*, *20*(4), 556–570.

Leenders, R. T. A., Van Engelen, J. M., & Kratzer, J. (2003). Virtuality, communication, and new product team creativity: A social network perspective. *Journal of Engineering and Technology Management*, *20*(1–2), 69–92. DOI: 10.1016/S0923-4748(03)00005-5

Leman, A., & Mott, R. (2023). Evaluating the outcomes of human-centered design in a virtual program development higher education course. *Journal of Human Sciences and Extension*, *11*(1), 15–30. https://scholarsjunction.msstate.edu/jhse/vol11/iss1/15/

Leonard, K., & Yorton, T. (2015). *Yes, and: How improvisation reverses no, but thinking and improves creativity and collaboration—Lessons from The Second City*. HarperCollins Publishers.

LePine, J. A., Buckman, B. R., Crawford, E. R., & Methot, J. R. (2011). A review of research on personality in teams: Accounting for pathways spanning levels of theory and analysis. *Human Resource Management Review*, *21*(4), 311–330. DOI: 10.1016/j.hrmr.2010.10.004

LePine, J. A., Hollenbeck, J. R., Ilgen, D. R., & Hedlund, J. (1997). Effects of individual differences on the performance of hierarchical decision making teams: Much more than g. *The Journal of Applied Psychology*, *82*(5), 803–811. DOI: 10.1037/0021-9010.82.5.803

LePine, J. A., Piccolo, R. F., Jackson, C. L., Mathieu, J. E., & Saul, J. R. (2008). A meta-analysis of teamwork processes: Tests of a multidimensional model and relationships with team effectiveness criteria. *Personnel Psychology*, *61*(2), 273–307. DOI: 10.1111/j.1744-6570.2008.00114.x

Lepisto, D. A. (2022). Ritual work and the formation of a shared sense of meaningfulness. *Academy of Management Journal*, *65*(4), 1327–1352.

Leroy, H., Buengeler, C., Veestraeten, M., Shemla, M., & Hoever, I. J. (2022). Fostering team creativity through team-focused inclusion: The role of leader harvesting the benefits of diversity and cultivating value-in-diversity beliefs. *Group & Organization Management*, *47*(4), 798–839. DOI: 10.1177/10596011211009683

Lewis, K. (2003). Measuring transactive memory systems in the field: Scale development and validation. *The Journal of Applied Psychology*, *88*(4), 587. PMID: 12940401

Liao, C. (2017). Leadership in virtual teams: A multilevel perspective. *Human Resource Management Review*, *27*(4), 648–659. DOI: 10.1016/j.hrmr.2016.12.010

Ligita, T., Nurjannah, I., Wicking, K., Harvey, N., & Francis, K. (2022). From textual to visual: The use of concept mapping as an analytical tool in a grounded theory study. *Qualitative Research*, *22*(1), 126–142. DOI: 10.1177/1468794120965362

Li, L. (2022). Reskilling and upskilling the future-ready workforce for industry 4.0 and beyond. *Information Systems Frontiers*. Advance online publication. DOI: 10.1007/s10796-022-10308-y PMID: 35855776

Lim, W. M., Gunasekara, A., Pallant, J. L., Pallant, J. I., & Pechenkina, E. (2023). Generative AI and the future of education: Ragnarök or reformation? A paradoxical perspective from management educators. *International Journal of Management Education*, *21*(2), 100790. DOI: 10.1016/j.ijme.2023.100790

Lin, X., & Sun, Q. (2024). Discussion activities in asynchronous online learning: Motivating adult learners' interactions. *The Journal of Continuing Higher Education*. Advance online publication. DOI: 10.1080/07377363.2022.2119803

Lisovska, L., Terebukh, A., & Hatsuk, M. (2019). Grounds of modern models and systems of organizational creativity support. *Journal of Lviv Polytechnic National University Series of Economics and Management Issues*, *6*(3), 99–112. DOI: 10.23939/semi2019.03.099

Liu, T., Wu, Q., Chang, L., & Gu, T. (2022). A review of deep learning-based recommender system in e-learning environments. *Artificial Intelligence Review*, *55*(8), 5953–5980. DOI: 10.1007/s10462-022-10135-2

Liu, Y., Keller, R. T., & Bartlett, K. R. (2021). Initiative climate, psychological safety and knowledge sharing as predictors of team creativity: A multilevel study of research and development project teams. *Creativity and Innovation Management, 30*(3), 498–510. DOI: 10.1111/caim.12438

Lohmann, G., Pratt, M. A., Benckendorff, P., Strickland, P., Reynolds, P., & Whitelaw, P. A. (2019). Online business simulations: Authentic teamwork, learning outcomes, and satisfaction. *Higher Education, 77*(3), 455–472. DOI: 10.1007/s10734-018-0282-x

London, M., Volmer, J., Zyberaj, J., & Kluger, A. N. (2023). Gaining feedback acceptance: Leader-member attachment style and psychological safety. *Human Resource Management Review, 33*(2), 100953.

Lotrecchiano, G. R., Bennett, L. M., & Vovides, Y. (2023). A framework for developing team science expertise using a reflective-reflexive design method (R2DM). *Humanities & Social Sciences Communications, 10*(1), 810. DOI: 10.1057/s41599-023-02298-2

Lott, A. J., & Lott, B. E. (1965). Group cohesiveness as interpersonal attraction: A review of relationships with antecedent and consequent variables. *Psychological Bulletin, 64*(4), 259–309. DOI: 10.1037/h0022386 PMID: 5318041

Luo, W., He, H., Liu, J., Berson, I. R., Berson, M. J., Zhou, Y., & Li, H. (2024). Aladdin's Genie or Pandora's Box for early childhood education? Experts chat on the roles, challenges, and developments of ChatGPT. *Early Education and Development, 35*(1), 96–113. DOI: 10.1080/10409289.2023.2214181

Lurey, J., & Raisinghani, M. (2001). An empirical study of best practices in virtual teams. *Information & Management, 38*, 523–544. DOI: 10.1016/S0378-7206(01)00074-X

Lynch, J., McGregor, A., & Benson, A. J. (2022). My way or the highway: Narcissism and dysfunctional team conflict processes. *Group Processes & Intergroup Relations, 25*(4), 1157–1171. DOI: 10.1177/1368430221100194

Maaravi, Y., Heller, B., Shoham, Y., Mohar, S., & Deutsch, B. (2021). Ideation in the digital age: Literature review and integrative model for electronic brainstorming. *Review of Managerial Science, 15*(6), 1431–1464. DOI: 10.1007/s11846-020-00400-5

Mach, M., Dolan, S., & Tzafrir, S. (2010). The differential effect of team members' trust on team performance: The mediation role of team cohesion. *Journal of Occupational and Organizational Psychology, 83*(3), 771–794.

MacPhail, L. H., & Edmondson, A. C. (2011). Learning domains: The importance of work context in organizational learning from error. In Hofmann, D. A., & Frese, M. (Eds.), *Errors in organizations* (pp. 177–198). Routledge.

Magistretti, S., Sanasi, S., Dell'Era, C., & Ghezzi, A. (2023). Entrepreneurship as design: A design process for the emergence and development of entrepreneurial opportunities. *Creativity and Innovation Management*, *32*(1), 5–21. DOI: 10.1111/caim.12529

Maguire, D., & Keceli, Y. (2024). The impact of formation and diversity on student team conflict. *Active Learning in Higher Education*, *25*(3), 409–423. DOI: 10.1177/14697874221144998

Majid, S., & Wey, S. M. (2011). Knowledge sharing behavior of graduate students. In Murray, E. J. (Ed.), *Global aspects and cultural perspectives on knowledge management: emerging dimensions* (pp. 113–125). Information Science Reference/IGI Global.

Makruf, I., & Tejaningsih, E. (2023). Overcoming online learning challenges in the COVID-19 pandemic by user-friendly platform. *Journal of Education and Learning*, *17*(2), 307–316. DOI: 10.11591/edulearn.v17i2.20513

Malhotra, A., Majchrzak, A., & Rosen, B. (2007). Leading virtual teams. *The Academy of Management Perspectives*, *21*(1), 60–70. DOI: 10.5465/amp.2007.24286164

Marcus, D. K., & Zeigler-Hill, V. (2015). A big tent of dark personality traits. *Social and Personality Psychology Compass*, *9*(8), 434–446. DOI: 10.1111/spc3.12185

Marks, M. A., Mathieu, J. E., & Zaccaro, S. J. (2001). A temporally based framework and taxonomy of team processes. *Academy of Management Review*, *26*(3), 356–376. DOI: 10.5465/amr.2001.4845785

Marlow, S. L., Lacerenza, C. N., & Salas, E. (2017). Communication in virtual teams: A conceptual framework and research agenda. *Human Resource Management Review*, *27*(4), 575–589. DOI: 10.1016/j.hrmr.2016.12.005

Marshall, T., Keville, S., Cain, A., & Adler, J. R. (2021). On being open-minded, wholehearted, and responsible: A review and synthesis exploring factors enabling practitioner development in reflective practice. *Reflective Practice*. Advance online publication. DOI: 10.1080/14623943.2021.1976131

Martínez-Peláez, R., Ochoa-Brust, A., Rivera, S., Félix, V. G., Ostos, R., Brito, H., Félix, R. A., & Mena, L. J. (2023). Role of digital transformation for achieving sustainability: Mediated role of stakeholders, key capabilities, and technology. *Sustainability*, *15*(14), 11221. DOI: 10.3390/su151411221

Maruping, L. M., & Agarwal, R. (2004). Managing team interpersonal processes through technology: A task-technology fit perspective. *The Journal of Applied Psychology*, *89*(6), 975–990. DOI: 10.1037/0021-9010.89.6.975 PMID: 15584836

Maryellen Weimer, P. (2017, June 28). *The Teaching Professor Blog Faculty Focus: Higher Ed Teaching Strategies.* Retrieved from Faculty Focus Magna Publications: https://www.facultyfocus.com/articles/philosophy-of-teaching/contradictions-think-teaching/?_hsenc=p2ANqtz-8urWzmYpvkRVyNY3i9fSYhmbEw8DtMXy_ImaAyTIHLJi8zWShbE90ZK2269Jys-wcnus45aExy3fo8EZaXRb1-XP93TQ&_hsmi=53632571

Ma, S., & Leman, A. (2023). Preparing career-ready students by building effective virtual teamwork skills. *NACTA Journal*, *67*(1), 50–56.

Maslov, I., Nikou, S., & Hansen, P. (2021). Exploring user experience of learning management system. *The International Journal of Information and Learning Technology*, *38*(4), 344–363. DOI: 10.1108/IJILT-03-2021-0046

Mathieu, J. E., Gilson, L. L., & Ruddy, T. M. (2006). Empowerment and team effectiveness: An empirical test of an integrated model. *The Journal of Applied Psychology*, *91*(1), 97–108. DOI: 10.1037/0021-9010.91.1.97 PMID: 16435941

Mathieu, J. E., Heffner, T. S., Goodwin, G. F., Salas, E., & Cannon-Bowers, J. A. (2000). The influence of shared mental models on team process and performance. *The Journal of Applied Psychology*, *85*(2), 273. PMID: 10783543

Mathieu, J. E., & Rapp, T. L. (2009). Laying the foundation for successful team performance trajectories: The roles of team charters and performance strategies. *The Journal of Applied Psychology*, *94*(1), 90–103. DOI: 10.1037/a0013257 PMID: 19186898

Mathieu, J. E., Tannenbaum, S. I., Donsbach, J. S., & Alliger, G. M. (2014). A review and integration of team composition models: Moving toward a dynamic and temporal framework. *Journal of Management*, *40*(1), 130–160. DOI: 10.1177/0149206313503014

Mathieu, J., Maynard, M. T., Rapp, T., & Gilson, L. (2008). Team effectiveness 1997-2007: A review of recent advancements and a glimpse into the future. *Journal of Management*, *34*(3), 410–476. DOI: 10.1177/0149206308316061

Matney, M. (2022). 2022 Global Virtual Teams Survey Report. RW3 Culture Wizard Global Inclusion Experts. www.rw-3.com/blog/global-virtual-teams-survey-report-2022

May, A., & Carter, C., & HUSAT Research Institute. (2001). A case study of virtual team working in the European automotive industry. *International Journal of Industrial Ergonomics*, *27*, 171–186.

Mayer, C., Sivatheerthan, T., Mütze-Niewöhner, S., & Nitsch, V. (2023). Sharing leadership behaviors in virtual teams: Effects of shared leadership behaviors on team member satisfaction and productivity. *Team Performance Management*, *29*(1/2), 90–112. DOI: 10.1108/tpm-07-2022-0054

Mayfield, C. O., & Valenti, A. (2024). Team satisfaction, identity, and trust: A comparison of face-to-face and virtual student teams. *Active Learning in Higher Education*, *25*(2), 213–226.

Maynard, M. T., Mathieu, J. E., Gilson, L. L. R., Sanchez, D., & Dean, M. D. (2019). Do I really know you and does it matter? Unpacking the relationship between familiarity and information elaboration in global virtual teams. *Group & Organization Management*, *44*(1), 3–37. DOI: 10.1177/1059601118785842

McAvoy, J., & Butler, T. (2008). The desire for cohesion in virtual teams: Be careful what you wish for. In Koch, N. (Ed.), *E-collaboration in modern organizations: Initiating and managing distributed projects* (pp. 220–241). Information Science Reference/IGI Global.

McCrae, R. R., & Costa, P. T. (1987). Validation of the five-factor model of personality across instruments and observers. *Journal of Personality and Social Psychology*, *52*(1), 81–90. DOI: 10.1037/0022-3514.52.1.81 PMID: 3820081

McEwan, D., & Beauchamp, M. R. (2014). The effectiveness of teamwork in sports settings: A meta-analytic review. *Journal of Applied Sport Psychology*, *26*(2), 200–217. DOI: 10.1080/10413200.2013.785887

McGrath, J. (1964). *Social Psychology: A Brief Introduction*. Holt, Rinehart & Winston.

McLarnon, M. J. W., O'Neill, T. A., Taras, V., Law, D., Donia, M. B. L., & Steel, P. (2019). Global virtual team communication, coordination, and performance across three peer feedback interventions. *Canadian Journal of Behavioural Science*, *51*, 207–218.

McLarnon, M. J. W., O'Neill, T. A., Taras, V., Law, D., Donia, M. B. L., & Steel, P. (2019). Global virtual team communication, coordination, and performance across three peer feedback strategies. *Canadian Journal of Behavioural Science/Revue Canadienne. Science et Comportement*, *51*(4), 207–218. DOI: 10.1037/cbs0000135

Mehmood, M. S., Jian, Z., Akram, U., Akram, Z., & Tanveer, Y. (2022). Entrepreneurial leadership and team creativity: The roles of team psychological safety and knowledge sharing. *Personnel Review*, *51*(9), 2404–2425.

Mengoni, M., Ceccacci, S., Giraldi, L., & Montanari, R. (2021). How to create engaging experiences from human emotions. *DIID*, *74*(74). Advance online publication. DOI: 10.30682/diid7421b

Mengue-Topio, H., Guedira, Y., Lepreux, S., & Kolski, C. (2024). Ideation, Focus Groups, and Brainstorming. In Stephanidis, C., & Salvendy, G. (Eds.), *User experience methods and tools in human-computer interaction* (pp. 34–70). CRC Press. DOI: 10.1201/9781003495161

Menon, S., & Suresh, M. (2021). Enablers of workforce agility in engineering educational institutions. *Journal of Applied Research in Higher Education*, *13*(2), 504–539. DOI: 10.1108/JARHE-12-2019-0304

Mercader, V., Galván-Vela, E., Ravina-Ripoll, R., & Popescu, C. R. G. (2021). A focus on ethical value under the vision of leadership, teamwork, effective communication and productivity. *Journal of Risk and Financial Management*, *14*(11), 522. DOI: 10.3390/jrfm14110522

Mesmer-Magnus, J. R., & DeChurch, L. A. (2009). Information sharing and team performance: A meta-analysis. *Journal of Applied Psychology, 94*(2), 535-546. DOI: 10.1177/001872088602800404

Mesmer-Magnus, J. R., & DeChurch, L. A. (2009). Information sharing and team performance: A meta-analysis. *The Journal of Applied Psychology*, *94*(2), 535–546. DOI: 10.1037/a0013773 PMID: 19271807

Mesmer-Magnus, J. R., DeChurch, L. A., Jimenez-Rodriguez, M., Wildman, J., & Shuffler, M. (2011). A meta-analytic investigation of virtuality and information sharing in teams. *Organizational Behavior and Human Decision Processes*, *115*(2), 214–225.

Methot, J. R., Rosado-Solomon, E. H., Downes, P., & Gabriel, A. S. (2021). Office chitchat as a social ritual: The uplifting yet distracting effects of daily small talk. *Academy of Management Journal*, *64*(5), 1445–1471.

Meyerson, D., Weick, K. E., & Kramer, R. M. (1996). Swift trust and temporary groups. In Kramer, R. M., & Tyler, T. R. (Eds.), *Trust in organizations: Frontiers of theory and research* (pp. 166–195). Sage Publications, Inc., DOI: 10.4135/9781452243610.n9

Mhlongo, S., Mbatha, K., Ramatsetse, B., & Dlamini, R. (2023). Challenges, opportunities, and prospects of adopting and using smart digital technologies in learning environments: An iterative review. *Heliyon*. Advance online publication. DOI: 10.1016/j.heliyon.2023.e16348 PMID: 37274691

Michalko, M. (2011). *Creative thinkering: Putting your imagination to work*. New World Library.

Mills, W. (2019, April 3). *Faculty Focus*. Retrieved from Faculty Focus: https://www.facultyfocus.com/articles/online-education/what-is-swift-trust-and-why-do-i-want-it-in-my-classes/

Mitchell, A. (2023). Collaboration technology affordances from virtual collaboration in the time of COVID-19 and post-pandemic strategies. *Information Technology & People*. Advance online publication. DOI: 10.1108/ITP-01-2021-0003

Mogavi, R. H., Deng, C., Kim, J. J., Zhou, P., Kwon, Y. D., Metwally, A. H. S., & Hui, P. (2024). ChatGPT in education: A blessing or a curse? A qualitative study exploring early adopters' utilization and perceptions. *Computers in Human Behavior: Artificial Humans*, *2*(1), 100027. DOI: 10.1016/j.chbah.2023.100027

Mohammed, S., & Dumville, B. C. (2001). Team mental models in a team knowledge framework: Expanding theory and measurement across disciplinary boundaries. *Journal of Organizational Behavior*, *22*(2), 89–106.

Mohtar, M., & Md Yunus, M. (2022). A systematic review of online learning during COVID 19: Students' motivation, task engagement and acceptance. *Arab World English Journal (AWEJ) 2nd Special Issue on COVID-19*.

Monge, P. R., Cozzens, M. D., & Contractor, N. S. (1992). Communication and motivational predictors of the dynamics of organizational innovation. *Organization Science*, *3*(2), 250–274. DOI: 10.1287/orsc.3.2.250

Moore, R. M. (1997). The positive effects of cohesion on the creativity of small groups. *International Social Science Review*, *72*(3/4), 84–93.

Morgan, N. (2018). *Can you hear me?: How to connect with people in a virtual world*. Harvard Business Press.

Morris, T. H. (2019, January 24). *Experiential Learning - A Systematic Review and Revision of Kolb's Theory*. Retrieved from Taylor & Francis Peer Reviewed Journals and Articles - Interactive Learning Environments: https://www.tandfonline.com/doi/abs/10.1080/10494820.2019.1570279

Morrison, E. W., Wheeler-Smith, S. L., & Kamdar, D. (2011). Speaking up in groups: A cross-level study of group voice climate and voice. *The Journal of Applied Psychology, 96*(1), 183–191. DOI: 10.1037/a0020744 PMID: 20718517

Morrison-Smith, S., & Ruiz, J. (2020). Challenges and barriers in virtual teams: A literature review. *SN Applied Sciences, 2*(6), 1–33.

Moser, K. S., & Axtell, C. M. (2013). The role of norms in virtual work. *Journal of Personnel Psychology, 12*(1), 1–6.

Moye, N. A., & Langfred, C. W. (2004). Information sharing and group conflict: Going beyond decision making to understand the effects of information sharing on group performance. *International Journal of Conflict Management, 15*(4), 381–410. DOI: 10.1108/eb022919

Mukerjee, J., & Metiu, A. (2022). Play and psychological safety: An ethnography of innovative work. *Journal of Product Innovation Management, 39*(3), 394–418. DOI: 10.1111/jpim.12598

Muller, P. C. (1999). *Team-based conceptualization of new products: Creating shared realities using information technological support* (Doctoral dissertation). University of Groningen.

Müller, S. (2023). How Slack Facilitates Communication and Collaboration in Seminars and Project-Based Courses. *Journal of Educational Technology Systems*. Advance online publication. DOI: 10.1177/00472395231151910

Mulye, A., Bhasin, A., Borger, B., & Fant, C. (2023). Virtual immediate feedback with POCUS in Belize. *Frontiers in Digital Health, 5*. Advance online publication. DOI: 10.3389/fdgth.2023.1268905 PMID: 38026838

Muñoz, M., Negrón, A. P. P., & Hernández, L. (2020). Gamification in virtual reality environments for the integration of highly effective teams. In A. Negrón, G. López, & H. Aguirre (Eds.), *Virtual reality designs* (pp. 151–175). CRC Press eBooks. DOI: 10.1201/9781003019589-7

Murmu, S., & Neelam, N. (2022). Impact of emotional intelligence and personality traits on managing team performance in virtual interface. *Asian Journal of Business Ethics, 11*(Suppl 1), 33–53. DOI: 10.1007/s13520-022-00154-1

Murphy, K. R., & Cleveland, J. N. (1995). *Understanding performance appraisal: Social, organizational, and goal-based perspectives*. Sage Publications, Inc.

Mutha, P., & Srivastava, M. (2021). Decoding leadership to leverage employee engagement in virtual teams. *The International Journal of Organizational Analysis*. Advance online publication. DOI: 10.1108/ijoa-07-2021-2856

Nahrgang, J. D., Morgeson, F. P., & Hofmann, D. A. (2011). Safety at work: A meta-analytic investigation of the link between job demands, job resources, burnout, engagement, and safety outcomes. *The Journal of Applied Psychology*, *96*(1), 71–94. DOI: 10.1037/a0021484 PMID: 21171732

National Association of Colleges and Employers. (2024, December 9). *What are employers looking for when reviewing college students' resumes?* https://naceweb.org/talent-acquisition/candidate-selection/what-are-employers-looking-for-when-reviewing-college-students-resumes

Nemiro, J. (2023). Virtual teams. In R. Reiter-Palmon & S. Hunter's (Eds.), *Handbook of organizational creativity: Group and individual influences,* 2nd edition (pp. 269–290). Elsevier Publishing.

Nemiro, J. (2007). The building blocks for creativity in virtual teams. In MacGregor, S., & Torres, T. (Eds.), *Higher creativity for virtual teams: Developing platforms for co-creation* (pp. 98–121). Information Science Reference.

Nemiro, J. (2023). Virtual teams. In Reiter-Palmon, R., & Hunter, S. (Eds.), *Handbook of organizational creativity: Group and individual influences* (2nd ed., pp. 269–290). Elsevier Publishing.

Nemiro, J. E. (2002). The creative process in virtual teams. *Creativity Research Journal*, *14*(1), 69–83. DOI: 10.1207/S15326934CRJ1401_6

Nemiro, J. E. (2026). *Creativity in virtual teams: Key components for success* (2nd ed.). Cognella Academic Publishing.

Nemiro, J. E., Ayala, A., Lee, J. S., & San Luis, B. (2023). Strategies for managing the challenges of student virtual teams in higher education: A case study. *Quarterly Review of Distance Education*, *24*(1), 55–77.

Neukam, M., & Bollinger, S. (2022). Encouraging creative teams to integrate a sustainable approach to technology. *Journal of Business Research*. Advance online publication. DOI: 10.1016/j.jbusres.2022.05.083

Nevicka, B., Ten Velden, F. S., De Hoogh, A. H., & Van Vianen, A. E. (2011). Reality at odds with perceptions: Narcissistic leaders and group performance. *Psychological Science*, *22*(10), 1259–1264. DOI: 10.1177/0956797611417259 PMID: 21931153

Newman, A., Donohue, R., & Evan, N. (2017). Psychological safety: A systematic review of the literature. *Human Resource Management Review, 27*(3), 521–535. DOI: 10.1016/j.hrmr.2017.01.001

Nguyen, T. H. (2023). Students' perceptions and practice of the blended learning approach to writing skills: Using Google Docs. *ICTE Conference Proceedings, 3*, 52–67. DOI: 10.54855/ictep.2335

Norcross, J. C., & Vangarelli, D. J. (1988). The resolution solution: Longitudinal examination of New Year's change attempts. *Journal of Substance Abuse, 1*(2), 127–134. DOI: 10.1016/s0899-3289(88)80016-6 PMID: 2980864

Norton, M. I. (2024, June 10). Strengthen teams with the power of rituals. *Harvard Business School Faculty Profile*. https://www.exed.hbs.edu/blog/strengthen-teams-with-power-rituals

Norton, M. I. (2024). *The ritual effect: From habit to ritual, harness the surprising power of everyday actions*. Scribner.

O'Neill, T. A., Aldana, A. J., Espinoza, J. A., Sperry, M. P., Brykman, K. M., & Donia, M. B. L. (2024). Conflict management styles assessment and feedback for student self-awareness and team development. *Assessment & Evaluation in Higher Education, 49*(8), 1091–1104. DOI: 10.1080/02602938.2024.2350682

O'Neill, T. A., & Allen, N. J. (2011). Personality and the prediction of team performance. *European Journal of Personality, 25*(1), 31–42. DOI: 10.1002/per.769

O'Neill, T. A., & Allen, N. J. (2014). Team task conflict resolution: An examination of its linkages to team personality composition and team effectiveness outcomes. *Group Dynamics, 18*(2), 159–173. DOI: 10.1037/gdn0000004

O'Neill, T. A., Boyce, M. A., & McLarnon, M. J. W. (2020). Team health is improved when peer evaluation scores affect grades on team projects. *Frontiers in Education, 5*, 1–10. DOI: 10.3389/feduc.2020.00049

O'Neill, T. A., Deacon, A., Gibbard, K., Larson, N., Hoffart, G., Smith, J., & Donia, B. L. M. (2018). Team dynamics feedback for post-secondary student learning teams. *Assessment & Evaluation in Higher Education, 43*(4), 571–585. DOI: 10.1080/02602938.2017.1380161

O'Neill, T. A., Hancock, S., McLarnon, M. J. W., & Holland, T. (2020). When the "SUIT" fits: Constructive controversy training in face-to-face and virtual teams. *Negotiation and Conflict Management Research, 13*(1), 44–59. DOI: 10.1111/ncmr.12154

O'Neill, T. A., Hoffart, G. C., McLarnon, M. M., Woodley, H. J., Eggermont, M., Rosehart, W., & Brennan, R. (2017). Constructive controversy and reflexivity training promotes effective conflict profiles and team functioning in student learning teams. *Academy of Management Learning & Education, 16*(2), 257–276. DOI: 10.5465/amle.2015.0183

O'Neill, T. A., Larson, N., Smith, J., Donia, M., Deng, C., Rosehart, W., & Brennan, R. (2019). Introducing a scalable peer feedback system for learning teams. *Assessment & Evaluation in Higher Education, 44*(6), 848–862. DOI: 10.1080/02602938.2018.1526256

O'Neill, T. A., Pezer, L., Solis, L., Larson, N., Maynard, N., Dolphin, G. R., Brennan, R. W., & Li, S. (2020). Team dynamics feedback for post-secondary student learning teams: Introducing the "Bare CARE" assessment and report. *Assessment & Evaluation in Higher Education, 45*(8), 1121–1135. DOI: 10.1080/02602938.2020.1727412

Obo-Rendón, R., Bruna Jofre, C., Lobos, K., Cisternas San Martin, N., & Guzman, E. (2022). Return to University Classrooms with Blended Learning: A Possible Post-pandemic COVID-19 Scenario. *Frontiers in Education, 7*, 957175.

Ogbeiwi, O. (2017). Why written objectives need to be really SMART. *British Journal of Health Care Management, 23*(7), 324–336. DOI: 10.12968/bjhc.2017.23.7.324

Oktavia, S., & Abdulkarim, A. (2022, January). The Use of the VCT Model in Civic Education to Build the Moral Awareness of Students in the Global Era. In *Annual Civic Education Conference (ACEC 2021)* (pp. 412-416). Atlantis Press.

Olson, J. R., & Olson, G. M. (Eds.). (2014). *Working together apart: Collaboration over the internet*. Morgan & Claypool.

Ong, C. W., Roberts, R., Arthur, C. A., Woodman, T., & Akehurst, S. (2016). The leader ship is sinking: A temporal investigation of narcissistic leadership. *Journal of Personality, 84*(2), 237–247. DOI: 10.1111/jopy.12155 PMID: 25487857

Ooms, W., Werker, C., & Caniëls, M. (2018). Personal and social proximity empowering collaborations: The glue of knowledge networks. *Industry and Innovation, 25*(9), 833–840.

Oo, T. Z., Kadyirov, T., Kadyjrova, L., & Józsa, K. (2024). Design-based learning in higher education: Its effects on students' motivation, creativity and design skills. *Thinking Skills and Creativity*. Advance online publication. DOI: 10.1016/j.tsc.2024.101621

Orazani, S. N., Reynolds, K. J., & Osborne, H. (2023). What works and why in interventions to strengthen social cohesion: A systematic review. *Journal of Applied Social Psychology*, *53*(10), 938–995.

Ortiz De Guinea, A., Webster, J., & Staples, D. S. (2012). A meta-analysis of the consequences of virtualness on team functioning. *Information & Management*, *49*(6), 301–308. DOI: 10.1016/j.im.2012.08.003

Oshri, I., Van Fenema, P., & Kotlarsky, J. (2008). Knowledge transfer in globally distributed teams: The role of transactive memory. *Information Systems Journal*, *18*(6), 593–616.

Owens, B. P., & Hekman, D. R. (2012). Modeling how to grow: An inductive examination of humble leader behaviors, contingencies, and outcomes. *Academy of Management Journal*, *55*(4), 787–818. DOI: 10.5465/amj.2010.0441

Ozenc, K. (2016, April 24). How do you design a ritual? *Medium – Stanford d.school*. https://medium.com/stanford-d-school/how-do-you-design-a-ritual-e4aeb3e17198

Ozenc, K. (2020, March 2). Designing well-being rituals for preventing workplace burnout. *Medium – Stanford d.school*. https://medium.com/stanford-d-school/designing-well-being-rituals-for-preventing-workplace-burnout-eafa577fe71b

Ozenc, K. (2023, January 4). Human-centered culture design: How to build better organizations. *Medium – Ritual Design Lab*. https://medium.com/ritual-design/human-centered-culture-design-building-better-organizations-70403398283d

Ozenc, K., & Fajardo, G. (2021). *Rituals for virtual meetings*. John Wiley & Sons.

Ozenc, K., & Hagan, M. (2019). *Rituals for work*. John Wiley & Sons.

Panteli, N., Yalabik, Z., & Rapti, A. (2019). Fostering work engagement in geographically-dispersed and asynchronous virtual teams. *Information Technology & People*, *32*, 2–17. DOI: 10.1108/ITP-04-2017-0133

Parović, M., Ansell, A., Vulić, I., & Korhonen, A. (2023). Cross-lingual transfer with target language-ready task adapters. *arXiv preprint arXiv:2306.02767*.

Paskevich, D. M., Brawley, L. R., Dorsch, K. D., & Widmeyer, W. N. (1999). Relationship between collective efficacy and team cohesion: Conceptual and measurement issues. *Group Dynamics*, *3*(3), 210.

Patricio, R., Moreira, A. C., & Zurlo, F. (2022). Gamification in innovation teams. *International Journal of Innovation Studies*. https://doi.org/DOI: 10.1016/j.ijis.2022.05.003

Paulhus, D. L., Harms, P. D., Bruce, M. N., & Lysy, D. C. (2003). The over-claiming technique: Measuring self-enhancement independent of ability. *Journal of Personality and Social Psychology*, *84*(4), 890–904. DOI: 10.1037/0022-3514.84.4.890 PMID: 12703655

Paulhus, D. L., & Williams, K. M. (2002). The Dark Triad of personality: Narcissism, Machiavellianism and psychopathy. *Journal of Research in Personality*, *36*(6), 556–563. DOI: 10.1016/S0092-6566(02)00505-6

Paul, R., Drake, J. R., & Liang, H. (2016). Global virtual team performance: The effect of coordination effectiveness, trust, and team cohesion. *IEEE Transactions on Professional Communication*, *59*(3), 186–202.

Paulus, P. B. (2000). Groups, teams, and creativity: The creative potential of idea-generating groups. *Applied Psychology*, *49*(2), 237–262. DOI: 10.1111/1464-0597.00013

Peeters, M. A., Van Tuijl, H. F., Rutte, C. G., & Reymen, I. M. (2006). Personality and team performance: A meta-analysis. *European Journal of Personality: Published for the European Association of Personality Psychology*, *20*(5), 377–396. DOI: 10.1002/per.588

Peña, J., Bravo, A., del-Río-Ortega, A., Resinas, M., & Ruiz-Cortés, A. (2021, June). Design patterns for board-based collaborative work management tools. In *International Conference on Advanced Information Systems Engineering* (pp. 177-192). Springer International Publishing. DOI: 10.1007/978-3-030-79382-1_11

Peter, C., & Brown, H. L. (2014). *Make It Stick: The Science of Successful Learning*. Belknap Press, Harvard University Press.

Petrescu, D., Enache, D., & Duta, L. (2022). Collaborative decision-making in online education. *Procedia Computer Science*, *199*, 1090–1094. DOI: 10.1016/j.procs.2022.01.138

Pew Research Center. (2021a, July 22). *Digital divide persists even as Americans with lower incomes make gains in tech adoption* [Report]. https://www.pewresearch.org/short-reads/2021/06/22/digital-divide-persists-even-as-americans-with-lower-incomes-make-gains-in-tech-adoption/

Pew Research Center. (2021b, July 16). *Home broadband adoption, computer ownership vary by race, ethnicity in the U.S.* [Report]. https://www.pewresearch.org/short-reads/2021/07/16/home-broadband-adoption-computer-ownership-vary-by-race-ethnicity-in-the-u-s/

Phelps, C., Heidl, R., & Wadhwa, A. (2012). Knowledge, networks, and knowledge networks: A review and research agenda. *Journal of Management*, *38*(4), 1115–1166. DOI: 10.1177/0149206311432640

Podgórska, M. (2022). Challenges and perspectives in innovative projects focused on sustainable industry 4.0—A case study on polish project teams. *Sustainability*. Advance online publication. DOI: 10.3390/su14095334

Porges, S. W. (2004). Neuroception: A subconscious system for detecting threats and safety. *Zero to Three (J)*, *24*(5), 19–24. https://chhs.fresnostate.edu/ccci/documents/07.15.16%20Neuroception%20Porges%202004.pdf

Pouthier, V. (2017). Griping and joking as identification rituals and tools for engagement in cross-boundary team meetings. *Organization Studies*, *38*(6), 753–774.

Prasad, A., DeRosa, D., & Beyerlein, M. (2017). Dispersion beyond miles: Configuration and performance in virtual teams. *Team Performance Management*, *23*(3), 186–204.

Prewett, M. S., Brown, M. I., Goswami, A., & Christiansen, N. D. (2018). Effects of team personality composition on member performance: A multilevel perspective. *Group & Organization Management*, *43*(2), 316–348. DOI: 10.1177/1059601116668633

Pritchard, A., & Woollard, J. (2013). *Psychology for the classroom: Constructivism and social learning*. Routledge.

Prochazka, J., Ovcari, M., & Durinik, M. (2020). Sandwich feedback: The empirical evidence of its effectiveness. *Learning and Motivation*, *71*, 101649. DOI: 10.1016/j.lmot.2020.101649

Purvanova, R. K., Charlier, S. D., Reeves, C. J., & Greco, L. M. (2021). Who emerges into virtual team leadership roles? The role of achievement and ascription antecedents for leadership emergence across the virtuality spectrum. *Journal of Business and Psychology*, *36*(4), 713–733. DOI: 10.1007/s10869-020-09698-0

Putnam, R. W. (2015). Recipes and reflective learning, "What would prevent you from saying it that way?" *Action Design*. https://actiondesign.com/resources/readings/recipes-and-reflective-learning

Radanliev, P., De Roure, D., Novitzky, P., & Sluganovic, I. (2024). Accessibility and inclusiveness of new information and communication technologies for disabled users and content creators in the Metaverse. *Disability and Rehabilitation. Assistive Technology*, *19*(5), 1849–1863. DOI: 10.1080/17483107.2023.2241882 PMID: 37585705

Rafaeli, A., Ravid, S., & Cheshin, A. (2009). Sensemaking in virtual teams: The impact of emotions and support tools on team mental models and team performance. *International Review of Industrial and Organizational Psychology*, *24*, 151–181.

Raghuram, S., Hill, N. S., Gibbs, J. L., & Maruping, L. M. (2019). Virtual work: Bridging research clusters. *The Academy of Management Annals*, *13*(1), 308–341. DOI: 10.5465/annals.2017.0020

Raginsky, M. (2023). Biological autonomy. *Biological Theory*, *18*(4), 303–308.

Rahim, A., & Bonoma, T. V. (1979). Managing organizational conflict: A model for diagnosis and intervention. *Psychological Reports*, *44*(3, Suppl.), 1323–1344. DOI: 10.2466/pr0.1979.44.3c.1323

Rapp, T. L., & Mathieu, J. E. (2007). Evaluating an individually self-administered generic teamwork skills training program across time and levels. *Small Group Research*, *38*(4), 532–555. DOI: 10.1177/1046496407300479

Rapp, T. L., & Rapp, A. A. (2021). Managing virtual sales teams: Challenges and evidence-based recommendations. *Organizational Dynamics*, *50*(1), 100821. DOI: 10.1016/j.orgdyn.2020.100821

Raskin, R., & Terry, H. (1988). A principal-components analysis of the Narcissistic Personality Inventory and further evidence of its construct validity. *Journal of Personality and Social Psychology*, *54*(5), 890–902. DOI: 10.1037//0022-3514.54.5.890 PMID: 3379585

Raven, B. H., & Rubin, J. Z. (1976). *Social psychology: People in groups*. Holt, Rinehart & Winston.

Reagans, R., & McEvily, B. (2003). Network structure and knowledge transfer: The effects of cohesion and range. *Administrative Science Quarterly*, *48*(2), 240–267. DOI: 10.2307/3556658

Reeve, J. M., & Tseng, C. (2011). Agency as a Fourth Aspect of Students' Engagement During Learning Activities. *Contemporary Educational Psychology*, *36*(4), 257–267.

Reiter-Palmon, R., Kramer, W., Allen, J. A., Murugavel, V. R., & Leone, S. (2021). Creativity in virtual teams: A review and agenda for future research. *International Journal of Business Communication*, *8*(1), 166–188.

Reyes, D. L., & Salas, E. (2019). What makes a team of experts an expert team? In Subotnik, R. F., Olszewski-Kubilius, P., & Worrell, F. C. (Eds.), *The psychology of high performance: Developing human potential into domain-specific talent* (pp. 141–159). American Psychological Association., DOI: 10.1037/0000120-007

Reyes, R. L., Isleta, K. P., Regala, J. D., & Bialba, D. M. R. (2024). Enhancing experiential science learning with virtual labs: A narrative account of merits, challenges, and implementation strategies. *Journal of Computer Assisted Learning*, *40*(6), 3167–3186. DOI: 10.1111/jcal.13061

Rietzschel, E. F., Slijkhuis, J. M., & Van Yperen, N. W. (2014). Task structure, need for structure, and creativity. *European Journal of Social Psychology*, *44*(4), 386–399. DOI: 10.1002/ejsp.2024

Ritual Design Lab. (n.d.). *Ritual Design Lab at Stanford University*. https://medium.com/ritual-design

Rizzo, J. R., House, R. J., & Lirtzman, S. I. (1970). Role conflict and ambiguity in complex organizations. *Administrative Science Quarterly*, *15*(2), 150–163. DOI: 10.2307/2391486

Roberts, R., & Woodman, T. (2017). Personality and performance: Moving beyond the Big 5. *Current Opinion in Psychology*, *16*, 104–108. DOI: 10.1016/j.copsyc.2017.03.033 PMID: 28813330

Robins, R. W., & Beer, J. S. (2001). Positive illusions about the self: Short-term benefits and long-term costs. *Journal of Personality and Social Psychology*, *80*(2), 340–352. DOI: 10.1037/0022-3514.80.2.340 PMID: 11220450

Rodríguez-Sánchez, A. M., Devloo, T., Rico, R., Salanova, M., & Anseel, F. (2017). What makes creative teams tick? Cohesion, engagement, and performance across creativity tasks: A three-wave study. *Group & Organization Management*, *42*(4), 521–547.

Rogers, B. A., Christian, J. S., Jennings, R. E., & Lanaj, K. (2023). The growth mindset at work: Will employees help others to develop themselves? *Academy of Management Discoveries*, *9*(1), 67–92. DOI: 10.5465/amd.2021.0144

Roos, C. A., Postmes, T., & Koudenburg, N. (2023). Feeling heard: Operationalizing a key concept for social relations. *PLoS One*, *18*(11), e0292865. DOI: 10.1371/journal.pone.0292865 PMID: 38032901

Rosenberg, M. B. (2015). *Nonviolent communication: A language of life* (3rd ed.). PuddleDancer Press.

Roth, P., & Doehne, M. (2024). Cohesion is lower in virtualized collaborations: A comparison of teams' network structure. *Small Group Research, 55*(4), 560–594.

Ruiz-Rojas, L. I., Salvador-Ullauri, L., & Acosta-Vargas, P. (2024). Collaborative working and critical thinking: Adoption of generative artificial intelligence tools in higher education. *Sustainability*. Advance online publication. DOI: 10.3390/su16135367

Ryan, R. M., & Deci, E. L. (2020). Intrinsic and extrinsic motivation from a self-determination theory perspective: Definitions, theory, practices, and future directions. *Contemporary Educational Psychology, 61*, 101860. DOI: 10.1016/j.cedpsych.2020.101860

Ryssina, V. N., & Koroleva, G. N. (1984). Role structures and creative potential of working teams. *R & D Management, 14*(4), 233–237.

Saad, E., & Agogué, M. (2023). Creativity in virtual teams: Systematic review, synthesis and research agenda. *Creativity and Innovation Management, 32*(1), 117–140. DOI: 10.1111/caim.12540

Salancik, G. R., & Pfeffer, J. (1978). A social information processing approach to job attitudes and task design. *Administrative Science Quarterly, 23*(2), 224–253. DOI: 10.2307/2392563 PMID: 10307892

Salas, E., DiazGranados, D., Klein, C., Burke, C. S., Stagl, K. C., Goodwin, G. F., & Halpin, S. M. (2008). Does team training improve team performance? A meta-analysis. *Human Factors, 50*(6), 903–933. DOI: 10.1518/001872008X375009 PMID: 19292013

Salas, E., Grossman, R., Hughes, A. M., & Coultas, C. W. (2015). Measuring team cohesion: Observations from the science. *Human Factors, 57*(3), 365–374. DOI: 10.1177/0018720815578267 PMID: 25875429

Salas, E., Shuffler, M. L., Thayer, A. L., Bedwell, W. L., & Lazzara, E. H. (2015). Understanding and improving teamwork in organizations: A scientifically based practical guide. *Human Resource Management, 54*(4), 599–622. DOI: 10.1002/hrm.21628

Salas, E., Sims, D. E., & Burke, C. S. (2005). Is there a "big five" in teamwork? *Small Group Research, 36*(5), 555–599. DOI: 10.1177/1046496405277134

Sánchez, J., Zornoza, A., Orengo, V., Peñarroja, V., & Chamakiotis, P. (2018, August). Team feedback intervention and team learning in virtual teams: A moderated mediation model of team cohesion and personality. In *IFIP International Conference on Human Choice and Computers* (pp. 136-148). Cham: Springer International Publishing. https://doi.org/DOI: 10.1007/978-3-319-99605-9_10

Saxena, D., & McDonagh, J. (2022). Communication breakdowns during business process change projects–Insights from a sociotechnical case study. *International Journal of Project Management*. Advance online publication. DOI: 10.1016/j.ijproman.2021.11.011

Schaubroeck, J., Lam, S. S. K., & Peng, A. C. (2011). Cognition-based and affect-based trust as mediators of leader behavior influences on team performance. *The Journal of Applied Psychology*, *96*(4), 863–871. DOI: 10.1037/a0022625 PMID: 21299271

Schippers, M. C., West, M. A., & Dawson, J. F. (2015). Team reflexivity and innovation: The moderating role of team context. *Journal of Management*, *41*(3), 769–788.

Schippers, M. C., West, M. A., & Edmondson, A. C. (2017). Team reflexivity and innovation. In Salas, E., Rico, R., & Passmore, J. (Eds.), *The Wiley Blackwell Handbook of the Psychology of Team Working and Collaborative Processes* (1st ed., pp. 459–478). Wiley. DOI: 10.1002/9781118909997.ch20

Schön, D. A. (Ed.). (1991). *The Reflective turn: Case studies in and on educational practice*. Teachers College Press.

Schrammel, M. (2024). Virtual Social Labs–Requirements and Challenges for Effective Team Collaboration. *Journal of Responsible Technology*. sciencedirect.comDOI: 10.1016/j.jrt.2024.100095

Schwarzer, R., & Jerusalem, M. (1995). *General Self-Efficacy Scale (GSE)* [Database record]. APA PsychTests.

Schwarz, R. M., & Bennett, L. M. (2021). Team effectiveness model for science (TEMS): Using a mutual learning shared mindset to design, develop, and sustain science teams. *Journal of Clinical and Translational Science*, *5*(1), e157. DOI: 10.1017/cts.2021.824 PMID: 34527296

Scott, C. P. R., & Wildman, J. L. (2015). Culture, communication, and conflict: A review of the global virtual team literature. In J. L. Wildman & R. L. Griffith (Eds.), *Leading global teams: Translating multidisciplinary science to practice* (pp. 13–32). Springer Science + Business Media. DOI: 10.1007/978-1-4939-2050-1_2

Senge, P. M. (2006). *The fifth discipline: The art and practice of the learning organization*. Currency Doubleday.

Senge, P. M., Kleiner, A., Roberts, C., Ross, R. B., & Smith, B. J. (2014). *The fifth discipline fieldbook: Strategies and tools for building a learning organization*. Crown/Archetype.

Serrat, O., & Serrat, O. (2017). Managing virtual teams. In *Knowledge solutions: Tools, methods, and approaches to drive organizational performance*, 619-625.

Setkhumbong, T., Na-Songkhla, J., & Tantrarungroj, P. (2020). A Literature Perspective of Key Factors Influencing Creativity and Conceptual Model for Virtual Learning Team Work. *Humanities, Arts and Social Sciences Studies*, 427-460.

Sherf, E. N., Parke, M. R., & Isaakyan, S. (2021). Distinguishing Voice and Silence at Work: Unique Relationships with Perceived Impact, Psychological Safety, and Burnout. *Academy of Management Journal, 64*(1), 114–148. DOI: 10.5465/amj.2018.1428

Shockley, K. M., Allen, T. D., Dodd, H., & Waiwood, A. M. (2021). Remote worker communication during COVID-19: The role of quantity, quality, and supervisor expectation-setting. *The Journal of Applied Psychology, 106*(10), 1466–1482. DOI: 10.1037/apl0000970 PMID: 34855422

Shuffler, M. L., Diazgranados, D., Maynard, M. T., & Salas, E. (2018). Developing, sustaining, and maximizing team effectiveness: An integrative, dynamic perspective of team development interventions. *The Academy of Management Annals, 12*(2), 688–724. DOI: 10.5465/annals.2016.0045 PMID: 30931078

Siebdrat, F., Hoegl, M., & Ernst, H. (2009). How to manage virtual teams. *MIT Sloan Management Review, 50*(4), 63–68.

Siltaloppi, J., & Ballardini, R. M. (2023). Promoting systemic collaboration for sustainable innovation through intellectual property rights. *Journal of Co-operative Organization and Management, 11*(1), 100200. DOI: 10.1016/j.jcom.2023.100200

Simmermeyer, E., Walsh, S., & Karcher, E. (2022). Associating Synchronous and Asynchronous Remote Teaching Formats with Student Situational Interest and Motivation. *NACTA Journal*. Advance online publication. DOI: 10.56103/4shou

Simons, T. L., & Peterson, R. S. (2000). Task conflict and relationship conflict in top management teams: The pivotal role of intragroup trust. *The Journal of Applied Psychology, 85*(1), 102–111. DOI: 10.1037/0021-9010.85.1.102 PMID: 10740960

Simunich, B., Gregg, A., & Ralston-Berg, P. (2024). *High-Impact Design for Online Courses: Blueprinting Quality Digital Learning in Eight Practical Steps*. Taylor & Francis.

Singh, J., Evans, E., Reed, A., Karch, L., Qualey, K., Singh, L., & Wiersma, H. (2022). Online, hybrid, and face-to-face learning through the eyes of faculty, students, administrators, and instructional designers: Lessons learned and directions for the post-vaccine and post-pandemic/COVID-19 world. *Journal of Educational Technology Systems*, *50*(3), 301–326. DOI: 10.1177/00472395211063754

Sisk, R. J. (2011). Team-based learning: Systematic research review. *The Journal of Nursing Education*, *50*(12), 665–669. PMID: 22007709

Sjöblom, K., Juutinen, S., & Mäkikangas, A. (2022). The importance of self-leadership strategies and psychological safety for well-being in the context of enforced remote work. *Challenges*. Advance online publication. DOI: 10.3390/challe13010014

Skilton, P. F., & Dooley, K. J. (2010). The effects of repeat collaboration on creative abrasion. *Academy of Management Review*, *35*(1), 118–134.

Smith, A. C. T., & Stewart, B. (2011). Organizational rituals: Features, functions and mechanisms. *International Journal of Management Reviews*, *13*(2), 113–133. DOI: 10.1111/j.1468-2370.2010.00288.x

Smuck, M., Odonkor, C. A., Wilt, J. K., Schmidt, N., & Swiernik, M. A. (2021). The emerging clinical role of wearables: Factors for successful implementation in healthcare. *NPJ Digital Medicine*, *4*(1), 1–8. DOI: 10.1038/s41746-021-00418-3 PMID: 33692479

Sokoloff, H., Dillon, D., & Dineen, P. (2016). "Debate, discussion, deliberative dialogue"—"3 D's" by Harris Sokoloff, David Dillon, and Patty Dineen. *NIFI*. https://www.nifi.org/en/catalog/product/debate-discussion-deliberative-dialogue-3-ds-harris-sokoloff-david-dillon-and-patty

Sole, D., & Edmondson, A. (2002). Situated knowledge and learning in dispersed teams. *British Journal of Management*, *13*(S2), S17–S34.

Sosa Díaz, M. J. (2021). Emergency remote education, family support and the digital divide in the context of the COVID-19 lockdown. *International Journal of Environmental Research and Public Health*, *18*(15), 7956. PMID: 34360248

Sperry, M.P., Aldana, A.J., O'Neill, T.A., Mimovic, A., Gibson, C.B., & McLarnon, M.J.W. (Under Review). Hybrid and remote team chartering: Creating clarity in an increasingly virtual world.

Stahl, G. (2023). *Computer support for collaborative learning: Foundations for a Cscl Community (cscl 2002 Proceedings)*. Routledge eBooks. DOI: 10.4324/9781315045467

Stajkovic, A. D., Lee, D. S., & Nyberg, A. J. (2009). Collective efficacy, group potency, and group performance: Meta-analyses of their relationships, and test of a mediation model. *The Journal of Applied Psychology*, *94*(3), 814–828. DOI: 10.1037/a0015659 PMID: 19450017

Stanford University. (n.d.). *Hasso Plattner Institute of Design (d.school)*. https://dschool.stanford.edu/

Steel Crate Games. (2015). *Keep Talking and Nobody Explodes*. Quest VR Games.

Stein, D. H., Schroeder, J., Hobson, N., Gino, F., & Norton, M. I. (2022). When alterations are violations: Moral outrage and punishment in response to (even minor) alterations to rituals. *Journal of Personality and Social Psychology: Interpersonal Relations and Group Processes*, *123*(1), 123–153. PMID: 33492153

Steiner, C., & Dick, J. (1995). *Original warm fuzzy tale: Fairytale*. Jalmar Press.

Stewart, V. R., Snyder, D. G., & Kou, C. Y. (2023). We hold ourselves accountable: A relational view of team accountability. *Journal of Business Ethics*. Advance online publication. DOI: 10.1007/s10551-021-04969-z PMID: 34812211

Stolz, R. C., Blackmon, A. T., Engerman, K., Tonge, L., & McKayle, C. A. (2022). Poised for creativity: Benefits of exposing undergraduate students to creative problem-solving to moderate change in creative self-efficacy and academic achievement. *Journal of Creativity*, *32*(2), 100024. DOI: 10.1016/j.yjoc.2022.100024

Stonehouse, L. P. P. A., Frick, R. A., & T. Codd, S. W. (n.d.). *Scholar*. Retrieved from Scholar.Google: Here is a link to multiple scholarly articles about the Socratic, experiential approach. https://scholar.google.com/scholar?q=socratic+and+experiential+learning+theory&hl=en&as_sdt=0&as_vis=1&oi=scholart

Stracke, C. M., Burgos, D., Santos-Hermosa, G., Bozkurt, A., Sharma, R. C., Swiatek Cassafieres, C., & Truong, V. (2022). Responding to the initial challenge of the COVID-19 pandemic: Analysis of international responses and impact in school and higher education. *Sustainability*, *14*(3), 1876. DOI: 10.3390/su14031876

Suherman, S., & Vidákovich, T. (2022). Assessment of mathematical creative thinking: A systematic review. *Thinking Skills and Creativity*. Advance online publication. DOI: 10.1016/j.tsc.2022.101019

Summers, I., Coffelt, T., & Horton, R. E. (1988). Work-group cohesion. *Psychological Reports*, *63*(2), 627–636. DOI: 10.2466/pr0.1988.63.2.627 PMID: 3406279

Swargiary, K. (2024). *Redefining reality: My vision for an education rooted in real-world experiences*. Scholar Press.

Swart, K., Bond-Barnard, T., & Chugh, R. (2022). *Challenges and critical success factors of digital communication, collaboration and knowledge sharing in project management virtual teams: A review*. AIS Electronic Library (AISeL). https://aisel.aisnet.org/ijispm/vol10/iss4/5/

Taggar, S., & Ellis, R. (2007). The role of leaders in shaping formal team norms. *The Leadership Quarterly*, *18*(2), 105–120. DOI: 10.1016/j.leaqua.2007.01.002

Taherdoost, H. (2024). Team Building in R&D Projects. In *Innovation through research and development: Strategies for success* (pp. 153–178). Springer Nature Switzerland. DOI: 10.1007/978-3-031-52565-0_8

Tannenbaum, S. I., Beard, R. L., & Salas, E. (1992). Team building and its influence on team effectiveness: An examination of conceptual and empirical developments. *Advances in Psychology*, *82*, 117–153. DOI: 10.1016/S0166-4115(08)62386-6

Tannenbaum, S. I., & Cerasoli, C. P. (2013). Do team and individual debriefs enhance performance? A meta-analysis. *Human Factors*, *55*(1), 231–245. DOI: 10.1177/0018720812448394 PMID: 23516804

Tanno, R., Barrett, D. G., Sellergren, A., Ghaisas, S., Dathathri, S., See, A., & Ktena, I. (2024). Collaboration between clinicians and vision–language models in radiology report generation. *Nature Medicine*, 1–10. DOI: 10.1038/s41591-024-03302-1 PMID: 39511432

Tao, X., Wang, C. L., Robson, P. J., & Hughes, M. (2025). How does team learning from failure facilitate new product performance? The double-edged moderating effect of collective efficacy. *Small Business Economics*, *64*(1), 133–155.

Taras, V., McLarnon, M., Steel, P., & O'Neil, T. (2024). Reducing freeloading in Global Virtual Teams: A quasi-experimental approach. *Journal of World Business*, *59*(5), 101566. DOI: 10.1016/j.jwb.2024.101566

Tasa, K., Taggar, S., & Seijts, G. H. (2007). The development of collective efficacy in teams: A multilevel and longitudinal perspective. *The Journal of Applied Psychology*, *92*(1), 17. PMID: 17227148

Tausworthe, R. C. (1979). The work breakdown structure in software project management. *Journal of Systems and Software*, *1*, 181–186. DOI: 10.1016/0164-1212(79)90018-9

Teh, A., Baniassad, E., Van Rooy, D., & Boughton, C. (2011). Social psychology and software teams: Establishing task-effective group norms. *IEEE Software*, *29*(4), 53–58.

Terenzini, P. T., Cabrera, A. F., Colbeck, C. L., Parente, J. M., & Bjorklund, S. A. (2001). Collaborative learning vs. lecture/discussion: Students' reported learning gains. *Journal of Engineering Education*, *90*(1), 123–130. DOI: 10.1002/j.2168-9830.2001.tb00579.x

Thenuwara, D., Sanjani, L. K. K., & Anuththara, K. (2023). The Digital Transformation of Higher Education in Sri Lanka due to COVID-19. *KDU Institutional Repository,* 224-232. http://ir.kdu.ac.lk/handle/345/7051

Thomas, K. W. (1992). Conflict and negotiation processes in organizations. In Dunnette, M. D., & Hough, L. M. (Eds.), *Handbook of industrial and organizational psychology* (Vol. 3, pp. 651–717). Consulting Psychologists Press.

Thompson, J. D. (1967). *Organizations in action*. McGraw-Hill. DOI: 10.4324/9781315125930

Tipmontree, N. S., & Tasanameelarp, N. A. (2021). Using role playing activities to improve Thai EFL students' oral English communication skills. *International Journal of Business and Society*, *21*(3), 1215–1225. DOI: 10.33736/ijbs.3345.2020

Tjosvold, D. (2008). Constructive controversy for management education: Developing committed, open-minded researchers. *Academy of Management Learning & Education*, *7*(1), 73–85. DOI: 10.5465/amle.2008.31413864

Tkalich, A., Šmite, D., Andersen, N. H., & Moe, N. B. (2022). What happens to psychological safety when going remote? *IEEE Software*, *41*(1), 113–122.

Ton, J. (2020, October 15). *Networking: It's Not What You Think*. Retrieved from Forbes Tech Council: https://www.forbes.com/councils/forbestechcouncil/2020/10/15/networking-its-not-what-you-think/

Trope, Y., & Liberman, N. (2010). Construal-level theory of psychological distance. *Psychological Review*, *117*(2), 440. PMID: 20438233

Tucker, C., Olsen, B., & Hale, R. T. (2023). Trust and commitment: A comparative study of virtual team communication across industries. *Team Performance Management*, *29*(1/2), 152–165. DOI: 10.1108/TPM-04-2022-0032

Tuckman, B. W. (1965). Developmental sequence in small groups. *Psychological Bulletin, 63*(6), 384–399. DOI: 10.1037/h0022100 PMID: 14314073

Tuckman, B. W., & Jensen, M. A. C. (1977). Stages of small-group development re-visited. *Group & Organization Studies, 2*(4), 419–427. DOI: 10.1177/105960117700200404

Tuohy, D., & Wallace, E. (2024). Ensuring effective intercultural communication in the emergency department. *Emergency Nurse*. Advance online publication. DOI: 10.7748/en.2022.e2122 PMID: 35266350

Turaev, S., Al-Dabet, S., Babu, A., Rustamov, Z., Rustamov, J., Zaki, N., Mohamad, M. S., & Loo, C. K. (2023). Review and analysis of patients' body language from an artificial intelligence perspective. *IEEE Access : Practical Innovations, Open Solutions, 11*, 62140–62173. DOI: 10.1109/access.2023.3287788

Turel, O., & Zhang, Y. (2010). Does virtual team composition matter? Trait and problem-solving configuration effects on team performance. *Behaviour & Information Technology, 29*(4), 363–375. DOI: 10.1080/01449291003752922

Twigg, A., & Valluri, N. (2024). Improving student team formation in design classrooms using a novel approach. In Zaphiris, P., & Ioannou, A. (Eds.), *Learning and Collaboration Technologies* (Vol. 14723, pp. 256–271). Springer Nature Switzerland., DOI: 10.1007/978-3-031-61685-3_19

Uday, S. (2022). *Potential of Collaborative Online Learning: A Guide for University Students*. Retrieved from University of Texas Collaborative Online: https://sites.utexas.edu/collaborated/potential-of-collaborative-online-learning/

Uitdewilligen, S., & Waller, M. J. (2018). Information sharing and decision-making in multidisciplinary crisis management teams. *Journal of Organizational Behavior, 39*(6), 731–748.

Valente, M. & MacMahon, M. E. (2020). Virtual communication for student group projects: The COVID-19 effect. *All Ireland Journal of Higher Education, 12*(3).

Van Dijk, J. A. (2017). Digital Divide: Impact of Access. *The International Encyclopedia of Media Effects*, 1-11.

Van Dyck, C., Frese, M., Baer, M., & Sonnentag, S. (2005). Organizational error management culture and its impact on performance: A two-study replication. *The Journal of Applied Psychology, 90*(6), 1228. PMID: 16316276

Van Dyne, L., & LePine, J. A. (1998). Helping and voice extra-role behaviors: Evidence of construct and predictive validity. *Academy of Management Journal, 41*(1), 108–119. DOI: 10.2307/256902

Van Hooft, E. A., & Van Mierlo, H. (2018). When teams fail to self-regulate: Predictors and outcomes of team procrastination among debating teams. *Frontiers in Psychology, 9*, 464. PMID: 29674991

Van Knippenberg, D. L., & Hoever, I. J. (2017). Team diversity and team creativity: A categorization-elaboration perspective. In *Team creativity and innovation* (pp. 41–60). Oxford University Press.

Verburg, R. M., Bosch-Sijtsema, P., & Vartiainen, M. (2013). Getting it done: Critical success factors for project managers in virtual work settings. *International Journal of Project Management, 31*(1), 68–79. DOI: 10.1016/j.ijproman.2012.04.005

Verduzco-Baker, L. (2018). Modified brave spaces: Calling in brave instructors. *Sociology of Race and Ethnicity (Thousand Oaks, Calif.), 4*(4), 585–592.

Vidolov, S. P. (2022). Virtual collaboration as co-enacting intercorporeality. *European Journal of Information Systems, 33*(2), 244–266. DOI: 10.1080/0960085x.2022.2152743

Vizeshfar, F., Rakhshan, M., Shirazi, F., & Dokoohaki, R. (2022). The effect of time management education on critical care nurses' prioritization: A randomized clinical trial. *Acute and Critical Care, 37*(2), 202–208. DOI: 10.4266/acc.2021.01123 PMID: 35545237

Vuchkovski, D., Zalaznik, M., Mitręga, M., & Pfajfar, G. (2023). A look at the future of work: The digital transformation of teams from conventional to virtual. *Journal of Business Research, 163*, 113912. DOI: 10.1016/j.jbusres.2023.113912

Wai, M., & Tiliopoulos, N. (2012). The affective and cognitive empathic nature of the dark triad of personality. *Personality and Individual Differences, 52*(7), 794–799. https://doi-org.ezproxy.net.ucf.edu/10.1016/j.paid.2012.01.008

Waizenegger, L., McKenna, B., Cai, W., & Bendz, T. (2020). An affordance perspective of team collaboration and enforced working from home during COVID-19. *European Journal of Information Systems, 29*(4), 429–442. DOI: 10.1080/0960085X.2020.1800417

Wallace, H. M., & Baumeister, R. F. (2002). The performance of narcissists rises and falls with perceived opportunity for glory. *Journal of Personality and Social Psychology, 82*(5), 819–834. DOI: 10.1037/0022-3514.82.5.819 PMID: 12003480

Waller, M. J., Zellmer-Bruhn, M. E., & Giambatista, R. C. (2002). Watching the clock: Group pacing behavior under dynamic deadlines. *Academy of Management Journal, 45*(5), 1046–1055. DOI: 10.5465/3069329

Walton, G. M., & Cohen, G. L. (2011). A Brief Social-Belonging Intervention Improves Academic and Health Outcomes of Minority Students. *Science, 331*(6023), 1447–1451. DOI: 10.1126/science.1198364 PMID: 21415354

Walton, H., Vindrola-Padros, C., Crellin, N. E., Sidhu, M. S., Herlitz, L., Litchfield, I., & Fulop, N. J. (2022). Patients' experiences of, and engagement with, remote home monitoring services for COVID-19 patients: A rapid mixed-methods study. *Health Expectations, 25*(5), 2386–2404. DOI: 10.1111/hex.13548 PMID: 35796686

Wang, B., Liu, Y., Qian, J., & Parker, S. K. (2021). Achieving effective remote working during the COVID-19 pandemic: A work design perspective. *Applied Psychology, 70*(1), 16–59. DOI: 10.1111/apps.1229 PMID: 33230359

Wang, M. L., & Hsu, B. F. (2012). A study to explore the team virtualization level and team effectiveness from the team personality composition. *Journal of the Knowledge Economy, 3*, 199–216. DOI: 10.1007/s13132-011-0079-y

Wang, S. L., & Lin, S. S. (2007). The effects of group composition of self-efficacy and collective efficacy on computer-supported collaborative learning. *Computers in Human Behavior, 23*(5), 2256–2268.

Wang, Y., Huang, Q., Davison, R. M., & Yang, F. (2018). Effect of transactive memory systems on team performance mediated by knowledge transfer. *International Journal of Information Management, 41*, 65–79.

Warren, T. (2020, March 26). Slack breaks user records as demand surges for remote working. *The Verge*. https://www.theverge.com/2020/3/26/21195092/slack-new-user-records-coronavirus-pandemic-remote-working-growth-concurrent-users

Watson, D., Clark, L. A., & Tellegen, A. (1988). Development and validation of brief measures of positive and negative affect: The PANAS scales. *Journal of Personality and Social Psychology, 54*, 1063–1070. PMID: 3397865

Watson-Jones, R. E., & Legare, C. H. (2016). The social functions of group rituals. *Current Directions in Psychological Science, 25*(1), 42–46. DOI: 10.1177/0963721415618486

Wegner, D. M., Giuliano, T., & Hertel, P. T. (1985). Cognitive interdependence in close relationships. In Ickes, W. J. (Ed.), *Compatible and incompatible relationships* (pp. 253–276). Springer-Verlag.

Wehrung, J. P. (2017). Displaying narcissism in a virtual team. *Management Review, 28*(4), 441–460. DOI: 10.5771/0935-9915-2017-4-441

West, M. A. (1990). The social psychology of innovation in groups. In West, M. A., & Farr, J. L. (Eds.), *Innovation and creativity at work: Psychological and organizational strategies* (pp. 309–333). Wiley.

West, M. A. (2012). *Effective teamwork: Practical lessons from organizational research*. BPS Blackwell.

Widiyanto, A., Pujiarto, B., Prabowo, N. A., Hanafi, M., Widyanto, R. A., Avizenna, M. H., Rodito, J., & Fadhilla, N. M. (2023). Influence of blockchain implementation for virtual meetings at Home Learning Indonesia. [iJET]. *International Journal of Emerging Technologies in Learning, 18*(06), 220–227. DOI: 10.3991/ijet.v18i06.37255

Wieland, B., de Wit, J., & de Rooij, A. (2022). Electronic brainstorming with a chatbot partner: A good idea due to increased productivity and idea diversity. *Frontiers in Artificial Intelligence*. Advance online publication. DOI: 10.3389/frai.2022.880673 PMID: 36213166

Wilson, J. M., Fletcher, T. D., Pescosolido, T., & Major, D. A. (2021). Extraversion and leadership emergence: Differences in virtual and face-to-face teams. *Small Group Research, 52*(5), 535–564. DOI: 10.1177/1046496420986620

Wilson, J., Oleary, M., Metiu, A., & Jett, Q. R. (2008). Perceived Proximity in Virtual Work: Explaining the Paradox of Far-But-Close. *Organization Studies, 29*, 979–1002.

Wu, T. (2022). Digital project management: Rapid changes define new working environments. *The Journal of Business Strategy*. Advance online publication. DOI: 10.1108/JBS-03-2021-0047

Xiao, X., Liu, F., Zhou, F., & Chen, S. (2018). Narcissistic leadership and employees' knowledge sharing: Influence of organizational identification and collectivism. *Social Behavior and Personality, 46*(8), 1317–1329. DOI: 10.2224/sbp.7034

Yang, J. (2007). The impact of knowledge sharing on organizational learning and effectiveness. *Journal of Knowledge Management, 11*, 83–90.

Yates, A., Pedersen Zari, M., Bloomfield, S., Burgess, A., Walker, C., Waghorn, K., & Palmer, F. (2022). A transformative architectural pedagogy and tool for a time of converging crises. *Urban Science (Basel, Switzerland), 7*(1), 1. DOI: 10.3390/urbansci7010001

Yoon, K., & Zhu, Y. (2022). Social Media Affordances and Transactive Memory Systems in Virtual Teams. *Management Communication Quarterly*, *36*(2), 235–260.

Yoo, Y., & Kanawattanachai, P. (2001). Developments of transactive memory systems and collective mind in virtual teams. *The International Journal of Organizational Analysis*, *9*(2), 187–208.

Zaccaro, S. J., Rittman, A. L., & Marks, M. A. (2001). Team leadership. *The Leadership Quarterly*, *12*(4), 451–483. DOI: 10.1016/S1048-9843(01)00093-5

Zacharaki, K., & Sebastian-Galles, N. (2021). The ontogeny of early language discrimination: Beyond rhythm. *Cognition*, *213*, 104628. PMID: 33618839

Zahra, A., & Febria, D. (2023). Online collaborative writing to enhance students' writing motivation and writing ability. *ENGGANG Jurnal Pendidikan Bahasa Sastra Seni Dan Budaya, 3*(2), 132–144. DOI: 10.37304/enggang.v3i2.9120

Zak, P. J. (2008). The neurobiology of trust. *Scientific American*. https://www.scientificamerican.com/article/the-neurobiology-of-trust/

Zamiri, M., & Esmaeili, A. (2024). Strategies, methods, and supports for developing skills within learning communities: A systematic review of the literature. *Administrative Sciences*. Advance online publication. DOI: 10.3390/admsci14090231

Zhang, H., Li, F., & Reynolds, K. J. (2022). Creativity at work: Exploring role identity, organizational climate and creative team mindset. *Current Psychology (New Brunswick, N.J.)*, *41*(6), 3993–4000.

Zhang, J., & Chen, Z. (2024). Exploring human resource management digital transformation in the digital age. *Journal of the Knowledge Economy*. Advance online publication. DOI: 10.1007/s13132-023-01214-y PMID: 40479358

Zhang, R., Duan, W., Flathmann, C., McNeese, N., Freeman, G., & Williams, A. (2023). Investigating AI teammate communication strategies and their impact in Human-AI teams for effective teamwork. *Proceedings of the ACM on Human-Computer Interaction, 7*(CSCW2), 1–31. DOI: 10.1145/3610072

Zhang, Y., Fang, Y., Wei, K., & Chen, H. (2010). Exploring the role of psychological safety in promoting the intention to continue sharing knowledge in virtual communities. *International Journal of Information Management*, *30*(5), 425–436.

Zhao, Y., & Liu, S. (2022). A Deep Learning Model with Virtual Reality Technology for Second Language Acquisition. *Mobile Information Systems*, *2022*, 1–7. DOI: 10.1155/2022/9686725

Zheng, S., Yan, M., Liang, Y., Chen, Y., Wei, Q., & Li, S. (2024). Understanding the positive and negative effects of team virtuality: A theoretical review and research agenda. *Human Resource Management Review, 34*(2), 101013. Advance online publication. DOI: 10.1016/j.hrmr.2024.101013

Zolfaghari, B., & Madjdi, F. (2022). Building trusting multicultural organizations: Rethinking the influence of culture on interpersonal trust development in the workplace. *Journal of International Management*. Advance online publication. DOI: 10.1016/j.intman.2022.100944

Zomorodi, M. (2020, September 30). How the Best Teacher Teaches Creativity. *Notes to Self podcast*. https://podcasts.apple.com/us/podcast/note-to-self/id561470997?i=1000451828638

About the Contributors

Jill E. Nemiro, Ph.D., is a professor of Organizational Psychology in the Psychology Department at California State Polytechnic University, Pomona. Dr. Nemiro's research interests are in organizational and team creativity, and the virtual workplace in both business and educational domains. As an organizational psychologist, Dr. Nemiro has widely published on ways to design virtual teams to be collaborative, creative, and high performing, including the newly released book, *Creativity in Virtual Teams: Key Components for Success*, Second Edition (2026). Before moving into academia, Dr. Nemiro spent many years working as a film editor in the entertainment industry. Dr. Nemiro has also worked as a consultant in creativity and virtual team training and instructional design. Dr. Nemiro received her Ph.D. in Organizational Psychology from Claremont Graduate University. She received her master's degree in psychology from California State University, Los Angeles, and a bachelor's degree from the University of California, Los Angeles in motion picture and television.

***

Aliza Aldana is a PhD student in Industrial-Organizational Psychology at the University of Calgary. Working in the Individual and Team Performance (ITP) lab under Dr. Thomas O'Neill's supervision, Aliza's research is focused on virtual and hybrid teamwork. Her master's thesis investigated experiences of interdependent teamwork in hybrid work teams. Aliza's other research interests include equity, diversity, inclusion, and accessibility, and high performance teamwork in other team types. Her work in the ITP lab also involves regular teamwork facilitations for university-level student teams embarking on team projects. As a certified teacher, Aliza also brings nearly a decade of experience with instructional design and execution.

Andi Asrifan is an accomplished educator and academic leader with a Doctorate in Education, specializing in English Language Education from Universitas Negeri Makassar. With a strong academic foundation, he holds a Master's degree in the same field and a Bachelor's degree in Secondary Education. His dissertation focused on developing bilingual educational materials, reflecting his commitment to enhancing language education. Dr. Asrifan has extensive experience in various educational roles, including serving as the Head of the International Affairs Office at Politeknik Negeri Nunukan and as the Head of the Institute for Student Development and Alumni at Universitas Muhammadiyah Sidenreng Rappang. He is also an active member of several professional organizations, including the Linguistics Society of Indonesia and TEFLIN. In addition to his administrative roles, Dr. Asrifan is a passionate advocate for educational innovation and has participated in numerous international conferences and webinars, sharing his insights on language teaching and curriculum development. His dedication to professional development is evident through his participation in various training programs.

L. Michelle Bennett, PhD, started her career as a molecular oncologist working at the laboratory bench. Over time she shifted focus to the use of collaborative approaches to maximize team and organizational effectiveness and catalyse partnerships. She is passionate about working at the leading edge of transdisciplinary research endeavours through consulting, facilitation, and as a team science architect. Michelle was the founding director of the National Cancer Institute's Center for Research Strategy, a role she relished until 2021. In that time, she worked with countless teams across different professions, and co-authored *Collaboration and Team Science: A Field Guide* which serves as a primer for investigators and staff who are building, participating in, or supporting collaborative research teams and institutions. Michelle is a certified Executive Coach and currently Principal and Owner of L.M. Bennett Consulting, LLC. During her 20-year career at the National Institutes of Health, Michelle held a number of leadership roles and gained extensive practical experience promoting collaboration and team-based approaches to strategic planning, identifying emerging areas of research, and assessing the impact of research investment. Routinely working across and beyond the organization, she brought individuals together with diverse backgrounds and expertise. She is now using this experience to help teams and organisations across a wide range of sectors, both in the US and on the international arena.

Jaelyn Rose Bentzinger is a rising sophomore at Creighton University pursuing her BA in psychology. In 2023 she started undergraduate research during her freshman year under Dr. Joshua Fairchild studying within the field of Industrial-

Organizational psychology. She is set to graduate with her BA in 2027 and intends to pursue her master's following graduation.

Lily Blocker is a tenured Associate Professor of Management at Stony Brook University and the director of the Leadership & Creativity Research Lab. She also serves as the Co-Director of the MBA Program in the College of Business. Her research in leadership, innovation, and conflict has been published in a variety of top peer reviewed research journals, including *Organizational Behavior and Human Decision Processes, The Journal of Organizational Behavior, The Leadership Quarterly, Advances in Developing Human Resources, Human Resource Management Review*, and *The Journal of Creative Behavior*. Her research has also been featured in *The Wall Street Journal, Fortune, Fast Company, Business Insider, Inc*, and *Pacific Standard Magazine*. Dr. Blocker received her Ph.D. and M.S. in Industrial-Organizational Psychology from Penn State University and a B.A. in Psychology from California State University, Fresno. For more information, please visit www.theLCLab.com.

C. Shawn Burke is a Professor (Research) and Director of the TRACE lab at the Institute for Simulation and Training, University of Central Florida. Her expertise includes teams and their leadership, team adaptability, team training, measurement, evaluation, and team effectiveness. Dr. Burke has published over 90 journal articles and book chapters related to the above topics and has presented/had work accepted at over 200 peer-reviewed conferences. Dr. Burke has received funding from the following agencies: Army Research Institute, Army Research Laboratory, Air Force Office of Scientific Research, Office of Naval Research, Army Research Office, National Science Foundation, DARPA, National Academies of Science/Gulf Oil Research Program, SLB, and NASA. Most recently, Dr. Burke has been funded by NASA to investigate issues related to team leadership, team roles, cultural diversity, and interpersonal relations within the context of teams operating in isolated, confined environments (e.g., long duration space exploration) with an eye towards fostering resiliency within such teams. All of the above work is conducted with an interest in team leadership and the training of teams operating in complex environments. She has also been funded by the Army Research Institute to investigate issues related to team composition and team resilience. Dr. Burke earned her doctorate in Industrial/Organizational Psychology from George Mason University and is an Associate Editor for the *Journal of Trust Research* and Consulting Editor for the *Journal of Business and Psychology*. She also serves as an ad-hoc reviewer for several journals, including: *Leadership Quarterly, Journal of Applied Psychology, Group and Organization Management, Organizational Psychology Review, Human Factors, Military Psychology, Small Group Research*, and *Human Resource Management*.

She has co-edited books on adaptability, advances in team effectiveness research, and intelligent tutoring for teams.

Joshua Fairchild is an associate professor of Industrial/Organizational Psychology at Creighton University. He received his PhD from The Pennsylvania State University in 2013, and joined the Department of Psychological Science at Creighton later that year. With a team of undergraduate scholars, Dr. Fairchild's research lab investigates factors underlying creativity, teamwork, and leadership, including the interplay of technology with these topics. His research has been published in a variety of outlets, and presented at numerous academic conferences.

Stacey Landreth Grau is associated with Texas Christian University, USA.

Başak Eda Hancı-Azizoglu gained her Ph.D. in English Language from Indiana University of Pennsylvania with a double major in Rhetoric and Applied Linguistics/ TESOL. She is an expert on global perspectives on language and literacy policies and English language learning and writing programs. She has given master's level courses to certified American school teachers to provide them leadership and skills on language teaching methods for their multicultural students. She is currently working as an associate professor in the English Language Teaching Department at Mediterranean University, Türkiye. Her research interests are artificial linguistic intelligence, linguistic analysis, the poetic and creative function of English as an additional language.

Trina Hoefling has an M.A. in Industrial/Organizational Psychology and an M.A. in Speech Communication from Southern Illinois University at Edwardsville. She is an associate adjunct professor at the University of Southern California, Bovard College, Human Resources Management master's program. In 2024, she was presented with the school's Teaching Excellence Award, selected by fellow faculty and students. Hoefling was previously an adjunct professor and online course developer for the University of Denver's University College Organization Leadership and Organization Development master's programs. She was granted Master Teacher status at the University of Denver. Hoefling provides coaching and training in remote team leadership and online learning engagement and was selected as a Visiting Fellow to deliver training workshops for the Department of Education Vocational Technical Training sector, Victoria, Australia.

Hüseyin Kafes holds an MA and a PhD in the field of foreign language education from Anadolu University. Dr. Kafes conducted his postdoctoral research on academic writing at Arizona State University. His research encompasses a range of topics, including academic writing, rhetoric, argumentation, genre analysis, and pronunciation. He actively participates in international conferences and engages in collaborative research projects, including TÜBİTAK-funded initiatives. Currently affiliated with Akdeniz University in Turkey, he serves as an Associate Professor in the Faculty of Education, where he has been contributing since 2013.

Addison LeGrand is an undergraduate student at Creighton University, majoring in Psychology, minoring in Studio Art, and has a concentration in Undergraduate Research and Scholarship. Addison is a member of the Creighton University Creativity, Teamwork, and Leadership Lab, and she is also a D1 athlete. Her academic research interests include athletic burnout, AI's impact on creativity and consumer behavior, and teamwork.

Kavita Mathad, a Gold Medalist in her post-graduation from Karnatak University, Karnataka, India, and an alumnus of Harvard Business School Online, holds rich academic and research experience. She has conducted several International Conferences, Business Conclaves, Webinars, and FDPs/MDPs and has actively participated in various webinars and FDPs MDPs as a resource person. To her credit, she has a good number of Scopus ABDC and Elsevier-indexed research papers and book publications, Major Research Projects, and consultancy done mainly in International Business, Digital Economy, and Sustainability. Dr Kavita Mathad has worked at the most eminent institutes and Universities Like XIME, Alliance University, IFIM Business School, CHRIST University, GIBS Business School, Presidency University, in Bangalore and Galgotias University, NCR, in various leadership positions and as a member of the core team of accreditations/rankings of NAAC, NBA and the QS Ranking. Dr. Kavita is known for her leadership acumen in building new perspectives and values in the HEIs ecosystem.

Thomas O'Neill is a professor of psychology and the director of the Industrial-Organizational Psychology program at the University of Calgary. He is a global research leader in the areas of high-performance teamwork, virtual team and leader effectiveness, flexible remote work, human-autonomy teaming, conflict and conflict management, personality, and assessment. His research funding exceeds $6M and he directs the Individual and Team Performance Lab of 15 members, which includes doctoral, post-doctoral, and master's candidates, as well as undergraduate students and staff members. Tom has published over 70 peer-reviewed articles in top academic journals and has worked extensively to translate the science of teamwork into practice through consultations, workshops, public lectures, training, and other resources. He collaborates closely with the University of Calgary's Schulich School of Engineering, working with faculty and students to improve team-based learning and help future engineers develop interpersonal and leadership skills critical for success.

Abdullah Özgel completed his degree in English Language Teaching at Mediterranean (Akdeniz) University, and he is currently engaged in postgraduate studies within the same area of discipline. His primary research interests lie in the fields of second language acquisition and the development of educational technology, particularly focusing on the application of artificial intelligence (AI) in English language teaching. He is specifically interested in exploring how AI can be integrated with social-emotional learning to create more engaging, personalized, and supportive language learning environments. Emphasizing the potential of immersive technologies such as virtual reality (VR), his research areas focus on enhancing learner motivation, reducing language anxiety, and facilitating effective language acquisition. His academic pursuits aim to bridge the gap between theoretical frameworks and applied classroom practices through inclusive technology and impactful learning experiences.

Amitava Pal is the Associate Dean at the International Institute of Sports Management (IISM), which received the prestigious President's Award in 2020. A seasoned academic and industry expert, he has guided pivotal industry reports in collaboration with organizations like FICCI, ASSOCHAM, and IMC. As Training and Research Head, he guided SOPs for the 37th National Games, Khelo India Youth Games, and Khelo India University Games. His research has been featured in leading publications, including Bonn University, Germany, and the University of California, and he received the Best Paper Award for Sustainability in Sports. Additionally, Amitava has mentored IIC fellows for the University of Chicago Harris School of Public Policy and spearheaded training, operation and implementation of the computer science curriculum researched and developed at IIT, Bombay for InOpen, SINE, IIT Bombay.

Katie Pfeiffer is a Psychology major in the Honors College at Creighton University. In addition, Ms. Pfeiffer is conducting research under the supervision of Dr. Joshua Fairchild. Ms. Pfeiffer plans to pursue a Psy.D after graduation in 2028.

M.Rajkumaris a highly experienced academician, with distinctive knowledge in business research techniques, marketing research, organizational behavior, and human capital management. At the center of his research is a persistent interest in leadership dynamics, motivation science, and organizational citizenship—threads he has pursued through multiple publications in Scopus-indexed journals and presentations given at global conferences. Aside from mentoring students and program management, Dr. Rajkumar is a peer reviewer for a leading academic journal (ABDC). He is also the Associate Editor for *The IUJ Journal of Management*. His proficiency in research methodologies, data analysis (SPSS, AMOS, SmartPLS), and structural equation modeling has been instrumental in conducting numerous workshops and faculty development programs.

Tracey Rockett is associated with Texas Christian University, USA.

McKenna Sperry recently completed her MSc in the Industrial-Organizational Psychology program at the University of Calgary, under the supervision of Dr. Thomas O'Neill. She has extensive facilitation experience and supports collaborative efforts between the Individual and Team Performance lab and the Schulich School of Engineering at the University of Calgary to help students develop essential teamwork skills. McKenna's master's thesis investigated neurodivergent engineering students' teamwork experiences, specifically focusing on what students think and do as they manage challenges and opportunities within team settings. Her other research interests include team processes and the impact of team interventions, as well as equity, diversity, inclusion, and accessibility.

Syahruddin, M.Kes., AIFO, is a distinguished professor and senior academic at Universitas Negeri Makassar (UNM), Indonesia, currently serving as Vice-Rector for Planning and Cooperation. His academic expertise lies in Physical Education, Health, and Recreation, with a strong interdisciplinary foundation in sports science and health physiology. Over his career, he has contributed significantly to education, research, and community service, focusing on the development of sport education models, kinesthetic learning, adaptive physical education, and performance optimization strategies for athletes. Prof. Syahruddin is an active lecturer in both undergraduate and postgraduate programs and has supervised numerous theses and dissertations. His scholarly works include multiple research projects, scientific publications in national and international journals, and the authorship of various academic books. Additionally, he has held leadership roles in national sports organizations and served as an assessor for educational accreditation bodies. Prof. Syahruddin continues to champion innovation, quality assurance, and academic excellence in sports education.

Krisztina Szabo is a doctoral student in the Industrial/Organizational Psychology program at the University of Central Florida. Her research primarily focuses on team resilience, team composition, and decision making. She earned her master's degree in Industrial/Organizational Psychology from the University of Central Florida.

Şevket Tekin is a talented independent researcher. He is currently pursuing his graduate degree in the field of foreign languages and education at Mediterranean (Akdeniz) University. He is highly interested in innovative language teaching methods. His research interests focus on the connections between technology and language pedagogy, with a particular focus on the applications of Virtual and Augmented Reality (VR/AR) in language education, the dynamics of Online Collaborative Learning, the role of Learning Styles and Cognitive Processes in technology-enhanced language acquisition, and the use of Autonomous Learning and Technology to support the language learning process.

Eşref Can Yılmaz is pursuing his graduate degree in English Language Teaching from Mediterranean (Akdeniz) University. His primary research interests lie in second language acquisition, educational technology, and the integration of virtual reality in innovative learning environments. Specifically, he explores how technological advancements can enhance language learning through the lens of neurolinguistics, with a focus on the cognitive and neurological foundations of language processing. His academic work aims to bridge the gap between theory and practice in technology-assisted language learning. The talented independent researcher contributes to a deeper understanding of how emerging tools can support more effective, personalized, and cognitively informed educational experiences.

Index

A

C

D

E

F

G

H

I

L

V

www.ingramcontent.com/pod-product-compliance
Lightning Source LLC
LaVergne TN
LVHW080608300926
849162LV00005B/1083